Advanced Software Testing—Vol. 2
2nd Edition

T0266830

About the Autor

With over 30 years of software and systems engineering experience, Rex Black is President of RBCS (www.rbcs-us.com), a leader in software, hardware, and systems testing. For 20 years, RBCS has delivered consulting, outsourcing, and training services in the areas of software, hardware, and systems testing and quality. Employing the industry's most experienced and recognized consultants, RBCS conducts product testing, builds and improves testing groups, and provides testing staff for hundreds of clients worldwide. Ranging from Fortune 20 companies to start-ups, RBCS clients save time and money through higher quality, improved product development, decreased tech support calls, improved reputation, and more.

As the leader of RBCS, Rex is the most prolific author practicing in the field of software testing today. His popular first book, *Managing the Testing Process*, has sold over 100,000 copies around the world, including Japanese, Chinese, and Indian releases, and is now in its third edition. His 11 other books on testing, *Advanced Software Testing: Volumes I, II, and III*, *Critical Testing Processes, Foundations of Software Testing, Pragmatic Software Testing, Fundamentos de Pruebas de Software, Testing Metrics, Improving the Testing Process, Improving the Software Process, and The Expert Test Manager* have also sold tens of thousands of copies, including Spanish, Chinese, Japanese, Hebrew, Hungarian, Indian, and Russian editions. He has written over 50 articles, presented hundreds of papers, workshops, and seminars, and given about 75 keynote and other speeches at conferences and events around the world.

Rex is the past President of the International Software Testing Qualifications Board and of the American Software Testing Qualifications Board.

Rex Black

Advanced Software Testing—Vol. 2

Guide to the ISTQB Advanced Certification as an Advanced Test Manager

2nd Edition

Rex Black (rex_black@rbcs-us.com)
Editor: Dr. Michael Barabas
Copyeditor: Judy Flynn
Layout and Type: Josef Hegele
Proofreader: Julie Simpson
Project Management: Matthias Rossmanith
Cover Design: Helmut Kraus, www.exclam.de

ISBN-13: 978-1-937538-50-7

2nd Edition (2nd Printing, September 2017) © 2014 by Rex Black

Rock Nook Inc.
1010 B Street, Ste. 350
San Rafael, CA 94901

www.rockynook.com

Library of Congress Cataloging-in-Publication Data

Black, Rex, 1964-
 Advanced software testing / Rex Black. -- Second edition.
    volumes ; cm
 ISBN 978-1-937538-50-7 (volume 2 : alk. paper : paperback)
1. Computer software--Testing. 2. Computer software--Examinations--Study guides.
3. Electronic data processing personnel--Certification. I. Title.
 QA76.76.T48B54813 2014
 005.1'4--dc23
                        2014013337

Distributed in the U.S. by Ingram Publisher Services
Distributed in the UK and Europe by Publishers Group UK

Acknowledgements

A complete list of people who deserve thanks for helping me along in my career as a test professional would probably make up its own small book. Here I'll confine myself to those who had an immediate impact on my ability to write this particular book.

First of all, I'd like to thank my colleagues on the American Software Testing Qualifications Board, the International Software Testing Qualifications Board, and especially the Advanced Syllabus Working Party, who made this book possible by creating the process and the material from which it grew. Not only has it been a real pleasure sharing ideas with and learning from each of the participants, but I have had the distinct honor of twice being elected president of both the American Software Testing Qualifications Board and the International Software Testing Qualifications Board. I continue to work on both boards. I look back with pride at our accomplishments so far, I look forward with pride to what we'll accomplish together in the future, and I hope this book serves as a suitable expression of the gratitude and sense of accomplishment I feel toward what we have done for the field of software testing.

Next, I'd like to thank the people who helped me create the material that grew into this book and the previous edition of it. The material in this book, in our Advanced Test Manager instructor-led training course, and in our Advanced Test Manager e-learning course was reviewed, re-reviewed, and polished with hours of dedicated assistance by Jamie Mitchell, Bernard Homés, Gary Rueda Sandoval, Jan Sabak, Joanna Kazun, Corné Kruger, Ed Weller, Dawn Haynes, José Mata, Judy McKay, Paul Jorgensen, and Pat Masters.

Now, once I had created the materials, the task of assembling the first draft of this book from scripts, slides, the syllabus, and a rough framework fell to Dena Pauletti, RBCS's extremely competent and meticulous senior system administrator. This book would have taken literally months longer to prepare without her intrepid and timely assistance.

Of course, the Advanced syllabus could not exist without a foundation, specifically the ISTQB Foundation syllabus. I had the honor of being part of that working party as well. I thank them for their excellent work over the years, creating the fertile soil from which the Advanced syllabus and thus this book sprang.

In the creation of the training courses and the materials that make up this book, I have drawn on all the experiences I have had as author, practitioner, consultant, and trainer. So I have benefited from individuals too numerous to list. I thank each of you who have bought one of my previous books, for you contributed to my skills as a writer. I thank each of you who have worked with me on a project, for you have contributed to my abilities as a test manager, test analyst, and technical test analyst. I thank each of you who have hired me to work with you as a consultant, for you have given me the opportunity to learn from your organizations. I thank each of you who have taken a training course from me, for you have collectively taught me much more than I taught each of you. I thank my readers, colleagues, clients, and students and hope that my contributions to each of you have repaid the debt of gratitude that I owe you.

For over 20 years, I have run a testing services company, RBCS. From humble beginnings, RBCS has grown into an international consulting, training, and outsourcing firm with clients on six continents. While I have remained a hands-on contributor to the firm, over 100 employees, subcontractors, and business partners have been the driving force of our ongoing success. I thank all of you for your hard work for our clients. Without the success of RBCS, I could hardly avail myself of the luxury of writing technical books, which is a source of pride but not a whole lot of money. Again, I hope that our mutual successes together have repaid the debt of gratitude that I owe each of you.

Finally, I thank my family, especially my wife, Laurel, and my daughters, Emma and Charlotte. The hectic work schedule entailed in running a global testing services company means little time for my family, and my bad habit of writing books reduces that time further. To Laurel, Emma, and Charlotte, know that I am aware that I can never fully repay the debt that I owe you for all that you give to me, but also know that my love for each of you is much greater than the time we get to share together.

Oh, yeah, and thanks to my dogs, Cosmo and Hank, for providing company and comic relief too. Sad to say, immediately prior to the final edits of this book, Cosmo, the senior RBCS mascot, left the office for the rewards that await good dogs after completing their work here on Earth. Maybe if I've been a good dog, too, I'll see you on the other side, buddy.

Table of Contents

Introduction

This is a book on advanced software testing for test managers. By that I mean that I address topics that a practitioner who has chosen to manage software testing as a career should know. I focus on those skills and techniques related to test analysis, test design, test execution, and test results evaluation. I assume that you know the basic concepts of test engineering, test design, test tools, testing in the software development life cycle, and test management. You are ready to increase your level of understanding of these concepts and to apply them to your daily work as a test professional.

This book follows the International Software Testing Qualifications Board's (ISTQB's) Advanced Level Test Manager syllabus. As such, it can help you prepare for the Advanced Test Manager exam. You can use this book to self-study for that exam or as part of an e-learning or instructor-led course on the topics covered in that exam. If you are taking an ISTQB-accredited Advanced Level Test Manager training course, this book is an ideal companion text for that course.

However, even if you are not interested in ISTQB certification, you will find this book useful to prepare yourself for advanced work in software testing. If you are a test manager, test director, test analyst, technical test analyst, automated test engineer, manual test engineer, or programmer, or in any other field where a sophisticated understanding of software test management is needed, then this book is for you.

This book focuses on test management. The book consists of eight chapters:

1. Testing Process
2. Test Management
3. Reviews
4. Defect Management
5. Improving the Test Process
6. Test Tools and Automation

7. People Skills – Team Composition
8. Preparing for the Exam

What should a test manager be able to do? Or, to ask the question another way, what should you have learned to do—or learned to do better—by the time you finish this book?

- Manage a testing project by implementing the mission, goals, and testing processes established for the testing organization.
- Organize and lead risk identification and risk analysis sessions and use the results of such sessions for test estimation, planning, monitoring, and control.
- Create and implement test plans consistent with organizational policies and test strategies.
- Continuously monitor and control the test activities to achieve project objectives.
- Assess and report relevant and timely test status to project stakeholders.
- Identify skills and resource gaps in your test team and participate in sourcing adequate resources.
- Identify and plan necessary skills development within your test team.
- Propose a business case for test activities that outlines the costs and benefits expected.
- Ensure proper communication within the test team and with other project stakeholders.
- Participate in and lead test process improvement initiatives.

In this book, I focus on these main concepts. I suggest that you keep these high-level outcomes in mind as you proceed through the material in each of the following chapters.

In writing this book and the companion volume on test analysis, I've kept foremost in my mind the question of how to make this material useful to you. If you are using this book to prepare for the Advanced Test Manager exam, then I recommend that you read Chapter 8 first and then read the other chapters in order. If you are using this book to expand your overall understanding of testing to an advanced level but do not intend to take the Advanced Test Manager exam, then I recommend that you read Chapters 1 through 7 only. If you are using this book as a reference, then feel free to read only those chapters that are of specific interest to you.

Each of the first seven chapters is divided into sections. For the most part, I have followed the organization of the Advanced Test Manager syllabus to the point of section divisions, but subsections and sub-subsection divisions in the syllabus might not appear in this book. You'll also notice that each section starts with a text box describing the learning objectives for the section. If you are curious about how to interpret those K2, K3, and K4 tags in front of each learning objective, and how learning objectives work within the ISTQB syllabi, read Chapter 8.

Software testing is in many ways similar to playing the piano, cooking a meal, or driving a car. How so? In each case, you can read books about these activities, but until you have practiced, you know very little about how to do it. So, I've included practical, real-world exercises for the key concepts. I encourage you to practice these concepts with the exercises in the book. Then, make sure you take these concepts and apply them on your projects. You can become an advanced software test management professional only by managing software testing.

1   Testing Process

Drill Sergeant: Gump! Why did you put that weapon together so quickly, Gump?

Forrest Gump: You told me to, Drill Sergeant.

Drill Sergeant: [Expressing surprise and looking at a stopwatch.] *This is a new company record! If it wouldn't be such a waste of a fine enlisted man, I'd recommend you for OCS! You are gonna be a general someday, Gump. Now disassemble your weapon and continue!*

Forrest Gump displays an innate ability to follow a process accurately and quickly in a scene from the movie *Forrest Gump*, screenplay by Eric Roth, from the novel by Winston Groom.

The first chapter of the Advanced syllabus is concerned with contextual and background material that influences the remaining chapters. There are eight sections.

1. Introduction
2. Test Planning, Monitoring, and Control
3. Test Analysis
4. Test Design
5. Test Implementation
6. Test Execution
7. Evaluating Exit Criteria and Reporting
8. Test Closure Activities

Let's look at each section and how it relates to test management.

1.1   Introduction

Learning objectives
Recall of content only

In the Foundation Level syllabus, the fundamental test process is defined as follows:

- Planning and control
- Analysis and design
- Implementation and execution
- Evaluating exit criteria and reporting
- Test closure activities

At the Advanced level, that process has been refined to separate certain activities, thus providing finer-grained resolution on the process as a whole as well as its constituent activities. This fine-grained breakdown allows us to focus refinement and optimization efforts, to tailor the test process better within the software development lifecycle, and to gain better insight into project and product status for responsive, effective test monitoring and control. The refined activities are as follows:

- Planning, monitoring, and control
- Analysis
- Design
- Implementation
- Execution
- Evaluating exit criteria and reporting
- Test closure activities

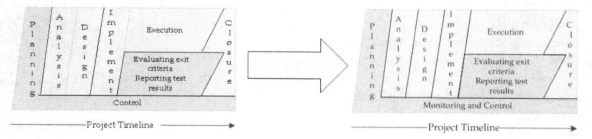

Figure 1–1   *Fundamental test process*

ISTQB Glossary

exit criteria: The set of generic and specific conditions, agreed upon with the stakeholders for permitting a process to be officially completed. The purpose of exit criteria is to prevent a task from being considered completed when there are still outstanding parts of the task which have not been finished. Exit criteria are used to report against and to plan when to stop testing.

test closure: During the test closure phase of a test process data is collected from completed activities to consolidate experience, testware, facts, and numbers. The test closure phase consists of finalizing and archiving the testware and evaluating the test process, including preparation of a test evaluation report.

test execution: The process of running a test on the component or system under test, producing actual result(s).

test implementation: The process of developing and prioritizing test procedures, creating test data and, optionally, preparing test harnesses and writing automated test scripts.

test planning: The activity of establishing or updating a test plan.

test process: The fundamental test process comprises test planning and control, test analysis and design, test implementation and execution, evaluating exit criteria and reporting, and test closure activities.

test script: Commonly used to refer to a test procedure specification, especially an automated one.

As at the Foundation level, remember that activities may overlap or be concurrent, in spite of the appearance of sequentiality in the syllabus—and in Figure 1–1?. In addition, it's usually necessary to tailor these activities, both in terms of the specific tasks performed and the order in which they occur in a project, based on the needs of the project and the type of system being tested. In fact, in my years as a test manager and test consultant, I can't remember ever seeing any testing done exactly according to the fundamental test process, but I have seen every activity and task described within the fundamental test process play an important part in at least one task. Therefore, in set theory terms, you can think of the fundamental test process as the union of all tasks that can be important in testing, organized into a hierarchy that corresponds roughly to the timeline of testing on a project following a sequential lifecycle.[1]

---

1. If you need to review the Foundation syllabus in detail, I suggest the book I coauthored with Dorothy Graham and Erik van Veenendaal, *Foundations of Software Testing*.

Since the fundamental test process was introduced at the Foundation level, I recommend that you review Chapter 1, section 4 of the Foundation syllabus prior to or immediately after going through this chapter. Remember that the Foundation syllabus material may be examined to the extent that it forms an underpinning of the Advanced material. If the Advanced material refines or modifies the Foundation material in any way, then you should expect the exam to follow the Advanced material.

While the fundamental test process includes tasks carried out by both managers and testers, in this book I will focus on the management perspective. That includes management tasks as well as the management of testers who are carrying out tester tasks.

1.2   Test Planning, Monitoring, and Control

Learning objectives

(K4) Analyze the test needs for a system in order to plan test activities and work products that will achieve the test objectives.

Test planning, monitoring, and control are management tasks. Let's start with test planning. I'll discuss the content of test planning documents and specific test control activities in Chapter 2, but for the moment let's focus on the process.

Test Planning

Test planning is the initial step of the fundamental test process. It occurs—to a greater or lesser extent and degree of formality—at every test level. Test planning is also an ongoing activity, with planning happening throughout the fundamental test process, even through closure. Planning should be about how to achieve the test mission and objectives—possibly as tailored for this particular project. (Note that Chapter 1 of the syllabus mentions the mission and objectives as being identified in the test strategy, but later in the syllabus it correctly places the main source of the mission and objectives as the test policy document.)

So, the mission and objectives address "what we want to achieve" with testing, while planning addresses "how we want to achieve that stuff." This includes the activities and resources necessary for the testing. Planning must also take into account the need to guide the testing itself, the project of product development or maintenance underway, and short-term and long-term process improvements, so planning should include the gathering and tracking of metrics. The use of these selected metrics will often require the support of tools, testers skilled in the proper input of the metrics information, and documentation about the metrics and their use, so planning must address these topics as well.

In Chapter 2, I'll address the different types of test strategies that can exist. Each of these test strategies has implications for test planning. In risk-based testing, the identified quality and project risks are addressed in the plan, such as increasing test coverage for risk areas that are seen as high risk as well as emphasizing elements of the test process that are seen as particularly effective at mitigating certain kinds of quality risks. In risk-based testing, the level of risk sets the priority and sequence of tests too; the means by which this prioritization is done must be addressed in planning. When blended test strategies are used—that is, the use of multiple test strategies at once to optimize the effectiveness and efficiency of testing—then the planning must handle the integration of all test activities across all strategies. So, if a combination of risk-based and reactive testing is adopted, then planning must address when, how, and by whom test charters will be defined.

Test planning should span all test levels to avoid a patchwork approach to testing across the project. Clearly defined goals and objectives, coverage criteria, entry and exit criteria, and techniques across all test levels will ensure optimal benefit from the testing and will maximize the ability to see a coherent picture of the test results across all levels.

Testing exists in a complex relationship with other parts of the project, and test inputs and outputs—for example, requirements specifications and test results—can have complex relationships as well, often many-to-many relationships. The needs of the project and the software development lifecycle have a strong influence here, too, and you'll see examples of that in just a moment. Effective test management in general—and test planning specifically—requires a good understanding of these inputs, outputs, and their relationships. Traceability between test inputs such as the test basis, intermediate test work products such as test conditions, and test outputs such as test status reports is essential to achieving test objectives such as confidence building, but it is sufficiently complex that it will not happen by itself or by accident. It will only happen when properly planned. If tools are needed, planning should address that too.

ISTQB Glossary

test control: A test management task that deals with developing and applying a set of corrective actions to get a test project on track when monitoring shows a deviation from what was planned.

test management: The planning, estimating, monitoring, and control of test activities, typically carried out by a test manager.

As with any project, the testing part of a project must have a clearly defined scope to stay focused and to avoid missing any important areas. Areas that are out of scope must be clearly stated to manage expectations. Each feature, risk area, or other element listed as within scope should be mappable to test work products such as groups of test conditions, perhaps in a test design specification.

Like test inputs and outputs, test environments can be quite complex, expensive, and protracted to procure. So, the smart test manager plans carefully, starting with collaboration with other project team members such as architects as to what the test environment should look like. That leads next to ensuring that the necessary resources will be available when needed and that the people who will configure and support the environment will also be available when needed. Cost, effort, and schedule for the test environment must be determined during planning.

As noted earlier, testing exists in a complex relationship with other parts of the project. Dependencies—in either direction—between testing and other members of the organization may exist. Project participants and stakeholders have expectations of the test team, and the test team has expectations of other participants and stakeholders too. Planning should identify these participants and stakeholders and address the dependencies.

Planning for Testing in Sequential Models

Sequential models like the V-model shown in ?Figure 1–2 are called sequential because the entire system is built at one time, in a sequence of activities that successively define, then implement, then test. All work products and activities associated with each phase are completed before the next phase begins. The two most common examples are the waterfall and the V-model.

You might have encountered the W-model too. The W-model depicts the test development activities for each test level—shown in the V-model as cross-

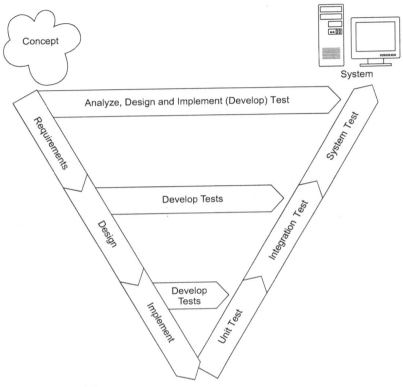

Figure 1–2   *V-model*

arms on the V—instead as a parallel track next to the requirements, design, and implementation activities and then explicitly shows bug fixing associated with the test levels as a parallel track next to the testing activities. Some find it clearer than the V-model, but I actually find the figure more confusing because it is more intricate.

The use of sequential lifecycle models creates certain issues for testing that the test manager must manage.

The first and most infamous issue is that of schedule compression at the end of the project, during testing. This tends to set up an unpleasant trade-off between quality and delivery dates during the always-hectic end game of the project. When the test manager is put in the position of "quality cop"—that is, the person who is supposed to approve a release—that becomes a no-win situation where the test manager is subjected to immense pressure to approve the release followed by howls of condemnation when the release proves bug-ridden in the field.

> **ISTQB Glossary**
>
> **test condition:** An item or event of a component or system that could be verified by one or more test cases, e.g., a function, transaction, feature, quality attribute, or structural element.
>
> **test design:** (1) See test design specification; (2) The process of transforming general testing objectives into tangible test conditions and test cases.
>
> **test design specification:** A document specifying the test conditions (coverage items) for a test item, the detailed test approach and identifying the associated high level test cases.
>
> **test specification:** A document that consists of a test design specification, test case specification, and/or test procedure specification.
>
> **test procedure specification:** A document specifying a sequence of actions for the execution of a test. Also known as test script or manual test script.

The second issue is the common problem of development groups, likewise pressured to achieve dates, delivering unstable and often untestable systems to the test team. This causes significant portions of the test schedule to be consumed by what is, effectively, retroactive unit testing. When compounded with a lack of adequate configuration management, this can render the high-level testing almost pointless since what is delivered doesn't work and it's not possible to determine what has been delivered.

A third issue is the common failure to include the activities shown in the crossbars of the V-model in Figure 1–2. Instead, due to other projects or a lack of management awareness, the test team is involved late. Very little preparation time is allowed. Testing typically devolves to an ad hoc or at best purely reactive strategy, with no defect prevention, no clear coverage, and limited value.

These issues are surmountable but require careful test planning and management.

Planning for Testing in Iterative Models

Iterative or incremental models are those where the system is built and tested iteratively in chunks, such as shown in ?Figure 1–3. The grouping of functions and capabilities into chunks can be done based on risk, in that the functions and capabilities most likely to fail get built in the first chunk, then the next most likely to fail, and so forth. The grouping into chunks can be done based on customer priority, in that the functions and capabilities most desirable to customers get built first, the least desirable last, and the others at some chunk in between. The grouping into chunks can also be influenced by regulatory requirements, design requirements, and other constraints.

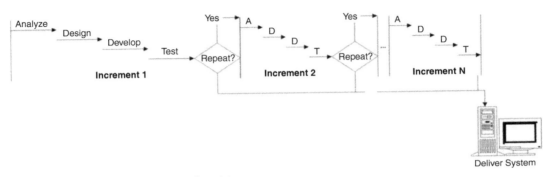

Figure 1–3   *Iterative or incremental model*

There are myriad examples of these models, including evolutionary and incremental. There is tremendous variation in terms of the size of the chunks, the duration of the iterations, and the level of formality. The common element is that fully integrated, working systems—albeit with only a portion of the functions and capabilities—are created earlier in the lifecycle than they would be in a sequential project.

The availability of testable systems earlier in the lifecycle would seem to be a boon to the test manager, and it can be. However, the iterative lifecycle models create certain test issues for the test manager.

First of these is the need, in each increment after the first one, to be able to regression test all the functions and capabilities provided in the previous increments. Since the most important functions and capabilities are typically provided in the earlier increments, you can imagine how important it is that these not be broken. However, given the frequent and large changes to the codebase—every increment being likely to introduce as much new and changed code as the previous increment—the risk of regression is high. This tends to lead to attempts to automate regression tests, with various degrees of success.

The second issue is the common failure to plan for bugs and how to handle them. This manifests itself when business analysts, designers, and programmers are assigned to work full-time on subsequent increments while testers are testing the current increment. In other words, the activities associated with increments are allowed to overlap; an increment doesn't need to be completed entirely before the next one starts. This can seem more efficient at first.

However, once the test team starts to locate bugs, this leads to an overbooked situation for the business analysts, designers, and programmers who must address them.

The final common issue is the lack of rigor in and respect for testing. That is not to say that it is universal—my consulting company, RBCS, has clients that follow excellent practices in testing and use iterative methodologies. These clients have found a way integrate formal testing into iterative lifecycles.

Again, these are all surmountable issues, but the test manager must plan for and manage them carefully, in conjunction with the project management team.

Planning for Testing in Agile Models

Agile models are a form of iterative lifecycles where the iterations are very short, often just two to four weeks (see Figure 1–4?). In addition, the entire team—including the testers—is to be engaged in the development effort throughout each iteration. Changes are allowed at any point in the project, and adjustments are to be made in scope (but not schedule) based on the changes.

One example of agile models is the Scrum process, which is basically a set of practices for managing iterations. Scrum includes daily meetings to discuss progress on an iteration, which is called a sprint, by a self-directed team. In practice, different organizations allow different degrees of self-direction. I have seen a number of groups that were using Scrum for managing the sprints but strong senior leadership from outside the team determined sprint content. In a number of these situations, the agile principle of "sustainable work pace" was violated when management refused to allow actual team velocity—that is, the rate of story points that can be achieved in a sprint—to determine the commitments made for each sprint. This led to test team crunches at the end of each sprint.

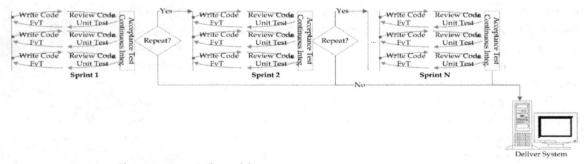

Figure 1–4   *Agile model*

Another example of agile models is Extreme Programming, or XP. XP provides a set of practices for programming in agile environments. It includes pair programming, a heavy emphasis on automated unit tests using tools like the x-unit frameworks, and again the concept of self-directed teams. Its originator, Kent Beck, is famous—or infamous, if you prefer—in testing circles for showing up at a testing conference in San Francisco in the late 1990s to proclaim that independent testing teams, and independent testers, were going to be rendered entirely obsolete by agile methods. Fifteen years later, testing as a profession is more recognized than ever.

Testing issues with agile methods are similar to those with iterative lifecycles, though the pace of the iterations makes the issues more acute. In addition, the exact relationship between the testers, the independent test team, and the agile teams is something that varies considerably from one organization to another.

Agile methods can create the following additional challenges for testers:

- Volume and speed of change. Testers must typically adopt lightweight documentation and rely more heavily on tester expertise than detailed test cases to keep up.
- Remaining effective in short iterations. Because time is at a premium, techniques such as risk-based testing can help focus attention on the important areas.
- Increased regression risk. Because of this, both at the unit level and at a system level, automated regression testing is important in agile projects.
- Inconsistent or inadequate unit testing. When developers short-change unit testing, this creates serious problems because it compounds the increased regression risk and exacerbates the time squeeze inherent in the short iterations.
- Poor, changing, and missing test oracles and a shifting test basis. Embracing change sometimes degrades into changing the content of a sprint or the way it should work without telling the testers, which can lead to a lot of confusion, ineffectiveness, and inefficiency.
- Meeting overload. In some organizations, an improper implementation of agile has led to lots of meetings, reducing the efficiency of the team, including testers.
- Sprint team siloing. On larger projects or system-of-systems projects, where different sprint teams are working on items that need to work—and be tested—together, it's important that a central test team provide the centripetal force needed to achieve a coherent final product.

■ The agile hype cycle and high expectations. Since agile is relatively new in terms of widespread use, the extent to which people are overhyping what it can accomplish—especially consultants and training companies who benefit the most from this hype—has led to unrealistic expectations. When these expectations are not achieved, particularly in the area of increased quality, testers are sometimes blamed.[2]

That said, agile methods also create testing opportunities:

■ Automated unit testing. When it is fully employed, the use of automated unit testing results in much higher-quality code delivered for testing.

■ Static code analysis. More and more agile teams use static code analysis tools, and this also improves the quality of code, especially its maintainability, which is particularly important given the increased regression risk.

■ Code coverage. Agile teams also use code coverage to measure the completeness of their unit tests and, increasingly, their automated functional tests, which helps quantify the level of confidence we can have in the testing.

■ Continuous integration. The use of continuous integration tools, especially when integrated with automated unit testing, static analysis, and code coverage analysis, increases overall code quality and reduces the incidence of untestable builds delivered for testing.

■ Automated functional testing. Agile test tools include a number of automated functional testing tools, some quite good and also free. In addition, automated functional tests can often be integrated into the continuous frameworks as well.

■ Requirements (or user story) reviews and test (acceptance criteria) reviews. In a properly functioning agile team, the user stories and the acceptance criteria are jointly reviewed by the entire team. This can help prevent surprises in terms of what's to be tested and how the software should behave, if the dysfunction mentioned earlier can be avoided.

■ Reasonable workload. While some agile teams abuse this, a properly implemented version of agile will try to keep work weeks within a 40-hour limit, including for testers, even at the end of a sprint.

---

2. See Gartner's web page, www.gartner.com, for an explanation of the hype cycle, which is a branded approach to thinking about new technologies and methodologies.

▨ Control of technical debt (via "fix bugs first"). Some agile teams have a rule that if bugs are allowed to escape from one sprint, they are fixed immediately in the next sprint, before any new user stories are implemented, which does an excellent job of controlling technical debt. [3]

Test planning and management should work to manage the issues and challenges while deriving full benefit from the opportunities.

Planning for Testing in Spiral Models

Finally, we have the spiral model, where early prototypes are used to design the system. The development work goes through a sequence of prototypes that are tested, then redesigned and reprototyped, and retested, until all of the risky design decisions have been proven (or disproven and rejected) through testing. The spiral model was developed by Barry Boehm.

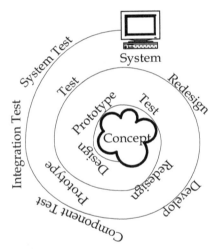

Figure 1–5   *Spiral model*

This model, shown in ?Figure 1–5, has seen service on the largest, most complex of projects, such as the United States' missile defense system, which is under development. I have also used it myself on small projects to develop e-learning packages with new technologies. It is quite useful when applied to projects with a large number of unknowns.

---

3. You can listen to recorded webinars on agile methodologies, and other topics, in the RBCS digital library at http://www.rbcs-us.com/software-testing-resources/library/digital-library.

> **ISTQB Glossary**
>
> **test case:** A set of input values, execution preconditions, expected results and execution postconditions, developed for a particular objective or test condition, such as to exercise a particular program path or to verify compliance with a specific requirement.

However, there are test issues created by it that the smart test manager must manage.

The first issue is that, by its very nature, the designs of the system will change. This means that flexibility is paramount in all test case, test data, test tool, and test environment decisions early in the project. If the test manager commits too heavily to a particular way of generating test data, for example, and the structure of the system data repository changes dramatically, say from a relational database to XML files, that will have serious rework implications in testing.

The second issue is the unique, experimental mode of early testing. Testing of early prototypes is all about finding out what we don't know, subjecting questionable designs to rigorous testing to see what might not work. Confidence building is not an objective, typically. These different test objectives for earlier testing, evolving into a more typical role of testing in the final stages, requires the test manager to change plans and strategies as the project progresses. Again, flexibility is key.

The final issue is that, given the spiral model's attempt to deal with unknowns through repeated prototyping, schedules can be quite unpredictable. This can make estimating and planning the testing work difficult, particularly if other projects are active at the same time.

Again, these are surmountable issues, but they are quite troublesome if not dealt with properly by the test manager.

Test Control and Monitoring

As testing work proceeds, we need to monitor it and, when needed, take control steps to keep it on track for success. During the planning process, the schedule and various monitoring activities and metrics should be defined. Then, as testing proceeds, we use this framework to measure whether we are on track in terms of the work products and test activities we need to complete. Of course, this framework must be aligned with the test strategy and test policy so that we can measure our success at achieving defined objectives. On a small or simple project, success is sometimes more self-evident, but on many projects the effort spent defining this framework is valuable. For example, being able to measure the coverage of risks, requirements, supported configurations, and other elements of the test basis can be very helpful in determining whether the product is ready for release.

When reporting test progress, results, and status, it's important to understand the perspective of project and business stakeholders and explain matters to them in a way that is relevant and clear. The work done during test planning in terms of setting up traceability between the test basis, the test conditions, and other test work products will pay off during test control and monitoring. Traceability will allow you to talk to stakeholders in terms of the extent to which quality risks are mitigated, requirements are met, and supported configurations work properly as well as operational business cycles, use cases, and so forth. This is far better than reporting purely based on defect counts and test case pass/fail status, which is often too far removed from most stakeholders' daily perspectives. I'll cover this topic in more detail later in Chapter 2.

If formal documentation of the system is lacking, then coverage must be established based on targets defined in collaboration with the stakeholders. In risk-based testing, this is done in terms of risks. In agile projects, user stories will provide the basis for testing. Testers should never assume that, since formal documentation of the system is not present, coverage metrics will not be needed. Testing must connect to the important elements of the system and measure for stakeholders the quality of those elements.

Lack of formal documentation can have the salutary effect of driving testers to establish earlier relationships with stakeholders in which the important elements, and how to report test status, are discussed. This earlier relationship leads to a closer alignment between stakeholders' needs and testers' activities throughout the project. So, even when formal documentation such as detailed requirements specifications is available, testers and test managers should make the effort to establish strong relationships with stakeholders right from the start.

The test manager is responsible for ensuring the success of the test effort, which ultimately means the achievement of the mission and objectives as well as the satisfaction of the key testing stakeholders' needs. When testing progresses in a manner that threatens success along one or more of these dimensions, the test manager must take appropriate control actions. As discussed at the Foundation level, those control actions may be local to the test team—in which case test managers can typically act on their own initiative—or involve other project participants—in which case test managers need to coordinate with their coworkers, peers, and senior managers. In the latter situation, having already built strong stakeholder relationships will help buffer the interactions, because control actions are sometimes taken in response to crises where stress levels can be high.

Proper planning helps set the stage for proper control. Proper planning allows for fine-grained visibility into the activities underway, which means deviations from a successful path are found sooner rather than later. Proper planning also provides better metrics, which allows a determination of the nature of the problem and the best way to solve it to be based on facts and data rather than subjective opinion.

Example: Lifecycle-Driven Entry Criteria

Let's look at an example of how development and test tasks interact in the lifecycle. This example, shown in ?Figure 1–6, is from a large, complex project to develop a system of systems providing an entertainment network in North America. These are the entry criteria for the System Integration Test phase, the last of the formal test phases before delivery of the system for operation.

Entry criterion 1 requires that the Pre-Integration Test phase has exited. This was an informal test phase to check, on a risk-driven basis, whether various intersystem interfaces were working properly.

1. Pre-Integration Test has exited.
2. Final, approved versions of the primary specification documents exist and have been provided to the individuals responsible for performing System Integration Testing.
3. This document [System IntegrationTest Plan] and the System IntegrationTestSuite documents are both final and approved.
4. The Network Team configures the [entire] live system for testing ... In addition, all integrated components, hardware and software, must be of the correct major and minor releases ...
5. All Development Teams provide revision-controlled, complete systems for Integration Test, with these products having completed at least one cycle of the applicable System Test.
6. All Development Teams provide all custom documentation needed [for] the software mentioned in entry criteria 5.
7. All Development Teams have plans in place to resolve all known "must-fix" bugs.

Figure 1–6   *Example: Life-cycle-driven entry criteria*

Entry criterion 2 requires that we have final, approved versions of the primary specification documents. This has lifecycle assumptions embedded in it, which is that we are following a lifecycle that would produce such documents.

Entry criterion 3 requires approval of the system integration test plan and the system integration tests. The development and project management teams were to review these documents and provide approval, which was to align development and test activities.

Entry criterion 4 requires that the live system be set up for testing. The lifecycle assumption here is that we would have access to the live system and that it would be ready well in advance of going into production so that we could use it for testing. Obviously, this is a unique criterion, one that only people working on deploying completely new systems would be able to have.

Entry criterion 5 requires that the development teams provide us with revision-controlled, complete systems, which imposes a level of formalism on configuration management. And, we further require that these systems have completed at least one cycle of the applicable system test. That's not to say that the system tests necessarily all pass, but at least enough of the system tests have been run that we're satisfied the systems will provide all major functions.

Entry criterion 6 requires that not only do we get systems, and tested systems, but also that we get whatever documentation is needed.

Finally, entry criterion 7 requires that there be a plan to resolve all known "must-fix" bugs. This imposes a requirement on development and the lifecycle that we not enter integration testing with no end in sight.

As you can see, these entry criteria provide a tight linkage between integration testing, previous testing activities, and the overall development lifecycle.

Test Planning, Monitoring, and Control Exercise

Read the HELLOCARMS system requirements document. Note that some of the sections are still to be completed, with the notation [TBD], meaning to be determined.

Assume that the project will follow an iterative lifecycle model. There will be five iterations. The features and capabilities built in each iteration are based on the priority of the underlying requirement.

Following the ISTQB fundamental test process, outline the test activities required for this project, including each iteration.

Test Planning, Monitoring, and Control Debrief

As a first step, let's review the ISTQB fundamental test process, as discussed in this chapter. It includes the following activities:

- Test Planning, Monitoring, and Control
- Test Analysis
- Test Design
- Test Implementation
- Test Execution
- Evaluating Exit Criteria and Reporting
- Test Closure Activities

In this exercise, you should have integrated the ISTQB fundamental test process activities into the iterative lifecycle.

There are activities in each of these seven areas of the fundamental test process. However, some iterations might not include all areas. Your solution could be structured as shown in ?Figure 1–7 and the subsequent figures. First, you see the work done during the initial project planning period, sometimes referred to as inception. As a test manager, you would define the system integration test plan as well as participate in the overall project planning work. You or a designated test analyst would work with stakeholders to do an initial, high-level quality risk analysis. Based on that analysis, the test analyst would outline the test suites—that is, the groups of tests—needed in each iteration, as a first step toward building out the tests.

```
    1. Initial Project Planning Period
        1.1 Test Planning, Monitoring, and Control
            1.1.1 Create system integration test plan
            1.1.2 Participate in overall project planning
        1.2 Test Analysis
            1.2.1 Perform quality risk analysis
            1.2.2 Outline test suites needed in each iteration
```

Figure 1–7   *Iterative model: initial project planning period*

In the first iteration, shown in ?Figure 1–8, the project team will build and test the very high-priority features. As the test manager, you must adjust the plan for this iteration, monitor test progress, and carry out control activities as needed. The test analysts refine the quality risk analysis, especially for features to be built in this iteration, and design and implement the necessary tests. Those tests are then run. As a test manager, you assess the status, including evaluating the exit criteria defined in the test plan. You periodically deliver this status information to management.

2. Iteration One (Very High Priority Features)
    2.1 Test Planning, Monitoring, and Control
        2.1.1 Adjust plan as needed for this iteration
        2.1.2 Guide testing work during this iteration
    2.2 Test Analysis: Adjust quality risk analysis
    2.3 Test Design: Design test suites and cases for this iteration
    2.4 Test Implementation: Implement test suites for this iteration
    2.5 Test Execution: Execute test suites for this iteration
    2.6 Evaluating Exit Criteria and Reporting
        2.6.1 Check test results against exit criteria in test plan
        2.6.2 Report test results to project management team

Figure 1–8   *Iterative model: iteration one*

Figure 1–9 shows the outline for the second iteration, which is much the same as the first.

3. Iteration Two (High Priority Features)
    3.1 Test Planning, Monitoring, and Control
        3.1.1 Adjust plan as needed for this iteration
        3.1.2 Guide testing work during this iteration
    3.2 Test Analysis: Adjust quality risk analysis
    3.3 Test Design: Design test suites and cases for this iteration
    3.4 Test Implementation: Implement test suites for this iteration
    3.5 Test Execution: Execute test suites for this iteration
    3.6 Evaluating Exit Criteria and Reporting
        3.6.1 Check test results against exit criteria in test plan
        3.6.2 Report test results to project management team

Figure 1–9   *Iterative model: iteration two*

Figure 1–10 shows the outline for the third iteration, which is much the same as the first.

4. Iteration Three (Medium Priority Features)
  4.1 Test Planning, Monitoring, and Control
    4.1.1 Adjust plan as needed for this iteration
    4.1.2 Guide testing work during this iteration
  4.2 Test Analysis: Adjust quality risk analysis
  4.3 Test Design: Design test suites and cases for this iteration
  4.4. Test Implementation: Implement test suites for this iteration
  4.5 Test Execution: Execute test suites for this iteration
  4.6 Evaluating Exit Criteria and Reporting
    4.6.1 Check test results against exit criteria in test plan
    4.6.2 Report test results to project management team

Figure 1–10   Iterativ model: iteration three

Figure 1–11? shows the outline for the fourth iteration, which is much the same as the first.

5. Iteration Four (Low Priority Features)
  5.1 Test Planning, Monitoring, and Control
    5.1.1 Adjust plan as needed for this iteration
    5.1.2 Guide testing work during this iteration
  5.2 Test Analysis: Adjust quality risk analysis
  5.3 Test Design: Design test suites and cases for this iteration
  5.4 Test Implementation: Implement test suites for this iteration
  5.5 Test Execution: Execute test suites for this iteration
  5.6 Evaluating Exit Criteria and Reporting
    5.6.1 Check test results against exit criteria in test plan
    5.6.2 Report test results to project management team

Figure 1–11   Iterative model: iteration four

Figure 1–12? shows the outline for the fifth iteration, which is much the same as the first.

6. Iteration Five (Very Low Priority Features)
    6.1 Test Planning, Monitoring, and Control
         6.1.1 Adjust plan as needed for this iteration
         6.1.2 Guide testing work during this iteration
    6.2 Test Analysis: Adjust quality risk analysis
    6.3 Test Design: Design test suites and cases for this iteration
    6.4 Test Implementation: Implement test suites for this iteration
    6.5 Test Execution: Execute test suites for this iteration
    6.6 Evaluating Exit Criteria and Reporting
         6.6.1 Check test results against exit criteria in test plan
         6.6.2 Report test results to project management team

Figure 1–12   *Iterative model: iteration five*

Finally, you see the work for the post-project period in Figure 1–13. There is some final test control work to be done, in terms of determining the extent to which you have varied from the plan and in participating in the project retrospective. You should also carry out the test closure activities, such as finalizing testware, documenting the test environment, and holding a separate test retrospective if needed.

7. Post Project Period
    7.1 Test Planning, Monitoring, and Control
         7.1.1 Document variances from plan
         7.1.2 Participate in project retrospective
    7.2 Test Closure Activities
         7.2.1 Finalize testware for archiving or handoff
         7.2.2 Document test environment configuration

Figure 1–13   *Iterative model: Post-Project period*

This solution was shown at a high level. You might have included another level of detail below each of the outlined elements in my solution, such as showing the particular test environments, test suites, and test data needed for each iteration.

1.3   Test Analysis

Learning objectives

(K3) Use traceability to check completeness and consistency of defined test conditions with respect to the test objectives, test strategy, and test plan.

(K2) Explain the factors that might affect the level of detail at which test conditions may be specified and the advantages and disadvantages for specifying test conditions at a detailed level.

In test analysis, we are determining what to test. The ISTQB terminology for "what to test" is *test condition*, and a set of test conditions will be produced via the test analysis activities. The question of how to test those test conditions is the realm of test design. The test team identifies these conditions through analysis. The analysis considers test basis documents and work products such as requirements specifications and user stories. It also considers the test objectives as defined in the test policy, strategy, and plans. The analysis can consider quality risks that were identified and assessed during product quality risk analysis sessions. The analysis should take into account the different stakeholders' perspectives on project and product success as well.

Since the test conditions are what we intend to test, then certainly part of being "done" with testing involves ensuring that the test conditions are covered and that the relevant test results are acceptable. So, exit criteria can involve checking the status of the test conditions. For example, one exit criterion could say "100 percent test coverage of each identified test condition must be achieved" and another exit criterion could say that "each test condition must have zero critical failed test cases and zero active must-fix defect reports associated with it." Measurement of these criteria requires traceability between the test conditions and their sources (e.g., the test basis documents) and between the test conditions and the tests and their results.

In the Advanced syllabus, analysis and design activities are separated in order to describe each in more detail. From a timing point of view, design can happen concurrently with analysis. Usually some degree of mental separation, if not temporal separation, makes sense, though, since the two types of activities are different. That said, it's often the case that design work reveals issues that lead to further analysis, so some level of iteration is typically unavoidable. Keep this in mind as you work through the next section on test design.

The Foundation syllabus discussed typical levels of testing, including the main areas of concern for each type of testing. Therefore, the answer to the question of "what to test" varies for each test level. For this reason, test analysis for each level occurs as a separate set of activities, though the results of the analysis for all test levels should be rationalized and aligned as you proceed. The test analysis for a given level of testing can start whenever you have the necessary inputs available. If you are following a requirements-based testing strategy, for example, then the requirements are a necessary input. If you are following a risk-based testing strategy, then the quality risk analysis results would be the input.

The more formal the test strategy and techniques, the more dependent the test team typically is on formal work products as inputs. This is one reason the test manager must carefully align the test strategy and test techniques with the overall development lifecycle and practices of the project that is to be served by the test team. It is a very common dysfunction for test teams to insist on receiving inputs that the project team has no intention or ability to provide. For example, I have seen numerous instances where the project team literally had no ability or motivation to write detailed requirements specifications. If the test team insists that such are necessary inputs to their analysis process, then the test team is at loggerheads with the rest of the project team and indeed has made itself an impediment rather than providing a valuable service.

Another important decision that the test manager must make regarding the test strategy and techniques at this point relates to how much detail to include in the test conditions. Do you want to have a large number of detailed test conditions or a small number of more general test conditions? Are the test conditions high-level descriptions of feature areas to be tested, risks to be covered, and configuration options to be included in the test environment? Or, alternatively, are the test conditions highly detailed, including specific values and variables? Or should the level of documentation be somewhere in between?

The right answer to these questions depends in part on the level of testing. For example, unit testing is typically less formal and not as well documented as system testing. The exception would be in agile teams that are carefully following best practices in terms of unit testing and feature acceptance testing, where some teams use automated tools and thoroughly document the areas of testing via the automated tests.

The level of detail in the test conditions also must be based on how much information the test team is provided during analysis. If you have limited information, testers won't be able to write highly detailed test conditions, even if they want to do so.

In general, the test manager should make smart decisions about the level of detail to be captured in test documentation. Too much detail is wasteful, because time spent documenting is time not spent doing other things. Too little detail can result in a higher rate of false positives and false negatives, though. A balance must be struck, and that must be documented in the test strategy so that testers have good guidance in terms of how to document test work products. When this guidance is not provided, what I usually see in organizations are situations where some testers are overdocumenting while others are under-documenting.

I'll revisit this issue of detailed versus cursory test conditions a little later in this chapter, but first let's look at the graphical view of the test analysis process.

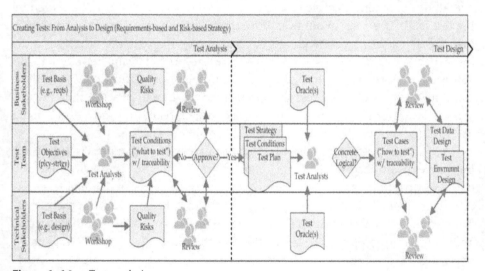

Figure 1–14   *Test analysis process*

Test Analysis and Design

Here you see Figure 1–14? depicting the test analysis process. In the situation shown in the figure, the test team is following a blended requirements-based and risk-based testing strategy. Figures in later sections of this chapter will show the addition of reactive elements to the strategy as well.

In the scenario shown in Figure 1–14?, technical stakeholders such as architects, database designers, and network administrators provide design specifications, metadata, and other technical information to the test analysts. Business stakeholders such as business analysts, product managers, and users provide requirements specifications, use cases, user stories, and other business-focused information to the test analysts. Both business and technical stakeholders participate in a quality risk analysis process that identifies quality risk items for the product and assesses the level of risk associated with each risk item. (I'll cover this process in more detail in the next chapter). Test analysts take all of these inputs, along with the test objectives defined in the test policy or strategy, and document the test conditions to the appropriate level of detail. Traceability between the test conditions and the test bases is captured.

At this point, the test conditions should be subjected to a review by business and technical stakeholders. This review is a bit different than those discussed at the Foundation level, in that it typically has at least the following three objectives:

- Finding defects in the test conditions, including both incorrect test conditions and missing test conditions, and perhaps discussing ways to repair these defects
- Educating the technical and business stakeholders about what is to be tested
- Obtaining stakeholder approval that the set of test conditions are sufficient to achieve their objectives for testing

As such, the review has the characteristics of a technical review and a management review. We'll return to the topic of reviews in a later chapter.

Once the test conditions are defined, they form an input to the test design activities. I'll describe the test design side of the figure in more detail in the next section. It's provided here to show how the analysis activities and their work products flow into the design activities. What is not shown—because it would make the graphic too complicated—is how some level of iteration and parallelism can exist between analysis and design, as mentioned earlier.

Example: SIT Condition Traceability

In Table 1–1?, you see an interesting representation of the test conditions to be covered in system integration testing of a large, complex system of systems. It consisted of seven constituents systems:

A. A custom hardware interactive voice response (IVR) server

B. A wide area network that was planned to span North America in production

C. A custom IVR application

D. A customer service application

E. The custom call center systems (excluding the customer service application running on the agent desktops)

F. A data warehouse used to analyze information from the IVR application and the customer service application

G. A content management system to allow users to create and edit audio content, which is subject to approval by customer service agents

Table 1–1   *Example: SIT condition traceability*

System	BB0	BB1	BB2	BB3	BB4	BB5
A. IVR HW	Alpha		Beta	Quad		Prod
B. Network	LAN					WAN
C. IVR App	C1-E1	C2-D1	C3-D2 C3-G3	C4-D3 C5-F1 C6-E4	C7-F2 C8-D6	C9-D8
D. Customer Service App		D1-C2	D2-C3	D3-C4 D4-G4 D5-E5	D6-C8 D7-F3	D8-C9 D9-F5
E. Call Center	E1-C1 E1-G1	E2-G2	E3-G4	E4-C6 E5-D5		
F. Data Warehouse				F1-C5	F2-C7 F3-D7 F4-G5	F5-D9
G. Content Mgmt	G1-E1	G2-E2	G3-C3 G4-E3	G4-D4	G5-F4	

Each of these systems is shown with a letter label in the table. The IVR server and the network provide the host environments. The other five systems communicate with each other via numbered interfaces. For example, in the second column from the left, in the IVR app row, you can see that interface 1 for the IVR app, labeled C1, communicates with interface 1 of call center system, labeled E1.

While the systems were being developed, we performed six integration builds, labeled BB0 through BB5 across the top. Each column beneath these labels shows the relevant interfaces first introduced in, and tested in, the corresponding build. The builds were cumulative in that each interface, once introduced, remained in all subsequent builds. In addition, the tests were cumulative in that we would repeat the tests of each interface from the previous builds in each subsequent build, which was done efficiently via test automation.

For the IVR server, we used the alpha model in BB0 and BB1, the beta model in BB2, the beta model equipped with quad-density telephony cards in BB3 and BB4, and the production hardware servers in BB5. For the network, we simulated the wide area network (WAN) using a local area network (LAN) for builds BB0 through BB4, switching to the WAN in BB5.

Table 1–1? provides, in a compact fashion, a complete listing of the interfaces tested for each system, when they were first tested, and in what hardware and network configuration.

How Much Detail in Test Conditions?

Let's return to the question of the level of detail to provide in test conditions, whether to be cursory or detailed. We'll start with factors to consider, and then proceed to advantages and disadvantages to detailed test conditions, along with enablers of detailed test conditions and enablers of cursory test conditions.

As I mentioned, different decisions regarding the level of detail in test conditions are made depending on the level of testing. As a test manager and consultant, I have rarely seen developers write detailed documents describing their test conditions for unit testing, except if well-documented automated unit tests are considered a form of detailed test conditions. The test conditions for system testing and system integration testing tend to be much more well documented.

In addition, if you think back to Figure 1–14, you'll remember that the analysis process took inputs from technical and business stakeholders in order to produce the test conditions. Some of these inputs are specifications, network diagrams, database metadata, and other written materials that make up the test bases. If the test basis is very vague, it may be difficult to produce detailed test conditions. If the test basis is relatively low quality, it may not make sense to extract and document detailed test conditions from the test basis because it would effectively be encoding defects in yet another location.

You should also remember from Figure 1–14 that we want to involve the project stakeholders in a review of the test conditions before test design begins. Their availability for this review, as well as their subsequent availability during the project, will influence your decision. For example, if the business stakeholders are highly available during analysis but will not be able to reengage with the test team until test execution begins, you might want to have detailed test conditions because your testers won't be able to ask them questions during test design and implementation.

The complexity of the software or system under test is also a factor. When systems are complex, it's easy to overlook something. You might choose to have more detailed test conditions as a way of ensuring that no important coverage areas are omitted.

The overall level of quality risk is a factor as well. With safety-critical systems such as medical devices, for example, test documentation must be highly detailed, to the extent that someone without in-depth knowledge of the project or product can audit the test documentation and be confident that everything important was covered.

Project risks are also a factor. When using an outsourced testing service provider, a major project risk can be their failure to cover important areas of the system. Detailed test conditions, given to the outsourced vendor and referenced in the contract as a prerequisite for payment, can help manage this risk. Cursory test conditions would simply leave too much to the judgment and interpretation of the vendor.

The need to mitigate a similar risk via detailed test conditions exists when testers with lower-than-ideal skills or experience must be used. With highly skilled and experienced testers, cursory test conditions may suffice.

You should also consider material factors such as the structure of the test basis documents themselves, the approach and tools used to capture traceability between the test conditions and the test basis, and the level of detail needed for test cases and other work products to be produced. For example, it's quite possible that the test management tools will have a built-in preference or default for the level of detail, and in some cases these tools can be uncooperative when attempts are made to override these defaults. On the whole, these considerations might make it clear that a higher or lower level of detail will be more efficient to implement.

The software lifecycle is also a factor. For agile lifecycles, lightweight documentation of all types—including test documentation—is preferred.

The maturity of the test process and other development processes is also a factor. It's not necessarily an obvious decision, since you can't always say, "Well, our test process is immature, and therefore we need to document more heavily to try to make up for it." You might find that the attempt to produce and maintain thorough documentation is beyond the maturity of your process. It might even be utterly unnecessary because the skills of the testers might lead you to determine that no such level of detail is needed.

Finally, keep in mind that, all other things being equal, detailed test conditions mean more test conditions. The syllabus provides a useful example. You might have a single general test condition, "test checkout," for an e-commerce application. If you wanted to have detailed test conditions, you'd need to have test conditions such as "test American Express checkout," "test Visa checkout," "test US destination," "test European destination," and so forth, providing specific test conditions for each payment method, destination country, and other relevant details.

Advantages of Detailed Test Conditions

Okay, so what advantages might detailed test conditions offer? Let's consider them.

First, consider the example in the previous section, where the "test checkout" condition was replaced by a dozen or more detailed conditions. When testers design, implement, and execute the tests to cover those conditions, they are less likely to miss something, and less likely to waste time trying to figure out what specifically to test, because the specific areas of desired coverage were indicated by the test conditions. In addition, when reporting results, if there is a problem with one of the "test checkout" tests, you can talk specifically about which of these conditions has failed.

This also has a manifestation in terms of clearer horizontal traceability. To continue the example, it's quite possible that the test condition "test checkout" maps back to a larger set of requirements. There would be a loss of resolution if we have "test checkout" with a one-to-many relationship with these requirements and then a one-to-many relationship between "test checkout" and the tests that cover it. The detailed test conditions could preserve a clearer trace from each individual requirement down to the tests, and the relationship between other test work products and the test conditions can be more clearly and cleanly captured.

Trying to create detailed test conditions is more work than creating general test conditions, of course, in part because a much closer inspection of the inputs must occur. Consider a situation where you are managing system test and part of the analysis process includes creating detailed test conditions from a requirements specification. The close reading of the requirements specification is likely to find more defects than a cursory reading would. Therefore, there is a defect prevention benefit to detailed test conditions, if they are created early in the development process.

In addition, detailed test conditions can have a defect-prevention benefit for testing as well. As shown in Figure 1–14?, we want test stakeholders to review the test conditions. If the test conditions are specific and detailed, the test stakeholders are more likely to notice omissions and mistakes as well as to understand exactly what you are proposing to test. When the test results are reported in terms of test conditions, that also contributes to stakeholder understanding of the results, in a way that is much more meaningful than simply reporting the number of test cases run, passed, and failed.

Finally, detailed test conditions can be useful to other project team members. For example, detailed test conditions provide not only a specific blueprint to testers in terms of what to test, they also provide that blueprint to developers who know what will be tested against their work products. So, when building their code, developers can refer to what will be tested as well as to the requirements and design specifications.

Using Detailed Test Conditions

Which situations enable the most effective use of detailed test conditions?

One example of a good fit for detailed test conditions is any situation where you will need to use lightweight test documentation during design or implementation. For example, you might have more time for analysis, but design and implementation timelines are short. Or, you have more budget for the resources performing the test analysis and less for the resources performing test design and implementation. Or, you are following an agile lifecycle where detailed acceptance criteria are seen as important but heavily documented test cases are not.

Another example of a good fit for detailed test conditions is where the test basis documents are scanty or entirely missing. While you cannot develop the detailed test conditions directly from the test basis documents, you can work with the business and technical stakeholders to try to elicit the details from them. These detailed test conditions can help fill in the gaps in the test basis documents during test design and implementation.

Finally, as mentioned earlier, another example of a good fit for detailed test conditions is where you have large, complex, or high-risk projects. In large and complex projects, you are likely to have thousands of test cases, and a direct relationship to the test basis and other development work products might be difficult to use and maintain. In high-risk projects, such as the regulated products I mentioned earlier, having fine-grained test conditions will support auditing.

Disadvantages of Detailed Test Conditions

Okay, so what disadvantages might be entailed in the use of detailed test conditions? Let's consider them.

First, to mention the obvious, you should expect to expend a lot of effort and thus money to develop detailed test conditions unless the project is very small. Extensive documentation requires extensive effort to create, and that effort is time not spent doing other things.

Second, not only are the initial costs and effort typically high, the long-term costs and effort associated with maintenance can also be high. This is especially true if you are working on a project where features are added, dropped, and extensively changed repeatedly throughout the project. I've worked on a few projects like this, and consulted with a number of clients working on such projects, and have found that all documentation, including test condition documentation, is best kept lightweight.

Finally, it's tough to get test analysts all marching to the same drummer in terms of test condition documentation when the format is very specific, very detailed, and very formal. You have to invest in training them in how to create and maintain the documentation. When new test analysts come on board, they must also be trained before they are allowed to work on the test conditions. While this seems like a minor matter, it's not. I've seen many situations where a lack of standardization in terms of test documentation leads to enormous variation in the level of detail captured.

Using Cursory Test Conditions

In which situations are general test conditions more effective?

One example of a good fit for general test conditions is any situation where the test basis maps cleanly to the tests being designed and implemented. You'll see a specific example of that in a bit. A clean mapping of the test basis to the tests themselves usually means three things. First, the tests for each test basis element are fairly obvious. Second, the pass/fail criteria are clear from the test basis (i.e., the test basis can also be used as the test oracle). Third, the relationship between test basis elements and tests is a one-to-few type of relationship. In other words, the relationship is hierarchical, where each test basis element maps to one or at most a handful of tests.

Another example of a good fit for general test conditions is component testing. Unless there are serious cohesion problems with the code, each class (in object-oriented systems) or function (in procedural languages) does only a few things. There simply aren't that many test conditions that apply, and they shouldn't be convoluted.

Yet another example of a good fit for general test conditions is acceptance testing if you have sufficiently detailed use cases. The details of the tests can be encapsulated in each use case. The test conditions simply summarize what is being tested, such as "test checkout" for an e-commerce application or "test saving and resuming a game" for a gaming application.

Example: Test Conditions Level of Detail

A few years ago, at RBCS, we went through a project to redesign our website. We hired a marketing firm to help us create the content and a web development company to implement the site.

We had a statement of work, included in the contract with the web development company. This included the requirements for the site.

As part of the project, we planned to do an acceptance test. This acceptance testing, like most such test levels, had the primary objective of demonstrating readiness for release. Since the requirements were the contract between RBCS and the web development company, we used a requirements-based testing strategy.

Based on this strategy, we developed a plan to cover all the stated and implied requirements. This involved documented test cases, though they were documented at the logical level, not the concrete level. We also used some amount of exploratory testing in areas where the requirements were vague or implied.

In Figure 1–15?, you can see an example of how two paragraphs in one section of the requirements specification became general test conditions. The mapping is clean, as mentioned in a previous section, and quite easy to follow.

Notice that the first two test conditions are relatively clear and unambiguous. There are a number of different specific test conditions possible in these test cases, which cause a lot of variation in terms of what was actually tested here. However, the test oracle—the definition of expected behavior—is clear: If a returning customer has to reenter billing or shipping information after signing in, or cannot sign in at all, that is a bug.

The third test case is, at first glance, ambiguous. What is the expected behavior? There are millions of e-commerce sites. Which one defines the standard? What we did in practice was to use Amazon.com as the reference site. You could say that it really didn't matter which major site we picked as long as we picked a major site, and I would agree.

Requirements excerpt	*Test conditions excerpt*
Returning customers can use the sign in page to avoid having to re-enter all of their shipping and billing information when they place an order. The sign in and customer account management features have a structure and functionality similar to what is becoming standard on most major e-commerce sites.	1. Returning customers can use the sign in page to avoid re-entering their shipping information
	2. Returning customers can use the sign in page to avoid re-entering their billing information when they place an order
	3. The sign in and customer account management features have a structure and functionality similar to...major e-commerce sites.
[Vendor] will provide a letter certifying PCI compliance, suitable for forwarding to Paymentech and/or credit card companies if needed.	4. [Vendor] will provide a letter certifying PCI compliance

Figure 1–15   *Test conditions*

The fourth test case is clear at first glance. Either there's a compliance letter, and it's professional in appearance, or there is not. However, if you ask, "Well, what does PCI compliance require?" then that opens up the question of what should this letter's content be? Ultimately, we had to trust that the vendor had done this before and checked the letter by submitting it to a credit card processing company.

Test Analysis Exercise

Assume you are using a risk-based testing strategy for the HELLOCARMS project. In a risk-based testing strategy, quality risks are identified and prioritized (usually in collaboration with technical and business stakeholders) for the system, and then tests are used to mitigate these identified risks until the remaining level of risk is acceptable.

One potential pitfall of such a strategy arises when significant quality risks are not identified. Describe ways to use traceability to check for gaps in the quality risk analysis.

Test Analysis Debrief

There are a number of ways to use traceability to check the completeness of the quality risk analysis:

- Categorize the quality risk items based on functional and nonfunctional attributes (e.g., functionality, performance, installation, etc.) or characteristics (e.g., using ISO 9126), organizing the list of risk items according to these categories. If no risk items are associated with a given category, check whether this indicates a gap, and if a gap is indicated, identify the quality risks in that category.

- Cross-reference the requirements specification against the quality risk items, ensuring that at least one risk item has been identified for each requirements specification element. (Note that many-to-many relationships will sometimes exist.) If any requirements elements exist that do not have associated risk items, identify one or more risk items related to those requirements elements. Establish traceability between the requirements elements and the risk items.

- As test execution proceeds, establish traceability between defects reported and risk items, especially for exploratory tests. If any defect is discovered that does not relate to a risk item, this indicates a gap in the risk item list. Identify the missing quality risk items, add them to the list, and take appropriate steps to address them with tests.

Notice that the traceability required here can be implemented in a test management tool, a database, or a spreadsheet. The use of a spreadsheet for traceability generally does not scale easily on large projects.

1.4 Test Design

Learning objectives

(K3) Use traceability to check completeness and consistency of designed test cases with respect to the defined test conditions.

In test design, we are determining how to test, based on the test conditions previously identified during analysis. We will take each condition—or perhaps a coherent set of conditions—and decide how to effectively and efficiently cover it with tests. Ideally, the test strategy or test plan will describe how that process works.

Let's look at an example. Suppose you are following a requirements-based test strategy for a browser-based e-commerce application. The requirements have described the screens on the application and each input field on each screen. From the requirements, a test analyst has identified the test condition "check rejection of invalid input values on all screens."

So, to create the tests, we would need examples of each screen. Mock-ups built using HTML could be used in this situation. For each screen, each input field would need to be shown. We would also need a description (hopefully in the requirements) of the valid values for each field.

Suppose a study of past projects has shown that most defects associated with accepting invalid inputs can be effectively found with equivalence partitioning and boundary value analysis. So, the next step would be to methodically apply these techniques to each field. Inputs representing invalid partitions or boundary values would be selected for testing.

These test values would then be associated with certain expected results, in this case error messages. Again, testers would look to the requirements to define what error messages should occur given certain specific invalid inputs. Testers would then document the inputs and their expected results in tests. This documentation should be consistent with the standards you as a test manager have defined, often in a test strategy document.

Test Design and Implementation

In Figure 1–16?, you see a graph depicting the test design process. To remind you, the test team is following a blended requirements-based and risk-based testing strategy. The addition of reactive elements to the strategy will arrive in a subsequent figure.

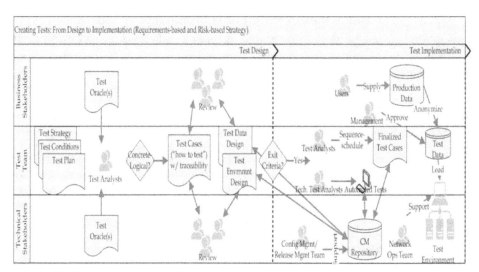

Figure 1–16   *Test design process*

As shown in Figure 1–16, the test analysts are using the test strategy, test conditions, and test plan as inputs into their test design process. The test analysts are also obtaining test oracles from the business and technical stakeholders if the test basis documents are not sufficient in themselves—and they often aren't.

With the test design inputs established, an important decision point is reached: Are we going to produce concrete or logical test cases? While you should remember these terms and concepts from the Foundation syllabus, this point is sufficiently important that I will address it in detail below.

Whichever level of detail is appropriate for the test cases, the test analysts then produce the test cases at that level of detail. The test cases should have traceability information captured as they are created, which is another topic I'll address again shortly. As part of test case design, the test analysts must also design the test data required for the test cases and the test environment in which the tests will run.

With these three major test work products drafted, the test analysts engage again with the business and technical stakeholders. Once again reviews occur, with similar objectives:

- Finding defects in the test cases, the test data design, and the test environment design, including both mistakes and omissions, and perhaps discussing ways to repair those defects
- Educating the technical and business stakeholders about how the testing will occur, at least to the extent they need to and want to understand
- Obtaining stakeholder approval and, for some stakeholders, a commitment to provide the necessary support, such as business stakeholders providing production data or technical stakeholders helping to configure and support test environments

Once these work products are approved as sufficiently complete and correct, you should check any other exit criteria that you (as the test manager) have defined for test design. If those other criteria are satisfied as well, then the test data design and test environment design should be checked into the project's configuration management repository. This repository is supported by the project's configuration management or release management team.

The test case designs are passed on to test analysts and technical test analysts for implementation. I'll describe the test implementation side of the figure in more detail in a later section. It's provided here to show how the design activities and their work products flow into the implementation activities. As I mentioned earlier, I have not shown the potential for iteration and parallelism.

Traceability

As I mentioned, testers frequently want to capture traceability information as tests are being designed. This can be done by relating the tests directly to the test basis elements they cover, skipping the test conditions, or it can be done indirectly through the test conditions. In the latter case, it's usually better that the test conditions be sufficiently detailed that no loss of resolution occurs when this traceability information is used for test monitoring and result reporting, as discussed earlier. A loss of resolution can happen when a number of requirements trace to a single test condition and that condition then traces to multiple tests. If a single test fails, it's unclear which of the requirements are not satisfied in this situation.

The traceability information should be bidirectional. That way, you can trace from an individual requirement, risk item, or other test basis element down to the tests and, during execution, their results. Test basis elements can also include strategic objectives, test objectives and other project or stakeholder criteria for success. You can also trace from individual tests and their results back to the test basis elements. This will allow you, as the test manager, to relate the tests to aspects of the project and product that stakeholders care about rather than talking in less meaningful—to test stakeholders anyway—abstractions such as test case counts and defect counts.

Consider this example. Suppose, for the e-commerce application mentioned earlier, marketing is telling people that the online store is robust and secure. They want testing to help them feel more confident about this claim. Robustness and security involve a number of factors, but one very important factor is the rejection of invalid inputs. As mentioned earlier, your team is designing tests for invalid inputs. If the testers capture proper traceability from these tests to marketing's objective for a robust, secure store, you will be able to report results in terms of the level of confidence marketing should have.

Inputs and Outputs for Test Design

The test conditions are one of the necessary inputs for test design. However, the test conditions only say "what to test" and not "how to test." As mentioned, if we have the test condition "check rejection of invalid input values on all screens," the test analyst needs examples of each screen and each field on each screen, the error messages for each field that are associated with invalid inputs, and a description of the valid values for each field. (Remember that the test analyst can use equivalence partitioning and boundary value analysis, as discussed in the Foundation syllabus, to infer the invalid values, given the valid values.)

In this example, the test analyst needs additional information about how the system behaves. In some cases, information about how the system is built is relevant. For example, if we have the risk item "slow system response time under maximum load," the technical test analyst will need not only information about acceptable response time and the various user screens but also system design and implementation information such as network and system resources, database design, and so forth.

As these two examples illustrate, the specific additional information needed will vary because different test types and techniques require different kinds of information. In addition, the degree of detail that testers will include in the test cases also influences the amount of information needed, with more detailed (or concrete) test cases requiring more information than less detailed (or logical) test cases. I'll return to the issue of concrete and logical test cases in a moment.

The test strategy should make clear the processes of gathering inputs, determining test types and techniques, producing outputs, and capturing those outputs at the appropriate level of detail. If any of these processes change in a given project, the test approach from the test plan should make those changes clear.

Logical or Concrete Test Cases

Let's return to this issue of logical and concrete test cases, beginning with the ISTQB glossary definitions of these terms.

A logical (high-level) test case is defined as "a test case without concrete (implementation level) values for input data and expected results. Logical operators are used; instances of the actual values are not yet defined and/or available."

A concrete (low-level) test case is defined as "a test case with concrete (implementation level) values for input data and expected results. Logical operators from high-level test cases are replaced by actual values that correspond to the objectives of the logical operators."

Let's consider the e-commerce example again. Logical tests could include annotated examples of each screen, with each input field highlighted and the valid values indicated. The tests would also specify that test analysts should use equivalence partitioning and boundary value analysis to identify the specific input test values. Finally, logical tests would specify where to find the expected results, in this case the error messages, though the tests would not include the messages themselves.

Concrete tests would go beyond logical tests by including all of the actual invalid values to be tested for each field. (Note that we'd no longer need to list the test techniques since those would already have been used to generate the values.) The specific error messages would be included and associated with each specific invalid value.

As you saw in Figure 1–16, the test analyst must understand which style of documentation is required before starting to produce the test cases; otherwise, substantial problems can occur. If concrete tests are written when only logical tests are required, the resulting overdocumented test cases are more expensive than necessary. They are also error prone when used by testers who feel excessively scripted because they tend to deviate from the tests and miss important areas. If logical tests are written when concrete tests are required, the resulting underdocumented tests are cheap to produce but very error prone when used by testers who cannot figure out how to follow the limited guidance given.

In reality, the concepts of "concrete tests" and "logical tests" are not binary states but rather extreme ends on a spectrum. Test managers must understand the trade-offs inherent in various degrees of documentation and define expectations clearly in the test strategy. Otherwise—as I have seen many times as a consultant—different testers will produce test cases with widely different degrees of detail, usually with a variance of two orders of magnitude separating the most detailed and the least detailed test cases.

In addition, the process of developing test cases is often stepwise. Logical test cases can be created first (during test design), with concrete test cases created later (during test implementation). In the case of reactive test strategies, the test charter is a logical test case, and the tester transforms the charter into a concrete test case—albeit an undocumented one, usually—at the time of test execution. Notice that all test cases ultimately do become concrete, in that specific values are supplied and some test oracle is consulted to evaluate the result. However, not all concrete test cases are documented.

Sequential or Iterative Process

While the syllabus describes the processes of analysis, design, implementation, and execution sequentially, considerable parallelism and even iteration are possible, as shown in Figure 1–17?. The test level and the test strategy have a great deal of influence on the degree of iteration that will occur. System test, system integration test, and acceptance test are typically more sequential, in part because the main test bases—requirements, quality risks, lists of supported configurations, and so on—are available so much earlier than the start of test execution in many cases. In unit test, where the main test bases—detail design and the code itself—are available right before test execution starts, test analysis and test design tend to occur in parallel and to iterate after test execution. An analytical test strategy, where careful analysis of the test bases occurs, tends to be more sequential, while reactive test strategies, where testers react to the system as delivered to them, are inherently iterative.

Even when a primarily sequential process is pursued, some overlap between test analysis, design, and implementation can be helpful. For example, proceeding from test data design to actually starting to generate test data—which is a test implementation activity—can often reveal subtleties to the test conditions. This can refine the test cases and possibly even lead to the discovery of new test conditions.

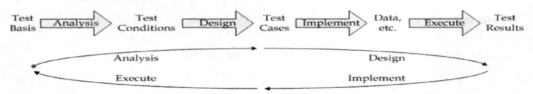

Figure 1–17   *Sequential versus iterative process*

Example: ISO 61508 Testing Implications

An interesting example of test design in the engineering of complex and/or safety-critical systems is found in the ISO/IEC standard 61508, which is mentioned in the Advanced syllabus. It is especially for embedded software that controls systems with safety-related implications, as you can tell from its title: "Functional safety of electrical/electronic/programmable electronic safety-related systems."

The standard is very much focused on mitigating quality risk through test analysis, test design, test implementation, and test execution, with careful traceability maintained throughout that process. Risk analysis is required. It considers two primary factors as determining the level of risk, likelihood and impact. During a project, we are to reduce the residual level of risk to a tolerable level, specifically through the application of electrical, electronic, or software improvements to the system.

The standard has an inherent philosophy about risk. It acknowledges that we can't attain a level of zero risk—whether for an entire system or even for a single risk item. It says that we have to build quality, especially safety, in from the beginning, not try to add it at the end, and thus must take defect-preventing actions like requirements, design, and code reviews.

The standard also insists that we know what constitutes tolerable and intolerable risks and that we take steps to reduce intolerable risks. When those steps involve test analysis, test design, test implementation, and test execution, the tasks and work products must be documented. These include software safety validation plans, software test specifications, software test results, software safety validation and verification reports, and software functional safety reports. The standard is concerned with the author-bias problem, which as you should recall from the Foundation syllabus is the problem with self-testing, so it calls for tester independence, indeed insisting on it for those performing any safety-related tests. And, since testing is most effective when the system is written to be testable, that's also a requirement.

The standard has a concept of a safety integrity level (SIL), which is based on the likelihood of failure for a particular component or subsystem and the impact that failure would have on the safety of the system. The safety integrity level influences a number of risk-related decisions, including the choice of testing and QA techniques.

Some of the techniques are ones we cover in *Advanced Software Testing–Vol. 1* (Rocky Nook), such as the various functional and black-box testing design techniques.

Many of the techniques are ones covered in *Advanced Software Testing–Vol. 3* (Rocky Nook), including probabilistic testing, dynamic analysis, data recording and analysis, performance testing, interface testing, static analysis, and complexity metrics. Additionally, since thorough coverage, including during regression testing, is important in reducing the likelihood of missed bugs, the standard mandates the use of applicable automated test tools.

Again, depending on the safety integrity level, various levels of testing might be required. These levels include module testing, integration testing, hardware-software integration testing, safety requirements testing, and system testing. If a level is required, the standard states that it should be documented and independently verified. In other words, auditing or outside reviews of testing activities can be required.

Continuing on in that vein of "guarding the guards," the standard also requires reviews for test cases, test procedures, and test results, along with verification of data integrity under test conditions.

Structural testing is a required test design technique. So, structural coverage is implied, again based on the safety integrity level. Because the desire is to have high confidence in the safety-critical aspects of the system, complete requirements coverage is required not once but multiple times, at multiple levels of

> **ISTQB Glossary**
>
> **test procedure:** A document specifying a sequence of actions for the execution of a test. Also known as test script or manual test script.
>
> **test script:** Commonly used to refer to a test procedure specification, especially an automated one.

testing. Again, the level of test coverage required depends on the safety integrity level. To demonstrate coverage, thorough traceability information must be captured throughout the test development and execution process.

Now, this might seem a bit excessive, especially if you come from a very informal world. However, the next time you step between two pieces of metal that can move—for example, elevator doors—ask yourself how much risk you want to remain in the software that controls that movement.

We'll return to this topic of risk in Chapter 2.

Traceability Exercise

Continue the scenario from the previous exercise.

A general problem with analytical testing strategies, such as risk-based testing, is that test conditions are identified and prioritized but not all of the necessary tests are created. Describe ways to use traceability to check for gaps in the coverage of the quality risk items.

Traceability Debrief

There are a number of ways to use traceability to check the completeness of the test cases with respect to the quality risk items:

- Ensure capture of bidirectional traceability between each quality risk item and the test(s) that cover it as tests are designed.
- Carry out reviews of each test, and include the traceability information and the covered quality risk item as part of the review. Ensure that the review participants evaluate (1) whether the test does cover that quality risk item and (2) whether the quality risk item is sufficiently covered.
- Monitor and control test design by periodically evaluating coverage achieved and coverage remaining to be achieved using the traceability information. Adjust the planned coverage if time constraints become an issue.

As before, the traceability required here can be implemented in a test management tool, a database, or a spreadsheet. The use of a spreadsheet for traceability generally does not scale easily on large projects.

1.5   Test Implementation

Learning objectives

(K3) Use risks, prioritization, test environment and data dependencies, and constraints to develop a test execution schedule which is complete and consistent with respect to the test objectives, test strategy, and test plan.

During test implementation, test analysts will organize the test cases to be ready to run. This can include preliminary assignment of ownership and proper formatting of the tests. In formal situations, high-risk products, projects where lower-skilled testers will execute the tests, and other settings in which formal documentation of the tests is required, logical tests produced during test design may be elaborated into concrete tests during implementation.

If an organization is following the IEEE 829 standard to the letter, then the test case specifications are separate from the test procedure specifications. The test case specifications include the inputs and expected results, while the test procedure specifications include the steps required to run one or more test cases. However, most organizations do not go to this extent but rather include the inputs, expected results, and steps in a single document, variously called a test case, a test procedure, or a test script.

The tests—whether documented at a logical or concrete level, and whether called cases, procedures, or scripts—should be prioritized during test implementation. In risk-based testing, this includes using the level of risk associated with each test to determine its priority. In the absence of any other considerations, the higher-risk tests come earlier and the lower-risk tests come later. That said, there usually *are* other considerations, which I'll discuss in a moment.

Test implementation also involves the implementation of the test data design created during test design. Since there's a fair amount of confusion about the test data versus test inputs, and the specific placement of various test data activities, let's review two relevant ISTQB glossary definitions.

First is the term *test data*, which is defined as "data that exists (for example, in a database) before a test is executed, and that affects or is affected by the component or system under test." As you can see, test data is clearly separated from test inputs by this definition. It's important to be clear that this distinction is not simply a matter of whether the data enters the system through a graphical user interface. If a test is operating at a command-line interface or an application programming interface, the test inputs are entering via that interface.

Second is the term *test data management*, which is defined as "the process of analyzing test data requirements, designing test data structures, creating and maintaining test data." Now, the first part of the process fits into analysis, the second part into design, the third part into implementation, and the fourth part, maintenance, into execution and beyond, so long as the data continues to exist. The test data that's being managed here can be in a flat file, a big data repository such as Hadoop, a relational database, a hierarchical or tree-structure data file, or what have you.

So, in implementation, test analysts create data that will be preloaded or otherwise provided to the system under test through an interface other than the interface through which the tests are being executed. There is often a need to document the test data more completely than was done in the initial test data design. That will also happen during test implementation.

Similar to test data, test implementation also involves the implementation of the test environment design created during test design. As with test data implementation, my experience is that test environment implementation is often—and in my opinion, ideally—started in parallel with test design. That way, test teams can avoid rude surprises in terms of the cost, configuration time, and testability of hardware and software in the environment.

Another way to visualize the implementation process is shown in ?Figure 1–18.

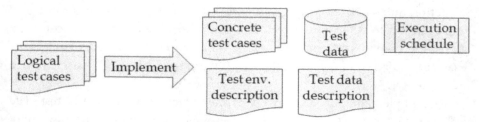

Figure 1–18   *Further elaboration of test cases in test implementation*

Test Implementation and Execution

Figure 1–19? depicts the test implementation process. To remind you, the test team is following a blended requirements-based and risk-based testing strategy through test design. With the entry into test implementation, the test team starts to add reactive elements to the strategy.

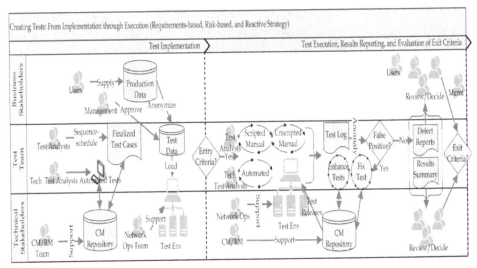

Figure 1–19   *Test implementation process*

Let's start with the role test analysts play at this point in the fundamental test process in terms of the test cases. During implementation, as shown in Figure 1–19?, test analysts will finalize the test cases, either as logical or concrete tests. If the organization is following a formal approach to test definition as set out in IEEE 829, then the test cases will be further elaborated into test procedures. Either way, the finalized tests should be checked into the configuration management repository along with the test conditions and all applicable test traceability information.

During implementation, technical test analysts should be automating tests where appropriate. We'll return to the question of which tests should be automated—and how—in Chapter 6. At this point, though, I'll mention that test automation ideally starts earlier than the finalization of manual tests, so the implementation tasks for automation are starting at an earlier point in time and asynchronously with the manual test process. As those automated tests are completed, though, they should also be checked into the configuration management repository, and similar traceability information should be captured.

Now, in terms of both automated and manual tests, the test environment should be set up according to the design created earlier. As mentioned previously, the set-up of the test environment may start well before the start of the implementation of the manual tests and even before the start of the implementation of the automated tests. This can be important for the automation work because development and debugging of the automated tests may well rely on the implementation of the test environment. In addition, early versions of both manual and automated tests may be required to determine whether the test environment is correctly configured, which is an essential part of test environment implementation. It is often the case that the test team needs the help of the organization's network operations team to configure and debug the test environment. As a test manager, you should make sure that this support is available when needed, and that must be considered during test planning. The implementation of a test environment is often a major effort in its own right, and the wise test manager will have carefully considered this point.

Similarly, the test plan should address how test data is implemented at this point. The overall design for the test data was completed during test design, and now that design must be implemented. In some cases, users will need to support this process by supplying production data. That production data often must be anonymized—that is, by the removal of personal identifying information—as part of this process. Management approval of this anonymization process and the subsequent use of the anonymized data is usually required in this case. The implementation of test data, whether anonymized production data or specially generated test data or both, is often a major effort in its own right, and the wise test manager will have carefully considered this point too.

As the test data is created, it should be loaded into the test environment. This process can be highly iterative and can reveal opportunities for improvement of the design of the test cases, the test data, and the test environment. In some cases, these opportunities involve ways to expand the coverage of the test cases and the test data, which must be backward-propagated to the test conditions and the traceability information. In the worst case, the loading of the test data reveals inadequacies in the test environment design, especially in terms of capacity. It's best to avoid this situation through careful test planning.

As the test cases, the test data, and the test environment are finalized, the test manager should start to check the entry criteria for test execution. These entry criteria should have been defined in the test plan (and, generically, in the test strategy). In addition, the entry criteria include elements beyond the control of the test manager, such as the readiness of the software to be tested. This topic will be addressed in future sections of this book.

Once the entry criteria are met, we are ready to move into test execution. The decision as to whether the entry criteria are met is often the subject of a management review with business and technical stakeholders. In this review, the test manager wants to obtain a stakeholder decision on whether test execution is ready to start. Some stakeholders must also commit to provide the necessary support for test execution once it starts, such as reviewing and prioritizing defects, evaluating test results and exit criteria, and helping to support test environments and test data.

I'll describe the right side of Figure 1–19 in more detail in later sections. It's provided here to show how the implementation activities and their work products flow into the execution activities. As I mentioned, I have not shown the potential for iteration and parallelism, which can lead to changes in the test analysis, test design, and test implementation. It is not always a failure of these predecessor processes when test execution reveals such necessary changes, but it can indicate such a problem. Therefore, the test manager should carefully evaluate any such changes to learn lessons for improvement on future projects.

Test Execution Schedule

As was shown in Figure 1–19?, the tests must be scheduled and sequenced during test implementation. There are a number of important considerations that must be kept in mind during this process.

The schedule must take into account both manual and automated tests, if you have both types of tests. I saw one instance where a tester ran automated tests overnight without coordinating with the manual testers, and the automated tests modified data that some of the manual testers had loaded the previous day. This resulted in a lot of confusion and false positives.

The schedule should attempt to honor the priorities assigned to the tests. These priorities can be based on the priority of the associated requirement, the level of the associated quality risk, stakeholder objectives, and other factors.

That said, the schedule has to take into account the various constraints that affect the practical order in which tests can be efficiently run. The availability of testers with the required skills is one such constraint. Another constraint can be whether a test environment must be reconfigured to run a different set of tests, because this can make it more efficient to run all the tests that share an environment before changing to a new environment. Dependencies between tests or between tests and test data create similar kinds of efficiency concerns.

Project risks should also be taken into account. If you have had problems with untestable builds being delivered for testing, having an automated smoke test that's run before other testing starts can help manage this risk.

Care must be exercised when creating a test schedule. The test manager should carefully review the schedule and ideally include the test team in the review. I have seen situations where attempts to run tests that weren't ready to run caused a great deal of waste. In some cases, testing has appeared blocked but actually tests could have been run had a different schedule been followed. If the wrong data is loaded based on the environment set up, you can get a situation where no tests can be run until either the data or the environment is changed.

Ready for Test Execution?

Part of the test implementation step includes making sure that you are indeed ready to start test execution. As a test manager, you should be very careful here, because assuming that everything is ready is a common mistake, and it leads to all kinds of unhappy outcomes. I've had these outcomes myself as a test manager, and I've seen them happen to clients. Here are some of the things you should check.

One of the important things to check is the test environment. I had a multimillion dollar test environment brought to a complete halt by the lack of a five dollar cable once, simply because I trusted someone outside of the test team to deliver it on time. Trust, but verify, as the Russian proverb goes. If, due to necessity, the test environment will evolve during test execution, double-check all changes that need to occur, including checking the test execution schedule. If a necessary component is due to arrive on a particular date, confirm that date and have a contingency plan in case it doesn't arrive.

Similarly, check the readiness of the test data. Even if the test data is loaded, that doesn't mean that you can be confident that it's ready. See if there are ways to check the data before testing can start.

You should also check quality and completeness and testability of the software. This is not entirely in your control, of course, so you need to listen carefully to other project participants and stakeholders. If you hear, directly or indirectly, that issues will exist in this area when you try to start testing, you should again consider what your contingency plan is. It'll be immensely frustrating to you and to other stakeholders on the project if your team is rendered dead in the water on the first day of test execution.

One best practice that has worked for me in terms of software, data, and environment readiness is the use of smoke tests or acceptance tests to check that all is indeed ready. Accepting an early release of the software, installing it in the test environment, and running some basic tests of functionality a few days prior to the start of test execution has worked well for me and for RBCS's clients.

Something that *is* in your control is the question of whether the tests are all ready to run. The tests should be written, to whatever level of detail is required. A review of the tests should have been completed, and you should check that they have been completed. Similarly, double-check the schedule, and again consider the constraints related to available people, environments, and data. If people outside the test team are required to support the execution of particular tests, do these people know that you are relying on them, and do they know when you'll need their help?

As part of test planning, you should have defined—and obtained consensus about—the entry criteria for testing. Each of these criteria should be checked. If any are not met, you should resolve the problems that you can resolve and escalate those problems that require outside assistance. There are often also implicit entry criteria, and you should check these too.

This list is by no means exhaustive. I've had various unexpected misfortunes occur during test execution that could have been avoided by careful checking beforehand. Try to anticipate what could go wrong during test execution and check it before it becomes a problem. You'll bolster your reputation as a competent manager if your group is the one that's seldom caught flatfooted by a predictable problem.

Example: Preconditions for Test Execution

Let's look at some examples of preconditions for starting test execution. In Figure 1–20, you can see the entry criteria for a test project that RBCS ran.

1. Bug tracking and test tracking systems are in place.

2. All components are under formal, automated configuration management and release management control.

3. The Operations team has configured the System Test server environment, including all target hardware components and subsystems. The Test Team has been provided with appropriate access to these systems.

Figure 1–20   *Test entry criteria*

These entry criteria focus on three typical test preconditions:

- Readiness of the test environment
- Configuration and release management for the system under test
- The readiness of a defect management and a test management system

Another typical test precondition, the readiness of the test cases, test data, and so forth, is not explicitly defined for this project in the test plan.

Detail and Complexity

With respect to the level of detail with which to document test implementation work products, as a test manager you should think about the same issues that were previously discussed with respect to test cases and test conditions. You also need to consider some additional factors.

If the tests will be archived as a way of documenting what was tested, then more details will be required than if the tests will not be saved. If tests will be reused—for example, for regression or confirmation testing—then you must capture sufficient detail for people other than the authors to run the test.

If testers with different skills or experiences will be involved in testing, you might need to capture more detail to make sure that everyone is able to use the tests.

Also, regulatory rules can dictate the need to document certain test work products at a certain level of detail. If these apply, you must be very careful to adhere to those rules, because failure to comply can lead to complete failure of the project, with the company unable to ship the product.

Test environment descriptions and test data descriptions also need to be captured, and the same considerations apply in terms of the degree to which these are documented.

As a test manager, it's critical that you define the standards for documentation that testers must follow. The appropriate level of detail and the complexity of documentation can vary from one project to another and from one organization to another. Without guidance, each individual tester will do what seems appropriate to them, and the likelihood of spontaneous emergence of consistency across these testers is very low.

Example: Regulated System

One of RBCS's clients builds regulated medical devices. The United States Food and Drug Administration rules apply to this organization and their products.

> **ISTQB Glossary**
>
> **test log:** A chronological record of relevant details about the execution of tests.

These regulations have the following implications for testing:

- Every one of its test cases is traceable to the requirements specification. The test case is the way in which the organization can prove that a requirement is met.
- Periodically, there is an audit of the organization to ensure compliance. This includes auditing of the tests and test results.
- In part to support this audit, the organization stores not only tests but also evidence of test results, including screen shots. The test execution schedule must ensure that every test is complete, and test logs must capture details of when and against which versions each test was run.

While this sounds quite formal, this organization uses the most lightweight possible documentation. It follows the Scrum lifecycle, an agile lifecycle model, but has modified it to support the documentation required.

Advantages of Early Implementation

As I've mentioned previously, implementation tasks can start before test design is completed, and in some cases people will proceed directly into implementation of concrete test cases and other detailed work products as soon as possible. What are the advantages and disadvantages of doing this? Let's start with the advantages.

Creating concrete test cases as soon as possible can provide useful fodder for discussion with business stakeholders, particularly experts, as well as with designers and programmers. When shown a test case, these stakeholders might realize that the requirements specification is quite ambiguous, or just plain wrong. When ambiguities exist, such test cases might be a way to resolve them, thus serving to guide design and development. In fact, for some applications that have been around a long time, the only reliable descriptions of system behavior *are* the test cases, so early implementation of concrete test cases can effectively patch a gappy requirements process.

Another advantage of early implementation is avoiding delays when it's finally time to start test execution. I've seen a number of situations where test teams were given early builds to test, or they were given builds on time that really didn't meet the entry criteria but they were asked to test them anyway. If your tests, your test data, and your test environments are ready not just on time but early, you are less likely to be caught out by such events.

Disadvantages of Early Implementation

That said, it's not all puppies and smiley faces when test cases, test data, and test environments are set up early. To the extent that requirements, supported configurations, and underlying data structures are changing, you will find your team continually shooting behind a moving target when changes occur. This is especially likely in agile lifecycles, which have the motto of "embrace change," and you might find that evolution, even during iterations, is the norm. The other iterative and incremental lifecycles will also allow change, or just add detail to previously vague requirements. I've worked on plenty of sequential life-cycle projects where change was not managed well and been surprised—and not pleasantly—by changes late in the project.

So, if you and your team have expended a lot of energy in finalizing concrete test cases, environments, and data, these changes will result in rework, at the very best, as you try to accommodate the changes. In the worst case, you might even have to throw some items away and rebuild them. Even if the test cases are modifiable to accommodate the change, it's often the case that detailed test work products can be hard to maintain without introducing defects into the tests themselves. At the very least, detailed work products require more effort to maintain.

These disadvantages may lead to a conclusion that implementation should start as late as possible. It's important that the test manager consider the alternatives for when to start implementation and how detailed the work products should be. Integration of test implementation into the lifecycle is also a factor, as is the overall predictability of the project and the features that will be delivered to you.

Example: Early Test Implementation

On one project, we followed a risk-based analytical test strategy. So, we implemented test cases early during the project, well before entering system test.

Shortly before system test was to start, the user interface team worked over a weekend. During that frenetic weekend, they changed the entire user interface. They did not communicate this action to the test team, either verbally or in email.

The next Monday morning we arrived and attempted to continue our tests. Since we didn't know why all the tests were failing in terms of the UI, we suspected a problem with configuration management. The entire test team—all eight people—spent the whole day researching this before a chance hallway conversation revealed what had actually happened.

The impact of this unmanaged change on our testing effort was twofold. Most immediately, there was the loss of one schedule day and 64 person-hours chasing down these false positives we thought at first were bugs. The longer and more significant impact was the approximately two person-weeks of effort spent updating the tests.

If I had to manage this test project again, knowing what would happen, would I still choose to have the testers implement the tests early in the project? Yes, I would. Here's why: The early test implementation revealed some important requirements specification defects. Without the detailed test implementation work we did, I don't think we would have found as many of those problems.

Execution Schedule Exercise

Continue the scenario from the previous exercise.

Describe a way to develop a test execution schedule that is consistent with a risk-based testing strategy for the HELLOCARMS project.

Execution Schedule Debrief

The requirements are prioritized, and the prioritization is used to group the features into five iterations. Within each iteration, you can look at the relative risk level for the risk items that are pertinent to the iteration. Through traceability, each test can inherit the risk level of the risk items that it covers, so you can use risk levels to develop an ideal schedule for the tests. You then check this ideal schedule against test environment and data dependencies and other constraints. If necessary, you make adjustments to the schedule to accommodate these constraints.

1.6   Test Execution

> ### Learning objectives
> (K3) Use traceability to monitor test progress for completeness and consistency with the test objectives, test strategy, and test plan.

At this point in the test process, we've reached the show. All the preparation is—we hope—complete and it's time to start executing the tests. In order for that to happen, though, some other group has to deliver a test-ready version of the system under test. That group is often called release engineering or configuration management, though in some cases the development team itself is in charge of building test releases. In higher levels of testing such as system test and system integration test, what is delivered for testing should be built and delivered through the same process and in the same package as it will be for the end users or customers so that installation can be tested. If you need such a realistic test release delivery process, be sure to incorporate that into the test plan and communicate that need to the appropriate parties.

Speaking of the test plan, yours should include entry criteria for testing. These criteria should be satisfied before test execution starts. In some cases, some entry criteria are waived for business reasons. In these situations, be sure to explain the risks and costs associated with such waivers, not with the objective of being an obstructionist pain in the neck but rather with the objective of helping project teams make an informed decision.

While some entry criteria are beyond your control, you should have your own ducks in a row, as the cliché goes, before test execution starts. Do you have all the tests ready to go, other than the reactive tests that will be created during test execution? Are the tests documented to the appropriate degree of detail? Is the test data ready, loaded, and documented? Is the test environment ready and documented, and have some preliminary tests been run to ensure that all these items are in order? Are all of the tools you will need to support test execution installed, with appropriate access granted to testers and other project participants, including test management, defect tracking, and test execution automation tools? Are the processes, standards, and expectations for the logging, tracking, metrics, and reporting of defects and other test results thoroughly defined (by you the test manager) and thoroughly understood (by the test team)? If you are wise, you'll make sure that these are all in order because it can be quite damaging, not only to test team efficiency but also your reputation as a competent manager, if your team spends the first days or even weeks of test execution tripping over their own mistakes left over from incomplete test design and implementation.

Test Execution and Closure

Figure 1–21? depicts the test execution process. As before, the test team is following a blended requirements-based, risk-based, and reactive test strategy during test implementation and execution.

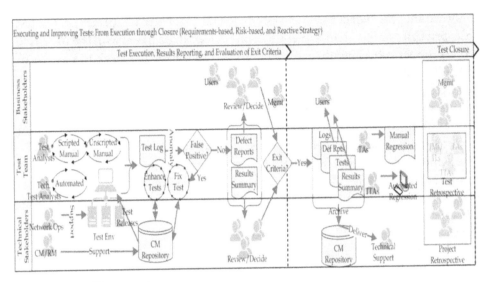

Figure 1–21   *Test execution process*

At the bottom of Figure 1–21?, you see two technical stakeholder groups. The upper group is the network operations team (or whatever they're called in your organization). This team provides support for the test environment. Below them you see the configuration management or release management or release engineering team (which again could be called something different in your organization). This team continues to provide support for the configuration management repository where test work products are stored, as during test implementation, but they are also responsible for delivering test releases. In some cases, these functional areas are actually part of the test team or in the same organization where the test team resides.

Once the first such release arrives—and the entry criteria are satisfied, as mentioned earlier—test analysts and technical test analysts start executing tests. Test analysts focus on running the scripted manual tests and, when following a reactive strategy, also run the unscripted manual tests using exploratory testing and other similar experience-based techniques. Test analysts may also run the automated tests, with the support of technical test analysts, or the technical test analysts may be responsible for doing so.

The results of these tests are captured in test logs. In some cases, the tests will indicate an anomaly (i.e., a discrepancy between actual and expected results). If so, then the appropriate test analyst must check the test to see if there is a false positive or a real failure. If a real failure has been detected, the analyst reports it into the defect tracking system. If a false positive has occurred, the test case, test data, or test environment will often need to be fixed, with the modified work product subsequently checked into the repository and the relevant test or tests rerun. It can also occur that testers realize the need to enhance tests during test execution, even if no false positive occurs, and this enhancement will trigger the same set of activities.

In many organizations, periodic meetings will occur to review defect reports. These ideally are attended by technical and business stakeholders. These meetings are intended to determine defect fix priority (or defect deferral in some cases) as well as to manage the proper flow of defects through their lifecycle. I'll cover the topic of defects and defect management in more detail in Chapter 4, but at this point I'll mention that the test manager should participate in these meetings.

The same or a similar set of stakeholders also typically review the overall test results reports. Based on what these results say about the progress of testing and the quality of the system, various project control decisions may occur in these meetings. I'll discuss this topic further in Chapter 2, but at this point I'll mention that the test manager should participate in these meetings.

Finally, as test execution winds down, these same or similar stakeholders evaluate the exit criteria to decide whether testing should be declared complete. As test manager, you should be ready to support that process by providing your own objective evaluation of the status. I'll talk more about this process in the next section.

I'll describe the activities on the right side of Figure 1–21 in detail at the end of this chapter. Here, it provides some insight into how test closure follows and relates to test execution. As with previous figures, it is not necessarily a problem if iteration occurs between test execution and test closure, but it can indicate problems, depending on the reason for the iteration. Therefore, the test manager should carefully evaluate the reasons for such iteration, especially if it was a surprise

Blending Reactive Test Strategies

In Figure 1–21?, the test team is following a blended test strategy that includes reactive elements. I generally recommend that all test approaches be blended, including reactive elements that comprise 10 to 20 percent of the test execution effort. I've found such blending to do an excellent job of offsetting weaknesses that exist in each test strategy because generally the strengths and weaknesses of the various strategies are complementary.

So, how should you go about blending reactive elements during test execution? First, I've found that giving testers permission to transcend the written tests cases while executing them is a quick and easy way to do this. I'll tell testers, "A test is a road map to interesting places in the software, and if you get to some place interesting, stop and look around." By using a timebox on the test case that includes sufficient time for executing the written test and spending another 15 to 30 minutes exploring, you can keep this process well under control while enjoying many benefits of exploratory testing, even with relatively inexperienced testers.

Second, use the more experienced testers on your test team to do mostly reactive testing, employing the experience-based and defect-based techniques discussed in the Foundation and Advanced Test Analyst syllabi. By using test charters (which I'll discuss in the next chapter) and careful timeboxing, you can manage this process effectively.

Third, make sure all testers understand the need for even better-than-usual defect reports during unscripted testing. Unlike with running a scripted test, you can't count on the details of a test case to answer any questions a developer might have about specific actions, inputs, environments, and data. I've seen multiple instances as a consultant where sloppy defect reporting during exploratory testing led to lots of waste, frustration, and rework during test execution. Indeed, much of my own professional reputation as being opposed to exploratory testing arose from my criticisms of these kinds of mistakes. In fact, I'm not at all opposed to exploratory testing—I've done it my entire career as a tester and test manager—but I'm opposed to doing it poorly and managing it badly, which I've seen done more than once by people who were otherwise very smart.

Earlier, I mentioned a general rule of thumb that 10 to 20 percent of test execution effort should be reactive. That's a pretty good rule of thumb that has worked for me and a number of my clients. However, if you are fortunate enough to have most of your predefined tests automated, the percentage of reactive testing should increase. This is because the automated tests will follow their defined procedures and you can't incorporate the kind of "stop and look around" exploration that I mentioned previously.

Test Manager's Role during Execution

Earlier, I described the role of the test analysts during test execution as well as the test manager's role in defect and test status review meetings. What else is the test manager doing?

Well, the test manager is actually quite busy managing the team and monitoring their progress. As a test manager, I usually tried to be accessible to my testers most of the day during test execution, except for when I am in meetings. (One of the reasons I recommend minimizing meetings during test execution is that I've seen testers and other individual contributors make mistakes when test managers were unavailable due to such excessive meetings.)

When managing a test team, I like to have a daily progress debrief with the entire team. In this short meeting, we discuss what tests were run, which passed, which failed, and whatever defects were reported during the day. As this information rolls in, I ensure that the test management and defect tracking tools are appropriately updated. I also compare where we are with where I'd expect us to be as well as consider how our progress relates to the test team's mission, objectives, and strategies and whether our progress is consistent with the larger organizational needs.

If the test team's progress has deviated from a successful path, the test manager must restore good direction through control actions. Even if testing is proceeding exactly according to the test plan, this might be necessary if the project is in trouble. I once had a test manager make an odd comment to me; he said that the project he felt most proud of was one where he managed to get the product canceled. To me, while such product cancellations are sometimes regrettable necessities, and while testing can indeed head off further trouble associated with an inappropriate product release, nothing succeeds like success, to use another cliché. Personally, I'm much prouder of the projects where early and ongoing feedback from testing helped the project to deliver a successful product.

How do we know whether we are succeeding? I discussed the need for bidirectional traceability in earlier parts of the process. It is now that the effort setting that up will pay off. Is a given requirement satisfied? With traceability, you can tell people the specific test results associated with that requirement. Is a given quality risk mitigated? Again, with traceability, you can tell people the specific test results associated with that risk item. Is a specific objective being met? Again, traceability to the rescue.

Or maybe not, if your test team did not capture traceability information earlier. If you think of the fairy tale of Hansel and Gretel, traceability is the trail of white pebbles that allowed them to find their way home successfully the first time. If traceability is not updated properly, it will be more like the trail of bread crumbs that they left the second time, which were eaten by birds.

Example: Simple Progress Monitoring

Figure 1–22? shows an example of progress monitoring on the website redesign project I mentioned earlier.

Pass Two Defect Status	
Verified	47
To be verified	1
Need RBCS approval	5
Deferred	21
Failed verification	3
Not a defect	8
New	18
Total	**103**

Figure 1–22   *Progress monitoring*

Generally, simple test projects can utilize simple test controls. In Chapter 2, I will illustrate complex test status reporting and control mechanisms. However, on this simple project, tracking of test case status and defect status was sufficient.

?Figure 1–22 shows the defect status at the end of the second pass of testing. We ran one pass of our tests, running each test case once, and found defects. We then let the vendor fix the defects and ran another pass. Ultimately, three passes of testing were required to fulfill the objective of compliance with requirements.

That said, you could say that the acceptance test failed in its objectives in a way. An acceptance test should not detect defects, typically. Certainly, in this case, since we had given the vendor our tests, we were highly disappointed in the test results. Failure of an acceptance test in a situation like this is tantamount to shifting costs of failure onto the customer. Costs of quality and the test management implications of them will be covered in Chapter 2, but at this point, I will say we are not a referenceable client for this web development company.

Metrics Exercise

Continue with the scenario in the previous exercise.

Describe one or more metrics that you could use to report on the remaining level of quality risk during test execution.

Metrics Debrief

There are a number of ways to report on the remaining level of quality risk during test execution:

- A table that lists the major risk items, along with the number of test cases planned, the number of test cases passed, and the number of test cases failed for each risk item
- The same table, but with two added numbers: the number of defects reported against the risk item and the number of those defects that are now closed
- A histogram graph showing the planned versus actual coverage of risk items by test cases
- The same histogram graph, with an additional set of bars representing the percentage of defects found for each risk item

Notice that you need traceability from risk items to test cases and/or defect reports for many of these metrics to work.

1.7   Evaluating Exit Criteria and Reporting

Learning objectives

(K2) Explain the importance of accurate and timely information collection during the test process to support accurate reporting and evaluation against exit criteria.

Testing, especially test execution, produces information—lots of information. Some of that information is extraneous, and some is relevant. The difference between relevance and irrelevance is often a matter of who is receiving the information, which I'll revisit in a moment. The test manager needs to make sure the right information is captured and ultimately delivered to the appropriate stakeholders.

The test manager should be able to relate the test results to the exit criteria. Are we done yet? If not, what obstacles exist to declaring the test execution complete? It's not enough to be kind-of, sort-of sure about what the results are telling us.

The test manager must also be able to report the test results to the stakeholders, as mentioned earlier. We'll revisit this topic in detail in Chapter 2, but again, it's not sufficient for the test results to be captured in a way that reflects only dimly on the status of the system under test.

Test managers need to have good solid information to support these activities of evaluating exit criteria and reporting test results. One central element is having test management, defect management, and other related tools properly selected and in place. However, tools by themselves are not sufficient, because the people using them—in this case the testers—must know how to use them to capture the necessary information. I've seen multiple situations where lots of time and money was spent setting up defect management and test management tools only to see nothing but noise in the test information because the testers didn't know how to use the tools. This is often the result of shortchanging the training elements of the budget when test tools are planned.

In addition, managers must be careful not to demotivate testers to gather accurate information. I heard an interesting example of such demotivation from one client. They had a defect management tool, and it wasn't set up too badly. When we did some analysis, it appeared that one group's software was much better than all the other groups' software because the incidence of severity one defects was much lower. However, it turned out that developers were punished on their annual performance evaluations if more than three severity one defects were filed against their code. So most developers found ways to convince testers not to report severity one bugs, often by assuring them that they would fix any bugs reported against their code, regardless of severity. Thus, we could not make meaningful judgments about the quality of the software.

This is a striking but hardly unusual example of how a breakdown in proper information-gathering reduces the value of testing. I've seen situations where test results reports were confusing or less meaningful because of noise in the test results information. I've even seen situations where the information was so bad that it was less than useful, either due to creating false confidence in the product or by being completely inscrutable to people outside of the test team.

Information Collection

So, how do we avoid these information problems?

First, plan carefully; know what information you need and how it should be collected. Clearly define what is to be collected, by whom, at what point in the test process. This can go into a test strategy document, if it's the same for each project, and you can document project-specific information needs in the test plan.

Second, as the information is being gathered, don't just assume it's okay. Check it. I once saw a situation where there were three different fields that could indicate whether a defect report was a false positive. Depending on which field you looked at, there were either just a few hundred or many thousands. Some of this conflicting data was entered by members of the test team, while some was entered by other project participants. Obviously, some bad practices had developed across various teams in that organization that made the information meaningless.

How do you know that good practices are being followed? First, the information should be complete. Missing classification information, terse or empty narrative fields, and the absence of traceability are typical data completeness problems. Second, the information should be accurate; inaccuracy was the problem in the example in the preceding paragraph. Third, the information should be entered promptly, not captured in a notebook and then entered three or four days later.

As a test manager, you should periodically monitor the test results information for any problems in these three areas. Running reports that cross-reference related fields can find inaccuracies, which is how I found the problem mentioned earlier. By randomly sampling a small percentage (say one percent or so) of the information, you can find patterns in terms of missing information. Checking for inexplicable delays in defect resolution can locate timeliness issues. When you find information problems, take prompt steps to adjust the information gathering requirements and methods to prevent those problems in the future. In some cases, this will involve working with other managers, as in the previous example where development managers were punishing developers based on defects reported by testers.

Frequency and Detail

In some cases, the information is solid and high quality, but test managers still have problems with results reporting. Why?

One major problem can be applying a one-size-fits-all approach to the amount of detail and the frequency of reporting. I've seen instances where test managers reported status by creating a gigantic Zip archive with every defect report, test case, and status summary and other test-related information, then sending that out daily as a email attachment with a cover note along the lines of, "Attached, please find current test status. Let me know if you have questions." When no questions arise, the test managers often assume that people have read and understood the results. However, it's far more likely that people find the

> **ISTQB Glossary**
>
> **test summary report:** A document summarizing testing activities and results. It also contains an evaluation of the corresponding test items against exit criteria.

volume of data overwhelming and the level of detail confusing, which means that they either don't read the information at all or end up less enlightened than they were before.

To avoid this, consider carefully who needs what information, at what level of detail, and how frequently. You should plan to monitor the exit criteria status closely, in detail, while reporting at a summary level for testing stakeholders. Of course, if they ask for details on one criterion or another, be ready to provide the details, but you typically shouldn't supply those as a matter of routine.

Test results reporting is primarily for the testing stakeholders, to help support decision making. Different stakeholders will need different information, depending on the way they approach their jobs as managers and the amount of time they have available.

As you can see, what we are doing here is providing information to others to support their work. This is different than the information you need to manage the test process, though test managers often confuse the two activities since both involve gathering and analyzing test results. A key difference is that, while your ability to control the test effort relies on information, outside stakeholders won't necessarily care whether they understand that information, provided you do understand it and you take the right control actions based on that understanding. For test results and exit criteria information, the outside stakeholders need to understand the information because it is they who will need to take the right control actions.

Therefore, you should work carefully with testing and other project stakeholders to define how results should be reported, what metrics you can gather and what these metrics mean, whether to provide fine-grained or coarse-grained information, and how frequently people want to receive that information. We'll return to this topic in Chapter 2.

Example: Sophisticated Results Reporting

Figure 1–23? shows an example of four kinds of test results reporting charts that you might deliver to testing and project stakeholders. We'll discuss each of these in detail in Chapter 2, but you might take a moment now to study them.

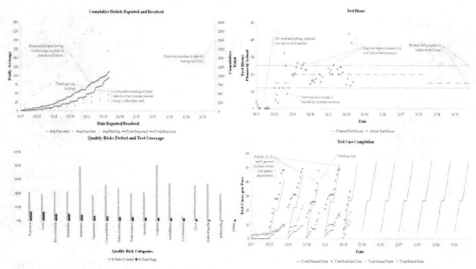

Figure 1–23   *Test results reporting charts*

1.8   Test Closure Activities

Learning objectives

(K2) Summarize the four groups of test closure activities.

(K3) Implement a project retrospective to evaluate processes and discover areas to improve.

Test closure work is the often-forgotten but important work at the end of the test process to guarantee and capture the remaining value available to the test team and the larger project team and the organization as a whole. There are four main types:

- Ensuring that test work is concluded
- Delivering test work products
- Participating in project retrospective
- Archiving test work products

As I mentioned, test closure is often forgotten, or at least one of these activities is often forgotten. In some cases, they are not so much forgotten as simply omitted, whether due to premature dissolution of the test or project team, immediate reallocation of resources to respond to schedule pressures on subsequent projects, or simple team burnout. For contract development, the contract should specify the closure activities to make sure they are not forgotten.

Let's look at each of these.

Test Completion Check

First is the simple act of checking to make sure you are really done. Given the complexity of managing testing—especially on large or distributed projects—it's easy to forget something.

So, smart test managers, as the testing draws to a close, double-check the test plan to make sure that everything planned was done. They check the test tracking information to make sure all planned tests were either run to conclusion or deliberately skipped (and approved for skipping). They check that all known defects were fixed (including the confirmation testing of the fix), deferred (with appropriate blessing from the project team), or accepted as permanent restrictions. They check that all stakeholders' test objectives were satisfied. They check that every exit criteria was either met or deliberately (and by the appropriate level of management) waived. They use traceability to check the status of all test conditions and verify that each was covered sufficiently.

Yes, this is a large task, especially when everyone seems ready to declare the testing done and move on to the post-project party or even the next project. However, given the amount of confusion and rushing about that can happen at the end of a project, it's really smart to invest a morning or afternoon making absolutely sure you're done.

Test Artifacts Handover

Next is looking for opportunities to reuse test work products. After they are released, many of these work products can be useful to other people on the project team, to people on support teams, or even to customers. For example, you can let users, customers, or support people know about known defects that were deferred or accepted. You can transfer tests and test environments to those who will perform maintenance testing. You can deliver automated or manual regression test packs to customers if they are integrating your system into a larger system of systems.

Yes, this is extra work for you and your team. But be sure to do it and to include it in your plan and schedule so it's work you already expected to do. Otherwise, your organization will be missing an opportunity to operate more effectively and efficiently. Teamwork is about helping each other.

Lessons Learned

The most common type of test closure activity is the use of project retrospectives to document lessons learned (both good and bad) from the project and to plan to manage the events, surprises, and problems of future projects better.

For example, during the analysis of a project retrospective, you might find that you saw many unexpected defect clusters during testing. This could lead you to plan for an expanded list of quality risk analysis participants on future projects.

You might find that your estimates were significantly off. This could lead to evaluating the root causes for this (more defects than expected, more test work than expected, etc.) and to adopt plans to resolve those causes in the future.

You might find trends and causes of defects that reveal many opportunities to find defects earlier, to reduce the number of defects, or to prevent defects entirely.

You might locate areas where testing, or the project as a whole, was inefficient or ineffective. You can then identify process, team, or tool improvements.

Keep in mind that retrospectives should apply to testing as well as the entire project and indeed the wider organization. Problems tend to be systemic, not isolated. Opportunities to improve often have enablers and disablers outside of the target improvement group.

Finally, draw conclusions and make recommendations based on data rather than simply opinion, wherever possible. Opinions about what went wrong, and why those things went wrong, are incorrect more often than you might think. Document the retrospective findings, including the conclusions and recommendations, and send those to other people in your organization.

Archiving

Finally, test closure includes safeguarding the information products. Testing delivers intermediate and final test results, test log files, test status reports, and other documents and work products. These should be placed into the configuration management system. In that system, the various test work products must be linked to the system under test (both in terms of names and versions).

For example, both the test plan and the project plan should be captured and archived along with the test cases, test procedures, test data, and test results.

Example: Lessons Learned

Here are some examples of things you can learn in a retrospective:

- If one or more unanticipated defect clusters is discovered late in the testing, consider what additional stakeholder groups and/or perspectives might need to be included in future quality risk analysis sessions.
- If the time, resources, number of defects found, number of tests needed, or other elements of the test estimate were underestimated, consider whether this is due to a systematic problem in estimation or merely anomalies of the project.
- If defects were found in high-level testing that could have been found in reviews or earlier levels of testing, demonstrate the business impact of this situation (using cost of quality), then work with the business analysts, requirements engineers, and developers to enhance these earlier bug filters.
- If defect trends indicate a large number of defects related to particular technologies, skills, or system attributes (e.g., security), evaluate ways to reduce the number of defects in these areas.
- If defect trends indicate a large number of defects related to staff turnover, recommend ways to reduce the "brain drain."
- Evaluate the metrics for effectiveness and efficiency with respect to the test objectives, and look for ways to increase test team capabilities.
- Ask yourselves what surprises occurred that should be considered in the future.

Example: Delivery of Work Products

As an example of valuable test work deliverables given to another party after the project, consider the Internet appliance project I've referred to already. Toward the end of the project, just before release, a tester was assigned the job of communicating all known issues to the technical support manager and key participants on the technical support team. This included detailed information on all failed test cases, to the point of the specific step in the test that failed, the actual result as opposed to expected result, and if possible, any workaround we had identified. It also included a complete review of all deferred or unresolved bugs.

According to the technical support manager, this resulted in a significant time savings, as much as 300 to 400 percent, for calls related to known failed tests and defects.

Retrospective Analysis

Figure 1–24? shows an example of a chart I created as part of a retrospective analysis of the testing of a project. The testing went rather poorly, and a number of reasons were revealed by this analysis.

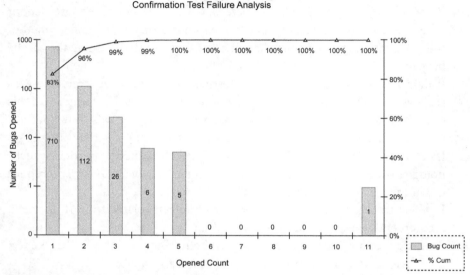

Figure 1–24   *Testing retrospective analysis*

In Figure 1–24?, you can see the number of times the various bug reports were opened. If a bug is discovered, reported, fixed by development, closed, and then never seen again, the bug count metric for that bug is one. If a bug is discovered, reported, allegedly fixed, reopened by test during confirmation testing, and then actually fixed, closed, and never seen again, the bug count metric for that bug is two. Alternatively, if the bug is discovered, reported, fixed, closed during confirmation testing, but then seen again later—due to regression, for example—and only the second time is it finally resolved, the bug count metric for that bug is also two. The scale, by the way, is logarithmic to prevent the large number of bugs from distracting attention to the key point of the chart.

The key point of the chart is the large number of bug reports that required attention more than once. As you can see, fully one in six (about 17 percent) of the bug reports were reopened at least once. How big a deal is this? Well, assume that each bug report requires at least one hour of effort to handle. I think that's a reasonable, conservative assumption. In that case, we can read the total waste associated with incomplete resolution of bugs, from left to right on the chart, starting with the second bar on the histogram, as follows:

- There were 112 bug reports opened twice. The second time was wasted time, so we can count 112 wasted hours for the bug reports opened twice.
- There were 26 bug reports opened three times. The second and third time were wasted time, so we can count 2 times 26, or 52 hours for the bug reports opened three times.
- There were 6 bug reports opened four times. The second, third, and fourth time were wasted time, so we can count 3 times 6, or 18 hours for the bug reports opened four times.
- There were five bug reports opened five times. The second, third, fourth, and fifth time were wasted time, so we can count 4 times 5, or 20 hours for the bug reports opened five times.
- There was one bug report opened 11 times. The 2nd through 11th time were wasted time, so we can count 10 times 1, or 10 hours for the bug report opened 11 times.

That totals more than 200 person-hours, or five person-weeks, of wasted effort associated with having to process and reprocess bug reports. The moral of this story is clear: Fix once and fix right.

Don't Forget!

To reiterate, a lot of organizations skip these test closure activities. Don't do it! They are valuable.

Part of avoiding a mistake is understanding why it happens. One major reason is that project staff are reassigned to other projects or perhaps removed from the organization if they are contractors or vendor employees. In the latter case, the loss of institutional knowledge is particularly profound. Another reason for omitting test closure activities is extreme pressure on resources and schedule, leading to a need for every individual to be engaged in urgent activity all of the time. Unfortunately, this results in repeating mistakes and re-creating things that already existed.

Finally, a massive sense of ennui and burnout can pervade the team at the end of a project, especially one that was poorly managed, and finding people who care enough about these test closure activities can be hard. If that's the problem on a project where you were the test manager, well, look in the mirror if you want to see one of the root causes. I'll admit to driving my teams too hard more than once, so I'm guilty too.

So, address these issues if they exist on your future projects. As I mentioned, make sure that you include test closure activities in the test plan and schedule. If you are using a vendor or testing services provider, make sure it's in the contract.

Retrospective Exercise

After the first release of the HELLOCARMS system, you hold a retrospective meeting. In researching the results, you discover the following:

- 27 percent of defects reported against reverse mortgage function were rejected as not actual problems.
- 25 percent of defects reported against optional life insurance feature were rejected as not actual problems.
- 37 percent of defects reported against LoDoPS were rejected as not actual problems.

The average defect report rejection rate is 5 percent for your team. You consider that acceptable, but anything above 10 percent is unacceptable.

List at least five potential improvements to investigate for the second and subsequent releases.

Retrospective Debrief

Your list should have included some of the following:

- Use training, hiring, or user assistance to increase reverse mortgage expertise in the test team.
- Evaluate whether the requirements associated with the particular rejected reverse mortgage defects were ambiguous or otherwise faulty.
- Check for a high incidence of field-reported defects associated with rejected reverse mortgage defects.
- Use training, hiring, or user assistance to increase life insurance expertise in the test team.
- Evaluate whether the requirements associated with the particular rejected life insurance defects were ambiguous or otherwise faulty.
- Check for a high incidence of field-reported defects associated with rejected life insurance defects.
- Use training, hiring, or user assistance to increase LoDoPS expertise in the test team.
- Evaluate whether the requirements associated with the particular rejected LoDoPS defects were ambiguous or otherwise faulty.

- Check for a high incidence of field-reported defects associated with rejected LoDoPS defects.
- Set up a meeting with developers to discuss why particular problems were rejected and to brainstorm ways to improve communication between the two teams.
- Have a defect review process so that each defect report is checked by one or more testers before the report is entered into the tracking system.

You can probably think of others as well. Remember, when considering improvements, the important thing is to use data.

1.9 Sample Exam Questions

To end each chapter, you can try one or more sample exam questions to reinforce your knowledge and understanding of the material and to prepare for the ISTQB Advanced Level Test Manager exam.

1. Assume you are a test manager working on a project to create a programmable thermostat for home use to control central heating, ventilation, and air conditioning (HVAC) systems. This project is following a sequential lifecycle model, specifically the V-model. Your test team is following a risk-based testing strategy augmented with a reactive testing strategy during test execution to ensure that key risks missed during risk analysis are caught.

   Of the following statements, identify all that are true about the test plan.

   A. The test plan should include risk analysis early in the process.

   B. The test plan should list the requirements specification as an input to the risk analysis.

   C. The test plan should assign specific bugs to specific developers.

   D. The test plan should not discuss the use of reactive test techniques because such tests are not preplanned.

   E. The test plan should specify overall project team metrics used to determine bonuses.

2. Which of the following is a test document in which you would you expect to find the preconditions to start executing a level of testing?

    A. Defect report

    B. Test plan

    C. Test case

    D. Project plan

3. Which of the following is the most likely reason a user might be included in test execution?

    A. Their management expertise

    B. Their testing expertise

    C. Their application domain knowledge

    D. Their technical expertise

4. You are the manager of a bank's quality assessment group, in charge of independent testing for banking applications. You have just concluded a project to implement an integrated system that will use three off-the-shelf systems to manage a bank's accounts receivable system. During the project, you found that one vendor's systems, while comprising approximately the same amount of functionality and of roughly the same complexity as the other two systems, had significantly more defects. Making no assumptions other than ones based on the information provided here, which of the following is a reasonable improvement to the test process for subsequent projects involving this vendor?

    A. Impose retroactive financial penalties on this vendor for the number of bugs delivered on this project.

    B. Perform an acceptance test for all systems received, with particular rigor for this vendor.

    C. Cancel the contract with this vendor and put it on an industry blacklist.

    D. Require the vendor's developers to attend training to improve their ability to write quality code.

2   Test Management

"Oh, we don't drink while we test."
"Right, Larry, we drink because we test!"

Two directors of large testing groups reacting to my story
about a group of testers at an Internet start-up who did testing work
while drinking beer.

Chapter 2, Test Management, of the Advanced syllabus contains the following
nine sections:

1. Introduction
2. Test Management in Context
3. Risk-Based Testing and Other Approaches for Test Prioritization and Effort
    Allocation
4. Test Documentation and Other Work Products
5. Test Estimation
6. Defining and Using Test Metrics
7. Business Value of Testing
8. Distributed, Outsourced, and Insourced Testing
9. Managing the Application of Industry Standards

2.1   Introduction

Learning objectives
Recall of content only

The ISTQB Advanced certifications are for people who have attained a certain level of seniority as testers and started to choose a specialty. It's assumed
that you are reading this book because you are moving along the test management track in your career. In this chapter, we focus on test management. It is

> **ISTQB Glossary**
>
> **test director:** A senior manager who manages test managers.
>
> **test leader:** The person responsible for project management of testing activities and resources, and evaluation of a test object. The individual who directs, controls, administers, plans and regulates the evaluation of a test object.
>
> **test management:** The planning, estimating, monitoring and control of test activities, typically carried out by a test manager.
>
> **test manager:** The person responsible for project management of testing activities and resources, and evaluation of a test object. The individual who directs, controls, administers, plans and regulates the evaluation of a test object.

meant for people in a test lead, test manager, or test director capacity. Collectively, the syllabus uses—and therefore I'll use—the term *test manager* to refer to these roles. In my experience as a consultant around the world, I've seen and heard a lot of different titles for people in test management roles, so don't be too concerned if your organization doesn't conform perfectly to the ISTQB terminology.

This chapter builds on the test management material introduced in the Foundation. I suggest that you reread Chapter 5 of the Foundation syllabus.

2.2 Test Management

Learning objectives
(K4) Analyze the stakeholders, circumstances, and needs of a software project or program, including the software development lifecycle model, and identify the optimal test activities.
(K2) Understand how development activities and work products affect testing, and how testing affects development activities and work products.
(K2) Explain ways to manage the test management issues associated with experience-based testing and non-functional testing.

As a test manager, in many ways your work will be like any other managers. You'll have to be able to get and apply resources to execute processes, and you must do this in such a way that the resources, through the processes, deliver valuable work products and information as well as product, project, and process improvement opportunities. The resources that you use will include people both inside and outside the test team; software such as operating systems, databases, and web application middleware; hardware such as servers, laptops, tablets, and smartphones; and infrastructure such as local area networks, the Internet, and cellular telephony networks. The processes may be formal or informal; they may be part of a small project or a large program; they may be used to deliver new software or systems or to maintain or operate existing ones.

As a test manager, the processes you use will be variations of the fundamental test process, as discussed in the previous chapter and as described in the Foundation and Advanced Test Manager syllabi. You'll apply these processes to increase the chances of project or program success by reducing the likelihood and impact associated with failures in production.

Your team will work within the context of this project or program, and so your team's processes, activities, and work products must be consistent and coherent. This means alignment with respect to the stakeholders and their needs, constraints, and objectives, such as budget limitations, target delivery dates, and customer satisfaction goals. It means alignment with respect to the activities and work product produced by others on the project or program, such as requirements specifications, project plans, and weekly status meetings. And it means alignment with respect to the software development, maintenance, or operations lifecycle in which the testing will occur, such as participating in planning sessions in a Scrum project or in phase exit meetings in a sequential project.

In this section, we'll look at how to achieve this kind of alignment successfully.

Testing Stakeholders

My work as a test manager and as a test management consultant has led me to a firm belief: in every case I've seen, testing can succeed only when it serves the needs of one or more stakeholders. Test teams that disappoint stakeholders end up reorganized, disbanded, or with new management. We're looking at optimizing the test process for its context in this section, and that's important. However, there's been a lot of focus on process in software engineering over the last couple decades, but too much of the discussion has been about what to do or not do and not enough about who we're doing it for. Since stakeholder satisfaction is such a critical topic, let's start our discussion in this section with them.

First, who are your test stakeholders? You might be surprised to find that there are more of them than you think, and probably even more than you've managed to meet so far. Anyone who has an interest in the testing activities you and your team do, whether through direct or indirect involvement, is a test stakeholder. Anyone to whom you give test work products, and anyone who gets those work products from someone else, is a test stakeholder. Anyone who is affected by the quality of the system, either by using the system themselves or by receiving products or services produced by the system, is a test stakeholder. I'll give you some examples of test stakeholders in the next section.

The process of contextual alignment of testing should start with the identification of your testing stakeholders, both broadly across the organization and for the particular project or program you are working on. Once you know who those stakeholders are, get to know them professionally if you don't already. Have a conversation with them—or better yet an ongoing series of conversations—that helps you understand how they relate to you and your team and what specific needs you and your team help them with. You'll use this information, together with your understanding of other project or program activities and work products that interact with testing, to determine the optimal mix and timing of activities, work products, and resources for your testing process.

In most cases, your stakeholders will be less knowledgeable than you are about testing. Most test stakeholders have never actually participated in or managed a testing team. As such, you need to be ready to educate them on points they need to understand and simplify matters where you can. Talking down to stakeholders or talking over their heads about testing, test results, quality, and other topics will quickly alienate them. Remember, each stakeholder probably knows more about something—for example, the application domain, the underlying system technology, the needs of the customer or user—than you do, and you'll need them to educate you and explain these topics to you in a way that you understand.

Typical Testing Stakeholders

In the previous chapter, I mentioned business and technical stakeholders and their participation in the test process. So who are some typical testing stakeholders? Let's start with some you probably already know and then get to some that you might not have thought of.

The first and most obvious group of stakeholders is those who develop the software or manage those who develop the software. Their work products are delivered to your team for testing. Your test results are delivered to them for information and for action, such as fixing bugs. Many testers have daily interaction with these technical stakeholders. Sometimes testers have very friendly working and even personal relationships with their development colleagues. This is a good thing, because it's usually easier to take bad news from a friend than from someone with whom you have a frosty relationship.

A less direct and less obvious group of stakeholders is those who design and architect the system. While you might not test their work products directly, you test them indirectly when you test the software or system. Of course, it's a best practice for qualified testers to review design and architecture documents, so part of alignment should include establishing the provision of that service to these stakeholders. These technical stakeholders also need to receive test results, and they might need to act on those results to improve the system's design.

Marketing and business analysis stakeholders often have a similar relationship with testing as the designer and architects. Test teams test software and systems that implement the marketing and business analysts' work products, which are the requirements and use cases and user stories and other descriptions of desired system behavior, features, and level of quality. In addition, qualified testers should—but don't always—participate in reviews of these work products. If they don't now, you should work to establish that. The business stakeholders have a strong interest in understanding and influencing decisions about the test conditions, risk items, and other test coverage elements. They will receive test results and make decisions on those results, such as prioritizing defects for repair, deciding where more testing is needed, and determining whether software can be released based on the measured level of quality.

Another group of business stakeholders comprises senior managers, product managers, and product sponsors. Like marketing and business analysis stakeholders, they are often involved in determining what should be tested. They have the same kind of roles and responsibilities in terms of evaluating and deciding based on test results as do the marketing and business analysis stakeholders, only more so because they often have the authority to make the final decisions on the questions of defect repair, extended test coverage, and software release.

Project managers are business stakeholders who tend to have regular and ongoing interactions with the test manager. If you're a test manager and you don't already know the project manager for the project on which you're working, drop this book right now and go introduce yourself! Just as the test manager is responsible for the success of the testing work on a project, the project manager is responsible for the overall success of the project. They must evaluate the relative progress and priorities of quality and features with respect to available schedule and budget. You will need to work closely with them at the beginning of the project to get resources for your testing. They should be work-

> **ISTQB Glossary**
>
> **risk:** A factor that could result in future negative consequences; usually expressed as impact and likelihood.
>
> **test condition:** An item or event of a component or system that could be verified by one or more test cases, e.g., a function, transaction, feature, quality attribute, or structural element.

ing with you when planning your testing, and they should be involving you in their project planning. You and the project manager will often need to collaborate on control decisions and actions.

Less well-known stakeholders, who are both business and technical stakeholders, are the technical support, customer support, or help desk staff. They will be the people who hear from users and customers about how well the software features, and the quality of those features, match their needs. These stakeholders have good ideas about what should be tested, so involve them in your test analysis. They also can make strong contributions in terms of defect prioritization and the evaluation of test results, so you should involve them in these processes where possible.

As a final example of a stakeholder, we have the user or customer. This person might use the software or receive outputs or services from the software. If they are happy with the features and quality of the software, they have you and your team to thank for that, at least to some extent. If they are not happy, that will eventually come back to you. Fair or not, their dissatisfaction will reflect on your team's capabilities. So, make it your team's job to know what these stakeholders want. Some test managers refer to their test teams as "the voice of the user in the project." I think we have to be careful with that metaphor because some test managers use that kind of perspective to rationalize opposing the interests and needs of other stakeholders. However, it's useful to think about such representation and advocacy as a part of your team's role.

This list is not exhaustive. I can and have provided more examples in the book *Beautiful Testing*.[1]Even that list wasn't exhaustive. This list should get you started thinking about your stakeholders. Consider factors such as the project, the product, the organization, and the risks. Consider the relationship between

---

1. See my chapter in the book *Beautiful Testing*, a collection of essays from various test authors and consultants.

your product and organization on the one hand and the users, customers, and society on the other hand.

Other Activities and Work Products

Activities outside of testing, often as part of an organized software development or maintenance lifecycle, produce one or more work products that are subsequently delivered for testing by the test team. Thus, these external activities and work products affect testing.

Testing evaluates the quality of these work products and delivers the result of that evaluation to the larger organization. These results, along with the testing activities themselves, affect these external activities and work products.

So, testing must be integrated and aligned with these other activities and with the work products. As a test manager, you must understand these reciprocating effects. The plan should take them into account. Your control actions must effectively manage the way these interactions between testing and the rest of the project or program will work out.

In the next few pages we'll look at some examples and further explore this idea of reciprocating effects. However, keep in mind that the specifics will vary from one project to another, from one lifecycle to another, from one organization to another, and so on. There are common patterns in the way test activities and work products affect and are affected by external activities and work products, but each situation displays its own nuances and variations.

Testing on Agile Projects

In an organization applying best practices within an agile lifecycle, I often find developers using test-driven development, or as some have now taken to calling it, behavior-driven development. This results in a nice set of automated unit tests. Those tests, along with the code, are integrated on an ongoing basis into the source code repository in the configuration management system. How should the test team respond to this situation?

Sometimes, test managers take an attitude along the lines of, "That's the developers' sandbox. We don't need to play around in it; we've got our own work to do." That's unfortunate, because it's a missed opportunity to integrate and align two related sets of activities and work products.

The best practice is for the test manager to include the development manager in the test planning process, looking for ways to involve testers. Testers with the appropriate expertise—which is different and more technical for agile organizations—can help to review the unit tests or maybe even engage in some pair unit testing with the developer. Professional, trained, certified testers can offer ideas on how to use white-box, black-box, experience-based, and defect-based test techniques to increase coverage for the tests. Testers can also explain how to make the tests better at finding defects because most tests created using test-driven development (TDD) or behavior-driven development (BDD) are more effective at confidence building than at defect finding.

This is not a one-way street that benefits the developers only. Of course, test teams benefit when software comes to them with fewer bugs, but that's not the only benefit. The individual testers gain much deeper knowledge of how the software works internally, which will also make their own tests more effective at finding defects, reducing risk, and building confidence. In addition, technical test analysts can look for ways to integrate the test team's automated tests into the continuous integration framework. Some of RBCS's clients have had particular luck doing this with automated functional tests.[2]

Example: Optimizing Test Activities

Figure 2–1 shows some key excerpts from the integration test strategy for a large system-of-systems project. On this project, we were testing a wide area network of interactive voice response (IVR) servers tied to a call center via the same wide area network. The integration of the call center servers and services with the IVR servers and services posed major risks.

Objective

Start integration testing immediately to accelerate integration defect discovery/removal and thus integration risk reduction.

Major Test Analysis, Design, and Implementation Tasks

-    Analyze the system design and risks to define the various backbones, which will consist of a subset of the servers and services, starting with the highest-risk backbone (BB0) and progressing to the lowest-risk (BB5).

-    Define and implement revision-naming for all backbone systems.

-    Define and implement bug tracking and resolution processes.

-    Define and implement backbone test environments and support.

-    Define test cycle duration.

-    Design and implement the integration tests for each backbone, including automated test harness and test data.

Figure 2–1   *Integration test strategy*

---

2. A good book to look at in this regard is *Agile Testing* by Lisa Crispin and Janet Gregory.

We wanted to begin integration testing as quickly as possible to reduce these risks. Therefore, we can classify our strategy here as a preventive strategy, as discussed in the Foundation syllabus and will be discussed later in this chapter.

Each build was called a "backbone." There were to be six backbones, starting with BB0 and progressing to BB5. To the extent possible, the systems and services would be added to each backbone in decreasing risk order. In other words, we wanted to start with the highest-risk systems and services.

Each backbone included the systems and services from the previous backbone. So, this is an incremental integration strategy, as discussed in the Foundation syllabus.

Notice that the test strategy is based on an analysis of the system design and the risks associated with it. Thus, it is an analytical test strategy.

As you can imagine, the test environments were complex and evolving. Therefore, skilled support teams were needed.

Testing Touchpoints

Let's review some of the major activities and work products that have interfaces with testing. Let's look at specific critical handoffs.

Requirements engineering and management. The volume of the requirements to be developed influences the size of the test effort, so the test manager has to be aware of requirements during planning and estimation. The extent of change to these requirements will heavily influence the test work that is ultimately done, so the test manager must use test control to adapt testing as these changes occur.

Project management. The test manager must work with the project manager in terms of test resources and schedule needs. To do so, the test manager will rely on the test analysts and technical test analysts to provide input to the planning and estimation process. As with requirements, changes to the project plan can have test implications that necessitate test control actions to keep the testing effort on track, so the test manager must remain vigilant for such events.

Configuration management, release management, and change management. Configuration management and release management are the means by which the test team receives the software that it will test, that is, the test object. The test manager should collaborate with the responsible parties in the project team to plan for the way in which such test releases will occur, and should capture that information in the test plan. It's often a good idea to look into the possibility of build verification tests, ideally automated and integrated into the configuration management system. This kind of thing is relatively easy to do in agile shops that are following the best practice of continuous integration and automated unit and functional testing, so be sure to leverage any work that's been done in that regard.

Software development and maintenance. The test team is going to test software built for it by developers, either as part of new development or maintenance. In the previous chapter, I talked about the need to put together a test execution schedule during test implementation. This will be heavily influenced by the specific content included in each test release, and the development manager is the person you should ask about that. As your team runs its tests, they'll find defects—they always do, don't they?—and so they'll be working with the developers to communicate the details of those defects, and the development manager is usually part of the defect review team.

Technical support. In Chapter 1, I mentioned the importance of communicating to the technical support team about any known failures, failed tests, and workarounds as part of the test closure activities. Technical support will also have definite opinions about what should be tested and what bugs should be fixed. In addition, you should plan to look at the failures that do make it out to production, ideally with the help of the technical support manager, because this is direct feedback on what your test process currently misses.

Technical documentation. Technical documentation, such as manuals, help screens, blog posts, and support articles online, should all be checked for accuracy, and ideally the test team has this within their scope. It's a mutually beneficial relationship because the technical documentation can prove an important resource for the testers during test design, implementation, and execution—both as a test basis and as a test oracle. When defects are found in the documentation, those defects need to be fixed as any other kind of defect would. During test planning, the test manager should work with the technical documentation manager to agree on how all these interactions will occur.

As you can see from this list, there are plenty of critical touchpoints. Neglecting any one of these can be a serious omission for a test manager, damaging the effectiveness and efficiency of the testing and the credibility of the test team and its manager. I have seen more than a few instances where these kinds of omissions had this effect. I recall one test manager being fired immediately from a test project because he didn't work properly with the technical documentation team to create acceptable records of testing that were suitable for auditing. Since the product was a regulated medical device, this omission would have resulted in the inability to ship it.

Testing in the Lifecycle

In Chapter 1, I discussed the need for test planning to consider the lifecycle being followed. This is essential because the lifecycle is a critical part of the context in which test activities occur and test work products are built. Let's review some highlights of how testing is integrated into the various lifecycles.

For sequential lifecycle models, all activities and work products for a given phase are completed before the next phase begins. Typical phases include requirements, design, implementation, unit test execution, integration test execution, system test execution, and acceptance test execution. Prior to each of these test execution phases, the test planning, test analysis, test design, and test implementation processes occur. For higher levels of testing, these preceding test process activities overlap project planning, business analysis, system design, and system implementation, respectively. For lower levels of test execution, such as unit test, overlap of these preceding test process activities with the earlier project phases is of course not possible.

For iterative or incremental models, we group features together, then design, implement, and test those features in these feature groups. (These feature groups are variously referred to as iterations or increments.) Sometimes the feature groups are worked on sequentially, with all the work on one group finished before work on the next group starts. Sometimes overlap occurs, so that some people are designing and implementing subsequent feature groups while test execution is happening for a preceding group. Either way, test levels will often overlap within groups, and entry and exit criteria should be set appropriately to enable this overlap. Test planning and analysis prior to work on the first group, during project initiation, is done in a general fashion. The specific test planning, analysis, design, and implementation work for each group is done on a group-by-group basis, typically with a lot of overlap and iteration. Test process activities for adjacent groups can overlap as well, with test planning of a subsequent group of features happening while test execution for the current group of features is continuing.

For agile models, the concept of iterative models is taken to its logical extreme—which is one explanation for the agile lifecycle type called Extreme Programming, or XP. Iterations are kept very short. Some of our agile clients use two weeks, some three weeks, some four weeks, but I've never seen anything longer than four. These iterations are often called sprints, especially when Scrum is used. The best practice—not universally practiced by any means—is for the sprint team to work collectively and sequentially on each iteration, with all the work on one iteration finished before work on the next iteration starts. All of the test levels are contained within each sprint, with the exception of system integration test for larger systems built this way. The test levels overlap extensively and entry criteria, even for higher levels of testing, are kept very flexible. Since sprint teams are supposed to be self-directing, for most of our clients the test manager assigns a tester into each team and then provides overall support and advice to the testers rather than day-by-day direction.

For spiral models, there is heavy use of prototypes to evaluate different ways to design and implement the system. The specific sequence of prototypes—that is, what we try first, what we try next, and so on—depends on considerations like business importance, the likelihood of problems with a particular design or implementation decision, and so forth. Basically, the experimental prototypes are used to get as much risk out of the project as early as possible. The testing of these prototypes must help the project team find and resolve any obstacles that will prevent them from succeeding, and to do so quickly. Once these obstacles

> **ISTQB Glossary**
>
> **test level:** A group of test activities that are organized and managed together. A test level is linked to the responsibilities in a project. Examples of test levels are component test, integration test, system test and acceptance test.

are resolved, the lifecycle will often revert to a standard sequential, iterative, or agile model, with the usual test considerations.

As you probably noticed, the different lifecycles have a profound effect on the timing and extent of the various fundamental test process activities. In a sequential lifecycle project, the early and complete implementation of a test environment is often essential to avoid significant waste and delays once test execution starts. In an agile lifecycle, a test manager would create an enormous obstacle to progress if they insisted that such a complete test environment be created before any test execution. Instead, test managers carefully plan for what's needed for the current iteration, not only in terms of test environments but also test data and test cases.

The lifecycles also affect the work products produced during the test process activities. Test results reporting and the evaluation of test completeness occurs repeatedly in iterative projects, at the end of each iteration, and typically the test manager will report in a much more lightweight fashion than in a sequential lifecycle. Test retrospectives can occur at the end of each iteration to decide on improvements for the next iteration, including changes in the work products produced for these subsequent iterations.

These have been simplified explanations of each lifecycle and how they affect testing. Whole books can be—and have been—written about how the lifecycles work, and some of those books even address testing. As a test manager, you should master all the details of the different lifecycle models that can occur in your organization. You and your team must be lifecycle promiscuous, as it were, ready to work effectively in whatever lifecycle you are injected into. Try to avoid some of the religious wars that rage around the selection of lifecycles. Remember, as a test manager, you'll need to play the hand you're dealt and work effectively within the context of the project, whatever that context may be.

A bit later in this chapter, we'll look at the concept and content of a test strategy document, which you might remember from the Foundation syllabus and from Chapter 1. One topic that a test strategy can address is the way in which testing is aligned with other activities and work products on a project, including alignment based on the selected lifecycle. This can vary from project to project, so you'll need to be careful to reevaluate this part of the test strategy as you work with the project manager during the test planning and project planning activities.

System Test Process Alignment for V-Model

Let's take another look at this concept of alignment using the V-model as a detailed example, as shown in Figure 2–2. We'll further assume that we are talking about the system test level.

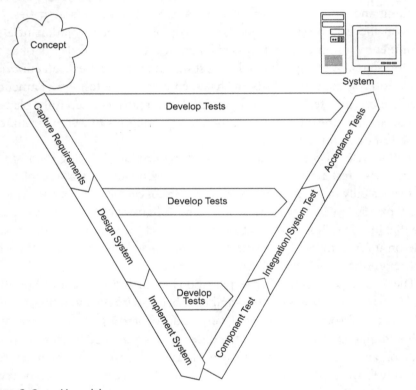

Figure 2–2   *V-model*

In the V-model, with a well-aligned test process, test planning occurs concurrently with project planning. In other words, the moment of involvement of testing is at the very start of the project.

Once the test plan is approved, test control begins. Test control continues through to test closure. Analysis, design, implementation, execution, evaluation of exit criteria, and test results reporting are carried out according to the plan. Deviations from the plan are managed.

Test analysis starts immediately after or even occurs concurrently with test planning. Test analysis and test design happen concurrently with requirements, high-level design, and low-level design. Test implementation, including test environment implementation, starts during system design and ends just before test execution begins.

Test execution begins when the test entry criteria are met. More realistically, test execution starts when most entry criteria are met and any outstanding entry criteria are waived. In V-model theory, the entry criteria would include successful completion of both component test and integration test levels. Test execution continues until the test exit criteria are met, though again some of these will often be waived.

Evaluation of test exit criteria and reporting of test results occurs throughout test execution.

Test closure activities occur after test execution is declared complete.

This kind of precise alignment of test activities with each other and with the rest of the system lifecycle absolutely *will not* just happen spontaneously or by accident. Nor can you expect to be able to instill this alignment continuously throughout the process, without any forethought.

Rather, for each test level, no matter what the selected software lifecycle and test process, the test manager must perform this alignment. Not only must this happen during the test and project planning, but also test control includes acting to ensure ongoing alignment.

No matter what test process and software lifecycle are chosen, each project has its own quirks. This is especially true for complex projects such as the systems-of-systems projects common in the military and among RBCS's larger clients. In such a case, the test manager must plan not only to align test processes but also to modify them. Off-the-rack process models, whether for testing alone or for the entire software lifecycle, don't fit such complex projects well.

Additional Test Levels

In the Foundation syllabus, four levels of testing are discussed:

- Unit testing (also called component testing). This often means testing of the smallest individually testable elements of the system, usually a class in object-oriented code such as Java or a function in procedural code such as C or COBOL. Just because a unit is independently testable does not mean it is independently executable; stubs, drivers, mock objects, and harnesses are usually required.

- Integration testing. This can mean one of two things. Component integration testing is sequential testing of an ever-increasing collection of units, as the complete set of units is assembled incrementally to compose the entire system. These collections, often called builds, are often not independently testable either, thus requiring harnesses. System integration testing is testing of interoperating systems of systems, generally after each of those systems has been independently tested. These systems of systems are independently testable.
- System testing. This is testing of a complete, integrated system.
- Acceptance testing. This can mean various things. For IT software, it includes activities such as user acceptance testing by the users and operational acceptance testing by system administrators and operators. For consumer, mass-market, and enterprise software, acceptance testing usually means alpha testing and beta (or field) testing. For both types of software, contractual and regulatory acceptance testing can apply.

While most projects can get by with just these levels of testing, on some projects there are additional levels required.

Hardware-software integration testing is required when custom-configured or custom-built hardware is part of the system. I have quite a bit of experience managing testing of such systems and can vouch for the fact that properly managed hardware-software integration testing is critical in these situations. A classic mistake that can occur is that the hardware and software are tested completely separately and the software is not tested on the custom hardware until the end, during an acceptance test. This will almost always result in disaster, because the functional and nonfunctional behaviors of the software will change, no matter how realistic the simulators used for testing the software. Instead of making this mistake, you should define a separate hardware-software integration test level. This level should start as soon as hardware prototypes are available and should include functional and nonfunctional tests that are designed to exercise the specific customizations and the way the software interacts with them.

As discussed in the Foundation syllabus, system integration testing can be required. Planning for system integration testing can reveal a number of challenges. Different systems are often developed and tested by different groups within the organization, or even entirely different organizations, which creates multifaceted issues during system integration testing: How to assign responsibility for fixing bugs? How to sequence the system integration testing in risk order when the systems are delivered for testing in whatever order they are ready? How to handle regression testing of systems when changes are needed, given that the project team that built the system may have already disbanded? How to work around defects found in commercial off-the-shelf (COTS) systems that are included? I've been involved in a few such projects and have consulted with many clients that sell systems of systems or have them in their data centers. System integration testing is always harder than anyone thinks it should be, and thus the tendency is to under-plan and under-resource. Don't make that mistake.

For large and complex applications especially, feature interaction testing may be required. For example, in a word processing application, features exist to allow the formatting of text; the creation of tables; the insertion of images and other figures; the automated generation of tables of contents, tables of figures, tables of tables, and indices; and the printing of the resulting document. All of these features can interact. Feature interaction can be tested as part of the functional and nonfunctional testing during component integration, system, and system integration test levels, or it can be organized as its own separate test level. Personally, I've always included feature interaction in other test levels, but circumstances could exist that make organizing it on a separate level a good idea. For example, if different teams are responsible for different features, there may be some value in having a specific level planned for feature interaction testing because you'll need to plan for close interaction of stakeholders and participants across different teams during this level of testing.

Finally, there is a somewhat rare test level, customer product integration testing. When I have seen clients using this test level, it is a special hybrid of system integration testing and field testing. It occurs when a system must be installed in a data center and must interact closely with other systems already installed in that data center. These interoperating systems are typically produced by vendors other than the vendor whose system is being installed, or they might be in-house applications created by the customer. The same challenges mentioned previously for system integration testing exist for customer product integration testing, as well as the obvious customer-relationship issues that can arise if customer product integration testing yields bad results (which might not be the test manager's fault) or is not properly managed (which certainly is at least in part the test manager's fault).

On any given project, you might find that you need some or all of these test levels. You might be surprised to hear that all could apply, but RBCS has a client that uses all of these levels except for hardware-software integration testing and another that uses all of them.

Well-Defined Test Levels

Simply deciding to use a test level does not mean that test level will succeed. As the management cliché goes, "Failing to plan is planning to fail." We'll address the topic of test plans in more detail later in this book, but since we're on the topic of test levels, let's talk about what needs to be covered in the plan for each test level.

Each test level needs clearly defined objectives. For example, defect detection is a typical objective for system testing. Not only do you need the objective clearly defined, but you also need an achievable goal, such as finding 95 percent of the defects. For acceptance testing, finding defects is usually not an objective but building confidence is. For confidence building, you might say that 100 percent coverage of the requirements and use cases is required during acceptance test, which would mean defining and executing at least one test case for every requirement element and use case.

You also must understand what is in scope and what is not in scope. This question of scope generally has three dimensions: test types, system attributes, and test items. As shown in Figure 2–3, for test types, you have to determine the appropriate mix and extent of coverage for dynamic tests, including white-box, black-box, defect-based, experience-based, and dynamic analysis, as well as the approach for static tests such as reviews and static analysis. For system attributes, you have to determine which functional and nonfunctional characteristics of the system you'll test. For test items, you have to determine what should be delivered to your team for testing.

By extension, you also must determine the appropriate test techniques and test basis for the selected test types. As a test manager, you should work with your test analysts and technical test analysts to define the test techniques and, as appropriate, the test tools needed to support those techniques. With the test basis selected, you can then define how you want to measure its coverage. For test bases such as requirements and quality risks, you can use traceability in your test management tool to measure coverage. For test bases such as code, you can use tools to measure the extent of coverage, as was discussed in the Foundation syllabus.

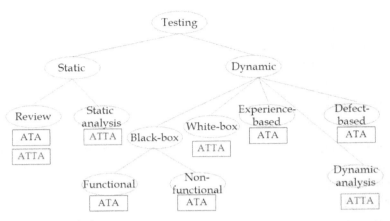

Figure 2-3   *Test techniques*

As was also discussed in the Foundation syllabus, test levels should have defined entry and exit criteria. Entry criteria help you ensure that all the enablers and preconditions for a test level are in place before you start executing that level of testing, which generally makes the testing more efficient and effective as well as prevents frustrating events where testing progress is abruptly slowed or halted. Exit criteria help you measure whether the objectives of the test level have been achieved and whether certain logistical and project management activities have been completed.

Reporting against entry and exit criteria is just one of the types of reporting that test managers typically must do during test projects. You should define measurements and metrics for each test level for these criteria, the defined objectives for the level, and the results of testing, including the extent to which your team has covered the selected test bases. We'll return to this topic later in this chapter.

The primary deliverables for testing are the results reports, which are typically delivered periodically. Another primary deliverable is the set of detailed defect reports, which are delivered as defects are discovered. Other deliverables can include test tools, test data, and test environments to be used by other teams, such as the users during user acceptance testing. To avoid confusion and perceptions of failure to deliver by the test team, each test level needs clearly defined deliverables.

Test activities are done by people and require resources. It's your job, as the test manager, to determine what resources and which people will be involved. Resources include both resources your team can create, such as test data, and

ISTQB Glossary

quality risk: A risk related to a quality attribute. As a comment from me, I'd point out that this term is actually a synonym for product risk, and is used that way in the Advanced syllabus.

quality attribute: A feature or characteristic that affects an item's quality.

resources provided and possibly supported by outside teams, such as test environments. Some of the people will be outside of the test team, so you'll need to plan to work cross-functionally with stakeholders throughout the organization.

For certain systems, there might be regulatory or contractual compliance issues that must be addressed by testing. For example, in medical systems regulated by the US Food and Drug Administration, detailed traceability of the tests and their results back to the requirements must be maintained throughout test execution. Test execution cannot conclude until every requirement can be shown to work by successful execution of every test planned for that requirement. In situations where compliance is an issue, it can be a fatal mistake for the test manager to fail to plan for it, or to plan for it incorrectly.

When RBCS performs assessments of test teams, we often find organizations that use test levels but perform them in isolation. This is usually very inefficient and confusing. I'll cover this topic in more detail later in this chapter. You'll see then that using documents like test policies and coordinating closely with test-related staff can coordinate the test levels to reduce gaps, overlap, and confusion about results.

As a final note, in some organizations following agile lifecycles, the word *plan* has become a near obscenity; the mere mention of it can bring on howls such as, "Plans aren't agile." This is ironic, actually, because most of our clients using agile are following much more rigorous and carefully choreographed development and testing processes than our clients that are not. In fact, one client manager, when I asked him how he liked agile, replied, "Well, I'm not crazy about it, but it's better than no process at all, which is what we had before." Keep in mind that it's possible to have a plan that describes how certain situations and activities will be organized without trying to specify the exact set of features to be built or otherwise squelch change during the project. The chosen lifecycle can change which of these test level elements must be defined in advance and which should be defined in each iteration, but still choices must be made for each element.

Managing Nonfunctional Testing

I previously mentioned the issue of test scoping with respect to both functional and nonfunctional characteristics. While functional testing is obviously important, test managers sometimes overlook nonfunctional testing, which can be just as important for many products. In some cases, the test manager is aware of the need for nonfunctional testing but is daunted by the cost associated with such tests. Whether through ignorance or a perception that the cost is too high, the omission of nonfunctional testing can lead to serious, sometimes even disastrous, consequences.

For example, some problems with laptop batteries led to the largest consumer-products recall in history. One laptop vendor, a client of ours, almost forgot about performance testing. Fortunately, representatives from the vendor called us just days before they were about to roll out the website they intended to use to manage the replacement of batteries for their laptops. We managed to successfully engage with them to do their performance testing, identifying in the process serious problems that would have caused major slowdowns and even crashes in production. A week of crazy effort paid off.

Another laptop vendor, not a client of ours, apparently didn't bother to performance-test its website. Once the recall started, the website was notoriously frequently down and slow for weeks. Perhaps this vendor felt that this recall was just something it had to do rather than something it wanted to do and therefore didn't really have to bother to do it well or spend a bunch of money on making sure the recall program would work properly? I felt at the time that it was unfortunate that the US regulatory agency overseeing the recall didn't issue massive fines for the vendor because the delivery of low-quality software and systems without consequence is, I believe, a major reason why software and systems continue to be so bad.

However, the dilemma is real. Nonfunctional testing can be quite expensive, especially if we want to do it well. So what's a test manager to do? What can help is to make visible the risks associated with not running nonfunctional tests and put those up against the costs and constraints that lead organizations to omit such tests. Sometimes organizations are unaware or in denial about such risks. The test manager can provide a forcing function to make the organization explicitly choose to either accept such risks or to mitigate them through testing. We'll talk more about a way to do that, risk-based testing, later in this chapter. Risk-based testing will also help the organization distinguish between relevant nonfunctional tests—that is, nonfunctional risks that could significantly affect the quality of the system—and those where the cost would outweigh the benefit.

> **ISTQB Glossary**
>
> **risk-based testing:** An approach to testing to reduce the level of product risks and inform stakeholders of their status, starting in the initial stages of a project. It involves the identification of product risks and the use of risk levels to guide the test process.

Another impediment to planning for nonfunctional testing is that many test managers are not sufficiently skilled to do so. In this case, test managers should collaborate with senior technical test analysts and test analysts on their team. These test team members should work with the test manager and with other project stakeholders to understand the key risks and requirements related to nonfunctional testing. They should identify the tools and test environments that will be needed. They should understand how organizational factors can affect the ability to run nonfunctional tests and look for creative solutions to organizational obstacles to such tests. For example, if insufficient hardware or operators are available to create a performance test environment, perhaps a cloud-based test environment can be used. Security considerations, such as the anonymization of production data used for testing, should also figure into the test plan.

In addition to using risk to select nonfunctional tests, risk should be considered when the tests are being prioritized and integrated into the project. There's a common misperception that nonfunctional tests can be run only at the end of the project, after all the functional testing is complete. This is simply another manifestation of a widespread testing worst practice, which is planning testing on the assumption that no bugs will be found. Of course, nonfunctional bugs *are* usually found, and if those bugs are critical, significant damage to the project's prospects for success can occur. I've personally seen firsthand two multiyear, multimillion dollar projects fail abruptly and with total loss of value when performance-related design defects were revealed late in the project. In both cases, the project failures were entirely preventable through early performance testing, including modeling and simulation of design decisions (i.e., static analysis) and by considering performance implications in reviews of code, architecture, and metadata.

I have seen early nonfunctional testing, including static nonfunctional testing, work. On one project where usability was a critical product characteristic, the project team included user interface experts. They built screen prototypes that we subjected to thorough reviews and then to actual dynamic testing with the target users. This allowed us to detect and remove usability defects that would have led to serious delays had they been revealed once we started the beta testing.

A particular challenge for designing, implementing, and executing non-functional tests occurs in iterative lifecycles, especially agile lifecycles. With agile lifecycles, you might find that certain nonfunctional test activities will not fit within a single iteration, and in fact don't really relate to the features being built in a single iteration. For example, setting up a realistic reliability and performance testing environment, assembling sufficient test data for such testing, and creating the automated tests can take more than just a couple weeks. In these cases, it's usually best to have a separate person or team working on these activities outside of the iteration team or teams. In fact, I recommend this approach for test automation generally, including functional test automation, in agile projects.

Example: Managing Performance Quality Risks throughout the Lifecycle

Two important concepts in the ISTQB approach are the ideas of testing integrated throughout the lifecycle and testing as a preventive activity. Here's an example of both, applied to an Internet appliance project.

On this project, performance and scalability were potential major risks. If the servers would not scale to handle the load of thousands of Internet appliances, a number of financial and customer-satisfaction disasters would ensue. So, on this project, we had four major activities to assure performance and scalability of the delivered system.

During the design phase, we did static performance tests of proposed designs, which basically consisted of reviews of spreadsheet models of load and performance.

Once those were done—but still during the design phase—we did static performance analysis, using commercial simulation tools, of the proposed designs.

As programming progressed, programmers were responsible for doing unit performance tests as they implemented the design. The harnesses used for these tests were also used to build system performance test tools.

Finally, once we had a feature-complete system, we started system test. (We followed a sequential lifecycle on this project.) At this point, we did system performance tests of the implemented design.

This approach reduced serious performance problems found during system test to a manageable number. That's not to say we didn't find performance defects—we found over a dozen—but they were all of the sort that could be fixed quickly and without major changes to the design—or the schedule.

Managing Experience-Based Testing

I discussed the selection of test types earlier in this chapter, including experience-based testing. As was mentioned in the Foundation syllabus, experience-based testing tends to be an efficient way of finding defects. Because it complements the other types of tests, it finds defects that other techniques miss. (The converse is also true, in that experience-based tests can miss defects that other techniques find.) The integration of experience-based tests can help identify any gaps in the other tests and rounds out a complete test set.

However, experience-based tests can be challenging to manage. This is especially true for exploratory testing because it is inherently the least predictable of the experience-based techniques. Part of the challenge is managing these tests in such a way that preserves their benefits while at the same time measures the coverage and provides for adequate reproducibility when needed. Reproducibility is especially difficult when multiple testers are involved since the lightweight documentation associated with experience-based tests might not provide enough guidance for other testers to re-create the testing work previously done.

A management technique called session-based testing addresses these challenges to some extent. Rather than testers being turned loose to work without guidance, their days are divided into test sessions that range from 30 to 120 minutes, depending on the scope of the testing to be done in a session. This is called *timeboxing*. The scope of the testing is defined in what's referred to as a *test charter* by the inclusion of either one or more test conditions or, less frequently, a very high-level logical test case. The test charter can be communicated verbally, though for purposes of traceability and reproducibility it is usually better that the charters be written. When the test conditions are divided across multiple test charters, the exploratory testing work can be spread across multiple testers without worrying about overlap. By defining the test conditions in the test charters, the test manager can be more confident that coverage goals were achieved.

Another technique for experience-based testing that I've used involves including experience-based testing within the execution of predesign logical or concrete tests, as I discussed in Chapter 1. Let's say that I have a written test that I think will take 90 minutes to execute from beginning to end, including time for capturing of the test results (e.g., defect reports and test logging). I can then add 30 minutes to the time allocated for the test, and this time is available to the tester to do exploratory testing within the scope of the test condition or conditions covered by the test. In these situations, I often tell the testers that they should consider the written tests to be road maps that will take them to interesting places in the software and, once they get somewhere interesting, they should stop and look around.

Similarly, you can also assign testers to run a mix of experience-based test charters and predesigned tests during each day. The charters can precede the predesigned tests, alternate with the predesigned tests during the day, or be run at the end of each day.

Yet another way to include the benefits of experience-based testing into your predesigned tests is by using the results of the experience-based tests to modify, expand, and, in some cases, redirect the predesigned tests. For example, if your testers find a lot of bugs in an area of the system undercovered by the predesigned tests, consider adding more written tests for that area.

Experience-Based Testing Sessions

What should a tester do during the test sessions? There are three main activities:

1. Session setup. This involves both setting up the test environment and making sure that the tester understands the area of the product or system to be tested. To some extent, this corresponds to creating the preconditions that occur when running scripted testing under a preventive test strategy. However, it also includes some test environment setup tasks that, in a preventive test strategy like analytical risk-based testing, would occur before test execution and off the critical path for release.

2. Test design and execution. This consists of designing and running tests against the test object in tight loops, looking for any problems. As the tester learns more about the application, and what works and what doesn't work, they modify their testing. The tester can apply structured test design techniques, but the techniques are selected based on what the tester is learning. If you are using exploratory testing, this is the "simultaneously learn the product, run the tests, and decide what to test next" activity that exploratory test proponents talk about. However, you could also be using Whittaker's software attacks approach under this method.[3] Notice that the

---

[3]. For more information, you can refer to James Whittaker's books *How to Break Software* and *How to Break Software Security*.

"design" activity is included here. Again, in a preventive test strategy like analytical risk-based testing, test design would occur before test execution and be off the critical path for release.

3. Defect investigation and results reporting. This same process would be triggered when a scripted test finds a problem. However, since we don't have a detailed written test case, it would not make sense to refer the developer to that test case. If anything, the defect reporting process under reactive test strategies must be even more meticulous and detailed in its outputs than the defect reporting process under preventive test strategies (that have produced test scripts and test data). The test results as a whole are logged throughout the session. If reproducibility of the test session by other testers is needed, the detail of these logs should increase, including the specific inputs, actions, and events.

While I have described these activities in a way that might sound sequential, in most cases they would overlap. In addition, depending on results of the debrief session, we might iterate this process for a given test charter.

In some cases, test managers will debrief testers after these sessions, which can influence and modify subsequent sessions and even the predesigned tests. However, if debriefs occur immediately after every session, this can negatively affect the scalability of the technique because an average of just 15 minutes for each debrief would mean that a test manager would probably spend 100 percent of their time on debriefs with a team of just four testers. I have used end-of-day debriefs personally, with testers free to ask me for on-the-spot advice when the test results are especially surprising.

Example: Exploratory Testing

Figure 2–4 shows an example of the kind of test results logging that I've had testers do for exploratory test sessions. This log replaces the written test and the log of its results, so as you can see, there's a lot less detail here about what was done. As I mentioned, if you need better reproducibility, you'll want to ensure that testers capture the steps, inputs, and expected results in an additional section of this log.

In Figure 2–4, you can see that we've captured the name of the tester, the date when the test was run, the time spent running the test, and the tester's assessment of whether they sufficiently tested the given test condition; that is, the test charter, also shown here. We also see references to the bug report IDs for the two bugs, along with summaries of those reports to make the log more of a free-standing document. Of course, for details about the bugs, you'd still need to go into the bug reports themselves.

```
┌─────────────────────────────────────────────────────────────────────┐
│                                                                       │
│                   Exploratory Testing Session Log                     │
│                                                                       │
│   Tester _Name_____Date _When_____             │
│                                                                       │
│   Time on-task _1:45_____Charter completed? _yes_____   │
│   ┌───────────────────────────────────────────────────────────────┐  │
│   │ Charter                                                         │  │
│   │                                                                 │  │
│   │ Test the security of the login page, see if it's possible to    │  │
│   │ log in without a password                                       │  │
│   └───────────────────────────────────────────────────────────────┘  │
│   ┌───────────────────────────────────────────────────────────────┐  │
│   │ Bugs reported                                                   │  │
│   │                                                                 │  │
│   │ 937 – Log in form vulnerable to SQL injection                   │  │
│   │ 939 – System identifies a valid username when the password      │  │
│   │ is wrong                                                        │  │
│   └───────────────────────────────────────────────────────────────┘  │
│   ┌───────────────────────────────────────────────────────────────┐  │
│   │ Issues that need followup                                       │  │
│   │                                                                 │  │
│   │ * Lockout feature on three unsuccessful login attempts doesn't  │  │
│   │ seem to work                                                    │  │
│   └───────────────────────────────────────────────────────────────┘  │
└─────────────────────────────────────────────────────────────────────┘
```

Figure 2–4   *Exploratory testing*

Finally, we have a section where the tester describes areas of interest for future sessions or issues that might be handed off to the test manager. In this example, we see that the tester saw behavior that was potentially buggy. Since it was outside the scope of the session, they didn't spend time on it. However, a subsequent test session had, as its test charter, testing the lockout feature of the login page.

Test Management in Context Exercise

Review your solution to the exercise in Chapter 1, section 1.2. Based on the discussion in this section, adjust your outline of test activities.

Test Management in Context Debrief

The following items could be added or adjusted:

- Specifying nonfunctional testing, including in early iterations
- Specifying experience-based testing in each cycle of test execution
- More details about aligning the component and component integration levels (done by developers) with the system and system integration test levels (done by your team)
- Identification of test stakeholders for this project
- Identification of test work products

This is only a partial list; other items are possible.

2.3   Risk-Based Testing and Other Approaches for Test Prioritization and Effort Allocation

Learning objectives

(K2) Explain the different ways that risk-based testing responds to risks.

(K2) Explain, giving examples, different techniques for product risk analysis.

(K4) Analyze, identify, and assess product quality risks, summarizing the risks and their assessed level of risk based on key project stakeholder perspectives.

(K2) Describe how identified product quality risks can be mitigated and managed, appropriate to their assessed level of risk, throughout the lifecycle and the test process

(K2) Give examples of different options for test selection, test prioritization and effort allocation.

Test Prioritization and Effort Allocation

What to test? What not to test? How much to test those things we do test? What should be tested first? What can be tested last? The hows and whys of answering those questions bedevil every test manager. The number of conceivable test conditions for any real-world system is huge, and the number of possible combinations of those test conditions is so large as to be infinite. Some people like to debate whether the number of tests is truly infinite or just practically infinite, but in case you think it matters, consider this example: engineers at the Sun Microsystems division of Oracle once calculated that the number of possible states in the Solaris operating system exceeded the number of atoms in the known universe. A quick check of the Internet shows that, if you could run a test as quickly as you could give the test ID number, it would still take 32,000 years before you'd run the trillionth test, which is not even a trillionth of a trillionth of the way to testing all of the possible states.[4]

---

4. This whimsical experiment made possible by searching the Internet for "how long to count to a trillion" and "how many atoms in the known universe."

So the test manager must establish a process to select a finite set of test conditions from this enormous set of possible tests. This process must also help to determine the appropriate time, effort, and resources to expend on each of the test conditions. Ideally, the process should also give guidance on the best sequencing of the tests, subject to the various constraints and realities of the project. In the absence of such a process, testing will be less effective and less efficient. In the worst case, testing degrades into an aimless shuffle through the product's features and behaviors.

In this section, we'll look at the various processes that have been developed over the years for smart selection, allocation, and prioritization of tests. Risk-based testing, which was introduced in the Foundation syllabus, is one strategy. Other test strategies also have ways to address this challenge. All of these strategies must adapt to the real-world constraints and priorities that exist on each project, so rarely is a pure solution achievable. It's important that you, as a test manager, keep in mind the need to successfully adapt chosen strategies to given circumstances.

Risk-Based Testing

Let's start with risk-based testing. First, we need to define some of the relevant terminology. A risk is any negative or undesirable outcome or event that could occur. There are two essential elements here:

- Possibility: Only events or outcomes that can occur are risks. That which is certain is not a risk, and that which is impossible is not a risk.
- Negativity: Only possible events or outcomes that are bad are risks. Possible events or outcomes that are good would be opportunities, and we are not talking about opportunity-based testing here.

In software testing, we are concerned with two specific types of risks. The first type of risk is a risk that, should it become an actual outcome, would reduce the product's perceived quality in the eyes of one or more customers, users, project participants, or project stakeholders. This type of risk is referred to in the ISTQB terminology as a quality risk, a product risk, or a product quality risk. Personally, I prefer *quality risk* because that term makes it clear that we are talking about a risk to the quality of the system.

The second type of risk is a risk that, should it become an actual outcome, would reduce the perception of the extent to which a project had succeeded, again from the perspective of one or more customers, users, project participants, or project stakeholders. This type of risk is referred to in the ISTQB

> **ISTQB Glossary**
>
> **product risk:** A risk directly related to the test object.
>
> **project risk:** A risk related to management and control of the (test) project, e.g., lack of staffing, strict deadlines, changing requirements, etc.

terminology as a project risk or planning risk. Personally, I prefer the term *project risk* because *planning risk* seems to indicate that the risks only arise due to a failure to plan sufficiently.

Now, you might be thinking, "Hmm, Rex, isn't a quality risk just a special type of project risk, since failing to deliver a quality product is one sign of an unsuccessful project?" Yes, that is true. However, it's very useful to make the distinction, because a quality risk can be mitigated by running a test against it, while a project risk cannot be mitigated in this way. I'll illustrate this with an example.

Suppose we have identified two risks for a project to develop an e-commerce application. The first risk involves the possibility of calculating incorrect totals during checkout. The second risk involves the possibility that a key piece of hardware needed for the test environment will not be available when needed.

Notice that we can develop a test to check the correctness of totals. If that test demonstrates that we have a defect, the project team is now aware of the defect, which is less risky than a situation where a defect is unknown. The project team can take advantage of the opportunities this awareness brings to either remove the defect or reduce the impact the defect can have on the customer. Of course, if the test passes, the project team can have a higher level of confidence in the correct operation of the system, at least under the tested conditions.

However, to manage the risk associated with test environment availability, we must do things such as careful test environment planning, thorough test environment implementation prior to test execution, and so on. The execution of a test is not a way to manage this risk because the risk itself threatens our ability to execute tests. Many test-related project risks have exactly this property; that is, the risk would impede successful test execution.

The example I gave, of a quality risk involving correctness of calculation, is a functional quality risk, specifically a risk to the system's accuracy. Quality risks can cover any functional or nonfunctional system attribute. The risk of a slow response when checking out would be a nonfunctional risk, specifically related to efficiency and response time. The risk of a user being unable to determine how to check out would be a nonfunctional risk too, specifically related to usability and understandability.

You can mitigate any quality risk by running a test against it. To run the test, of course, it must first be designed and implemented. So, let's put this in the context of the fundamental test process.

First, during test analysis, we identify the quality risks. Quality risks have different degrees of importance, based on the degree of risk each poses to the quality of the system, so we must also assess the level of risk for each quality risk. This is best done in a collaborative fashion, working with stakeholders, as I'll explain further in a moment. Given the assessed list of quality risks, we can then select appropriate test conditions, the effort appropriate to each test condition, and the priority and sequence for testing each condition.

Next, during test design we determine how to cover each quality risk with tests. During test implementation, we create the test environments and test data needed to run those tests. We also sequence those tests, trying to run the high-risk tests as early as possible, given project constraints.

Finally, during test execution, we run the tests, mitigating the covered risks as we proceed. As mentioned, the failing tests mitigate risk by exposing problems that we can address, and the passing tests mitigate risk by reducing the likelihood of undetected failures in the area tested. We can report test results based on risk. If we have used risk measurements as part of our exit criteria—and we should—we can make a risk-aware decision about when to declare testing sufficiency.

Risk-based testing delivers four main benefits:

- First, consider an ideal testing project. In such a project, you would find every bug in exact order of importance, starting with the most important bug and ending with the least important bug. You would, in short, find the scary stuff first. Now, while no testing strategy, including risk-based testing, can guarantee such perfect bug discovery, risk-based testing allows us to run tests in risk order, giving the highest likelihood of discovering defects in severity order.
- Second, remember the problem of test selection I mentioned earlier. As testers, we must pick the right tests out of the infinite cloud of possible tests.

We can't have perfect confidence in the system when we release it; we can only hope to manage the most important risks to quality. Risk-based testing allows us to allocate test effort based on risk. This is the most efficient way to minimize the residual quality risk upon release.

- Third, it's not enough to minimize the residual risk; a project team must also know what the residual risks are. In this way, we can decide to release when the risk of further testing (which would delay the release) is in balance with risk of dissatisfaction associated with possible quality problems. Risk-based testing allows us to measure test results based on risk. Thus, the project team knows the residual level of quality risk throughout test execution. Based on this knowledge, we can make smart release decisions.

- Fourth, as testers we are all familiar with the problem of test execution schedule pressures. If we are pressured to reduce our test coverage, we'd want to give up tests we worry about the least. So, if schedule requires, risk-based testing allows us to drop tests in reverse risk order. This reduces the test execution period with the least possible increase in quality risk in the delivered product.

All of these benefits allow the test team to operate more efficiently and in a targeted fashion, especially in time-constrained and/or resource-constrained situations.

Risk-Based Testing Process

I mentioned earlier that risk-based testing is one process for smart test condition selection, test effort allocation, and test execution prioritization. Further, it should be clear from what I just wrote that this process uses an analysis of quality risks as its foundation. In fact, it's not just one process but rather a family of related processes. Each of these different techniques tends to have its own inputs, outputs, tempo, templates, standards, styles of collaboration, and level of formality. These variations affect the way in which risks are identified, assessed, documented, communicated, verified, traced to other test basis documents, traced to tests and test results, and otherwise managed from initial identification to final mitigation.

Regardless of the different techniques, the objective is the same: reduce risk through testing to an acceptable level. All testing has the effect of mitigating the overall level of quality risk. However, testing without an awareness of risk—that is, without performing quality risk analysis—will lead to a higher and unknown level of risk at the end of the testing.[5] In risk-based testing, we can organize the testing in a way that minimizes the residual level of quality risk remaining for any given amount of testing effort. In addition, we can report test results in terms of the residual level of quality risk at any time. Once management is more comfortable with accepting the residual level of quality risk than they would be with continuing the testing effort, we can say that we have achieved the optimal level of testing in terms of risk mitigation. Some of the techniques for risk-based testing do a better job of giving project stakeholders insight into the residual level of quality risk than others, as you'll see.

Earlier, I put the process of risk-based testing into the context of the fundamental test process, at a high level. Over the next few pages in this book, I'll focus on the constituent activities associated with risk-based testing. These activities are as follows:

- Risk identification
- Risk assessment
- Risk mitigation
- Risk management

While I will discuss these in a sequential fashion, it's important to keep in mind that project teams will need to iterate these activities on most projects. New facts come to light and projects change, which will affect the risks that can be identified, the assessed level of risk, how those risks should be mitigated, and what steps should be taken to manage the risks. In addition, the activities tend to overlap. For example, during the assessment of risk levels, new risks are often identified.

Risk-Based Testing Participants

Before we start discussing the process and the activities within it, let me address a topic that is much more important. I have been doing risk-based testing using various techniques for about 20 years now. Over those years, I have honed a technique that I feel works well for me. However, I have found that the most important success factor for risk-based testing is the participation of the right

---

5. As one of the reviewers, Jamie Mitchell, mentioned, "Certainly people are always making (consciously or unconsciously) choices as to what is important while they test. They may not be aware of this thing called risk-based testing formally. It is possible they will make some good choices, mitigating some risks." I agree that some risks will be mitigated, but without a clear inventory of quality risks to measure the mitigation against, the level of risk is not known, and without broad stakeholder involvement, fewer risks will be identified.

set of cross-functional stakeholders in the risk identification and risk assessment activities. Attempts by testers alone, or testers together with only one or two other people, to identify the risks and determine the level of each risk will result in a lot of mistakes. These mistakes include missing a lot of risks, overestimating the level of some risks while underestimating the level of other risks, and failing to get stakeholder consensus on the catalog of quality risks that is produced.

Who are these stakeholders who must participate? Well, I addressed the topic of the stakeholders in testing and quality in section 2.2 earlier in this chapter. It turns out the list is very much the same. Anyone with an interest in the quality of the product and the success of the project is a stakeholder who has an awareness—to a greater or lesser extent—of the risks. As noted previously, we can talk about two categories of such stakeholders. Business stakeholders include customers, users, operation staff, and help desk and technical support staff. A business stakeholder understands the problem we're trying to solve with the system and can see risks that would affect how well we've solved that problem and how bad it would be if we failed to solve some aspect of the problem. Technical stakeholders include developers, architects, database administrators, and network administrators. A technical stakeholder understands how failures can occur and thus can see risks associated with such failures and the likelihood of various failures occurring.

Now, you don't have to get every stakeholder to participate in the quality risk analysis process because many will have the same perspective, based on the group they are in. What you do need to have is a qualified representative of each group. A qualified representative is someone who is most likely to have the best understanding of the quality risks that are relevant to the group as well as the perceived authority—which need not be managerial authority—to speak on behalf of the group.

It's sometimes the case that you can't get a qualified representative for certain groups. For example, customers and users might not exist for a product still under development, or senior management may be really queasy about having frank discussions about quality risks with existing customers or users. In such situations, you need to identify a surrogate who can speak for that group. As mentioned, a qualified surrogate representative is someone who understands the quality risks that affect the group they represent and who is seen by others on the project team as a good spokesperson for that group.

> **ISTQB Glossary**
>
> **risk analysis:** The process of assessing identified risks to estimate their impact and probability of occurrence (likelihood).
>
> **risk assessment:** The process of assessing a given project or product risk to determine its level of risk, typically by assigning likelihood and impact ratings and then aggregating those ratings into a single risk priority rating.
>
> **risk identification:** The process of identifying risks using techniques such as brainstorming, checklists, and failure history.
>
> **risk level:** The importance of a risk as defined by its characteristics impact and likelihood. The level of risk can be used to determine the intensity of testing to be performed. A risk level can be expressed either qualitatively (e.g., high, medium, low) or quantitatively.
>
> **risk management:** Systematic application of procedures and practices to the tasks of identifying, analyzing, prioritizing, and controlling risk.
>
> **risk mitigation:** The process through which decisions are reached and protective measures are implemented for reducing risks to, or maintaining risks within, specified levels.
>
> **risk impact:** The damage that will be caused if the risk become an actual outcome or event.

In some cases, a stakeholder can be both a business stakeholder and a technical stakeholder, which is often true of testers and sometimes of business analysts. In fact, testers tend to be very aware of quality risks, even when they have never done risk-based testing explicitly, because they must spend their time thinking about possible failures, which of course are just quality risks. Therefore, testers should at least be actively involved in the process. Usually I recommend that a senior tester, test lead, or test manager be in charge of the quality risk analysis process.

Risk Identification

Okay, so you've assembled the right group of stakeholder representatives for the quality risk analysis process, which is made up of the risk identification and risk assessment activities. How do you start identifying quality risks? Is it enough to simply send an email to every representative saying, "Right, now tell me what you're worried about?" That won't work in most situations, especially the first time someone participates in risk-based testing, because the question is too wide ranging and vague.

Instead, what we recommend for clients is to either organize a group brainstorming session with all of the representatives at one time or conduct a sequence of one-on-one interviews with each representative. The group brainstorming sessions will typically last an entire day and sometimes even two days for large, complex products. That significant time commitment often leads our clients to choose the one-on-one interview approach, which requires only about 90 to 120 minutes from each representative. Of course, the time commitment for the person leading the interviews could be larger because interviewing 10 different representatives could take 20 hours, but that's usually an acceptable investment. The brainstorming session does have the advantage of building consensus about the risks during the meeting itself, so if you choose to use the interviews, you need a final review of the quality risk catalog that is produced, including the assessed levels of risk for each risk item, to make sure everyone has seen and approved the final list.

As an intermediate approach, you could arrange risk workshops with small groups of stakeholder representatives. Each such workshop lasts about four hours, and two or three workshops will typically be required. This can balance the benefits of the brainstorming sessions against the problems of getting people to invest an entire day.

In some cases, especially with new products that the existing team has never built before, or when first starting risk-based testing at an organization, it helps to bring in outside experts for the identification and assessment processes. These experts can be consultants such as myself or some of my colleagues at RBCS, or they can be other similarly experienced testers who have applied risk-based testing in other organizations, possibly people who have applied this technique within the organization on previous projects.

Whether using the interviews, the brainstorming sessions, or the risk workshops, the person leading the risk identification process will typically need to guide the process. In other words, just getting the right people together is still not enough because simply asking people to tell you what they're worried about is still too open ended. Instead, we have a checklist of 24 typical quality risks categories such as functionality, performance, reliability, usability, and so on. Each category includes a general description of the types of quality risks that fit into it. We've also found that it can be useful for the person leading the process to identify one or more quality risks in each category before the interviews or brainstorming starts. This serves as a quality risk checklist that helps us avoid missing risk items in any given category. Records from project retrospectives, as well as test and production defects from previous projects, can be a good source of ideas for such examples of quality risks for each category.

Senior test analysts, test leads, or test managers often serve as the leader of this risk identification and assessment process. When using an expert to guide the process, the leader of the process can rely on this expert's guidance and advice.

In the case of the brainstorming session, the leader starts by describing each category and the sample risk they have identified. If, for a given category, no sample risk can be identified, that category can be described as a candidate for omission. I've found it useful to write the categories on a whiteboard and then let the participants put sticky notes or index cards on the whiteboard near the relevant category.

In the case of interviews, the leader should walk through the list of categories and sample risks, inviting the interviewee to identify as many quality risks as possible in each category before moving to the next category. This can also be a good way to organize the workshops or group brainstorming sessions. Whether in interviews, workshops, or brainstorming sessions, people should be encouraged to call upon their past experience as well as their understanding of the product, its uses, and its users and any other good source of ideas.

However, I would encourage you to avoid a mechanical translation of the requirements into risks. Anyone can simply walk through a requirements specification and restate each requirement in the negative. You should try to think beyond the requirements during the initial risk identification sessions. What you should do, once the risk identification interviews, workshops, or brainstorming sessions are complete, is go through the requirements and establish traceability between each requirement element and one or more risk items. If you find requirement elements that have no identified risks, those indicate gaps in the list of risks. You should add the relevant risks to the risk catalog before starting the risk assessment activity. You can do this same traceability exercise with use cases, design specifications, user stories, or any other description of system behavior or implementation.

In addition to the list of quality risk categories, at RBCS we have a typical template that we use to capture the risks and their assessments. I'll explain that template shortly. Both the template and the risk category list are available for free download from the RBCS website, in the basic[6] and advanced[7] libraries.

If you have included a good, broad cross section of stakeholders in the process, this process will typically identify a good solid set of risks. You'll miss a few quality risk items—no process is perfect—but usually the important ones will be there. In fact, if you use the interview process rather than the workshop or brainstorming session, you can see the list falling into place. Each interviewee will identify typically more than 10 and fewer than 50 quality risk items. No two interviewees will identify the same set of risks, unless you invite two stakeholders from the same stakeholder group. However, as you proceed through the interviews, each new interviewee will identify fewer and fewer previously unidentified risks. By the time you get to the last two or three interviews, you might find that only one or two new risk items are identified. I refer to this phenomenon as convergence, and I rely on convergence to tell me that the risk identification work is done. It is an advantage of the interview process over the group brainstorming process that in part makes up for the lack of consensus building in the interview process.

In addition to identifying quality risks, risk identification activities identify other by-products. These by-products include defects in reference documents such as requirements specifications, design specifications, use cases, and user stories. They also include questions, issues, and assumptions about the project or product. And they include project risks. All of these by-products should be captured as part of documenting the findings of the risk identification work. However, rather than acting on these by-products directly, you should direct them to the appropriate people. For example, business analysts should receive the list of requirements defects and project managers should receive the list of project risks. The only exception is test-related project risks, which you as the test manager should handle in the test plan. I'll talk more about managing test-related project risks and developing test plans later in this chapter.

Risk Assessment

After risk identification, you can start risk assessment. The syllabus refers to categorization of the identified risk items as part of risk assessment. My prefer-

---

6. You can find the RBCS Basic Library at http://www.rbcs-us.com/software-testing-resources/library/basic-library.
7. You can find the RBCS Advanced Library at http://www.rbcs-us.com/software-testing-resources/library/advanced-library.

ence is to integrate that work into the risk identification, categorizing risks as they are identified. In some cases, you'll find that some of these risks are miscategorized after the risk identification is complete, and you'll want to move them.

I use my list of two dozen quality risk categories as the framework for this categorization work. If your organization is following the International Organization for Standardization (ISO/IEC) 9126 standard, you might want to use that instead, during both risk identification and risk assessment. Personally, I think doing so creates more work because you have to make sure everyone understands the ISO 9126 standard before the risk identification starts.

Usually, it doesn't matter too much which category a risk is placed in, unless the categorization also implies ownership, that is, who is responsible for mitigating the risk. If a separate risk analysis is done for each test level, then usually a single manager will be responsible for all the risks identified for that level. In more mature implementations of risk-based testing, a risk analysis will cover all levels of testing. In this case, risk assessment involves identifying the test level or levels at which a risk should be mitigated, which then determines the responsible manager or managers.

Either way, once you know the manager who owns all of the risks or a subset of them, the manager can then assign groups of risks—perhaps by category—to particular testers. Those testers should design and implement the tests that will cover those risks. Those testers might be the same ones who execute the tests, but sometimes you'll want to reassign tests to achieve the optimal test execution sequence. I'll come back to the topic of risk-based test sequencing in a bit.

The most important and tricky part of risk assessment, in my opinion, is evaluating the likelihood and impact of each identified risk. For a risk, the likelihood refers to the probability that one or more defects related to the risk will exist in the system when it is delivered for testing. The impact refers to the severity of the effect that one of these defects would have on users, customers, or other stakeholders if the system were to be delivered with such a defect still in the system, whether known or unknown.

Assessing the likelihood of a risk is mostly based on technical considerations related to the product, the risk, the project, and so on. Assessing the impact of a risk is mostly based on business considerations related to the product, the risk, the project, and so on. There are a number of factors that affect likelihood and impact, which we'll now examine.

Likelihood and Impact Factors

Let's start with factors to consider when assessing the likelihood of a risk:

- Complexity of technology and teams: Complicated stuff is simply harder for business analysts, designers, and programmers to get right. Complicated teams make more mistakes than simple teams, especially when you look at how miscommunication increases with team size and complexity.
- Personnel and training issues among the business analysts, designers, and programmers. Personnel issues would include problems with attitudes or behaviors. As one example, if you have a programmer who is going through a messy and painful divorce, that person may be distracted and error prone because of it, depending on their personality type. Training issues include problems with skills. For example, if someone is working on their first agile project and has not been trained in agile methods, they are more likely to make mistakes.
- Conflict within the team. People who are unhappy, angry, or hostile toward each other usually don't communicate effectively. Miscommunication is the root cause of many defects.
- Contractual problems with suppliers. When vendors build some or all of the components of the system, failures to be explicit about what is needed and failures to hold the vendor accountable for delivering a quality product are common. This increases the likelihood of bugs in those components.
- Geographically distributed team. Having people on the project spread around, often in disparate time zones, can create communication problems, especially if native languages are different.
- Legacy versus new approaches. While new methodologies and technologies are cool and fun to work with, in many cases people will still be learning them. That feeling of learning new things is part of what makes the work fun, but it's also true that people will make more mistakes during their learning-curve phase.
- Tools and technology. When good tools and technologies are available to support the software development process, fewer bugs will be introduced, and more bugs will be caught shortly after introduction. With bad tools and technologies, or no tools at all, these opportunities for early testing are lost.
- Weak managerial or technical leadership. When leaders don't give good guidance, their people will make more mistakes. This is especially true for the more-junior team members. Remember that *weak* in this context means bad, not necessarily bad by virtue of being excessively lax. Excessively strict

managerial or technical leadership—micromanaging, creating a climate of fear, punishing more frequently than praising, punishing publicly rather than privately, and so on—will also tend to result in mistakes, generally mistakes of omission rather than commission.

Time, resource, budget, and management pressure. This is an ironic factor because when the pressure's on, that's when we need people to do their best work. Some people really do shine under conditions of pressure, and these people form the foundation of the "individual heroics" cultures that are both the short-term saviors and the long-term bane of many organizations. Unfortunately, many people tend to choke under pressure, to develop performance anxiety, especially when they start to fixate on the pressure on them to not make mistakes. Think about it: if management is constantly sending explicit and implicit messages about tight deadlines, unavailable resources, lack of funds, or the absolute criticality of not making any mistakes, does that actually help? Of course, people need to be made aware of project constraints and realities, and yes repetition is the key to recollection, but constantly harping on people will have the opposite of the desired effect, typically.

Lack of earlier quality assurance activities. This one is sort of a no-brainer, so you're unlikely to forget it. The fewer reviews of requirements specifications, design specifications, and code, the more infrequent the use of static analysis, and the more cursory the lower levels of testing, the more bugs you'll find in the higher levels of testing.

High change rates. This factor can manifest itself in many ways. Code that is frequently changed has a higher risk of regression. Requirements that change during development can result in miscommunication about what is to be built. Changes in project resources can result in early quality assurance and testing not occurring. Changes in tools and technologies can create opportunities for mistakes.

High earlier defect rates. It's important to remember that the more defects you have when you go into any testing activity, the more defects you'll have when you come out of it. If unit testing has a defect detection effectiveness of 25 percent, say, an industry average figure, then imagine the difference between starting with 100 bugs versus starting with 1,000 bugs. In the former situation, 75 bugs escape to the next level of testing, while in the latter situation, 750 bugs escape. We had an example of this with a course we paid a contractor to build for us. It was not built to our usual quality standards, and in spite of our meticulous efforts at testing it, we were still finding defects in it three years later when we decided to update the course.

- Interfacing and integration issues. The more the number and variety of different interfaces, the more the opportunity for misunderstanding how to use those interfaces. The more components or systems that must be integrated, the more the opportunity for integration mistakes.

Let's move on to factors to consider when assessing the impact of a risk:

- Frequency of use of the affected feature. If a feature is used frequently, problems with that feature will have a greater impact on the benefit that users or customers receive from the system, or at least on the perceived quality of the system. Imagine a bug that affects the home screen or the most frequently used feature of a browser-based or mobile application. Consistent exposure to the resulting failure will be a constant reminder of the poor quality of the application, and will sap the users' overall confidence.
- Criticality of the feature to accomplishing a business goal. Even an infrequently used feature can be the home of a high-impact risk if that feature is essential to the value of the application. Consider a bug in a financial system that affects a company's ability to send accurate year-end reports to its shareholders. This only needs to happen once a year, but when it happens, it has to be right.
- Damage to reputation. Sometimes the effect of bugs is more about embarrassment than anything else. For example, one client told me about a bug they had in the welcome screen of an application. This bug didn't affect the functionality of the system at all because it was a simple spelling error. Unfortunately it was the project sponsor's name that was misspelled, and it was literally the first thing she saw when the client did a demo of the application for her.
- Loss of business. Some bugs can cause immediate and measurable impact. For example, a reliability bug in a bank's ATM network would reduce the daily fees collected on out-of-network withdrawals because potential customers would simply go elsewhere.
- Potential financial, ecological, or social losses or liability. Software that controls emissions monitoring and reduction systems for factories would be an example of where this risk factor could apply.
- Civil or criminal legal sanctions. When software is custom-developed under contract, the customer can potentially sue the vendor when certain features don't work.

- Loss of license. Software that is produced under regulations, such as US Food and Drug Administration regulations, or that is used to carry out some sort of regulated activity, is exposed to this risk factor.
- Lack of reasonable workarounds. A failure that can be addressed by using the system differently to accomplish the same task is less severe than a failure that completely incapacitates some portion of the application.
- Visibility of failure leading to negative publicity. A bad Twitter post, Facebook entry, or YouTube video can ruin a company's day. In a non-software example, a few years ago United Airlines got some bad publicity when it broke a musician's guitar, which was in checked baggage, and then refused to pay for the repair. The musician wrote a song called "United Breaks Guitars" and then did a clever music video for it, which he posted on the Internet. The "cost" to the company's reputation far outweighed the cost of replacing the guitar.
- Safety. If a particular feature in an application makes objects move in the real world, or affects critical decisions that have real-world consequences, safety can be involved. For example, one of our clients makes elevators, which are controlled by software. If the elevator were to start moving without the door being completely closed, that would create a significant safety hazard for passengers.

Note that these factors can influence likelihood and impact assessments for both quality risks and project risks. In addition, these lists of factors are not exhaustive.

Quantitative or Qualitative?

Some organizations try to do quantitative risk assessment. In other words, they try to assign dollar values to impacts and percentage values to likelihoods. These numbers can then be multiplied together to give an expected cost associated with a risk, just as insurance companies do. If you have statistically valid data about past failures on sufficiently similar projects, these quantitative assessments can be accurate, at least to some degree of precision. This requires relatively large amounts of data, though. While many of our clients do accurate quantitative estimation of the number of test cases required or the number of bugs they expect to find—a topic we'll revisit when we discuss estimation later in this chapter—we've yet to see a situation where we felt the volume of defect data was sufficient for quantitative risk assessment. If quantitative risk assessment is done where the data is insufficient to support it, the result is a misleading number that can create false confidence in the extent to which you understand risk.

What does work, and quite well, is qualitative risk assessment. In other words, rather than dollar values and percentages, assign a relative rating for likelihood and impact. Over the years, I've developed a preference for using a five-point ordinal scale: very high, high, medium, low, and very low.[8] This scale reflects the stakeholders' best estimate and understanding of the relative likelihood and impact. You can then create an aggregate risk rating from these two ratings. The easiest way to do so is to translate the ratings into numbers—I use 1 to 5, with 1 being the highest risk—and then multiply those numbers together. This gives a risk priority number ranging from 1 to 25. A risk with a priority number of 1 is scary because it's a risk that is very likely to occur and the outcome will be bad if it does. A risk with a priority number of 25 is almost unworthy of consideration because it's very unlikely and trivial even if it does occur.

Unless you are doing truly quantitative risk assessment based on statistically valid data, your assessments are based on the stakeholders' perceptions, past experience, fears, and opinions. That's not a reason to disregard the ratings, but rather an acknowledgement of the source. You will need to work with the stakeholders to make sure all of them use the same mental scale and criteria to determine how to assess likelihood and impact. Otherwise, what constitutes a "very high impact" for one person will not be the same for another.

Even with clear criteria established, reasonable people can have different opinions about the level of risk, based on their past experience or the constituency they represent. When disparate opinions about likelihood or impact ratings emerge—and they always do—you'll need to work with stakeholders to try to reach a consensus on the proper rating. In some cases, consensus is not obtained, so it's often a good idea to have some deadlock-resolution mechanism. For example, if people do not agree on the impact or likelihood, you can use the average, median, or mode value.[9]

In addition to problems with reaching consensus, another problem that can arise during risk assessment is clumping or skewing of the ratings. If the likeli-

---

8. Jamie Mitchell commented during the review of this material that "Google makes a pretty good point about using a four-point system to avoid people reflexively choosing a three." I haven't had this problem, if the criteria are clear, but you do have to watch for clustering of the scores.
9. The average rating is the total of all ratings divided by the number of ratings. The median rating can be found by sorting the ratings from lowest to highest and then selecting the middle value. The mode rating is found by again sorting the ratings from lowest to highest and then selecting the value that occurs most often in the list.

hood or impact ratings are not distributed in an approximately normal (i.e., bell curve) fashion, you'll get a distribution of overall risk ratings that is not well dispersed across the various ratings. This effectively limits the value of the risk assessment because it provides less discrimination in terms of test effort allocation and priority. As a client of mine once said, "Without prioritization, there are no priorities." I show how to handle this in the subsection "Example: Risk Priority Number Distribution" later in this chapter.

Example: DO 178B Mandated Coverage

Table 2–1 shows an example of risk-based testing found in a testing standard. The United States Federal Aviation Administration provides a standard called DO-178B for avionics systems. In Europe, it's called ED-12B.

Table 2–1   *Risk-based white-box testing in DO-178B*

Criticality	Potential Failure Impact	Required Coverage
Level A: Catastrophic	Software failure can result in a catastrophic failure of the system.	Modified Condition/Decision, Decision, and Statement
Level B: Hazardous/ Severe	Software failure can result in a hazardous or severe/major failure of the system.	Decision and Statement
Level C: Major	Software failure can result in a major failure of the system.	Statement
Level D: Minor	Software failure can result in a minor failure of the system.	None
Level E: No effect	Software failure cannot have an effect on the system.	None

The standard assigns a criticality level based on the potential impact of a failure. Based on the criticality level, a certain level of white-box test coverage is required.

Criticality level A, or Catastrophic, applies when a software failure can result in a catastrophic failure of the system. For software with such criticality, the standard requires Modified Condition/Decision, Decision, and Statement coverage.

Criticality level B, or Hazardous and Severe, applies when a software failure can result in a hazardous, severe, or major failure of the system. For software with such criticality, the standard requires Decision and Statement coverage.

Criticality level C, or Major, applies when a software failure can result in a major failure of the system. For software with such criticality, the standard requires only Statement coverage.

Criticality level D, or Minor, applies when a software failure can only result in a minor failure of the system. For software with such criticality, the standard does not require any level of coverage.

Finally, criticality level E, or No effect, applies when a software failure cannot have an effect on the system. For software with such criticality, the standard does not require any level of coverage.

This makes a certain amount of sense. You should be more concerned about software that affects flight safety, such as rudder and aileron control modules, than you are about software that doesn't, such as video entertainment systems. Lately there has been a trend toward putting all of the software, both critical and noncritical, on a common network in the plane, which introduces enormous potential risks for inadvertent interference and malicious hacking.

Moreover, there is a risk of using a one-dimensional white-box measuring stick to determine how much confidence we should have in a system. Coverage metrics are a measure of confidence, it's true, but we should use multiple coverage metrics, both white-box and black-box.

By the way, if you found this material a bit confusing, note that some of the white-box coverage metrics used in this standard were discussed in the Foundation syllabus, in Chapter 4. If you don't remember these coverage metrics, you should go back and review that material in that chapter of the Foundation syllabus.

Risk Mitigation

So far, I've talked about the analysis activities of risk-based testing; that is, the activities that are logically part of the analysis step in the fundamental test process. Those activities are the identification and assessment of risks to the quality of the software product. In risk-based testing, the results of that analysis will form key inputs into the test planning process as well as the test estimation process.

The estimate will determine the resources, people, and time required to cover the risks sufficiently with tests. For each risk, the level of risk determines the extent of test coverage required. The more intensive techniques, such as pairwise testing and other combinational testing techniques, will apply to the

> **ISTQB Glossary**
>
> **master test plan:** A test plan that typically addresses multiple test levels.
>
> **test estimation:** The calculated approximation of a result related to various aspects of testing (e.g., effort spent, completion date, costs involved, number of test cases, etc.) which is usable even if input data may be incomplete, uncertain, or noisy.

higher risks. Lower risks will receive testing that requires less effort, such as equivalence partitioning, exploratory testing, or even simple sampling. In addition, in the estimated schedule, the higher-risk tests should be developed and executed first. (See the sidebar titled "Matching Techniques to the Extent of Testing" later in this chapter.)

The plan will specify how these tests should be designed, implemented, and executed. Planning may also involve taking additional measures to help mitigate quality risks. One such measure would be using reviews and static analysis more heavily, or using more formal types of reviews, for areas of high risk. Another such measure would be assigning more experienced testers to design and implement (and possibly execute) high-risk tests. Yet another such measure would be defining the confirmation test and regression test procedures in the test plan so that these change-related tests are more rigorous and extensive when they relate to high-risk areas. Finally, if testing is being planned across multiple levels, the master test plan should ensure that all high-risk areas are tested by independent testers.

As mentioned earlier, the understanding of risks, as well as the risks themselves, will change over the course of the project. We learn about new risks that were overlooked during the initial identification. We learn that an existing risk has a higher or lower likelihood or impact than we thought. We learn that a new feature has been added or an existing feature removed, resulting in the creation or deletion of risks. The test team should always be watching for these situations, and the test manager must ensure that the team is alert to any event and information that changes the risks on the project.

In addition to on-demand adjustments, the test manager should plan for periodic re-reviews of the quality risk analysis. At the very least, these should occur at every major project milestone and probably once test execution is about one-third to one-half complete. These re-reviews should specifically look at the following topics:

> **ISTQB Glossary**
>
> **test policy:** A high-level document describing the principles, approach, and major objectives of the organization regarding testing.

- What new quality risks exist and what existing quality risks have we just become aware of? Those risks should be added to the risk catalog and assessed as described earlier.
- Which likelihood and impact ratings need to be adjusted up or down? Careful (but not paralyzing) analysis of the current ratings should occur, and changes should be made where needed. If test execution is happening, checking the test results—especially in terms of the number and severity of defects found—against the risk analysis can be particularly instructive.
- How effective is our risk mitigation so far? If tests have been run or reviews performed, we should consider how well those activities have reduced risk. This could influence changes in risk ratings as discussed. In well-managed projects, significant quality risk mitigation occurs as part of early project activities, such as requirements and design reviews, code reviews and static analysis, performance modeling, automated unit testing, and continuous integration, so those activities must be taken into account.

If ratings are changed as a result of these reviews, rechecking the distribution of the ratings is important. In addition, if ratings are changed, the new test priorities and effort allocations must be implemented.

Risk Management in the Lifecycle

While we were helping them get started doing risk-based testing, some of our clients have pointed out that there is no reason for the benefits of risk awareness to be limited to higher-level testing such as system test or system integration test. They often ask, "Shouldn't this awareness and management of risk really be happening across the entire team, continuously in the project, throughout the lifecycle?" The answer is, of course, yes. You, as the test manager, can help make this happen.

What would the ideal situation look like? Part of the solution is making sure the process for risk management is clearly communicated. Since testing will always play a critical role in quality risk mitigation, the test policy document (which describes what testing is about) and the test strategy document (which describes how testing should be done) provide the objectives and process for quality risk mitigation via testing, at all levels of testing. In addition, the way test-related project risks are managed should be covered.

However, it wouldn't end there. The entire project or product team—business analysts, architects, database designers, network administrators, programmers, marketing staff, and so on—would be aware of risk and the activities that can be used to manage risk. The test team would still focus on executing high-risk tests earlier, but, as previously mentioned, high-risk areas would also be addressed through earlier levels of testing and other quality assurance activities.

I saw an excellent example of this on a project where performance was a high risk. Not only did we run system tests for performance earlier in the test execution period, but there was static performance testing through design reviews, spreadsheet models, and network simulation models before system implementation was even started. During system implementation, programmers did careful resource utilization and performance testing as part of their unit testing and integration testing. By the time we got the software, much of the serious performance risk had already been mitigated.

Not only should we mitigate risks that exist, but we can also figure out ways to eliminate risk, or at least to significantly reduce the likelihood of risks. For example, when defects are found during any testing or quality assurance activity, it's not enough to ask, "How do we fix it?" We also must ask, "How did it come to be here in the first place?" In other words, we need to do root cause analysis. This root cause analysis should not apply only to defects but also to process and project breakdowns and inefficiencies. Truly mature organizations are engaged in continuous process improvement to increase the quality of their work products and the effectiveness and efficiency of their work processes.

Mature organizations also study risk more deeply. You can see this especially if you look at organizations like the United States Marine Corps, which is of course engaged in an inherently high-risk endeavor, warfare. The Marine Corps has an entire group devoted to finding ways to continuously improve the way it goes about its work, the Marine Corps Center for Lessons Learned. Very few of our clients have groups or cross-functional panels that focus on learning from and improving processes based on risks encountered and managed (or mismanaged) on projects, but the most mature ones do. In the most mature organizations, managing risk is not a siloed activity limited to test teams and periodic project review meetings but instead would span the entire team, every project, and all programs.

So how to get to this ideal situation? Step by step. First, get a successful risk-based testing process in place. Involve the appropriate stakeholders and demonstrate the benefits to them. Create risk-management evangelists by showing these stakeholders how well this works. Then, set the stage for rolling out risk management in a wider fashion. You can start by doing quality risk analysis that spans all levels of testing, from unit testing to acceptance testing. After that is in place, look at using risk awareness to drive reviews and static analysis.

Risk Management during Test Execution

Let's turn our focus back to testing, specifically how we use information about risk during execution.

The first area to consider is sequencing of tests. As a general rule, the higher the risk, the earlier we run the test, and the lower the risk, the later we run the test. This leads to two of the main benefits of risk-based testing. First, we will have tested the most risky parts of the system early, leading to the fastest possible reduction in the overall level of quality risk. Second, since the level of risk is determined by the likelihood of defects and the impact those defects would have, risk-based test sequencing also means that we have the highest possible chance of finding the most important defects early in the testing.

To accomplish this risk-based test sequence, during test design, each test case inherits the risk priority number of the risk that it covers. Then, during test implementation, we use the risk priority number (RPN) associated with the test to determine when to run it. If the tests are run in strict risk order—that is, all the RPN one tests first, then the RPN two tests, then the RPN three tests, and so forth—then this is referred to as *depth-first* sequencing, because we are going to test deeply in the highest-risk areas before moving to lower-risk areas.

Depth-first sequencing has the advantage of producing the greatest reduction of residual quality risk as quickly as possible. However, there is a test-related project risk associated with it. To the extent that the quality risk analysis is flawed, especially in terms of missing risk items and overrated risks, the testing will be misguided, and there is no way of discovering those flaws until later in the project, when fewer options remain to resolve them.

So, some people prefer to use an approach called *breadth-first* sequencing. In breadth-first sequencing, we break the test execution period into segments. The number of segments can vary, but for this example assume we have three segments: start, middle, and end. In the start segment, we run mostly high-risk tests, but we also make sure every functional area and every risk item has at least one test executed against it. In addition, we use exploratory testing to address some areas for which no specific tests are planned, just to see if we have missed risk items in those areas. In the middle segment, we run mostly medium-risk tests, along with any remaining high-risk tests. We also again test every functional area and risk item and do some exploratory testing. In the end segment, we run whatever tests remain, along with some exploratory testing.

Throughout each segment, we monitor for findings that indicate problems in our risk analysis, as discussed earlier. In addition, at the end of the start and middle segments, we carefully evaluate our findings and make adjustments to our risk analysis as warranted. Those adjustments can lead to changes in the plan for the rest of the testing.

In a subsequent section in this chapter, we'll look at ways to report test results. Three of the types of results reporting we'll examine are histograms, pie charts, and tables that tell the project team how much of the quality risk has been mitigated through testing and how much quality risk remains. These reports can tell the project team about quality risk at a high level, across all the risks, and at the detailed level, risk by risk. It's important that you work with the different project stakeholders to make sure they receive the presentation and level of detail that fits their needs.

What I've found is that project teams really value this information and have a much deeper understanding of the test results when the reporting includes insights on the remaining level of risk. As test execution proceeds, the project team can use this insight into the remaining level of risk to monitor and control the project. This includes making a risk-informed release decision.

For example, suppose you and your test team have gotten to the end of the test execution period but, due to a higher-than-expected number of defects, you have not finished running all of your tests. In addition, some of those defects are still to be resolved. In that case, management can look at the tests that remain unrun and the defects that remain unfixed and assess which of two organizational risks they prefer. They can accept the risks—and costs—associated with extending the test execution and bug fixing period if they feel that releasing the software is unacceptable. Alternatively, they can choose to release the software, effectively transferring the costs and risks inherent in the untested and known-to-be-broken areas of the system onto users, customers, technical support, and operational staff.

Lightweight Risk-Based Testing Techniques

There are various risk-based testing techniques, ranging from very informal to very formal. For reasons I'll explain further a little later on, the very informal techniques don't fully deliver the benefits of risk-based testing.

So if the very informal techniques fail to deliver, does that mean we must use very formal techniques, which can be ponderous and expensive? Fortunately, no. Over the years, test consultants and practitioners have found a middle ground, crafting lightweight, inexpensive risk-based techniques that nonetheless deliver the benefits of risk-based testing. The Advanced Test Manager syllabus mentions three such techniques: Pragmatic Risk Analysis and Management (PRAM),[10] Practical Risk Management (PRisMA),[11] and Systematic Software Testing (SST).[12] Since I am the primary creator of PRAM, my primary focus in this book is on PRAM. However, the techniques have common features.

The techniques are not theoretical but rather were evolved by their progenitors as they worked on actual projects. It took me about five years to evolve PRAM from its initial basis, failure mode and effect analysis (FMEA), stripping off layers of formality until what remained was the lowest level of structure, documentation, and formality that could deliver the full benefits of risk-based testing. My desire to strip down the technique to the lowest possible level of formality was driven by our clients' focus on efficiency and cost savings. The lightweight nature also has the side benefit of a low learning curve. My associates and I can usually launch risk-based testing in an organization within one week.

While all risk-based testing techniques work best when cross-functional stakeholders, with business and technical perspectives, are involved, PRAM, along with PRisMa and SST, are heavily reliant on their inputs. The reason is that the more formalized techniques, such as FMEA, require the extensive study of all identified risks to determine their sources and potential effects, which allows an individual performing that study to improve their imperfect understanding of the quality risks on a project. PRAM does not require such extensive study, because the cost is too high. Instead, during risk identification and assessment, it substitutes exhaustive research by one with the collective wisdom of many.

---

10. PRAM is covered in my book *Managing the Testing Process, 3rd Edition*.
11. PRisMa is covered in Erik van Veenendaal's book *Practical Risk-Based Testing*.
12. SST is covered in *Systematic Software Testing* by Rick Craig and Stefan Jaskiel.

The involvement of the stakeholders can provide a nice side benefit of building a collective consensus about what should be tested, in what order, and how extensively, as well as what should not be tested. However, there are two prerequisites to getting this benefit. The first is that each stakeholder group has to fully engage in the process. Desultory participation by the delegated representative for a stakeholder group, or the delegation of an unqualified representative, will lead to gaps in the risk analysis and a lack of consensus about the level of risk. It's important that you, the test manager, sell each group on the benefits of risk-based testing and how those benefits will affect their team. In addition, when disagreements arise about likelihood or (more typically) impact assessments, make sure you have an agreed-upon—and agreeable—process for resolving the differences in opinion. The best possible outcome is to be able to convince the stakeholders on a common rating for each risk.

These lightweight techniques are also most effective and efficient when initiated early, either at the requirements specification phase in a sequential lifecycle or at the beginning of each iteration in agile or incremental lifecycles. This gives the testers the longest period of time to align their testing with the risks as well as giving the rest of the project team the opportunity to act on the findings of the risk analysis. For example, if risk analysis determines that a particular user story will require a huge amount of effort to test sufficiently, that might motivate the project team to reclassify that story as an epic and break it down into a series of smaller stories across multiple iterations. Such a decision would minimize risk by means other than testing.

These techniques are truly risk based in the sense that the risk catalog (also called a risk matrix or risk analysis table), containing all the risks with their associated level of risk, is the predominant test basis. Other test bases may be used to fill out the risk catalog, as mentioned earlier, but the risk catalog is the kingpin. The test conditions either are the risks themselves or are all generated from the risk items. The test estimate and test plan is based around the activities required to cover the risks to the extent necessary to mitigate them. Throughout the entire test process, the primary goal is the mitigation of those risk items.

The techniques are especially concerned with the risk-based results reporting mentioned earlier. Risk-based results reporting can be done at all levels, if the risk analysis is done for all levels rather than simply for the higher levels. However, if the risk analysis is done for only one level, such as system test or system integration test, then the results reporting can be done for that level alone.

As I mentioned earlier, we can rate likelihood and impact on a five-point scale, from very high to very low. I mentioned the translation of those ratings into numbers from 1 to 5 and then the creation of an overall risk priority number by multiplication of the two numbers. In the case of PRAM, I evolved this simple two-factor qualitative rating system from the much more complex and ponderous three-factor, 10-point quantitative rating system in FMEA. PRAM's qualitative approach might not be mathematically pure, but it is simple and easy to learn. Another example of similar simple qualitative scales is the use of planning poker on agile teams.

It is also possible to use other formulas beyond simple multiplication for calculation of the risk priority number, especially if the project team wants to weight one factor—likelihood or impact—more heavily than the other. This can be useful if risk-based testing is used across all levels of testing because we might want to focus on high-likelihood bugs during unit and integration testing and on high-impact bugs during system and system integration testing. This would have the effect of shifting the emphasis of earlier testing on the objective of defect detection, especially in the removal of defect clusters, while making later testing emphasize the objective of confidence building. This approach is consistent with the principles of testing.

Whether a weighted formula or the simple multiplication is used, my associates and I have found that this simple qualitative rating system delivers the benefits of risk-based testing as well as or maybe even better than the FMEA rating system. It is flexible. I have worked with clients around the world to get risk-based testing started and have never found a situation where PRAM would not work, regardless of the type of industry or whether the software was built for sale or for in-house use. My associates and I have found that even the most inexperienced test teams could learn how to use the technique properly. Just as critically, because the process is so similar to other intuitive problem-solving approaches people use in everyday life, even nontechnical people and business stakeholders have no trouble grasping the essence of the technique and contributing meaningfully during risk identification and assessment.

For SST, the requirements specifications are a required input to the process because the risk items are generated from the requirements. PRAM and PRisMa can work either with specifications as an input or purely based on stakeholder input. If requirements specifications are used as an input to these techniques, they effectively become blended risk-based and requirements-based test strategies. These requirements specifications can be very useful, especially if the prioritization of the requirements was done well. Properly prioritized requirements make determining impact easier, and impact is generally the more difficult of the risk assessments to perform.

However, since requirements are often flawed, you have to ensure that the technique operates to avoid these flaws. For example, the use of the standard list of quality risk categories I mentioned earlier will help the person leading the quality risk analysis to ensure the inclusion of functional and nonfunctional risk categories. The latter category is particularly easy to miss because requirements often underspecify nonfunctional behaviors.

A Risk Catalog Template

In Figure 2–5 you see a template you can use—and that my associates and I have used often—to capture the risk catalog during risks identification and risk assessment. I would put this in a spreadsheet, for reasons that will become clear in the next few pages. Let me explain each column.

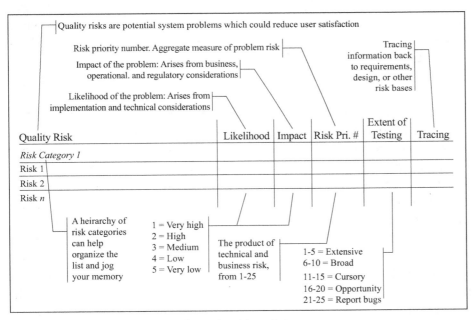

Figure 2–5   *Annotated template for quality risk analysis*

First, down the left side of Figure 2–5, you have the list of risks. They are grouped into categories, using the classic quality risk category list I mentioned earlier. Of course, prior to the first interview or the start of the brainstorming session, the catalog contains only the categories, the explanation of each category, and the example risk generated by the tester leading the quality risks analysis process.

In the second and third columns you have the likelihood and impact. These follow the five-point rating system I've described. Figure 2–5 shows the use of a descending scale, with 1 representing "very high" and 5 representing "very low." You can invert both scales to have an ascending scale if you prefer, but since most bug-tracking tools use a descending scale for severity and priority, and since severity and priority are analogous to likelihood and impact, I prefer the descending scale.

The fourth column is the risk priority number, an aggregate measure of the overall level of risk associated with each risk item. If you populate the active rows with a formula for risk priority number—whether simple multiplication or some weighted formula—this cell should self-calculate the RPN for you.

The fifth column is the extent of testing. It shows the level of effort that should be allocated to design, implement, and execute tests for the risk, based on a range of risk priority numbers. If the risk priority number for a risk item is between 1 and 5, we allocate extensive testing effort. If it's between 6 and 10, we allocate broad testing effort. If it's between 11 and 15, we allocate cursory testing effort. If it's between 16 and 20, we test opportunistically. If it's between 21 and 25, we do not test and report bugs only if we see them.

Let me explain these extent-of-testing categories further, using an example.

Suppose you are testing a word processor application. You are specifically considering a risk item in the functionality category "cannot open supported file type." Assume that this word processor, like most, can open a number of different file types. Assume also that this word processor, like most, can manage a number of different types of objects in the files it supports, including text, formatting, fonts, embedded pictures, tables, tables of contents, and so forth.

In this case, extensive testing would cover every possible combination of supported file type with the types of objects that can occur in that file. Broad testing would cover every supported file type and every supported object type, but not every object and file combination. Cursory testing would cover only the most important file and object types. Opportunity testing would cover opening files as part of another test. If you were only to report bugs, you would not test opening files, but you would report any bugs related to an inability to open a supported file type that you might see.

The final column allows you to capture traceability information between the risk items and other test basis inputs you might consider. I've discussed the importance of this process earlier.

Example: Risk Catalog

Table 2–2 shows an example of a risk catalog with two sample risk items in each risk category. The risk categories include both functional and nonfunctional types of risks. You might spend a moment reviewing this example closely.

Table 2–2   *Risk catalog example*

Quality Risk	Tech. Risk	Bus. Risk	Risk Priority	Extent of Testing
Functionality				
User login and authentication fails	2	1	2	Extensive
User can't view transactions in accounts	3	1	3	Extensive
Localization				
Spanish language translation doesn't fit fields	2	3	6	Broad
Spanish language messages wrong, insulting, etc.	4	3	12	Cursory
Usability and User Interface				
User gets "stuck" in screen flows, esp. on error	4	2	8	Broad
User finds interface too complex	4	1	4	Extensive
Reliability				
Less than 95% availability from 4:00 AM to 2:00 AM.	4	2	8	Broad
Performance				
System responses >0.5 seconds under full load	5	2	10	Broad
Supportability				
Patches and releases won't install correctly	5	4	20	Opportunity
Patches and releases require extensive downtime	5	3	15	Cursory

Matching Techniques to the Extent of Testing

In the Pragmatic Risk Analysis and Management process, the following extents of testing are defined, in decreasing order of thoroughness:

- Extensive
- Broad
- Cursory
- Opportunity
- Report bugs only
- None

Risk-based testing does not prescribe specific test design techniques to mitigate quality risks based on the level of risk because the selection of a test design technique for a given risk item is subject to many factors. These factors include the suspected defects (what Beizer called the "bug hypothesis"), the technology of the system under test, and so forth. However, risk-based testing does give guidance in terms of the level of test design, implementation, and execution effort to expend, and that *does* influence the selection of test design techniques. This sidebar provides heuristic guidelines to help test managers and engineers select appropriate test techniques based on the extent of testing indicated for a risk item by the quality risk analysis process. These guidelines apply to testing during system and system integration testing by independent test teams.

Extensive

According to the quality risk analysis process template, for risks rated to receive this extent of testing, the tester should "run a large number of tests that are both broad and deep, exercising combinations and variations of interesting conditions." Because combinational testing is specified, testers should select test design techniques that generate test values to cover combinations. These techniques are either (a) domain analysis or decision tables or (b) classification trees, pairwise testing, or orthogonal arrays. Domain analysis and decision tables are appropriate where the mode of interaction between factors is understood (e.g., rules determining output values). Classification trees, pairwise testing, and orthogonal arrays are appropriate where the mode of interaction between factors is not understood or indeed interaction should not occur (e.g., configuration compatibility). For each technique selected, the strongest coverage criteria should be applied, such as, for example, all columns in a decision table, including the application of boundary value analysis and equivalence partitioning on the conditions in the decision table. The use of these combinational techniques guarantees deep coverage.

In addition, testers should ensure that, for all relevant inputs or factors, tests cover all equivalence partitions and, if applicable, boundary values. This contributes to broad coverage.

Testers should plan to augment the test values with values selected using experience-based and defect-based techniques. This augmentation can occur during the design and implementation of tests or alternatively during test execution. This augmentation can be used to broaden test coverage, to deepen test coverage, or both.

If available, use cases should be tested, and the tester should cover all normal and exception paths.

If they are available, the tester should use state transition diagrams. Complete state/transition coverage is required, 1-switch (or higher) coverage is recommended, and in the case of a safety-related risk items, state transition table coverage is also recommended.

In some cases—for example, safety-critical risks, risks related to key features, and so on—the tester may elect to use code coverage measurements for risks assigned this extent of coverage and to apply white-box test design techniques to fill any code coverage gaps detected by such measures.

As a general rule of thumb, around 50 percent of the total test design, implementation, and execution effort should be spent addressing the risk items assigned this extent of testing.

Broad

According to the quality risk analysis process template, for risks rated to receive this extent of testing, the tester should "run a medium number of tests that exercise many different interesting conditions." Testers should create tests that cover all equivalence partitions and, if applicable, boundary values. Testers should plan to augment the test values with values selected using experience-based and defect-based techniques. This augmentation can occur during the design and implementation of tests or alternatively during test execution. This augmentation should be used to broaden test coverage.

If available, use cases should be tested, and the tester should cover all normal and exception paths.

If state transition diagrams are available, the tester should use state them. Complete state/transition coverage is required, but higher levels of coverage should be used only if doing so won't greatly expand the number of test cases.

If decision tables are available, the tester should use them but strive to have only one test per column.

Other than the possible use of decision tables, combinational testing typically should not be used unless it can be done without generating a large number of test cases.

As a general rule of thumb, between 25 and 35 percent of the total test design, implementation, and execution effort should be spent addressing the risk items assigned this extent of testing.

Cursory

According to the quality risk analysis process templates, for risks rated to receive this extent of testing, the tester should "run a small number of tests that sample the most interesting conditions." Testers should use equivalence partitioning or boundary value analysis on the appropriate areas of the system to identify particularly interesting test values, though they should not try to cover all partitions or boundary values.

Testers should plan to augment these test values with values selected using experience-based and defect-based techniques. This augmentation can occur during the design and implementation of tests or alternatively during test execution.

If available, use cases should be used. The tester should cover normal paths, though the tester need not cover all exception paths.

The tester may use decision tables but should not try to cover columns that represent unusual situations.

The tester may use state transition diagrams but need not visit unusual states or force unusual events to occur.

Other than the possible use of decision tables, combinational testing should not be used.

As a general rule of thumb, between 5 and 15 percent of the total test design, implementation, and execution effort should be spent addressing the risk items assigned this extent of testing.

Opportunity

According to the quality risk analysis process templates, for risks rated to receive this extent of testing, the tester should "leverage other tests or activities to run a test or two of an interesting condition but invest very little time and effort." Experience-based and defect-based techniques are particularly useful for opportunity testing because the tester can augment other tests with additional test values that fit into the logical flow of the tests. This can occur during the design and implementation of tests or alternatively during test execution.

In addition, testers can use equivalence partitioning or boundary value analysis on the appropriate areas of the system to identify particularly interesting test values, though they should not try to cover all partitions or boundary values.

As a general rule of thumb, less than 5 percent of the total test design, implementation, and execution effort should be spent addressing all of the risk items assigned this extent of testing. In addition, no more than 20 percent of the effort allocated to design, implement, and execute any given test case should be devoted to addressing any risk item assigned this extent of testing.

Report Bugs Only

According to the quality risk analysis process templates, for risks rated to receive this extent of testing, the tester should "not test at all, but if bugs related to this risk arise during other tests, report those bugs." Therefore no test design, implementation, or execution effort should occur, and it is a misallocation of testing effort if it does.

None

According to the quality risk analysis process templates, for risks rated to receive this extent of testing, the tester should "neither test for these risks nor report related bugs." Therefore, no test design, implementation, or execution effort should occur, and it is a misallocation of testing effort if it does.

Other Risk-Based Testing Techniques

Beyond PRAM (which I highly recommend and can vouch for), SST, and PRisMa, what other risk-based testing techniques exist?

At the informal end of the scale, we can say—and some do say—that exploratory testing is by its nature risk based, in the sense that during exploratory test execution, you analyze the application to look for areas that are likely to contain defects, especially important defects, and you continually refine your understanding of the quality risks as you proceed. This can be structured by following a list of areas to attack or a predefined set of test charters or by using the concept of tours through the application, its structure, and its behaviors.[13]

While these techniques have their place, as a primary technique for risk-based testing they are fatally flawed in three ways. First, few testers can resist the bright shiny object of defects, and thus these test sessions often become more focused on likelihood than impact. In other words, exploratory testers will often

---

13. For example, see James Whittaker's books *Exploratory Testing* and *How to Break Software*.

gravitate toward bug clusters and then perseverate on the testing of those clusters, even while important areas of the application get undertested.

Second, as I mentioned earlier, while collectively all the stakeholders can identify most of the risks and assess their likelihood and impact with reasonable accuracy, individually any one stakeholder's understanding of the quality risks is limited and their assessment often inaccurate. This includes even the smartest testers. So without the collective wisdom present in cross-functional stakeholder risk analysis, the testing is to some extent misguided, unable to achieve the full benefits of risk-based testing.

The third, and somewhat related, flaw is that, in the professional community of testers, there are many, many more junior testers than senior ones. The extent to which an individual tester's risk analysis is flawed decreases significantly based on skills and experience, and a junior tester would have little idea about where to perform exploratory testing based on risk. Even the most senior tester often has their own particular bugbears and pet peeves about software and will tend to overtest those areas. Therefore, the subjectivity and dependence on skills of these techniques further undermines the value received from them.

Now, while I believe PRAM lies at the sweet spot between informal and formal techniques, since some organizations do use these very formal techniques and do benefit from them, let me review a few of them.

The first is hazard analysis. This technique uses the results of the analysis process to identify the hazards that underlie each risk. Understanding the underlying hazards can help the project team remove the sources of risk, or at least reduce the level of risk associated with them. However, large, complex products can have so many risks, and so many hazards, that the identification of the hazards can become difficult.

Another formal technique option is cost of exposure. In this approach, the stakeholders' assessment process determines two quantitative factors for each quality risk. First, the likelihood of a failure related to the risk item is specified as a percentage. Second, the cost of the failure occurring in production is specified as a dollar, euro, or other relevant currency amount. Then, the testers estimate the cost of testing for such failures prior to release. We calculate the cost of exposure by multiplying the cost of the failure by its likelihood. (This is referred to as the expected payout in the insurance industry.) Where testing costs less than the cost of exposure, you should test for that risk. If you can do quantitative risk assessment—and that's a big "if" for the reasons I've already mentioned—and if the consequences of failure are purely financial, then this technique can work. However, if safety, personal rights, or other nonfinancial considerations apply, this analysis understates the importance of testing.

The most formal approach to risk-based testing is called failure mode and effect analysis (FMEA) and its variants.[14] FMEA is expensive to implement, in terms of training costs, documentation creation and upkeep, and time spent performing the analysis. While certainly the cost can be justified for safety-critical or mission-critical products, for most it cannot. Some attempts to implement FMEA eventually fail due to the inability of the organization to sustain the costs associated with the technique. I've also had clients ask us to help them launch PRAM—which in all cases we did successfully—after they had failed when attempting to implement FMEA within their companies.

A somewhat less formal approach is called Quality Function Deployment (QFD). This technique is part of Total Quality Management and is popular in Japan. It is primarily an organization-wide quality risk management technique with testing implications. QFD is focused on eliminating situations where an incorrect or insufficient understanding of the customers' or users' needs leads to quality risks. QFD requires a detailed study, through decomposition, of each requirement to ensure deep understanding. It draws on a concept called voice of the customer (VOC) to flesh out exactly what's needed in terms of the specific and important functions (demand items) and quality attributes (demand qualities). These demand items and demand qualities are initially expressed abstractly and then refined in terms of how they'll be implemented and how they relate to the quality characteristics. The work product from QFD is a quality table. The table has a triangular form on the top, which looks something like a roof. This has given rise to the nickname "house of quality" for the work product and even the technique. The "house of quality" is mostly an input for system design and implementation. However, it can be used as a test basis and does provide strong insights into the impact associated with certain areas of failure.

The last of the formal techniques we'll look at is Fault Tree Analysis (FTA). FTA, as the name implies, involves the study of actual failures, those observed in testing and, if applicable, in production. You also include in the analysis potential failures. Once this complete list of actual and possible quality risks is compiled, the quality risks analysis team performs root cause analysis on each risk. Each risk is associated with a tree structure. The base of the tree is the risk. The branching starts with the defects that could cause the failure. We branch out to

---

14. See *Failure Mode and Effect Analysis* by D.H. Stamatis.

the errors or defects that could cause each defect. This continues until the various possible root causes are identified. (As you can see, this part of the process is similar to hazard analysis.) The analysis should consider defects regardless of location: software, hardware, or data. Defect interaction should also be considered. As with QFD, it is mostly an input for system design and implementation. However, it can be used as a test basis and does provide strong insights into the impact associated with certain areas of failure.[15]

Example: FMEA

In Figure 2–6, you see an example of a quality risk analysis document. It is a case study of an actual project. This document—and the approach we used—followed the failure mode and effects analysis approach.

System Function or Feature	Potential Failure Mode(s)- Quality Risk(s)	Potential Effect(s) of Failure	Critical?	Severity	Potential Cause(s) of Failure	Priority	Detection Method(s)	Detection	Risk Pri No	Recommended Action	Who/ When?
Shreds Swap Files	Fails to Shred	Security Breach	Y	1	Program Error	1	Test; Debug Trace; Code Review	1	1	Test; Debug Tracing; Code Review	
Shreds Swap Files	Shreds Excessively	Data Loss	Y	1	Program Error	1	Test; Debug Trace; Code Review	1	1	Test; Debug Tracing; Code Review	
Compression Compatibility	Damages Data	Data Loss	Y	1	Program Error	1	Test	2	2	Test	
Compression Compatibility	Hangs System	Data Loss	Y	1	Program Error	1	Test	2	2	Test	
Compression Compatibility	Shreds Improperly	Data Loss	Y	1	Program Error	1	Test	2	2	Test	
Internet Files Recognition	Recognizes Incorrectly	Data Loss	Y	1	Program Error	1	Test; Debug Trace; Code Review	2	2	Test; Rules Validation	
Network Compatibility	Shreds Network	Data Loss	Y	1	Program Error	1	Test	2	2	Test Selected/ Improve Network Coverage	
Removes File Name	Damages FS	Data Loss	Y	1	Program Error	1	Test; Debug Trace; Code Review	2	2	Test; Debug Tracing; Code Review	
Removes File Name	Fails to Remove	Security Breach	Y	1	Program Error	1	Test; Debug Trace; Code Review	2	2	Test; Debug Tracing; Code Review	

Table title: Failure Mode and Effects Analysis (Quality Risks Analysis) Form--RPN Sorted / Inital FMEA--RPN Sorted

Figure 2–6   *Quality risk analysis document*

15. This material on QFD and FTA is summarized from *Guide to the Software Quality Body of Knowledge (SQuBOK)*, from the Union of Japanese Scientists and Engineers, http://www.juse.or.jp/software/pdf/squbok_eng_ver1.pdf. I thank my friend and colleague Kenji Onishi for providing good insights on how these techniques are used in practice in Japan.

As you can see, we start—at the left side of the table—with a specific function and then identify failure modes and their possible effects. Criticality is determined based on the effects, as is the severity and priority. Possible causes are listed to enable bug prevention work during requirements, design, and implementation.

Next, we look at detection methods—those methods we expect to be applied anyway for this project. The more likely the failure mode is to escape detection, the worse the detection number. We calculate a risk priority number based on the severity, priority, and detection numbers. Smaller numbers are worse. Severity, priority, and detection each range from 1 to 5. So, the risk priority number ranges from 1 to 125.

This particular figure, Figure 2–6, shows the highest level risk items only because it was sorted by risk priority number. For these risk items, we'd expect a lot of additional detection and other recommended risk control actions. You can see that we have assigned some additional actions at this point but have not yet assigned the owners.

During testing actions associated with a risk item, we'd expect that the number of test cases, the amount of test data, and the degree of test coverage would all increase as the risk increased. Notice that we can allow any test procedures that cover a risk item to inherit the level of risk from the risk item. That documents the priority of the test procedure, based on the level of risk.

Tips for Successful Risk-Based Testing

So far, we've discussed about 10 techniques for risk-based testing. Clearly, I prefer PRAM, having created it myself and finding it useful in a wide variety of situations. However, I've also used FMEA, and I can see why some situations would call for that level of formality. In a highly time-constrained situation, even the very informal techniques might make sense, especially if the overall level of risk is seen as low.

We can use less-formal techniques at lower levels of testing and more-formal techniques at higher levels. For example, on a system-of-systems project, you might see informal risk analysis for unit and component integration testing. PRAM or a similar technique could apply at the system and system integration levels. User acceptance testing might rely on very informal risk analysis by the users.

Even with PRAM, we have options for the level of documentation. For our clients using PRAM with safety-critical products, the level of documentation is higher, and traceability from each risk back to one or more requirements is necessary. Automating this process of capturing traceability from requirements to risks, and from risks to tests and test results, is essential for audits.

PRAM and other lightweight techniques can be adapted to different lifecycles. For our clients doing agile development, we've created a different process than the one used for our clients doing sequential development because each agile iteration needs a lightweight risk analysis on the user stories at the beginning of each iteration. The relevant risks effectively become part of the user story.

Whichever technique you select, the best practice is to have the inputs, processes, and outputs defined, either in a test strategy document or in the test plan. Those inputs, processes, and outputs do differ depending on the technique, and they can even differ for a single technique depending on the project, process, and product involved, as discussed previously. As a test manager, you need to ensure that these inputs, processes, and outputs are supplied, carried out, and delivered, respectively.

I've discussed the inputs fairly extensively so far. Stakeholder insights are gathered during risk analysis in the form of identified risks and assessed likelihood and impact. The quality risk analysis leader should also look at specifications, past test results, and production failures to identify additional risks and to establish traceability to requirements and design elements.

So far, I've focused mostly on the risk identification and risk assessment parts of the process. However, keep in mind that, as the test manager, you need to ensure that the proper risk control steps are subsequently carried out. Test design and test implementation must appropriately cover the quality risks. The test plan should put in place controls for the test-related project risks, and you should execute the mitigation and contingency actions for those risks as appropriate. Test execution must carry out the planned tests as well as include the reevaluation actions I've mentioned. Test results reporting and the evaluation of exit criteria must enable risk-aware decision making. Test closure, which I'll discuss in detail shortly, should ensure that risk-based testing was successfully performed.

During risk analysis, the main output will be the quality risk catalog. As you've seen, it should include a categorized collection of risk items. Each risk should have an assessed likelihood and impact or perhaps other assessed ratings, depending on the technique. Each risk must have a calculated aggregate measure of risk and an appropriate allocation of test effort. In most cases, each requirement should trace to one or more risks, and if an objective is to force the removal of gaps in the requirements, the project team can require that every risk be traceable back to one or more requirements. The outputs will also include the by-products discussed earlier, such as the defects found during input document analysis, questions, issues or implementation assumptions about the product or project, and project risks. Those by-products should be directed to the appropriate people on the project promptly after they are identified.

As I've discussed throughout, and would like to stress one last time, the most important thing you can do to improve the odds of successful risk-based testing is to involve the right team of business and technical stakeholders in the risk identification and assessment steps of the process. I've been doing risk-based testing for two decades now. At first I focused on getting the process right, but I soon learned that getting the people right was the key. This is especially true of a lightweight technique like PRAM: the process is robust and resilient, but it will not give good results if the right people are missing.

When you're trying to get stakeholder groups to commit to sending a qualified representative, remember to sell them on the benefits, not the process. In other words, avoid sending them meeting invitations that drone on about how risk-based testing works. Instead, pick up the phone and relate a benefit of risk-based testing to something the stakeholder cares about. For example, development managers really hate it when testers find critical bugs right at the end of a project, so you can sell risk-based testing to them via the benefit of earlier detection of important defects.

This selling should not be only at the front end, when you're trying to get stakeholders to participate. If you want them to continue to participate, and to support the process in general, make sure to follow up with them afterward. Demonstrate the value achieved. Make sure they feel that they received the benefit they were promised. Make sure they feel it was time well spent and that they did not exceed the amount of time they could afford to spend. Successful engagement of the stakeholders means that not only do they know *how* to participate, but also they *want* to participate and are *able* to participate. Without these three things—knowledge, desire, and ability—for all relevant stakeholders, long-term implementation of risk-based testing cannot succeed.

A strength of this broad cross section of stakeholders is that they have different perceptions and priorities and concerns, each complementing and effectively completing all the others. However, this strength can also lead to divergent opinions and even arguments. Stakeholders can argue about what is or isn't a risk and what the right ratings for a risk should be. What I've learned is to not worry about consensus on the risk items but do worry about the ratings. If someone—anyone—of the stakeholders considers something to be a quality risk, and it is indeed a quality risk as opposed to some other kind of risk, then include it in the risk catalog. However, if people disagree about ratings, as I mentioned before, work hard to try to resolve the disagreement, following a process that is fair but that also does not pander. An example of a pandering process is one where the highest-risk rating is always accepted as the right rating.

Pandering will lead to risk inflation, which is part of the other thing you need to worry about, rating distribution. You want to see a nice normal or bell-curve type of distribution. If you have all the risks clumped together, the technique loses its power to help you sequence tests and allocate effort differently based on different levels of risk. Another thing that can create clumping or skewing problems with the ratings distribution is an inadequate, or inadequately understood, scale for likelihood and impact. Don't just define the five points on the scale, also define product-appropriate criteria that help people make objective decisions on the ratings. Otherwise, people will do the rating based on their own understanding of the scale, which will differ from one stakeholder to the next, and this makes consistency in the ratings very unlikely.

Example: Risk Priority Number Distribution

Let me illustrate this concept of ratings distribution problems with an example. In Figure 2–7, you see a histogram that shows the distribution of risk priority numbers after the likelihood and impact assessments were completed. On this project, both likelihood and impact were rated on a five-point scale, so risk priority numbers ranged from 1 to 25, with 1 being the most risky and 25 the least risky.

As I mentioned earlier, one potential problem with quality risk analysis is a clumping of risk ratings. This can occur when teams consistently skew the impact of risk items by basing their ratings on worst-case outcomes. It also can occur when teams use a scale with poorly defined distinctions.

To check for clumping, use a histogram to analyze the risk ratings. This use of a histogram to check the ratings is one reason capturing quality risk analysis information in a spreadsheet is such a good idea.

Figure 2–7 shows the histogram of RPNs. Ideally, this would look more like the normal distribution shown superimposed on the histogram.

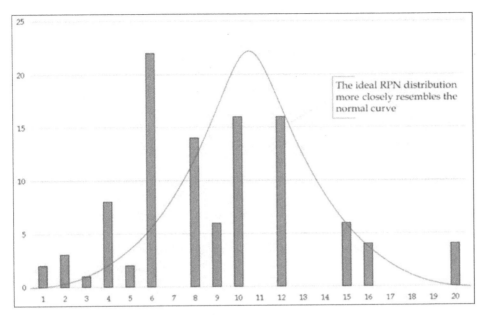

Figure 2–7   *Risk priority number distribution*

Note that some of the dead zones exist because there are no two integers between 1 and 5 that when multiplied together yield 7, 11, 13, 14, 17, 18, 19, 21, 22, 23, or 24. We didn't have a single risk item with a risk priority number of 25 because we had no very unlikely risks that we would not fix. (Notice that the averaging of ratings mentioned earlier as a means to resolve disagreements over the ratings would tend to remove some of the dead zones.)

We did, however, see a strong skewing toward the left side of the histogram, with many risk items rated with a value of 6.

To check for the underlying cause, we looked at the number of risk items with each possible likelihood and impact rating, as shown in Table 2–3.

Table 2–3   *Likelihood and impact rating counts*

Likelihood	Count
1	5
2	9
3	25
4	39
5	26

Impact	Count
1	10
2	52
3	32
4	8
5	2

On the left half of Table 2–3, the likelihood ratings at first look skewed. But the product we were working with was a mature, well-established product with a maintainable, solid code base and a rock-solid development team. For a newer product, such a distribution would likely be wishful thinking.

The right half of Table 2–3, on the other hand, may be more problematic. More than half of the risk items received an impact ratings of 2, which means "schedule for attention and resolution as quickly as possible."

To address this clumping, we adjusted the distinction between an impact rating of 2 and an impact rating of 3.

For those risk items that could trigger product bugs that were must-fix and had no workaround, we adjusted the rating to 2. This included issues that led to loss of important functionality with no workaround, which needed to be scheduled for attention and resolution as quickly as possible.

For those risk items that could trigger product bugs that were must-fix but had a workaround, we adjusted the rating to 3. This included issues that led to loss of important functionality but for which there was a workaround. These would be scheduled for attention once the impact 2 and 2 issues were resolved.

The other ratings, being acceptable in their distributions, were not adjusted.

These adjustments achieved a much better distribution of impact, as you can see from the histogram in Figure 2–8.

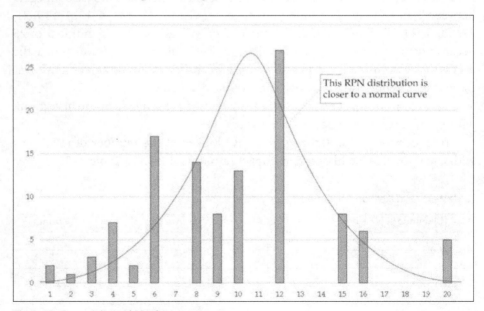

Figure 2–8   *Adjusted RPN histogram*

Measuring the Benefits of Risk-Based Testing

Earlier in this discussion about risk-based testing, I mentioned four main benefits. Along the way, I've mentioned other side benefits that accrue too. However, the main benefits—the ones you want to commit to achieving—should be measured during test closure. This allows you to improve the process as well as to give stakeholders confidence that you are delivering the benefits.

The first main benefit of risk-based testing is finding defects, especially the dangerous ones. To demonstrate this value, calculate the defect detection effectiveness for all defects. Then, calculate the defect detection effectiveness for important defects only. For example, suppose your testers find 90 defects during testing and, in the first 90 days after release, users find 10 defects. Your defect detection effectiveness is therefore 90 percent. Suppose that, of the 90 defects your testers found, 19 are important, while only 1 production defect was important. In that case, your defect detection effectiveness for important defects is 95 percent. Note that you can use any criteria you want to define defects as important, provided that all the stakeholders agree with the criteria used.

The second main benefit of risk-based testing is the early detection of the most important defects. To demonstrate this value, calculate the percentage of important defects that were found in the first quarter or third of the test execution period. You'd like that to be a large percentage, certainly at least half and ideally closer to two-thirds or even three-quarters.

The third main benefit of risk-based testing is the ability to report test results based on the residual level of risk. I'll discuss the exact means for doing this later in the book. In terms of measuring how well you're doing here, the best metric I've found is to ask the project stakeholders, especially managers, if they feel they understood the level of quality risk, based on your reports, and whether that understanding allowed them to better manage the project.

Finally, the fourth main benefit of risk-based testing—which isn't always needed—is the ability to triage or drop tests based on an understanding of risk. Here, the metric to look at is whether any tests were run that had a lower risk level than any tests that were skipped. Now, this metric gets a bit unreliable when you use breadth-first test sequencing, so you'll want to set a threshold percentage for lower-risk tests.

In situations where projects have badly defined or completely undefined requirements, proper participation of a cross-functional team of stakeholders in risk-based testing provides an essential benefit to you as the test manager. The involvement of the stakeholders in this process is going to provide you with a reliable and credible test basis, something you wouldn't have without their help. Thus, your testing will be less contentious and it will achieve a higher level of defect detection effectiveness. While improved defect detection effectiveness is generally true for test teams that adopt risk-based testing, it's especially notable in those organizations that have systemically bad requirements specifications. This is harder to measure, but it's just as important to testers and test managers as any of the others.

When you first start doing risk-based testing, establish your metrics for success as discussed here. After the first pilot of risk-based testing, measure how you did. Set those measures as a baseline for future projects. However, on each project, consider implementing improvements that will lead to somewhat better performance. Also, consider ways to make risk-based testing more efficient, perhaps by tightening the process, improving the templates, or getting better tool support. Of course, this technique applies to the entire test process, not just the risk-based part of it.

Other Techniques for Test Selection, Prioritization, and Effort Allocation

So far, I've talked about using a risk-based testing strategy to select tests, prioritize those tests, and allocate effort for those tests. However, these are not the only test strategies in use to solve these problems. While later in this chapter I'll talk more extensively about test strategies, let's spend a moment on a few other strategies and how they solve this selection problem.

The most widely known approach for selecting tests is another analytical strategy, requirements-based testing. In requirements-based testing, testers go through the requirements, ideally as part of the larger requirements review process. The testers might use a checklist for ambiguity and other typical requirements problems.[16] Testers can also use specification-based test design techniques such as those discussed in the Advanced Test Analyst syllabus.

One of our associates, Gary Mogyorodi, finds cause-effect graphing particularly useful. This is a technique that identifies important combinations of test conditions for testing. According to Gary, it produces a manageable number of tests that will ensure that all of the functionality of the system will be tested. He says he has found it very useful in identifying defects in requirements. However, my own experience with the technique is that it has a pretty steep learning curve, and that most people prefer the tabular equivalent, the decision table.

---

16. A good discussion is found in *Software Requirements 2* by Karl Wiegers.

As a by-product of preparing for the review and perhaps through the use of these test design techniques, the tester documents a set of test conditions, as discussed in Chapter 1. If the requirements are relatively good, you should get a good set of test conditions. However, gaps are common in requirements specifications, especially in terms of nonfunctional behaviors. These gaps become gaps in your test conditions. Untestable or ambiguous requirements cannot be translated into test conditions either. You should flag ambiguous, untestable, and missing requirements as defects and try to get them resolved. This means that you need a way of tracking the defects you and other reviewers found because you'll have to revise your list of test conditions once the requirements are updated. If you can't get these problems resolved, you're best off switching to another test strategy rather than endlessly harping on people about the general lousiness of the requirements specifications.

If the requirements were prioritized, then the test conditions can inherit the priority of the requirement from which they derive. This test condition priority can be used the same way the risk priority number is used in risk-based testing, to determine the priority and effort for the tests. However, one very common problem with requirements is an unrealistic distribution of priorities for requirements, with the highest priorities heavily represented and very few of the lowest priorities. If these priorities are used for testing, you'll end up in the same situation I discussed when I talked about the bad distribution of RPNs. Another very common problem with requirements is, instead of a bad distribution of priorities, a total absence of priorities! Either way, you might have to resort to augmenting the requirements analysis with quality risk analysis to address the selection problem.[17]

Another strategy for testing, model-based testing, would involve testers creating operational or usage profiles for the system. These operational profiles include use cases, defined types of users, typical inputs and outputs, and often mathematical models for how these elements interact. For example, the percentage of users that will be logged into the system will vary based on time of day, day of the week, and week of the year. The objective is to have a realistic model for how the system will be used and then to use that model for testing various characteristics. The model must be built with the test type in mind; a model of functional usage will be incomplete if you try to use it for performance testing.

---

17. See, for example, *Systematic Software Testing* by Rick Craig and Stefan Jaskiel.

Ideally, the model is built during test analysis, with the test cases then created from the model during test design and implementation. The model is imperfect, as all models are, but then again so is risk analysis. The goal is to have a model that is accurate enough, in terms of its predictions of actual usage, to support the type of testing it's designed for.[18] We test what the model tells us will happen in the real world. If the model is based on production data, it can be quite accurate. For example, large e-commerce organizations such as Amazon.com have detailed web logs that allow them to build accurate models for performance, reliability, and functional testing.

Another test strategy that deals with the test selection problem is the methodical strategy. In a methodical strategy, a checklist of high-level test conditions is provided for the testers. Ideally, the test conditions are prioritized so that the testers know how to sequence the resulting tests and the amount of effort to associate with testing each test condition. The same checklist is used from one project to the next, which is fine if that the checklist is good and the product doesn't change much. If the checklist isn't very good—for example, it has gaps, it's too ambiguous about what should be tested, it has wrong or missing priorities, and so on—or if the product is rapidly changing, this strategy will tend to fail.

Finally, there are the reactive approaches. I discussed the management challenges associated with reactive test strategies earlier in this chapter. Remember that, in a reactive approach, much of the analysis, design, and implementation work occurs during test execution. This is because the essence of a reactive approach is to react to the system that you receive. This includes deciding what to test, in what order, and how much and deciding what not to test at all. Because it is so different from the other strategies, and because skilled and experienced testers can get so much value from it, I always recommend using it as a complement to the other test strategies. Typically, I recommend that 10 to 20 percent of the test effort be dedicated to exploratory testing. However, as a primary test technique, it tends to be too bug-focused and gappy, as I've mentioned.

Example: Blending Risk-Based and Reactive Testing Strategies

Let's look a little more closely at this idea of complementing another strategy with reactive testing, using an example. In one project, we mixed our risk-based analytical test strategy with reactive testing. The reactive strategy involved the

---

18. This topic is covered in John Musa's *Software Reliability Engineering, 2nd Edition.*

use of chartered, exploratory test techniques during test execution. The analytical strategy involved the prior design and implementation of test scripts based on a risk analysis performed in parallel with test planning and project planning. During test execution, the test manager and the three test engineers, who together had over 20 years total experience, did the exploratory testing. Test technicians ran the scripted tests. Some of the test technicians had no testing experience and others had just a little.

During test execution, the technicians each spent about six hours per day running test scripts. The rest of the time, three to four hours per day, was spent reading email, attending meetings, updating bug reports, doing confirmation testing, and the like.

The engineers and manager, being heavily engaged in other tasks, could spend only one to two hours per day doing exploratory testing. Even so, due to their heavy experience, the experienced testers were the most efficient bug finders.

However, if you examine test coverage, you see a different situation. The technicians ran roughly 850 test scripts over the three months of system test. That covered a lot of ground, well-documented ground yielding well-documented results that we could show to management. The exploratory testing produced very little clear documentation. We weren't using the session reports that I showed earlier, in part because we were relying on the technicians to gather the coverage evidence with the scripts.

Now, not only did scripted testing cover more ground, it also involved more hours of testing and megabytes of test data. We didn't measure this, but I estimate that the manual scripted tests resulted in somewhere between 5 and 10 thousand inputs of various kinds—strings, dates, radio buttons, and so on—while the exploratory testing was probably at most a fifth of that volume. Similarly, scripted tests involved more distinct results being explicitly checked. On a per-hour basis, the exploratory testing might have been equally effective, but it would have been less effective if we'd had to produce the session reports because that would have slowed us down.

So, which was better? Ah, it wasn't that kind of experiment. It wasn't an experiment at all; it was a proven way of mixing two strategies, each with different strengths.

The exploratory testing was effective at finding bugs on an hour-per-hour basis, and we found a number of bugs that wouldn't have been found by the scripts. The reusable test scripts gave us good regression risk mitigation, good overall risk mitigation, and good confidence building—in sum, a successful blended approach.

In fact, the approach was more blended than it first appears. In Table 2–4, I'm simplifying by creating a sharp division between scripted and exploratory testing. The reality is that the difference is entirely one of degree, not of kind. The more verbose your test charter, the more scripted your testing. The less detailed your test script, the more exploratory your testing.

Table 2–4   *Comparing risk-based scripted tests with exploratory tests*

Staff	Seven technicians	Three engineers + One manager
Experience	<10 years total	> 20 years total
Test type	Precise scripts	Chartered exploratory
Test hrs/day	42	6
Bugs found	928 (78%)	261 (22%)
Bug effectiveness	22	44
Scripts run	850	0
Inputs submitted	~5,000–10,000	~1,000
Results verified	~4,000-8,000	~1,000

On this project, as on many projects, the test technicians were given latitude to vary their execution of the test scripts, as I've mentioned before. We told them, "A test script is a road map to interesting places; when you get somewhere interesting, stop and look around." We included some time in our planned test time—which we could easily have called a "test session"—for them to explore the system. In addition, as the test technicians became more experienced, we had them start writing test scripts themselves and doing some of the exploratory testing.

It's been good marketing for some of the advocates of exploratory testing to insist that exploratory testing is nothing like scripted testing. That's a good marketing position because you have to differentiate your services. However, the reality is not so black and white. I have seen advocates of exploratory testing produce test charters that were much more detailed than many test cases that my associates and I have written for scripted testing. The reality is that the level of detail in the test cases, as well as the point in time at which they are created, is a complicated question that you'll have to struggle with on your projects as a test manager.[19]

Select, Allocate, and Prioritize: In the Process

So, to return to the broader point, the test manager must pick the appropriate strategy—ideally a mix of strategies—and that strategy will tell the testers, the test manager, and other project stakeholders how we intend to select test conditions, allocate the effort to test those conditions, and prioritize the resulting tests. The test manager must then implement that strategy within the context of their test process and the larger project. For example, in sequential lifecycles, the selection, allocation, and prioritization should occur in parallel with the requirements specification process, while in an agile project the selection, allocation, and prioritization should occur at the beginning of each sprint. Your test plan should specifically address how you will implement the strategy on your project, particularly considering how your team should handle an evolving understanding of how best to select, allocate, and prioritize.

Now, remember that the selection, allocation, and prioritization are basically the analysis part of the fundamental test process. You need to avoid a common disconnect that occurs, which is where analysis works just fine but the work product of analysis has no influence on the design, implementation, and execution of tests. For example, risk analysis occurs, but the testers proceed to design and implement whatever the heck they want to test. This happens more often than you might think, so be sure to monitor the proper implementation of the strategy.

During test execution, the testers should use whatever prioritization scheme you've picked. If you're doing risk-based testing, that means either breadth-first or depth-first sequencing. Remember that your understanding of risks, and the risks themselves, continues to evolve during the project, so be prepared to revise your selection, allocation, and prioritization. This can be true for models, checklists, and requirements too.

As test execution proceeds, evaluate and report the test results and the status of the exit criteria. Depending on the selection technique, you'll need to be able to report risk status, requirements status, usage profiles status, checklist status, and so on. For example, has each requirement been tested? If so, did all the tests for each requirement pass? If the answer is no to either question, what's the

---

19. You can find the discussion on level of detail in my book *Managing the Testing Process, 3rd Edition* and also in my article "I Take It (Almost) All Back," www.rbcs-us.com/documents/I-Take-It-All-Back.pdf.

plan for finishing? If you're going to run out of time before you finish, what is the best possible outcome, in terms of which tests should be dropped and which kept? For risk-based testing, the same set of questions can be asked for each risk. Your test results reports should be able to answer those questions.[20]

Once test execution is complete, test closure can and should start. Part of test closure should be looking at metrics for the success of the chosen selection technique. I discussed the way to do this in risk-based testing earlier, and similar approaches can be applied to each of the other selection techniques. The important thing is that the metrics be based on the test stakeholders' objectives. As discussed in section 2.2, effective, efficient, and satisfying testing is determined by the extent to which stakeholder needs and expectations are met.

Functional Quality Risks Analysis Exercise

Read the HELLOCARMS system requirements document, which is a document for a hypothetical project that nonetheless is derived from a real project that RBCS helped to test.

Perform quality risks analysis for this project. To help manage the time required for this exercise, identify and assess risks for *functional* quality characteristics only. Use the template shown in Table 2–5.

Table 2–5   *Functional quality risk analysis template showing quality risk categories to address*

	Quality Risk	Likeli-hood	Im-pact	Risk Pri. #	Extent of Testing	Tracing
1.1.000	**Functionality: Suitability**					
1.1.001	*[Functional risks related to suitability go in this section.]*					
1.2.000	*Functionality: Accuracy*					
1.2.001	*[Functional risks related to accuracy go in this section.]*					
1.3.000	*Functionality: Interoperability*					
1.3.001	*[Functional risks related to interoperability go in this section.]*					
1.4.000	*Functionality: Security*					
1.4.001	*[Functional risks related to security go in this section.]*					
1.5.000	*Functionality: Compliance*					
1.5.001	*[Functional risks related to functional compliance go in this section.]*					

---

20. For a discussion of this topic, see my book *Critical Testing Processes*.

Functional Quality Risks Analysis Debrief

You can see my solution to the exercise in Table 2–6. Immediately after that table are two lists of by-products. One is the list of project risks discovered during the analysis. The other is the list of requirements document defects discovered during the analysis.

Notice that I didn't list any compliance risks in the last section of risks in Table 2–6, but of course there would be some. A regulatory expert would be the right person to consult for these risk items.

Table 2–6   *Functional quality risk analysis for HELLOCARMS*

	Quality Risk	Likeli-hood	Im-pact	Risk Pri. #	Extent of Testing	Tracing
1.1.000	*Functionality: Suitability*					
1.1.001	Reject all applications for home equity loans.	5	1	5	Extensive	010-010-010
1.1.002	Reject all applications for home equity lines of credit.	5	1	5	Extensive	010-010-010
1.1.003	Reject all applications for reverse mortgages.	5	1	5	Extensive	010-010-010
1.1.004	Fail to properly process some home equity applications.	3	1	3	Extensive	010-010-190
1.1.005	Fail to properly process some home equity line of credit applications.	3	2	6	Broad	010-010-200
1.1.006	Fail to properly process some home equity reverse mortgage applications.	3	3	9	Broad	010-010-210
1.1.007	Fail to properly process some combined products (e.g., home equity and credit cards).	3	4	12	Cursory	010-010-220
1.1.008	Fail to properly process some original mortgage applications.	3	5	15	Cursory	010-010-230
1.1.009	Fail to properly process some preapproved applications.	3	4	12	Cursory	010-010-240
1.1.010	Scripts not available for all fields and screens.	4	2	8	Broad	010-010-020
1.1.011	Customer source data not collected.	3	2	6	Broad	010-010-030
1.1.012	Customer source data categories not well defined.	2	2	4	Extensive	010-010-030
1.1.013	Accepts invalid data at input fields.	1	1	1	Extensive	010-010-040
1.1.014	Existing trade lines not displayed and/or processed properly.	3	1	3	Extensive	010-010-050 010-010-100
1.1.015	Trade line payoff details not passed to LoDoPS.	2	1	2	Extensive	010-010-050 010-010-100
1.1.016	Loan to be paid off included in debt-to-income calculations.	4	3	12	Cursory	010-010-110
1.1.017	Cannot resume incomplete/interrupted applications.	3	2	6	Broad	010-010-060
1.1.018	Applicant not asked about existing relationship.	5	2	10	Broad	010-010-070
1.1.019	Applicant existing relationship not passed to GLADS.	3	2	6	Broad	010-010-070
1.1.020	Loan status information lost after initiation.	3	2	6	Broad	010-010-080

Table continues

	Quality Risk	Likeli-hood	Im-pact	Risk Pri. #	Extent of Testing	Tracing
1.1.021	Cannot abort or abandon an application cleanly (i.e., must close browser).	4	3	12	Cursory	010-010-090
1.1.022	Cannot retrieve existing application by customer ID.	4	4	16	Opportunity	010-010-120
1.1.023	Loans over $500,000 not transferred for approval.	4	1	4	Extensive	010-010-130
1.1.024	Loans over $500,000 automatically denied.	3	1	3	Extensive	010-010-130
1.1.025	Property valuation over $1,000,000 not transferred for approval.	4	2	8	Broad	010-010-140
1.1.026	Property valuation over $1,000,000 automatically denied.	3	2	6	Extensive	010-010-140
1.1.027	Inbound telemarketing operations fail in supported region.	1	2	2	Extensive	010-010-150
1.1.028	Outbound telemarketing operations fail in supported region.	1	2	2	Extensive	010-010-150
1.1.029	Branding for brokers and other business partners not supported.	4	2	8	Broad	010-010-160
1.1.030	Untrained users (e.g., end customers) cannot enter applications via Internet.	4	3	12	Cursory	010-010-170
1.1.031	Product operations for retail bank branches not supported.	4	4	16	Opportunity	010-010-180
1.1.032	Flexible pricing schemes not supported.	4	5	20	Opportunity	010-010-250
1.2.000	*Functionality: Accuracy*					
1.2.001	Customer presented with products for which they are ineligible.	3	1	3	Extensive	010-020-010
1.2.002	Customer not presented with products for which they are eligible.	4	1	4	Extensive	010-020-010
1.2.003	Application decisioning inconsistent with Globobank credit policies.	3	1	3	Extensive	010-020-010
1.2.004	Risk-based pricing miscalculated based on credit score, loan-to-value, and debt-to-income.	4	1	4	Extensive	010-020-020
1.2.005	New loan payment not included in credit scoring.	3	2	6	Broad	010-020-030
1.2.006	Pricing add-ons not calculated correctly.	3	3	9	Broad	010-020-040
1.2.007	Government retirement income not handled properly.	3	1	3	Extensive	010-020-050
1.2.008	Duration of additional income not captured.	4	3	12	Cursory	010-020-060
1.3.000	*Functionality: Interoperability*					
1.3.001	Can't pull information from GloboRainBQW into HELLOCARMS.	2	2	4	Extensive	010-030-010
1.3.002	HELLOCARMS and Scoring Mainframe reject joint apps.	3	1	3	Extensive	010-030-020
1.3.003	HELLOCARMS and Scoring Mainframe cannot handle/resolve duplication of information on joint apps.	1	2	2	Extensive	010-030-030
1.3.004	HELLOCARMS trade line communication to LoDoPS fails.	3	1	3	Extensive	010-030-040 010-030-070
1.3.005	Loan status information from LoDoPS to HELLOCARMS lost or corrupted.	5	2	10	Broad	010-030-050 010-030-140

Table continues

	Quality Risk	Likeli-hood	Im-pact	Risk Pri. #	Extent of Testing	Tracing
1.3.006	HELLOCARMS can't continue if the Scoring MF indicates an undischarged bankruptcy or foreclosure.	4	3	12	Cursory	010-030-060
1.3.007	HELLOCARMS communication of government retirement income to LoDoPS fails.	5	1	5	Extensive	010-030-080
1.3.008	HELLOCARMS application information not passed to Scoring MF properly.	3	1	3	Extensive	010-030-090
1.3.009	HELLOCARMS does not receive information from Scoring MF properly.	3	1	3	Extensive	010-030-100
1.3.010	Decisioning requests not queued for Scoring MF as needed.	4	2	8	Broad	010-030-110
1.3.011	Tentatively approved, customer-accepted loans not passed to LoDoPS.	5	2	10	Broad	010-030-120
1.3.012	Declined applications not passed to LoDoPS.	5	2	10	Broad	010-030-130
1.3.013	Changes made in loan information in LoDoPS not propagated back to HELLOCARMS.	5	2	10	Broad	010-030-140
1.3.014	Computer-telephony integration not supported.	3	5	15	Cursory	010-030-150
1.3.015	Applicant existing relationship not passed to GLADS.	4	3	12	Broad	010-010-070
1.4.000	*Functionality: Security*					
1.4.001	Agreed-upon security requirements not supported.	1	2	2	Extensive	010-040-010
1.4.002	"Created By" and "Last Changed By" audit trail information lost.	3	1	3	Extensive	010-040-020
1.4.003	Outsourced telemarketers see actual credit scores and other privileged information.	3	2	6	Broad	010-040-030
1.4.004	Internet applications insecure against intentional attacks.	1	2	2	Extensive	010-040-040
1.4.005	Internet applications insecure against unintentional attacks.	3	2	6	Broad	010-040-040
1.4.006	Anonymous browsing on Internet not permitted.	2	4	8	Broad	010-040-050
1.4.007	Fraud detection too lenient.	3	1	3	Extensive	010-040-060
1.4.008	Fraud detection too strict.	3	1	3	Extensive	010-040-060
1.5.000	*Functionality: Compliance*					
1.5.001	*[Functional risks related to functional compliance go in this section.]*					

In the course of preparing the quality risk analysis document, I observed the following project risk inherent in the requirements.

> Given the lack of clarity around security requirements (see 010-040-010), there's a strong chance that the necessary infrastructure won't be in place as needed to support this project's schedule.

How many project risks did you notice?

In the course of preparing the quality risk analysis document, I observed the following defects in the requirements.

- For 010-010-150, what are the supported states, provinces, and countries?
- For 010-010-150, the phrase "all support States" should be "all supported States."
- For 010-020-020, the phrase "dept-to-income" should be "debt-to-income".
- For some requirements, the ID number is duplicated; e.g., 010-030-140.
- Not all requirements are prioritized; e.g., 010-030-150.
- For 010-040-010, what are the agreed-upon security approaches discussed here?
- There doesn't appear to be any direct mention of regulatory compliance requirements, though certainly many would apply for a bank.

How many requirements problems did you notice?

2.4   Test Documentation and Other Work Products

Learning objectives

(K4) Analyze given samples of test policies and test strategies, and create master test plans, level test plans, and other test work products that are complete and consistent with these documents.

(K4) For a given project, analyze project risks and select appropriate risk management options (i.e., mitigation, contingency, transference, and/or acceptance).

(K2) Describe, giving examples, how test strategies affect test activities.

(K3) Define documentation norms and templates for test work products that will fit organization, lifecycle, and project needs, adapting available templates from standards bodies where applicable.

You can—and should—use techniques such as those discussed earlier for quality risks in order to identify as many test-related project risks as possible. When you identify non-test project risks, you should escalate those to the project manager. A specific list of all possible test-related project risks would be huge, but includes issues like these:

- Test environment and tool readiness
- Test staff availability and qualification
- Low quality of test deliverables
- Too much change in scope or product definition
- Sloppy, ad hoc testing effort

Test-related project risks can often be managed by preemptive actions, which should be addressed in the test plan. We'll discuss test plans shortly.

Options to Manage Risks

How can you address project risks, or any risk for that matter? You have four main options for risk control:

- Mitigation, where you take preventive measures to reduce the likelihood and/or the impact of a risk. Notice that testing prior to a release mitigates quality risk because it reduces the likelihood of undiscovered serious defects. For a test-related project risk such as a skills deficit, using training and cross-training to build better skills would mitigate the risk.
- Contingency, where you have a plan or perhaps multiple plans to reduce the impact if the risk becomes an actuality. Notice that having a technical support team is a form of contingency for quality risk because you can act on defects found in production. For a test-related project risk such as the lack of adequate test environments, you could have a contingency plan to use cloud resources for testing. In that case, you'd need to set a trigger—a date on which you'd decide to start configuring the cloud environment—and an owner responsible for carrying out this contingency plan.
- Transference, where you get another party to accept the consequences of a risk. For quality risks, shipping with known defects, or untested areas, is a form of transference. For test-related project risks, I have found that transference usually doesn't work. Saying that a delay in the start of test execution will result in a delay in the end of it is all well and good, but if you've been in this business any length of time, you know it usually doesn't happen.
- Finally, you can ignore or accept the risk and its consequences. This is often the best option for risks with low likelihood and low impact because the cost of dealing with the risk could easily exceed the damage associated with consequences.

For any given risk item, selecting one or more of these options creates its own set of benefits and opportunities as well as costs and, potentially, additional risks associated with each option. Done wrong, risk control can make things worse, not better.

Test-Specific Project Risk Management

What are some common ways to manage test-related project risks?

You can accelerate the moment of test involvement and ensure early preparation of testware. This can help ensure that your team is ready to start test execution when the product is ready. In addition, as was mentioned in the Foundation syllabus and elsewhere in this book, early involvement of the test team allows test analysis, design, and implementation activities to serve as a form of static testing for the project, which can prevent bugs from showing up later during dynamic testing, such as during system test. Detecting an unexpectedly large number of bugs during high-level testing like system test, system integration test, and acceptance test creates a significant risk of project delay, so this bug-preventing activity is a key project risk-reducing benefit of testing.

You can make sure that your team checks out the test environment before test execution starts. This can be paired with another risk-mitigation activity, that of testing early versions of the product before formal test execution begins. If you do this in the test environment, your testers can test the testware, the test environment, the test release and test object installation process, and many other test execution processes in advance before the first day of formal test execution.

You can also define tougher entry criteria to testing. That can be an effective approach *if* the project manager will slip the end date of testing if the start date slips. Often, project managers won't do that, so making it harder to start testing while not changing the end date of testing simply creates more stress and pressure on the test team.

You can try to institute requirements for testability. For example, getting the user interface design team to change editable fields into noneditable pull-down fields wherever possible—such as on date and time fields—can reduce the size of the potential user input validation test set dramatically and help automation efforts.

To reduce the likelihood of being caught unaware by really bad products, and to help reduce bugs in the product, test team members can participate in reviews of earlier project work products, such as requirements specifications. You can also have the test team participate in problem and change management.

Finally, during the test execution effort—hopefully starting with unit testing and perhaps even before, but if not, at least from day one of formal testing—you can monitor the project progress and quality. If you see alarming trends developing, you can try to manage them before they turn into end-game disasters.

Example: Test-Related Project Risks

In Figure 2–9 you see the test-related project risks for an Internet appliance project that has served as a recurring case study in this book. These risks were identified in the test plan and steps were taken throughout the project to manage them through mitigation or respond to them through contingency.

Risk	Mitigation/Contingency
Unable to staff test team on time.	Reduce scope of test effort in reverse-priority order.
Release management not well-defined, resulting in a test cycle's results being invalidated.	Define a crisp release management process.
Test environment system administration support not available or proficient.	Identify system administration resources with pager/cell availability and appropriate ... skills.
Test environment shared with development.	[TBD]
Buggy deliverables impede testing progress.	Complete unit...testing. Adherence to test entry and exit criteria. Early auditing of vendor test and reliability plans and results.
Test and product scope and definition changes impede testing progress.	Change management or change control board.

Figure 2–9   *Example: Test-related project risks*

Let's review the main project risks identified for testing on this project and the mitigation and contingency plans put in place for them.

We were worried, given the initial aggressive schedules, that we might not be able to staff the test team on time. Our contingency plan was to reduce scope of test effort in reverse-priority order.

On some projects, test release management is not well defined, which can result in a test cycle's results being invalidated. Our mitigation plan was to ensure a well-defined crisp release management process.

On some projects, we have had to deal with test environment system administration support that was either unavailable at key times or simply unable to carry out the tasks required. Our mitigation plan was to identify system administration resources with cell phone availability and appropriate Unix, QNX, and network skills.

As consultants, my associates and I often encounter situations where test environments are shared with development, which can introduce tremendous delays and unpredictable interruptions into the test execution schedule. In this case, we had not yet determined the best mitigation or contingency plan for this, so it was marked [TBD].

Of course, buggy deliverables can impede testing progress. In fact, more often than not, the determining factor in test cycle duration for new applications (as opposed to maintenance releases) is the number of bugs in the product and how long it takes to grind them out. We asked for complete unit testing and adherence to test entry and exit criteria as mitigation plans for the software. For the hardware component, we wanted to mitigate this risk through early auditing of vendor test and reliability plans and results.

It's also the case that frequent or sizeable test and product scope and definition changes can impede testing progress. As a contingency plan to manage this should it occur, we wanted a change management or change control board to be established.

Example: Controlling Project Risks

In addition to having to manage product quality risks through testing during the test execution period, we have to control test-related project risks that might affect our ability to execute tests. Table 2–7 shows an example of that, from a real laptop development project.

Table 2–7   *Example: Controlling project risks*

Risk	Impact	Trigger
CD-ROM failure in C-Test boards delays testing due to rework.	Testing end slips out to 11/28 for First Customer Ship critical path items.	11/14
PC Cards initialize, but don't work under Windows.	If this problem is must-fix, it must be resolved in time to finish this test by 11/22. Given that this test takes five days, we need resolution by 11/15.	11/15
The "golden candidate" BIOS, Q3A11, will not enter testing until 11/19.	This is a risk in two ways: we might find showstoppers in the last three or four days of testing before 11/22, and the golden BIOS might ship with very little compatibility testing done against it. Vendor did not deliver a new BIOS on 11/19 as previously scheduled. This increases both risks mentioned above.	11/19

This lists three project risks that could affect our ability to run tests. The first has to do with a potential problem with the DVD drives on the laptop. If that happens, it would delay the end of testing. You see the trigger date, which is the point at which we will know if the risk has become an event. In some cases, if the trigger date is reached and the risk has become an event, that "triggers" (hence the name) a contingency plan.

The next risk is actually both a product risk and a project risk at the same time. Notice that the trigger date is actually a deadline.

The final risk in Table 2–7 has to do with a vendor's failure to deliver the BIOS on schedule. (The BIOS is the built-in software that helps a computer boot.) This project risk has *created* a product quality risk because insufficient testing will occur.

HELLOCARMS Test Project Risks Exercise

Review the HELLOCARMS system requirements document, focusing specifically on identifying test-related project risks. You can also look for other project risks if you'd like.

Document the test-related project risks along with the control option(s) you'd choose to take.

HELLOCARMS Test Project Risks Debrief

I'll review the test-related and other project risks I identified in my review of the HELLOCARMS system requirements document. For the test-related project risks, I have identified control activities. We'll start with some test-related project risks inherent in the requirements, together with risk-control options for each one.

First, unable to secure a true replica of the production environment (see section 000) for testing, leading to restrictions/blockages in testing.

- Mitigation: Identify quality risks that require a replica of the production environment for testing purposes; report to project management.
- Mitigation: As the test environment is assembled, identify tests that cannot be run due to discrepancies between test and production environments; report to project management.
- Mitigation: Explore options for outsourcing performance and reliability testing since the application architecture is common.
- Transfer: If test environment discrepancies remain during test execution, escalate the test coverage holes inherent in these limitations to the project team.

- Contingency: If certain interoperating systems will not be available (e.g., the Scoring Mainframe), arrange for test harnesses that will allow simulation of these interactions.

Next, unable to acquire and deploy adequate and workable performance and reliability testing tools (see sections 020 and 040).

- Mitigation: Determine budgetary and other constraints during test planning and use these constraints during tool evaluation.
- Mitigation: Immediately start tool evaluation in parallel with test planning.
- Transfer: If performance and reliability cannot be tested due to lack of tools, escalate the test coverage holes inherent in these limitations to the project team.

Unable to run tests, including basic functionality and interoperability tests, at start of formal testing due to insufficient quality (including uninstallability) of the test releases.

- Mitigation: Use of an iterative lifecycle model with relatively short iterations, focused on achieving basic functionality and interoperability in the first iteration.
- Mitigation: Continuous integration, nightly builds, and automated smoke tests by the development team.
- Mitigation: Test installations of test releases into the test environment regularly during test implementation (i.e., prior to test execution) to evaluate the test environment and the installability/testability of the test releases prior to the start of test execution.
- Mitigation: Design tests to cover both end-to-end, complex workflows and relatively simple (e.g., screen-by-screen) capabilities to make tests robust in the face of poor-quality software.
- Contingency/transfer: If tests are blocked on entry, triage test cases based on risk priority and escalate reduction in coverage to the project team.

Changes in product in second and later iterations require extensive retesting, invalidate test results, and require test updates.

- Mitigation: Use maintainable automated tests to regression-test existing functionality as new iterations occur, adding new automated tests to the regression suite for each iteration. (Note that this mitigation plan has automated test design implications as well as test team staffing implications.)

- Mitigation: For manual testing, use testers with domain and testing expertise, limit extent of test case documentation to reduce test update effort, and maintain a significant (10 to 20 percent) mix of exploratory test execution with test charters used to document exploratory coverage after execution.
- Contingency/transfer: Where regression testing is not possible, triage test effort based on risk and escalate reduction in coverage to the project team.

Blank spots in requirements specification (e.g., section 020) completed too late to allow for adequate test preparation.

- Mitigation: Work backwards from the start of the first test execution cycle to identify the date by which all key specification areas must be complete to avoid impact on testing, and work with project management to ensure completion by that time.
- Mitigation: Make reasonable assumptions about the requirements that would apply where not currently specified; define lightweight tests, allowing for the possibility of test updates during test execution.
- Mitigation: Appoint one test team member to monitor requirements changes/completions so the appropriate test cases can be identified for changes/maintenance.
- Transfer: Where insufficient information is provided to define any tests whatsoever, escalate holes in coverage to the project team.

Misconfigurations of the complex test environment result in a large number of false positives (i.e., incident reports related to the environment, not the software itself).

- Mitigation: Ensure adequate skills and availability in the assigned system administration support staff.
- Mitigation: Test installations of test releases into the test environment regularly during test implementation (i.e., prior to test execution) to evaluate the test environment and the installability/testability of the test releases prior to the start of test execution. (Note that this is a repeat of a previous mitigation.)
- Contingency: Monitor environment-related false positives during test execution; increase test system administration skills through contractors/consultants if needed.

Gaps in test coverage result in an unacceptable defect detection percentage (i.e., less than 95 percent) with a high rate of field failures.

- Mitigation: Use quality risk analysis to guide the testing.
- Contingency: Use a significant (10 to 20 percent) mix of exploratory test execution, including in areas not considered key risks; use exploratory test results to check for any gaps in the risk analysis and thus the test cases; and refactor the tests based on any gaps discovered.
- Transfer: Escalate gaps in testing related to key (high likelihood and/or impact) risks to management.

Delays in the start of test execution without corresponding delays in the end date result in compression of test periods.

- Mitigation: Adhere to iterative lifecycle model; reduce number of iterations rather than compressing iteration times through reduced test scope.
- Contingency/transfer: Where test compression does occur, triage test effort based on risk and escalate reduction in coverage to the project team.

Budget or staffing constraints make it impossible to assemble a fully suitable test team and/or test environment.

- Mitigation: Explore outsource possibilities to reduce costs (e.g., performance, reliability, and compatibility testing).
- Mitigation: Structure test effort so that discrete, separable test areas can be stripped away while maintaining an ability to do some useful testing in a realistic time frame.
- Contingency/transfer: Where test compression does occur, triage test effort based on risk and escalate reduction in coverage to the project team.

Use of the test environment for debugging causes unpredictable delays, lost test time/effort, and ultimately test compression for the test team.

- Mitigation: Work with project management to ensure adequate debugging environments for the development team (which would also have the positive side effect of lowering the risk of installability problems if the software were first installed in the development environment).
- Contingency/transfer: Where test compression does occur, triage test effort based on risk and escalate reduction in coverage to the project team.

Here are some non-test-related project risks inherent in the requirements:

- Given the lack of clarity around security requirements (see 010-040-010), there's a strong chance that the necessary infrastructure won't be in place as needed to support this project's schedule.

- A higher-than-expected number of escalations to Senior Telephone Bankers (see sections 001 and 004) undermines the ability of the system to service the expected number of customers.
- Availability of developers and other Globobank employees assigned to other interoperating systems (e.g., Scoring Mainframe, LoDoPS, etc.) to resolve cross-system problems is insufficient, leading to delays in defect resolution and production environment setup, delaying first release.
- There are changes/upgrades to interoperating systems that are not coordinated with this release.

As I mentioned, these should be escalated to the appropriate person on the project team.

The ISTQB Test Management Documents

While managing testing properly certainly involves more than creating documents, it is necessary to put some structure around the test process, and this typically involves documents.

Creating test management documentation is a common duty—though perhaps some would call it a chore—but it can be hard for us test professionals to communicate about the documents that we create. It seems that everyone has a somewhat different name for these documents, and many times the same name refers to different documents in different organizations.

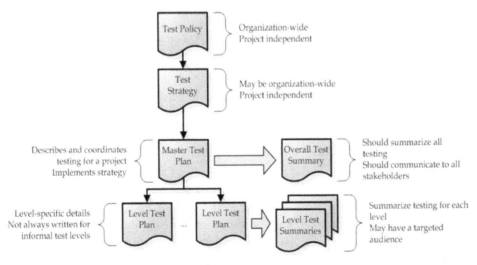

Figure 2–10   *ISTQB test management documents*

In the ISTQB Advanced syllabus, we try to put some structure around this by defining six key management document types (Figure 2–10) that we believe occur when organizations follow testing best practices.

- **Test policy**: The document that describes the organization's philosophy, objectives, and key metrics for testing—and possibly quality assurance as well.

- **Test strategy:** The document that describes the organization's general method of testing. This document would ideally be independent of any specific project but rather would lay out the approach to testing across most projects. This would include product and project risk management; the organization of testing steps, levels, or phases; and the main activities that occur during testing, such as those described in the ISTQB fundamental test process. You might find this document name a bit confusing because we also talk about test strategies in the sense of a set of organizing principles for testing, such as risk-based analytical testing strategies and dynamic testing strategies. Notice that this document elaborates those organizing principles into an actionable—if general—methodology.

- **Master test plan (or project test plan):** The document that describes the application of the test strategy to a particular project. This would include the specific test levels that will occur and the relationship among those levels, including how gaps and overlap between the levels are to be managed and avoided. It would also address those activities, like bug reporting, that are common across levels, unless those activities are already described in sufficient detail in the test strategy. Notice that because different teams might own the different test levels, this is a cross-functional document. Test managers are wise to work cross-functionally when creating such documents.

- **Level test plan (or phase test plan):** The document that describes the specific activities for each test level. It expands on the master test plan for the specific level addressed, such as the system test plan, the integration test plan, and so on.

  These first four documents are created during the planning step of the fundamental test process. During evaluation of exit criteria and results reporting, two additional types of documents are created.

- **Overall test summary**: This is a high-level summary of all the testing on a project, ideally spanning and including all levels of testing. The best practice is to keep these simple. For example, I created an overall test summary

> **ISTQB Glossary**
> **level test plan:** A test plan that typically addresses one test level.

for a client that was targeted at executive and senior management and senior project stakeholders. It consisted of four intuitive graphs and was called "the Core 4," logically enough.

- **Level test summaries**: These are more detailed reports about the results of testing for a particular level. For example, in agile projects, it's not unusual for programmers to talk about their unit testing in terms of the status of each individual acceptance criteria and the percentage of code coverage achieved. This is a level of detail aimed at fellow individual contributors and at line managers.

I refer to these as documents, though they are more typically presentations involving graphs and charts. I'll discuss these more thoroughly in a later section of this chapter and show you many examples. In the rest of this section, we'll look at the four planning documents in detail.

Are you a bad test manager if you don't have all six types of documents, addressing exactly the topics described? No. The information in these documents can be combined into one document or spread across multiple documents. In some cases, it might not be documented at all, though that's a risky approach for all but the smallest, shortest, and most transient projects.

Test Policy

The test policy describes the "why" of testing for an organization, independent of means, projects, and test levels.

A test policy describes the organization's overall objectives for testing. In some cases, it's even broader, describing the quality assurance objectives, from the beginning to the end of the lifecycle. It should reflect the organizational values and goals as they relate to testing and perhaps also quality assurance.

Senior managers, both test managers and test stakeholder managers, work collaboratively to establish the test policy—not the test team by itself. However, the test team as a whole should review the test policy, and in some cases the test team as a whole drafts the policy and submits it to management for approval, promulgation, and establishment. Like any policy that establishes direction, the test policy should be written.

The test policy can be a component in a broader quality policy. Alternatively, they can be distinct policies, but in that case, they should be complementary and well aligned.

The audience for the test policy document is not only the test team, nor is it only the technical people; it's also the entire organization, from management on down. In the case of a product development organization, the organization might choose to make the test policy accessible to customers and users.

A test policy document is not a long document. The best ones are short, about one to two pages. They are high-level documents.

Test Policy Topics

Test policies should briefly discuss the following topics:

- The business value of testing, both tangible and intangible. I'll talk about how to define and measure testing value later in this chapter.
- The objectives of testing, such as building confidence in the system, detecting defects, generating information, and managing quality risks. These objectives must be consistent with the stakeholder objectives discussed earlier in this chapter.
- Various metrics for measuring the effectiveness and efficiency of testing for all of the defined objectives. For example, in terms of defect detection, the test policy might mention defect detection effectiveness as an effectiveness metric and the relative cost of defects detected in testing as opposed to after release as an efficiency metric. Stakeholder satisfaction metrics can be defined as well. Reasonable goals for these metrics can also be defined in the test policy. Sometimes the test policy defines quality targets, if the document is addressing quality assurance.
- The organization's basic, generic, fundamental test process, following the ISTQB process or some other process.
- Approaches for metrics-driven, experience-based improvements to the test process, such as checking the metrics for effectiveness and efficiency during a project retrospective, and then applying test process improvement models such as Critical Testing Processes (CTP), Test Process Improvement Next (TPI Next), or Testing Maturity Model integration (TMMi) to improve.

The test policy should address new development and maintenance, large projects and small.

In some cases, where applicable, the test policy can address optional or mandatory standards. For example, a company producing safety-critical medical software, regulated by the FDA, would need to explain the importance of adherence to FDA standards for testing and traceability. The test policy can also reference standard terminology, such as using the ISTQB glossary as the standard for testing terms.

As an RBCS consultant, I can say that the test policy document is more often missing than present. That creates real problems for test organizations because there is both a lack of agreement on what the test team is supposed to accomplish and no measurement toward goals.

Example: Test Policy

In Figure 2–11, you see the first page of a sample test policy my associates and I helped put in place for a client. We have a high-level mission statement to begin with. Next, we summarize the testing strategy for the test team. You'll see more details on this test strategy, from the company's test strategy document, later in this section.

Sample Test Policy

Mission of Testing

To effectively and efficiently provide timely, accurate, and useful quality risk management information and services.

[Company Name Here] Risk-Based Testing Strategy

Depending on project objectives, [company name] selects the degree of quality risk mitigation desired. Quality risks are identified, and risk items are assessed to determine their level of risk. The level of risk determines test effort and test sequencing. Test results are reported in terms of mitigated and unmitigated risks.

Sequential Test Levels Performed by the Best-Qualified Participants

Test levels promote mitigation of quality risk as early as possible and to the highest practical extent.

Level	Owner	Objective(s)	Key Areas of Testing
Unit	Development	• Detect defective code in units • Reduce risk of unit failure in Production	Functionality and resource utilization
Integration	Development	• Detect defects in unit interfaces • Reduce risk of dataflow and workflow failures in Production	Functionality, data quality, unit inter-operability and compatibility, performance
System	Risk Mitigation and Quality Assurance	• Detect defects in use cases and end-to-end scenarios • Assist in mitigating risk of unmet business requirements in Production	Functionality, data quality, performance, reliability, usability, resource utilization, maintainability, installability, portability and interoperability
Acceptance	Business	• Demonstrate readiness for deployment • Detect defects in user workflows*	Functionality

Figure 2–11   Sample test policy, page 1

Next, we have a table that shows how the test levels are distributed across different teams. Development owns unit and integration testing, the test team—titled "Risk Mitigation and Quality Assurance"—owns system testing, and the business stakeholders own acceptance testing. We have clearly defined, appropriate objectives for each test level, and we also have defined the key software attributes tested at each level.

In Figure 2–12, you see the second page of the test policy. We define the overall test process for each level, calling for involvement from day one of the project. This organization chose to follow the Critical Testing Processes (CTP) framework rather than the ISTQB fundamental test process.

Next we have a statement about the need to establish effectiveness and efficiency metrics—referred to here as KPIs, or key performance indicators—for each test level. It also discusses the need for test process improvement.

The Test Process for Each Test Level

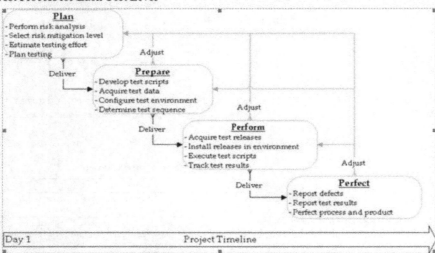

The degree of formality for the various activities will depend on the level of risk associated with the project as a whole.

Key Process Indicators (KPIs)

Each group responsible for one or more test levels shall establish KPIs for test activities that address the following areas:

- Defect detection effectiveness
- Risk coverage and sequencing

In consultation with IT management, each group manager shall develop and execute plans for project-by-project alignment of KPIs across groups and long-term plans for test process improvement at each level and across levels.

Figure 2–12   *Sample test policy, page 2*

Test Strategy

The test strategy describes, at a high level, independent of any specific project, the "how" of testing for an organization.

The test strategy describes the organization's methods of testing. It can cover the options that the organization can use to manage product and project risks during testing. For example, what are the typical product quality risks that we try to address with testing, and how do we do so? How do those quality risks relate to the high-level test objectives? What are the typical project risks that can affect testing, and how do we manage those risks?

A test strategy document can also provide more detail on the various testing levels or phases to be used. For example, it might discuss the general entry and exit criteria for the various levels. It could describe how unit testing, integration testing, and system test are managed.

In describing each test level, it might lay out the high-level test activities to be performed.

Since the test strategy provides the "how" details for the test policy's "why" statements, it must be aligned with the test policy. Further, it should provide generic test requirements for each test level and for the testing as a whole. For example, in a risk-based approach, it would specify the generic quality risk areas to be examined during quality risk identification and assessment.

A test strategy is not project dependent. It spans projects. That is, the document describes an approach to testing that applies to many if not all test efforts undertaken during a project. It also spans responsible groups, laying out the approach to take for all levels of testing across the different groups responsible. For example, it can discuss unit testing, integration testing, and system testing and which group is responsible for each level.

Different organizations and even different projects within the same organization might need different test strategies. A test strategy document is not about creating a "one size fits all" approach to testing but rather about creating an approach that can be tailored.

A test strategy can address both short-term and long-term needs. Since those needs could change, the test strategy should address the reasons for those needs to change and how those changes affect testing.

The test strategies can change depending on the project, application, and chosen lifecycle. A security-critical or safety-critical application requires a more rigorous, intensive, and perhaps standards-compliant strategy. A small agile project will certainly require much less rigor.

Test strategy documents are also more often missing than present. This means that people don't address some of the important topics mentioned in this section. Alternatively, the absence of information about those topics results in questions being asked twice, three times, four times, or more, perhaps once for each project, with inconsistent decisions made each time. There's nothing wrong with rationally and deliberately tailoring the approach for each project, but having to figure out fundamental aspects of testing over and over again because no one can be bothered to document an overarching test strategy is inefficient and, on many projects, reduces the effectiveness of the testing.

Types of Test Strategies

Some test strategies are in the form of written documents, and some are just oral tradition or institutional knowledge within a company. While they come in different forms, there are identifiable *types* of test strategies. Understanding these types can help you think more clearly about how you should select, blend, and devise your organization's test strategy.

You should recall from the Foundation syllabus that we can classify test strategies as either preventive or reactive. Preventive test strategies are those that focus on early involvement of the test team and use test planning, analysis, and design activities to identify problems in the project plan, the product requirements and design, and other project work products. This allows the organization to resolve these problems before test execution, thus preventing the late discovery of a large number of defects, which is a leading cause of project failure.

Reactive test strategies are those that focus on responding to the system as it is actually presented to the test team. This allows the organization to avoid costs associated with development of test work products that might not be useful if the actual system differs from what was initially planned.

As you can see, for projects that are predictable, carefully planned, and executed according to plan, the preventive strategies have the advantage. Why do all the test planning, analysis, and design in parallel with test execution—or perhaps not at all—if you can do this work earlier in the project?

For projects that are chaotic, poorly planned, or in constant fundamental change, the reactive strategies have the advantage. Why create a bunch of test work products that will have to be maintained or completely re-created when the system delivered turns out to be a total surprise?

Now, this classification of a strategy as preventive or reactive is a simplification. In actuality, a given test strategy will fall somewhere along a spectrum and will often incorporate both preventive and reactive elements.

In my book *Pragmatic Software Testing*,[21] I surveyed the types of test strategies that we find in actual use. That survey is the basis of the list of test strategies in both the Foundation and Advanced syllabi. Let's look at the various types of test strategies that exist.

In analytical strategies, such as risk-based testing, the test team analyzes a test basis to identify the test conditions. The results of the analysis form the basis of the test effort, from design and implementation to execution and reporting of results. Analytical test strategies tend to be thorough, excellent for quality risk management, and good at finding bugs. Analytical test strategies are primarily preventive and require significant early-project time and effort.

In model-based strategies, such as those relying on operational profiles, you design, implement, and execute your tests based on models of system behavior. If the models capture the system's essential elements, your tests will be good. Therefore, model-based strategies rely on the ability of the tester to develop good models. These strategies fail when the models, or the testers building the models, fail to capture the essential or risky aspects of the system.

In methodical strategies, such as those that follow checklists of quality characteristics, you follow some standard catalog of test objectives. Methodical strategies are lightweight and effective for stable systems and for systems that are similar to ones you've tested previously. However, significant changes will make these strategies ineffective, at least unless some adjustment to the catalog of test objectives occurs.

In process- or standard-compliant strategies, such as those based on IEEE 829 or agile methods, you follow some process or standard promulgated by a standards committee or group of wise people somewhere. These strategies can save you the time and energy of devising your own methodologies. However, if your overall mission of testing is different from the one that the creators of the standard had, or if the test problems you are struggling with are not those that the creators of the standard have resolved, you'll find that this borrowed approach fits about as a well as a borrowed tuxedo.

In reactive strategies (also sometimes called dynamic or heuristic strategies), such as those based on bug taxonomies or software attacks, you use general rules

---

21. Rex Black 2007.

about how software fails; lists of important software areas, features, and behaviors; or lists of common software data structures and operations to make educated guesses to focus the testing. These test strategies will minimize structure, maximize flexibility, and typically, focus on finding bugs rather than building confidence or reducing risk. The lack of structure and documentation means that they lack detailed coverage information, do not systematically reduce quality risks, or do not incorporate any preventive elements. These weaknesses aside, using a purely reactive strategy is better than not testing at all. Better yet, you can blend reactive strategies with analytical strategies, providing a good way to check for gaps in the analytically designed tests.

In consultative strategies, such as those where users or programmers determine what is to be tested, the test manager trusts that some other group of people knows best what should be tested. The test manager asks them for the test conditions to cover and covers those conditions. The other group also acts as the primary test oracle, in that we'll ask them to determine the expected results. This strategy can be appropriate when the test team is brought in primarily to serve as the hands and eyes of another group, such as with some types of outsourced testing.

Finally, in regression averse strategies, such as those that rely on extensive functional test automation, we focus on test repetition and smart test selection to try to minimize the risk of breaking something that already works. For stable systems that are changing only slowly, these strategies can make sense. However, there is always the risk that new features will be poorly tested and, should the rate of change accelerate, the test coverage for recently added features will be left behind. In addition, even given a good approach for test automation, a rapidly increasing automated regression test set can overwhelm the abilities of the test team to run and analyze all the test results.

As with the classification of strategies as preventive or reactive, remember that these strategies exist on a continuum. Also, remember that strategies are not philosophies or religions—you don't have to choose just one and stay with it. Strategies may be combined. It is smart to spend some time as a test manager carefully selecting and tailoring your test strategies. You can adopt general strategies for your test team and modify or completely rework those for a particular project, too.

Other Contents of Test Strategy Documents

A test strategy can provide various details on the test process. It might discuss the following areas:

- The integration procedures, such as top-down, bottom-up, functional, or risk based.
- The test specification techniques, including the test design concepts discussed in Advanced Software Testing: Volumes 1 and 3, as well as the level of documentation details required.
- The degree of independence needed in various testing activities, which may vary depending on level.
- Any mandatory and optional standards to be followed in testing. These would probably have been introduced in the test policy, but their actual use would be described in the test strategy.
- The various test environments used for different types of testing.
- The application of test automation to various types of testing.
- The need for and means for reusability of software work products and test work products, such as test cases, test data, and test plans.
- The approach for confirmation testing and regression testing, which might intersect with the test automation topic.
- The means for performing and gathering information for test control and reporting.
- The test measurements and metrics to be gathered, and frequency and means of communication.
- How defect management is to be performed, including reporting of defects, prioritization of defects, and management of defects.
- How to carry out configuration management for the testware.
- The relationship between groups performing testing and other groups on the project, and the deliverables that flow between those groups.

Addressing these types of topics can be quite useful when projects are similar because it reduces the amount of project-specific documentation needed. A test team can simply refer to the test strategy rather than redocument these issues in each test plan.

Example: Test Strategy and Activities

In Table 2–8, you see an excerpt from the test strategy document that my associates and I helped a client create. It is the client for which the test policy document shown earlier was created.

Table 2–8   *Test strategy and activities*

Initial Risk	Approach	Entry Criteria	Coverage/ Risk Mitigation	Exit Criteria	Residual Risk
Very High	Pl	No process, unit test, review variance	MC: Extensive Non-MC: Broad Regr: Automated	High coverage, confidence, quality	Low to Very Low
High	Au	Little process, unit test, review variance	MC: Broad Non-MC: Cursory Regr: Manual	Good coverage, confidence, quality	Low to Very Low
Medium	Ag	Some process, unit test, review variance	MC: Cursory Non-MC: Opportunity Regr: None	Fair coverage, confidence, quality	Low to Very Low
Low	Pb	Discretionary process, unit test, review variance	MC: Opportunity Non-MC: None Regr: None	Low coverage, confidence, quality	Low to Very Low
Very Low	Hg	-	No testing	-	Very Low

In Table 2–8, we define the appropriate extent and approach for testing a given project based on the initial level of risk posed by the application being created or maintained by the project team. The initial level of risk is determined after the quality risk analysis is performed, by evaluating the list of risk items and the distribution of risk ratings. Based on that information, the project stakeholders assigned an initial risk on a five-point scale, from very high to very low.

Based on that initial risk, we suggest one of five general approaches to testing, to which we gave suggestive metal names:

- Pl, the chemical symbol for platinum. For this approach, all best practices of software development processes must be followed, including good unit testing and requirements, design, and code reviews. During system test, mission-critical (or MC) applications receive extensive testing, non-mission-critical applications receive broad testing, and regression (Regr) testing is automated. The exit criteria are defined in the test plan to support high test coverage, a high level of confidence, and a high-quality release. The residual level of risk is expected to be low or very low upon release.

- Au, the chemical symbol for gold. For this approach, all best practices of software development processes should be followed, including good unit testing and requirements, design, and code reviews, but some minor variance is allowed. During system test, mission-critical applications receive broad testing, non-mission-critical applications receive cursory testing, and regression testing is manual. The exit criteria are defined in the test plan to support good test coverage, a good level of confidence, and a good-quality release. The residual level of risk is expected to be low or very low upon release.

- Ag, the chemical symbol for silver. For this approach, all best practices of software development processes are recommended, including good unit testing and requirements, design, and code reviews, but variance is allowed. During system test, mission-critical applications receive cursory testing, non-mission-critical applications receive opportunity testing, and regression testing is omitted. The exit criteria are defined in the test plan to support fair test coverage, a fair level of confidence, and a fair-quality release. The residual level of risk is expected to be low or very low upon release.

- Pb, the chemical symbol for lead. For this approach, best practices of software development processes may be followed, including good unit testing and requirements, design, and code reviews, but significant project team discretion is allowed. During system test, mission-critical applications receive opportunity testing, non-mission-critical applications are not tested, and regression testing is omitted. The exit criteria are defined in the test plan to support low test coverage and a low level of confidence and to allow for release even if the overall quality is low—after all, this is a low-risk project. The residual level of risk is expected to be low or very low upon release.

- Hg, the chemical symbol for mercury. The level of risk is not deemed sufficient to justify any testing at all.

Notice that this table provides general guidance for creating the test plan to the test manager as well as giving test stakeholders a summary view of the test expectations, activities, and ultimate effect on the residual level of quality risk

Table 2–9 shows the residual risk consequences of selecting particular approaches that vary from the suggested initial risk/approach combinations shown in Table 2–8. Selecting a weaker approach will leave a higher level of risk in exchange for a quicker release. I suggest you study Table 2–9 and perhaps go back to the previous one for reference once or twice as you do. A lot of information is packed into these two tables.

Table 2–9   *Trading off time and quality risk*

Initial Risk	Selected Approach and Consequent Residual Risk				
	Pl	Au	Ag	Pb	Hg
Very High	Low to Very Low	Medium to Low	High to Medium	Very High to High	Very High
High	Very Low	Low to Very Low	Medium to Low	High to Medium	High
Medium	Very Low	Very Low	Low to Very Low	Medium to Low	Medium
Low	Very Low	Very Low	Very Low	Low to Very Low	Low
Very Low	Very Low	Very Low	Very Low	Very Low	Very Low

Master Test Plan

The master test plan describes the "how" of testing for a single project, spanning multiple levels of testing. It describes how we intend to apply the test strategy to a specific project. When the testing is decomposed into multiple levels, such as unit test, integration test, system test, and acceptance, the master test plan should describe the relationship between these levels and the division of work across the levels.

The master test plan should be aligned with the test policy and strategy. However, in some cases, the master test plan will deviate from policies or strategies for specific reasons. Those reasons should be explained in the test plan.

Across the project or operation that the testing serves, we want to ensure that the master test plan complements the project plan or operations guide. It should describe the testing effort as part of the larger project or operation. It should ensure that testing is organized in a way that serves the purposes and goals of the project or operation as well as the broader organizational objectives for testing.

Testing is downstream of most other activities on a project. This means that chaos and disorder in other areas of the project can leak into the testing effort if we're not careful. If during test planning, you identify a situation where disorder elsewhere in the project will affect your testing, then your master test plan or a detail test plan might need to fill the gaps in other project documents. For example, if the configuration management process is not documented, you can expect to have challenges with test item delivery, test item transmittal reports, revision numbering, and other related release engineering topics. Therefore, the test plan should specify how test objects will be delivered to the test team.

In some cases, the master test plan and level test plans can be combined into a single document. This is common if only one level of testing is a formal level. For example, if we have a formal system test performed by an independent test team but informal component and integration testing performed by programmers and informal acceptance testing performed by customers under the name of a beta program, then the system test plan is probably the only written test plan.

Contents of the Master Test Plan

The specific content and structure of a master test plan can vary. However, most of the good ones I've seen and written tended to address a core set of topics. Let's review those important topics here.

It's important that scope be clear in test plans, so I like to see a section that addresses this topic, in terms of both items to be tested and not to be tested and quality attributes to be tested and not to be tested. It should be specific about this topic overall as well as for each test level.

The test plan should address the testing schedule and budget, and those should be consistent with the project or operational budget. Again, when multiple test levels are used, we need to make sure this definition of scope is clear for each level described.

Because miscommunications and mistakes often occur when we're trying to coordinate the delivery of test items, the execution of test cycles, and the ultimate completion of the test cycles, the test plan should describe in some detail the test execution cycles and their relationship to the software release plan. Under what circumstances are we ready to start a level of testing, under what circumstances might we suspend and resume a level of testing, and under what circumstances are we ready to declare a level of testing completed? In general, foul-ups are always more likely during handoffs across the project team, so the test plan should discuss relationships and deliverables that will pass between testing and other people or departments.

The test plan should address directly, or by reference to the test policy and/or test strategy documents, the organizational objectives of testing, the business justification for testing, and value of the test work to be done. What are the quality risks that we are covering with testing? What are the project risks that might affect testing?

The test plan should also address the test-related project risks and how they will be managed, as discussed earlier.

Finally, the whole topic of test governance should be addressed. This includes escalation processes to use when plan breakdowns occur, how defects are managed, to whom results are reported, how test course-correction occurs, and so forth. While these topics are often discussed in general in the test strategy, they should be made specific here, particularly in terms of assigning specific project participants' names to specific roles.

Level Test Plan

The level test plan describes, for a single test level on a single project, the "how" of testing. For example, we can have a system test plan. Sometimes these test plans describe a test type, such as a performance test plan. In agile projects, there might be a test plan for each iteration, though my usual advice is to have a general test plan for each level that applies across all sprints and then instantiate that with lightweight documentation for each sprint.

The level test plan will describe the particular activities for a test level or test type. Theoretically, there would be a detail test plan for each level of testing, and it would expand on the master test plan for that level.

The level test plan provides level-specific schedule, task, and milestone details. If there are level-specific standards and templates, then the level test plan should cover that.

Now, though theory calls for a master test plan and then four or more level test plans, one for each level, when working on an informal project or operation, you might find that a single level test plan is the only test management document actually written down. If that's the case, it has to address the topics that would theoretically be covered in a master test plan—and potentially even in the strategy and policy documents.

Other Work Products

As shown earlier in this section, test managers are responsible for documenting—or helping to document—test policies, test strategies, test plans, and test results reports. Testers—specifically, test analysts and technical test analysts—are responsible for the other major test work products, including defect reports, test specifications, test logs, and so forth.

In the Advanced Test Analyst syllabus, significant detail is given on these various work products that testers must produce. However, as a test manager, you have to manage the production of these test work products. What is your role in that process?

The Test Manager's Role

As with any manager, you are responsible for the consistency and quality of the work done by your team. For example, bug reports should contain all necessary information, be consistent in their level of detail, and be found informative and valuable by all stakeholders and project participants who read them. One or two weak testers, polluting the defect tracking system with lousy bug reports, can damage the entire test team's reputation—I've seen it happen a number of times.

If you manage a large test team or are a director of testing, you might be thinking, "Well, I have a lot of people who work for me. I certainly can't review and revise every single work product from my team." Fortunately, there are ways to put metrics in place that will tell you whether the process is working smoothly and quality is being delivered. For example, measuring the rate of duplicate and rejected bug reports is a good way to see if there might be problems with defect reporting.

In addition to setting up ways to monitor for problems, take proactive steps to prevent them. A team effort to select and customize useful templates, with input from key stakeholders, can go a long way to ensure consistency across the team in terms of content. Then, you can work with the team again—and again with key stakeholders—to define standards for the content, which will help ensure quality. For example, you could select the IEEE 829 standard for the content of defect reports and then define the various fields mentioned in that template. We'll return to this topic—creating good defect reports—in a later chapter.

In addition, while you might not be able to review every single work product, remember that reviews are an appropriate way to improve work product quality for all work products, including test work products. On test teams that I've managed, I have a simple rule: at least two pairs of eyes. In other words, nothing is considered complete and ready for release outside the test team until at least one other tester has reviewed it, including defect reports. For more elaborate or farther-reaching deliverables, such as risk catalogs produced by quality risk analysis, I might want the entire test team—at least the senior testers—to review it before we release it for project-wide review.

Now, consistency is good, and in general it's to be desired across test work products. Standardization across testers improves efficiency because training is simplified and mistakes are reduced. However, standardization can reduce effectiveness in situations where project-specific variables make the standards less apt. For example, the software development lifecycle, applicable regulations, and quality and project risks associated with a particular system being developed can, if different from other projects, make particular elements of a standard or even the entire standard inappropriate. For example, many organizations use different documentation standards for defect reports in agile projects than they do in traditional lifecycles to avoid costly overhead that slows down sprints. You need to be ready to do appropriate tailoring while ensuring that important information is still captured and documented.

Case Study: Test Plan for Simple PC App

We've reviewed test plans at a high level, looking at outlines and major topics. Let's now take a closer look at selected sections of a test plan. This plan addressed testing of a simple PC application. The application was designed to allow comparative PC performance testing during PC evaluation and purchase. It resided on a dedicated USB drive.

RBCS served as the test team for this project. We were performing what we called a component test on the user interface of the application. It was a relatively short, low-cost, low-risk test project, so formalism and rigor is low, as you'll see in the plan.

In this case study as before, the non-RBCS names have been changed to anonymize the client and the participants.

Case Study: Resources

The excerpt in Table 2–10 shows the resources section. In it, we define the test team, plus the client contact. Given the simplicity of the project, the only outside interaction the test team had was with Quincy Adams.

Table 2–10   *Resources Section of the Test Plan*

Title	Roles	Name
Test Manager	Plan, track, and report on test execution. Conduct end-of-day debrief, status update, and results posting to client contact and test team. Secure appropriate resources. Review bug reports and test results.	Rex Black
Lead Test Engineer	Execute tests. Guide the other test engineers. Act as test manager when needed. Review bug reports and test results.	Nabi Berri
Test Engineers	Execute tests. Report results to the lead test engineer or test manager as needed. Review bug reports and test results.	Amit Harare Laurel Becker
Test System Admin	Ensure proper configuration of all the test environments.	Joe Maxim
Client Contact	Deliver test release. Receive test results. Guide resolution of bugs for Phase II. Act as liaison for any blocking test issues not resolvable by the test team.	Quincy Adams

Case Study: Test Execution Process

Figure 2–13 shows the test execution process section of the test plan. Let me highlight some key ideas here. You might want to read Figure 2–13 completely first.

Notice that in the first sentence we establish the objective of testing. This project has a single objective, that of finding bugs. Because this is a one-off project, not an ongoing test team, this statement, which would otherwise occur in a test policy document, is found here in this test plan.

We also define our strategy briefly here, which is a combination of consultative testing (the test charters were supplied by the client), object-based analytical testing (analyzing the use cases the client provided to identify test conditions), and reactive (using exploratory testing). We define the receipt of releases, the test cycles, and the mapping of test cases to test cycles in this paragraph as well.

> The objective of the [testing project] is to find bugs in the [application] user interface. The RBCS test team intends to do so by running a set of test charters and exploratory tests against two test releases, one release for each of the two Component Test Phases. The test team shall run every test case exactly one time as part of each of the two Component Test Phases.
>
> To track the testing, the test team shall use…Test Case Summary worksheets… At the beginning of each test cycle, the Test Manager…shall assign a "basket" of test cases to each tester. In Phase II, the Test Manager…shall attempt to assign a different basket to each tester, to minimize the risk that any invalid assumptions on one tester's part result in a test escape. Once assigned their basket of tests, these testers shall follow the process described in the rest of this section to execute each test case, and repeat the process until they have exhausted their list.
>
> If they empty their basket prior to the end of a cycle, they are to assist other testers by coordinating a reassignment of some of those testers' test cases to themselves.

Figure 2–13   *Test execution process section*

The next paragraph describes the test assignment and tracking processes as well as the process for the tester to run the tests. Notice that workload balancing is covered as well.

Case Study: Use Case and Test Charter

Table 2–11 shows an example of the use cases and test charters supplied by the client. Again, I recommend taking time to read Table 2–11 before proceeding.

Table 2–11   *Use cases and test charters*

Name:	Test Current Computer
User Goal:	To calculate and see True Performance Scores for the computer into which [the application USB drive] is currently plugged.
Starting Point:	Test Current Computer can be initiated from any application state.
Path:	User clicks Test in the Primary Function area. The Animation runs in the Content area while the [performance test] executes and the True Performance Scores display is created. As soon as the True Performance Scores display is created, the Animation stops and the current computer's True Performance Scores are displayed in the Content area.
Ending Point:	The current computer's True Performance Scores are displayed in the Content area.
Notes:	Clicking Test always causes the [performance test] to execute and a new True Performance Scores display to be built, even if this scenario has already been executed one or more times for the current computer.
Test Charter:	Verify the Path from Starting Point to Ending Point, including the specified error conditions.

As you can see, there are many opportunities for test design and exploratory testing here. For example, the use case says that this action can be initiated from any application state. Hmm, how many different states are there? Have we tested them all?

Notice too how concise the test charter is. This gives the tester many different ways to explore the use case.

Case Study: Schedule of Milestones

Table 2–12 shows the schedule of milestones. Again, you might want to quickly read Table 2–12 before continuing.

Table 2–12   *Schedule of milestones*

Date	Milestones
9/30	Delivery of the Test Charters to RBCS.
10/7	Delivery of the System Test Plan for the AMD DIPstick Test Project by RBCS.
10/13	Delivery of the First Test Release (assumed to be feature complete) to RBCS.
10/13	Delivery of the shell DLL needed to [create test data] to RBCS.
10/14 - 10/20	Testing Phase I by RBCS.
10/21	Delivery of Phase I Test Results and Bug Reports by RBCS.
10/27	Delivery of the Second (Final) Test Release to RBCS.
10/28 - 11/3	Testing Phase II by RBCS.
11/4	Delivery of Phase II Test Results and Bug Reports by RBCS.

Notice that the test basis—the use cases and test charters—are delivered at the start of the project. We analyze those and develop a plan. We then have two one-week test cycles, with a week in between cycles to allow for bug fixes.

The entire project is just a little over one month long.

Case Study: Risks and Contingencies

Finally, in Table 2–13 you see the risks and contingencies for the project. The risks are quite simple for this simple project. Notice, too, that we don't have a lot of ability to control the risks. Most of the contingencies result in reduced testing, delay of testing, or both.

Table 2–13   *Risk and contingencies*

Risk	Contingency
Test release very buggy during test Phase I or II.	Run whatever tests are not blocked. Allow mid-phase test release during test phase, complete as many tests as possible.
Component remains very buggy at end of Phase II.	There is no provision within the scope of the project for additional testing, so this is an unmitigated risk.
Schedule slip in start of Phase I or Phase II.	Delay start of test phase. Since tester availability is now closely tied to specific schedule days, a delay in a phase start date may result in a disproportionately long delay in the phase end date.

HELLOCARMS Test Plan Exercise

Review the HELLOCARMS system requirements document. Using the IEEE 829 template, outline a combined master test plan and level test plan covering system test and system integration test, based on your earlier risk analysis exercises and your analysis of the HELLOCARMS project. Use a bullet-item level of detail, two to four bullet items per section.

HELLOCARMS Test Plan Debrief

Here's the outline I created for this exercise.

I.   **Test plan identifier:** Adhere to whatever document naming/numbering standard exists at Globobank.

II. **Introduction:**
   a. Describe project at a high level.
   b. Describe testing at a high level.

III. **Test items:**
   a. HELLOCARMS system components:
      i.   SQL and other items for database server
      ii. Java and other items for application server
      iii. Java, HTML, Flash, and other items for web server
   b. HELLOCARMS system integration components:
      i.   LoDoPS interface
      ii. Decisioning mainframe interface
      iii. Other interfacing components
   c. All of these items must be packaged in the same way they will be packaged for delivery to the data center.

IV. **Features to be tested:**
   a. Home equity loan, home equity line of credit, and reverse mortgage functionality

b. Rejection of undesirable applicants

c. End-to-end transaction handling

d. Error handling and recovery

e. Security

f. Regulatory compliance

g. HELLOCARMS/Scoring Mainframe interfaces

h. HELLOCARMS/LoDoPS interfaces

i. HELLOCARMS/GLADS interfaces

j. HELLOCARMS/GloboRainBQW interfaces

V.   **Features not to be tested:**

a. [At this point, only functional quality characteristics are identified.]

VI.   **Approach:**

a. Primary test strategy is analytical risk-based testing, accounting for 60 percent of the test execution effort, with the effort allocated relative to risk item level.

b. Secondary test strategy is reactive, using software attacks and exploratory testing, accounting for 20 percent of the test execution effort.

c. Confirmation testing to validate bug fixes and check for success with testing previously failed test cases, accounting for 20 percent of the test execution effort.

d. System testing and system integration testing will be handled by the HELLOCARMS independent test team, assuming some basic unit testing and component integration testing by development.

VII.   **Item pass/fail criteria**

a. I would include this in the test criteria section in terms of measured product quality.

VIII.   **Test criteria (e.g., entry, exit, suspension, and resumption)**

a. Need to define entry criteria for system and system integration test levels based on the following:

  i. Readiness of testware, test environments, test team

  ii. Demonstrated quality of test items (unit and component integration test results, smoke tests, build verification tests, etc.)

  iii. SDLC lifecycle model rules

    b. Need to define exit criteria for system and system integration test
       levels based on the following:
       i.   Product quality using bug metrics
       ii. Completeness of testing using test case completion metrics
       iii. Test efficiency using test hours metrics
       iv. Thoroughness of testing using test coverage metrics
       v.   Residual level of risk
       vi. Resolution of known defects
       vii. Management acceptance of residual risk
    c. Define the four or five test results dashboard charts and supporting
       data delivered to project management during test execution.
    d. Define the detailed information delivered to technical support, devel-
       opment, etc. during test execution.
    e. Define the testware, test environments, test processes, etc. that will be
       delivered for maintenance testing at the end of test execution.

IX.   **Test tasks**
    a. Refer to the test estimate work breakdown structure.

X.   **Environmental needs**
    a. Replica (as close as possible) of the data centers and call centers shown
       in Figure 1 of the HELLOCARMS system requirements document
    b. Test interfaces to the Scoring Mainframe, LoDoPS, GLADS, and
       GloboRainBQW, with sufficient control over the data interchange to
       produce all necessary inputs and outputs

XI.   **Responsibilities**
    a. Define test team members and their roles.
    b. Define major non-test participants.

XII.   **Staffing and training needs**
    a. Define the team, perhaps by reference to the previous section.
    b. Discuss technical, testing, or domain training needed for team.

XIII. **Schedule**
    a. Refer to the test estimate work breakdown structure.

XIV. **Risks and contingencies**
    a. Refer to the quality risk analysis document for quality risks.
    b. Refer to the project risk identified in the first exercise of this section
       ("HELLOCARMS Test Project Risks Exercise").

XV.   **Approvals**
    a. Add a signature section here if needed.

2.5   Test Estimation

Learning objectives

(K3) For a given project, create an estimate for all test process activities, using all applicable estimation techniques.

(K2) Understand and give examples of factors which may influence test estimates.

To quote an aphorism often misattributed to Yogi Berra but which was actually coined by Neils Bohr, "Prediction is difficult, especially about the future." However, project stakeholders and especially project sponsors—those who foot the bill—tend to have this pesky need to know how long the various project activities will take and how much those activities will cost. The same is true for ongoing operations once a system is put into production. As a test manager, you'll be involved in putting some target dates and costs in place for testing activities. If you don't like that reality, you've probably taken a wrong turn somewhere in your career.

On a serious note, though, why do test managers dislike estimation? Generally, I find there are three reasons:

- They weren't properly trained to do estimation, so what they are doing is just making a politically loaded guess.
- They find the constant pressure for lower cost and quicker test completion dates during the estimation process to be an excruciating form of wheedling, especially when they are trying to defend an estimate that is as much guess as prediction.
- When the test execution drags on and delays the project due to the poor quality of the software, test managers are often blamed for having a bad estimate and creating a project crisis.

Relief is on the way. In this section, you'll learn some tips that will help you make good predictions, do smart negotiations with managers, and ensure that quality problems are taken into account in your estimates.

Let's start with a discussion of what a good estimate is. First, a good estimate is one that is assembled collectively by the manager with the team of people who will participate in the work. The same kind of collective wisdom that was tapped when doing quality risk analysis will be employed in estimation. Since the participants are involved in the creation of the estimate, they are more likely to put in extra effort when needed to achieve dates that seemed reasonable when the estimate was made but prove difficult to achieve in practice.

A good estimate is also specific and detailed. You should decompose the testing work to be done, from the activities in the fundamental test process all the way down to individual tasks. Ideally, each task should be one, two, or maybe three days in duration; have a clearly defined deliverable or other way of measuring completion; and have a single owner. The resources and other costs associated with each task should be clearly defined. If there are other people whose participation is required to complete a task—for example, stakeholders who must review a test plan before it's finalized—then that should be clearly identified in the estimate (as well documented in the test strategy or test plan).

A good estimate should not be missing anything. Remember to include all activities within the fundamental test process. That includes the test closure tasks—you'll often have to fight for this, but do so because that supports greater efficiency on the next project.

Finally, a good estimate is not optimistic. Yes, you heard that right. As Fred Brooks wrote in *The Mythical Man-Month*, unwarranted optimism is the bane of the manager's life because it sets up situations in which disappointment is inevitable. Instead, the duration, effort, and cost associated with each task must be predicted with hard-eyed realism. If that results in a cost that is too high or a date that is too late, then the thing not to do is to pretend that the impossible outcome that is desired can somehow by ineffable magic be achieved. No, the thing to do is to descope to fit within cost and schedule constraints. Realistic estimation can be the start of a negotiation that includes such descoping.

Yes, this is politically difficult. Yes, it is hard work to create good estimates. However, by following best practices and by staying focused on achieving the test objectives for the project within defined constraints, it can be done.

Test Execution Estimation

"When will we ever finish testing?" Many test managers have heard some version of this question, usually with a greater or lesser degree of exasperation depending on how far beyond the original estimated end date of test execution the project has gone. During the estimation process, project participants and managers will carefully scrutinize the test manager's estimated test execution cost, effort, and—above all—duration.

This scrutiny is something of a Murphy's Law scenario for the test manager because estimation of test execution is particularly hard to do—at least to any degree of reliability. Test execution increases in cost, effort, and duration when the size of the system increases, assuming that the scope of testing is proportional to the size of the system. Test execution increases in cost, effort, and duration when the quality of the system decreases, especially if most of the defects found during test execution are to be fixed. Therefore, estimating test execution should involve the following two steps:

- First, estimate the number of tests based on the size of the system. Ideally, you can use historical data such as the average number of tests per requirement or per quality risk from similar past projects to produce this estimate. Then, using the average number of testing hours per week per tester, and the average number of effort hours per test, you can calculate how long it will take to run each test at least once.
- Next, factor in the quality of the software. Again, using historical data such as the average number of defects per developer-hour on similar past projects, estimate the number of defects you'll find. Using historical data from past test execution efforts, determine how long it will take to find those defects and for those defects to be fixed.

These estimates can be done using relatively simple spreadsheets. There are examples of such spreadsheets in the Basic Library and Advanced Library[22] on the RBCS website.

To the extent that you made any assumptions during these two steps, be sure to document those assumptions and discuss them with project participants and stakeholders.

Estimation Factors

A large number of factors can affect the cost, effort, and duration of tasks throughout the test process. As a test manager, you need to take these factors into account; otherwise, a reasonable-sounding estimate can prove woefully inaccurate. Let's review these factors here, in no particular order:

- The required level of quality of the system. When testing a safety-critical system such as elevator control software, or a mission-critical system such as a banking application, or a system that affects many people such as a massive multiplayer game, the quality of the final deliverable must be high. This means not only must the test coverage be thorough on multiple dimensions but also most if not all the defects found by testing must be repaired.

---

22. You can find the RBCS Advanced Library at http://www.rbcs-us.com/software-testing-resources/library/advanced-library.

- The size of the system to be tested. As noted earlier, the size of the system influences the number of tests needed to achieve a given level of coverage and confidence. That probably struck you as a pretty obvious comment. What might not be obvious is that the increase in testing effort is generally nonlinear as the size of the system increases. A system of systems with five component systems is going to take much more time and effort to test than the total time and effort that would be required to test all of the component systems by themselves.
- The quality of the software delivered. As also noted earlier, the more the bugs, the longer the testing takes. The test manager should consider the practices of the business analysts, software architects, programmers, and others on the team. If you can expect to receive high-quality deliverables, the entire test process will go more smoothly.[23]
- Historical data on the testing time, cost, and effort required on previous projects. The availability of such data is very helpful, not only for estimating test execution as noted earlier but also for estimating other parts of the test process. This data can be augmented with industry data or benchmark data from other organizations, but you should be careful when doing so. Unless you control for the other factors mentioned here, you can get reasonable-sounding but entirely inaccurate estimates by using other people's data.
- Process factors. Some of these factors are internal testing factors, such as the test process described in the test strategy and the process maturity of that test process. Other factors are external, such as the software lifecycle in use in the organization and the process maturity of that lifecycle. In addition, since the overall project estimate is often an input to the test estimation process, the accuracy of that estimate matters too.
- Material factors. Again, some of these factors are internal to the test organization, such as the extent of test automation; the utility, cost, and availability of tools and test environments; and the ability to produce and perhaps even reuse test data, test scripts, and other test work products. Other factors are external. For example, if the developers have sufficient environments, they won't need to impinge on the test environments to debug their software. If business analysts and software architects provide sufficient information in terms of requirements and designs, testers will find it easier to design, implement, and execute valid and sufficient tests.

---

23. There's great data on the impact of quality (or lack of it) in *Economics of Software Quality* by Capers Jones and Olivier Bonsignour.

- People factors. These factors can be the most important influences on the success or failure of a project, and that includes the ability to hit schedule, cost, and effort targets derived during estimation. To maximize the likelihood of success, everyone from the individual contributors to the project managers and from senior technical staff to executives and senior management must help move the project forward. This includes making and keeping commitments, having realistic expectations about what can be achieved, bringing the proper technical, business, and testing skills to each task, having experience with similar past projects, and maintaining a positive, solutions-oriented attitude. The project team should be stable, with minimal turnover, and when turnover is unavoidable, proper knowledge transfer should occur during the transition. Within the project team, including between testers and non-testers, positive and supportive relationships should be cultivated and sustained. Adequate and timely support should be available for the test and debugging environments. When outside contractors and consultants are required, successful projects include people who are a good fit in terms of skills, attitude, past experience, and the ability to form good relationships with the team.
- Complexity. Increased complexity, like increased size, has a nonlinear impact on the cost, effort, and duration of projects. Complexity in this context does not refer solely to code complexity, though that can also be a factor. Complex processes, whether the complexity is necessary such as on a regulated project or unnecessary such as when people are micromanaged, lead to inefficient overhead activities and typically mistakes. Complex organizational structures or project team compositions likewise lead to more overhead and more opportunities for miscommunication and overlooked project stakeholders. This includes situations where the project team is distributed in a complex fashion, such as when there is little or no overlap in normal working hours between the various locations. Complex technology often brings with it a higher level of defects, simply because it's harder for the programmers to get it right the first time. Even when all testing and project stakeholders are known, a large, complex, diverse set of such stakeholders will have disparate goals, requirements, and expectations, making it harder to succeed in the eyes of all stakeholders.
- Significant ramp-up, training, and orientation needs. In general, a team that has the right skills, has worked together before, and has done similar projects will work much more effectively and efficiently.

- Newness. While people typically like to work on projects that have new attributes—tools, technology, processes, techniques, custom hardware, testware, and so on—each new attribute brings with it elements of the unknown. Learning about new things is great, but test managers should remember that it takes longer than doing familiar tasks.

- Detailed test documentation. This factor is pretty obvious, but people do forget about it. If you have to write detailed test plans and the testers must write detailed tests, that adds time and effort. This is especially true in regulated or contractual situations because the risk of missing some important detail is so high that even more effort must be spent checking the documents. If the regulatory or contractual standard is new to the test team, the effort will be even more considerable.

- Complex timing. I worked on a project once where the test environment was highly complex and being built as we proceeded through the project, for reasons of cost and availability of components. We had numerous delays and inefficiencies when essential elements of the test environment weren't ready. This affected our ability to develop our tests—which were heavily automated using custom-built tools that required testing in the test environment—as well as to execute the tests.

- Fragile test data. When data must be regenerated after each use, when data cannot be shared by multiple testers during test execution, when data has time-dependent elements that must be adjusted to the precision of a day (or worse yet down to a second), that data is fragile and will require a lot of extra effort.

Example: Estimation Factors

In Figure 2–14, we revisit the deviation-from-plan test log. I'm focusing on one specific deviation from the plan, the one related to the TIBCO licenses.

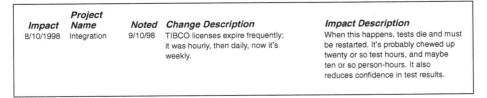

Impact	Project Name	Noted	Change Description	Impact Description
8/10/1998	Integration	9/10/98	TIBCO licenses expire frequently; it was hourly, then daily, now it's weekly.	When this happens, tests die and must be restarted. It's probably chewed up twenty or so test hours, and maybe ten or so person-hours. It also reduces confidence in test results.

Figure 2–14   *Deviation-from-plan test log*

In our plans and estimates, we had assumed a stable test environment. This hypothetical test environment was one where all infrastructure was properly configured and no false positives or test-blocking events occurred. Of course, this assumption was inaccurate. This inaccurate assumption led to an inaccurate estimate and a flawed plan.

As an interesting side note, about two months after this note was entered in the test log, we discovered that a license key had not been properly installed at the beginning of testing. You might say, "Well, Rex, if you had a better pre-test checklist, you might have caught this." That's true for smaller, simpler, more stable test environments. On this project, we actually had a database that tracked complex dependencies between test cases, hardware, infrastructure, and software in the test environment and testers. Even with such a database, there's a limit to how fine-grained you can be in what you track. As a manager, you can—and should—try to mitigate test-related project risks. However, to assume that you will be able to mitigate all test-related project risks is a dangerous, optimistic fantasy that will result in inaccurate, unrealistic estimates.

Estimation Techniques

Both bottom-up and top-down approaches can be used for estimation. Bottom-up estimates are based on each task; that is, you estimate each task individually and then derive the project estimate from those estimates. Top-down estimates are based on the overall project; that is, you estimate for the test effort or perhaps for the high-level test activities all at once.

There are various test estimation techniques in use:

- Intuition, guesses, and experience
- Work breakdown structures, such as Gantt charts and tools like Microsoft Project
- Team estimation sessions, either unstructured or structured with some approach like the Delphic oracle, three point, or wideband
- Test Point Analysis, which is usable when function points are available
- Company standards and norms, which can influence and in some cases determine test estimates
- The typical or believed-typical percentages of the overall project effort or staffing level, such as the infamous tester-developer ratio
- Organizational history and metrics, including proven tester-developer ratios within the company
- Industry averages, metrics, and other predictive models

> **ISTQB Glossary**
>
> **Wide Band Delphi:** An expert-based test estimation technique that aims at making an accurate estimation using the collective wisdom of the team members.

Achieving Good Estimation

As a test manager, you can create a good estimate yourself, with the assistance of your team and ideally good historical metrics from similar past projects. However, you can't use that estimate—you cannot achieve good estimation, in effect—without the approval of management. Whether working as an employee within an organization or as an outside testing services provider, you'll need to go to management for approval of your estimate.

It's a good idea to be ready to justify your estimate. Why will it take that long? Why will it cost that much? Why is that level of effort required? Be ready to discuss, in detail, the benefits and objectives served by the testing you are proposing. We'll talk more about how to create a business justification for testing later in this chapter, in section 2.7.

Even when you have a solid business case, in my experience, negotiation typically ensues (I have rarely gotten approval for the first estimate I delivered). At that point, a new set of relevant questions arises. What if we reduce the resources? What if we reduce the time, especially the time for test execution? Are there other options that will reduce cost? As you discuss these questions with management, be sure to highlight the trade-offs that they are making with these reductions. Renegotiate goals for the objectives. For example, if you typically have a goal of 95 percent defect detection effectiveness, make sure people understand that, if the test execution period is cut in half, you will not be able to achieve that same level of effectiveness.

I encourage you to have a positive, can-do attitude throughout this process. Work with management to achieve a practical plan for testing. At the same time, politely but firmly refuse to commit to something you can't do or commit to achieve with half the resources the goals that you know would require all the resources. State up front the need to achieve the proper balance of quality, schedule, budget, and features. You can also mention that management has other options to reduce the cost of testing, such as ensuring thorough requirements or user story reviews, implementing good automated unit testing and continuous integration practices together with code coverage targets, and in some cases outsourcing expensive types of testing such as performance and usability testing.

Another important topic to discuss with management is the level of uncertainty inherent in the estimate based on the level of information available. The cone of uncertainty is a widely discussed project management concept that refers to a high level of imprecision inherent in early estimates. That level of imprecision goes down as the project proceeds and more information is available. Of course, on many projects, the irony is that the precision comes too late because precise numbers were needed for the estimate up front. Agile lifecycles deal with this problem by providing certainty in terms of schedule and budget targets in exchange for uncertainty in terms of specific feature delivery. In sequential lifecycles, the cone of uncertainty means that you have to estimate conservatively at the beginning and refine the estimate as you get new information.[24]

Some Rules Derived from Jones

Industry averages are also useful in estimation. In Figure 2–15, you see figures derived from Capers Jones's book *Estimating Software Costs*.[25] Jones has gathered data from thousands of projects across hundreds of clients, which makes his figures quite useful.

Task, activity, and size estimation rules		Project effort ratios (testing includes bug fixing)	
Person-months for the project	$(FP/150) \cdot FP^{0.4}$	Coding:testing:other (10 FP)	2:1:1
Effort to develop a test case	1 person·hr	Coding:testing:other (100 FP)	4:3:3
Number of test cases needed	$FP^{1.2}$	Coding:testing:other (1 KFP)	3:3:4
Number of bugs to expect	$FP^{1.25}$	Coding:testing:other (10 KFP)	2:3:5
U.S. average bugs per function point	5.00	Coding:testing:other (100 KFP)	1:2:3
Bug origin, req:des:code:doc:regress	3:4:5:2:1	Coding:testing:other (end-user)	6:3:1
DRE for a formal design inspection	65%	Coding:testing:other (MIS)	1:1:2
DRE for a formal code inspection	60%	Coding:testing:other (systems)	2:3:5
DRE for a well-designed test suite	30%	Coding:testing:other (commercial)	2:3:3
U.S. average DRE across project	85%	Coding:testing:other (military)	1:1:3

DRE (defect removal effectiveness): proportion of bugs present in the system (at the time some quality control activity took place) removed by that activity

Figure 2–15   *Estimation rules derived from Capers Jones's industry data*

---

24. You can find more on the cone of uncertainty in Steve McConnell's book *Software Estimation*.
25. You can find a number of useful metrics and data in *Estimating Software Costs, 2nd Edition*, by Capers Jones.

Jones uses function points for some of his figures. Function points are based on counting the size of an application based on its requirements, in a rigorous and defined fashion. You can also convert from lines of code to function points—and vice versa—according to Jones. For reference, one function point is about 125 lines of C code and about 55 lines of C++ code.

Let's look at some particularly interesting metrics here. For example, Jones has found that, on average, there are five bugs per function point. That equates to one bug for every 25 lines of C code and one bug for every 11 lines of C++ code.

Where do bugs come from? Jones has found that, typically, 20 percent of bugs were introduced in requirements, 25 percent of bugs were introduced in design, 33 percent were introduced in coding, 15 percent were introduced in documentation, and 7 percent were introduced as bad fixes (regressions).

Look at the defect removal effectiveness figures. DRE, or defect removal effectiveness, is the proportion of bugs that were present in the system at the time that some quality control activity took place and were removed by that activity. For example, Jones has found that formal design inspections remove on average 65 percent of the defects present in the design at the time of the review.

The right-hand side of the table includes effort ratios relating coding, testing, and other activities. One thing to keep in mind about the testing figures is that they include the development time required to fix the bugs.

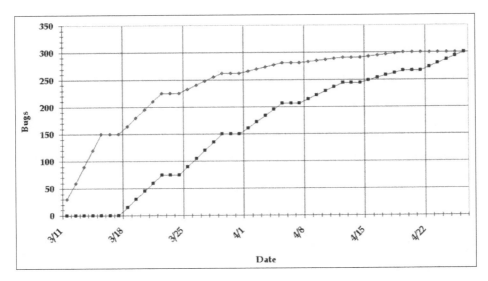

Figure 2–16 *Use of historical metrics to predict defects*

Predicting Bug Find/Fix/Confirm Duration

In Figure 2–16, you see an example of the use of historical metrics to estimate the time required to find, fix, and confirm as fixed the critical bugs, which is a critical part of the test execution estimate. In the source spreadsheet that creates this chart, I used some historical data from a couple of past projects along with some simple models for bug find and fix rates. The model is parameterized so that it responds to the number of testers and developers assigned. At their core, models like this one rely on historical data, formulas, and constants derived from previous projects. The more data you have, the more accurate your model can be and the more you can predict the accuracy of the estimate.

1. Initial Project Planning Period
  1.1. Test Planning, Monitoring, and Control
    1.1.1. Create system integration test plan (5d)
    1.1.2. Participate in overall project planning (5d)
  1.2. Test Analysis
    1.2.1. Perform quality risk analysis (5 d)
    1.2.2. Outline test suites needed in each iteration (1 d)
2. Iteration One (Very High Priority Features)
  2.1. Test Planning, Monitoring, and Control
    2.1.1. Adjust plan as needed for this iteration (1 d)
    2.1.2. Guide testing work during this iteration (on-going)
  2.2. Test Analysis: Adjust quality risk analysis (1 d)
  2.3. Test Design: Design test suites and cases for this iteration (30 d)
  2.4. Test Implementation: Implement test suites for this iteration (30 d)
  2.5. Test Execution: Execute test suites for this iteration (duration 6 weeks)
  2.6. Evaluating Exit Criteria and Reporting
    2.6.1. Check test results against exit criteria in test plan (on-going)
    2.6.2. Report test results to project management team (on-going)
3. Iteration Two (High Priority Features)
  3.1. Test Planning, Monitoring, and Control
    3.1.1. Adjust plan as needed for this iteration (1 d)
    3.1.2. Guide testing work during this iteration (on-going)
  3.2. Test Analysis: Adjust quality risk analysis (1 d)
  3.3. Test Design: Design test suites and cases for this iteration (30 d)
  3.4. Test Implementation: Implement test suites for this iteration (30 d)
  3.5. Test Execution: Execute test suites for this iteration (duration 6 weeks)
  3.6. Evaluating Exit Criteria and Reporting
    3.6.1. Check test results against exit criteria in test plan (on-going)
    3.6.2. Report test results to project management team (on-going)

Figure 2–17   *Adding estimated effort for planning and iterations one and two*

HELLOCARMS Estimation **Exercise**

Revisit your solution to the exercise in Chapter 1, section 1.2. Develop an estimate for the testing work, using the activities you outlined in that solution. You should also consider your quality risk analysis and test plan.

Decompose down to major tasks (3–10 days).

Document any assumptions you make.

HELLOCARMS Estimation **Debrief**

To create this solution, I proceeded in two steps. First, I went through the solution to the Chapter 1, section 2 exercise, adding estimated effort in person-days to each task.

The estimated effort for planning and iterations one and two are shown in Figure 2–17. They are shown for iterations three and four in Figure 2–18 and for iteration five and the post-project period in Figure 2–19.

```
4.  Iteration Three (Medium Priority Features)
    4.1. Test Planning, Monitoring, and Control
         4.1.1.  Adjust plan as needed for this iteration (1 d)
         4.1.2.  Guide testing work during this iteration (on-going)
    4.2. Test Analysis: Adjust quality risk analysis (1 d)
    4.3. Test Design: Design test suites and cases for this iteration (30 d)
    4.4. Test Implementation: Implement test suites for this iteration (30 d)
    4.5. Test Execution: Execute test suites for this iteration (duration 6 weeks)
    4.6. Evaluating Exit Criteria and Reporting
         4.6.1.  Check test results against exit criteria in test plan (on-going)
         4.6.2.  Report test results to project management team (on-going)
5.  Iteration Four (Low Priority Features)
    5.1. Test Planning, Monitoring, and Control
         5.1.1.  Adjust plan as needed for this iteration (1 d)
         5.1.2.  Guide testing work during this iteration (on-going)
    5.2. Test Analysis: Adjust quality risk analysis (1 d)
    5.3. Test Design: Design test suites and cases for this iteration (30 d)
    5.4. Test Implementation: Implement test suites for this iteration (30 d)
    5.5. Test Execution: Execute test suites for this iteration ( duration 6 weeks)
    5.6. Evaluating Exit Criteria and Reporting
         5.6.1.  Check test results against exit criteria in test plan (on-going)
         5.6.2.  Report test results to project management team (on-going)
```

Figure 2–18 *Adding estimated effort for iterations three and four*

```
6.  Iteration Five (Very Low Priority Features)
    6.1. Test Planning, Monitoring, and Control
         6.1.1.  Adjust plan as needed for this iteration (1 d)
         6.1.2.  Guide testing work during this iteration (on-going)
    6.2. Test Analysis: Adjust quality risk analysis (1 d)
    6.3. Test Design: Design test suites and cases for this iteration (30 d)
    6.4. Test Implementation: Implement test suites for this iteration (30 d)
    6.5. Test Execution: Execute test suites for this iteration (duration 6 weeks)
    6.6. Evaluating Exit Criteria and Reporting
         6.6.1.  Check test results against exit criteria in test plan (on-going)
         6.6.2.  Report test results to project management team (on-going)
7.  Post Project Period – Test Closure
    7.1. Check completion and document variances from plan (5 d)
    7.2. Participate in project retrospective; hold test retrospective (2 d)
    7.3. Finalize testware for archiving and hand off (20 d)
    7.4. Document test environment configuration (10 d)
```

Figure 2–19   *Adding estimated effort for iteration five and the post-project period*

Some comments on these estimates:

- I am assuming a skilled test team that can work with relatively high-level, logical test cases.
- I am assuming approximately equal content size for each iteration, with two person-months of test design and implementation work for each iteration and a six-week test execution period, consisting of three two-week test passes.

Second, I put this into Microsoft Project, setting up the appropriate dependencies between iterations and major activities. You would need to do this by using sticky notes on a white board if you did not have access to such a tool. By the way, I chose January 1 as the arbitrary start date for the project.

Here are some comments on this work breakdown structure:

- I am assuming one test manager, two test leads, and six test analysts in the test team.
- I don't have a lot of information on the amount of development effort or the number of bugs I will find, so this is a first estimate.
- I would need to align this with the project plan and development plan, to ensure that they were consistent.
- If we assume that I will receive weekly test releases during test execution, then I should try to overlap the analysis and design tasks of each subsequent iteration more completely with the previous iteration so that test execution always starts on a Monday.

The Gantt charts produced by Microsoft Project are shown in Figure 2–20, Figure 2–21, and Figure 2–22.

ID	Task Name	Duration	Start	Finish
1	Start of Project Pl anning	0 days	1/1	1/1
2	Initial Project Planning Period	10 days	1/1	1/14
3	Test Planning and Control	10 days	1/1	1/14
4	Create System and system integration testplan	5 days	1/8	1/14
5	Participate in overall project planning	5 days	1/1	1/7
6	Test Analysis and Design	6 days	1/1	1/8
7	Perform quality risk analysis	6 days	1/1	1/7
8	Outline test suites needed in each iteration	1 day	1/8	1/8
9	Iteration One (Very High Priority Features)	42 days	1/15	3/13
10	Test Planning and Control	40 days	1/15	3/11
11	Adjust plan as needed for this iteration	1 day	1/16	1/15
12	Guide testing work during this iteration	8 wks	1/15	3/11
13	Test Analysis and Design	6 days	1/16	1/23
14	Adjust quality risk analysis	1 day	1/16	1/16
15	Design test suites and cases for this iteration	1 wk	1/19	1/23
16	Test Implementation and Execution	35 days	1/26	3/13
17	Implement test suites for this iteration	1 wk	1/26	1/30
18	Execute test suites for this iteration	6 wks	2/2	3/13
19	Evaluating Exit Criteria and Reporting	30 days	2/2	3/13
20	Check test results against exit criteria in test plan	6 wks	2/2	3/13
21	Report test results to project management team	6 wks	2/2	3/13
22	Iteration Two (High Priority Features)	42 days	3/2	4/28
23	Test Planning and Control	40 days	3/2	4/24
24	Adjust plan as needed for this iteration	1 day	3/2	3/2
25	Guide testing work during this iteration	8 wks	3/2	4/24
26	Test Analysis and Design	6 days	3/3	3/10
27	Adjust quality risk analysis	1 day	3/3	3/3
28	Design test suites and cases for this iteration	1 wk	3/4	3/10
29	Test Implementation and Execution	35 days	3/11	4/28
30	Implement test suites for this iteration	1 wk	3/11	3/17
31	Execute test suites for this iteration	6 wks	3/18	4/28
32	Evaluating Exit Criteria and Reporting	30 days	3/18	4/28
33	Check test results against exit criteria in test plan	6 wks	3/18	4/28
34	Report test results to project management team	6 wks	3/18	4/28

Figure 2–20   Gantt for planning and iterations one and two

ID	Task Name	Duration	Start	Finish
35	Iteration Three (Medium Priority Features)	42 days	4/15	6/11
36	Test Planning and Control	40 days	4/15	6/9
37	Adjust plan as needed for this iteration	1 day	4/16	4/16
38	Guide testing work during this iteration	8 wks	4/15	6/9
39	Test Analysis and Design	6 days	4/16	4/23
40	Adjust quality risk analysis	1 day	4/16	4/16
41	Design test suites and cases for this iteration	1 wk	4/17	4/23
42	Test Implementation and Execution	35 days	4/24	6/11
43	Implement test suites for this iteration	1 wk	4/24	4/30
44	Execute test suites for this iteration	6 wks	5/1	6/11
45	Evaluating Exit Criteria and Reporting	30 days	5/1	6/11
46	Check test results against exit criteria in test plan	6 wks	5/1	6/11
47	Report test results to project management team	6 wks	5/1	6/11
48	Iteration Four (Low Priority Features)	42 days	5/29	7/27
49	Test Planning and Control	40 days	5/29	7/23
50	Adjust plan as needed for this iteration	1 day	5/29	5/29
51	Guide testing work during this iteration	8 wks	5/29	7/23
52	Test Analysis and Design	6 days	6/1	6/8
53	Adjust quality risk analysis	1 day	6/1	6/1
54	Design test suites and cases for this iteration	1 wk	6/2	6/8
55	Test Implementation and Execution	35 days	6/9	7/27
56	Implement test suites for this iteration	1 wk	6/9	6/15
57	Execute test suites for this iteration	6 wks	6/16	7/27
58	Evaluating Exit Criteria and Reporting	30 days	6/16	7/27
59	Check test results against exit criteria in test plan	6 wks	6/16	7/27
60	Report test results to project management team	6 wks	6/16	7/27

Figure 2–21   Gantt for iterations three and four

ID	Task Name	Duration	Start	Finish		1st Quarter			2nd Quarter			3rd Quarter			4th Q
					Dec	Jan	Feb	Mar	Apr	May	Jun	Jul	Aug	Sep	Oct
61	Iteration Five (Very Low Priority Features)	42 days	7/14	9/9											
62	Test Planning and Control	40 days	7/14	9/7											
63	Adjust plan as needed for this iteration	1 day	7/14	7/14											
64	Guide testing work during this iteration	8 wks	7/14	9/7											
65	Test Analysis and Design	6 days	7/15	7/22											
66	Adjust quality risk analysis	1 day	7/15	7/15											
67	Design test suites and cases for this iteration	1 wk	7/16	7/22											
68	Test Implementation and Execution	35 days	7/23	9/9											
69	Implement test suites for this iteration	1 wk	7/23	7/29											
70	Execute test suites for this iteration	6 wks	7/30	9/9											
71	Evaluating Exit Criteria and Reporting	30 days	7/30	9/9											
72	Check test results against exit criteria in test plan	6 wks	7/30	9/9											
73	Report test results to project management team	6 Wks	7/30	9/9											
74	Post Project Period	5 days	9/10	9/16											
75	Test Planning and Control	5 days	9/10	9/16											
76	Document variances from plan	1 wk	9/10	9/16											
77	Participate in project retrospective	1 day	9/10	9/10											
78	Test Closure Activities	5 days	9/10	9/16											
79	Finalize testware for archiving or handoff	1 wk	9/10	9/16											
80	Document test environment configuration	1 wk	9/10	9/16											

Figure 2–22   *Gantt for iteration five and the post-project period*

2.6   Defining and Using Test Metrics

Learning objectives

(K2) Describe and compare typical testing related metrics.

(K2) Compare the different dimensions of test progress monitoring.

(K4) Analyze and report test results in terms of the residual risk, defect status, test execution status, test coverage status, and confidence to provide insight and recommendations that enable project stakeholders to make release decision.

Many clichés are clichés because they are true, and the management cliché that says what gets measured gets done is perhaps the truest of all. The act of measuring something focuses attention on the factors that affect it, and since attention is limited, that has the side effect of taking attention away from other things. Since those things that are not measured will not be noticed, they are easily ignored—sometimes with dangerous results. So, when setting up metrics for any activity, we must be very careful to anticipate the consequences of our chosen measures and what we've chosen not to measure.

Just to get the terminology straight, let's review the ISTQB definitions for some words I'll be using in this section. First is *metric*, which is defined as "a measurement scale and the method used for measurement." This leads us to the next term, *measurement scale*, which is defined as "a scale that constrains the type of data analysis that can be performed on it." Also, there's *measurement*, which is defined as "the process of assigning a number or category to an entity to describe an attribute of that entity." Finally, there's *measure*, which is defined as "the number or category assigned to an attribute of an entity by making a measurement."

Those definitions are a bit abstract, so let's look at an example, a temperature metric. If we select Celsius as the measurement scale, that is a numeric scale, specifically decimal numbers. The measure can be any decimal number, provided it is at least ?273.15 (which is absolute zero) and no more than a temperature referred to as "absolute hot" (which is the temperature at which the laws of physics break down). If I'd chosen Kelvin as the scale, then negative measures are not allowed. So, you can see that the scale constrains the analysis. Using a thermometer is a way of performing a measurement, and a specific temperature value on that thermometer at a given point in time is a measure.

As a test manager and consultant, I have seen four categories of test metrics in use:

- Project metrics: These are metrics used to determine how we are doing in terms of achieving the goals of the project. In testing, these metrics often have a direct relationship to established exit criteria in the test plan or test strategy document. One example of a project metric is the percentage of tests run, typically further broken down into the percentage passed and percentage failed. Another example of a project metric is the percentage of test effort expended compared to the work breakdown structure.
- Product metrics: These are metrics used to measure the product. In testing, these metrics will often relate to the quality of the product or the degree to which the quality has been assessed. Examples of product quality metrics are defect density and failure rate. An example of product quality assessment metrics is the percentage of requirements and risks that have been covered by testing.
- Process metrics: These are metrics used to measure the effectiveness or efficiency of a process or the degree of stakeholder satisfaction with that process. In testing, these metrics can measure the test process specifically or the development process as a whole. One example is the defect detection effectiveness metric discussed in section 2.3 earlier in this chapter. Another example is the cost of internal failure, which I'll discuss in the next section.

■ People metrics: These are metrics used to measure a person or group, often tied to some agreed-upon goals. In testing, we might choose to measure the percentage of the test team holding an ISTQB Foundation level or Advanced level certificate. These people metrics can be particularly dangerous if misused or if a process metric is mistakenly confused as a people metric. People can become demotivated when measured unfairly, or they will find ways to game the metric so that they benefit. Since this is such a sensitive topic, we'll return to the topic of assessing, motivating, and managing people in Chapter 7.[26]

While these are categories of metrics, note that they are not orthogonal categories. In other words, a particular metric could belong in multiple categories. The syllabus gives the example of a defect trend chart that shows the daily arrival rate of defects. That chart can be used to assess project progress if we are referring to an exit criterion that says we should test for at least one week without finding any defects. That chart can also be used to assess the quality of the product, because a decreasing or zero rate of defect detection can—assuming sufficiency of test coverage and continuing test execution—indicate a product that has few undiscovered remaining defects. That chart can also be used to assess the test process, because the largest number of defects will be found early in an efficient test execution process. That chart should not be used to assess people though. For example, showing a breakdown of defects by individual tester can create a dysfunctional contest between testers to see who can find the most bugs, distracting attention away from the other objectives of testing.

In this section, we are going to focus primarily on project metrics, with some of those metrics also having process and product attributes or implications. As I mentioned, I'll cover people management issues, including people metrics, in Chapter 7.[27]

Using Test Metrics

Early in my career as a test manager, I was lucky enough to work for a company that did contract software development for IBM, including its mainframe operating system team. This is the same group that Fred Brooks once managed, and Fred is at least a patron saint if not a minor deity for software engineers. (If

---

26. I discuss this in even more detail in my upcoming book *Expert Test Manager*.
27. More information on the management use of product and process metrics is found in the Expert Test Management syllabus. More information on the use of process metrics is found in the Expert Improving the Test Process syllabus.

you're not familiar with Fred, you should be; every test manager should read *The Mythical Man-Month*, which I was fortunate to read at UCLA while getting my computer science and engineering degree.) That team has always been on the leading edge of software engineering best practices and their testing practices were no exception.

I learned a number of things from that job, but one of the most important was how to set up a consistent, meaningful set of metrics to track test progress and report test results, because we modeled our test management and reporting systems on IBM's. During test execution, I attended a daily project status meeting where all the managers (including me) had to present their current status. The metrics I used were very effective in helping everyone, from technical staff to executive managers, understand test progress and status. Using the metrics, I would explain where we were in our testing plan and what the results were telling us. Being relatively new to test management—with only three years experience at that point—sometimes I made mistakes in my guidance of the team and of the test process. The senior and executive managers in that meeting did not scruple to point that out. While that was sometimes embarrassing, it had the desired effect because I never made the same mistake twice.

The choice of proper metrics is especially critical for testing because testing measures the quality of the system. These measures are necessarily indirect because quality ultimately is an experience that customers, users, project participants, and other stakeholders will have or not have, in a manner of degrees. In other words, people are usually not completely dissatisfied or completely satisfied, but they have some level of satisfaction with quality. Testing measures quality, and quality is not only to some extent amorphous and ineffable, quality is also multidimensional, and the different quality attributes mean different things and have different levels of importance to different stakeholders. So when putting metrics in place, you must consider a number of factors very carefully.

Don't make the mistake of simply taking whatever canned graphs and metrics your test management tool produces and spraying those out via email on a daily basis to all project stakeholders. That's a sure way to drown people in irrelevant tactical details and to invite micromanagement of the testing. Instead, aim to have a limited set of relevant metrics. Create a small set of metrics that relate directly to specific objectives. These objectives can be exit criteria from the test plan as well as the higher-level objectives defined in the test policy. It should be possible to explain why each metric matters and how it relates to a key project, process, or product objective.

Make sure the metrics are balanced, in the sense that if the project is in trouble, at least one chosen metric will point out the problem. For example, if one of your metrics shows the cumulative number of defects found and resolved on a daily basis, that metric might show that the daily defect discovery rate has been at zero for a week. That could be good news, but what if your team's not finding defects because they are completely stuck and can't run any tests? You need another metric that shows the test execution progress, which would reveal the problem. Usually, having a good set of objectives that relate clearly to the chosen metrics will help promote balance.

You should define the metrics you use to be clear and understandable, but don't assume that people will understand them without any explanation or education. The best practice is to work through a process of teaching the stakeholders what the metrics are, how they relate to various objectives, what each metric tells you, and how to recognize common signs of trouble in each metric. Doing this prior to starting test execution will reduce the kind of confusion and wishful thinking that can lead to test results being misunderstood, sometimes with disastrous consequences. The usual problem here is that stakeholders fail to recognize trouble, or they put their heads in the sand and pretend the metrics aren't telling them bad news. It's easier to get away with pretending not to see bad news that's staring you in the face when most of the people around you are confused.

When tracking the agreed-upon metrics, take advantage of tools where possible to make the process more efficient, but don't use tools as a substitute for thinking. I saw a test manager eviscerate his credibility in a project status meeting when he showed up with a set of graphs he clearly hadn't studied carefully prior to the meeting. A project manager asked, "What does it mean that the closure period for defects has been steadily increasing for the last two weeks? Why is that happening?" There was no obvious explanation for the delay in defect repair, and the test manager was not ready to answer this important question. He looked stupid. So, as you track the metrics, compare what the metrics say *is* happening to what you and other stakeholders would *expect* to be happening. If there is a divergence, make sure you understand, and can explain, the reason or reasons.

In some cases, the reason for divergence is a problem in the data. Invalid data can be a real problem with meaningful metrics. I worked with one client to define a testing dashboard. As we started to populate the dashboard with real test data, we found myriad problems such as a failure to establish proper traceability between tests and requirements, not properly associating defect reports with test cases, and other types of internal consistency issues. Invalid data can make the status appear either unrealistically negative *or* unrealistically positive, or in some cases it can make some of the metrics unrealistically negative while others look unrealistically positive. Never report test status using metrics that are based on underlying data that you suspect—or worse yet, know—is invalid. It's better to go into a meeting and say, "We're having some trouble with our test result data right now and I'll get you updated metrics as soon as we fix it," than to put up charts and tables you know are wrong and hope to get away with it. Not only is the latter behavior unethical, you're quite likely to be caught at it, especially when your audience includes detail-oriented and savvy senior managers. These people didn't get to be senior managers by being stupid and easily gulled.

In terms of reporting of metrics, remember that your objective in presenting on test progress and status is to provide insight to the audience. It is not an exercise in dazzling them with your command of tactical details or impressing them with how much you know. Ask your stakeholders if your test status reports are easily understood and provide them with the information they need. If they answer no, find out why immediately and fix the problem. As long as that problem persists, you are wasting your time and breath giving a presentation no one but you understands.

Sometimes the problem with a metric is how you choose to present it. In some cases a table that shows details about the current status or a histogram that summarizes current status—either is effectively a snapshot of a moment in time—is a good way to present information. In other cases, people really need to see trends that are emerging, in which case a time-based graph is the way you want to go. If in doubt, you might want to try both ways of presenting the same information and see which approach people prefer.

Dimensions of Test Progress Metrics

So, let's get more specific about metrics for measuring test progress. As I mentioned, these are metrics that allow us to measure project status, and often they have some relevance in terms of product and process too.

Ideally, a set of test progress metrics will have five main dimensions:

- Quality risks. One or more of the metrics should help people understand what the current status is in terms of quality risk. Which of the risks are fully mitigated? Which risks are associated with known defects? Which risks are not yet fully tested? We should be able to answer these questions if our testing strategy includes risk-based testing. I've had good results using histograms to show this information.

- Defects. One or more of the metrics should help people understand the current status in terms of defects. How many have been found? How many have been resolved? Typically, this is better displayed in a trend chart than in a table or histogram.

- Tests. One or more of the metrics should help people understand the current status in terms of test execution progress. How many tests have been run? How many pass? How many fail? How many are blocked? I've seen this done either in tables or in trend charts, though my preference is for a trend chart because tables are often too detailed and invite micromanagement.

- Coverage. One or more of the metrics should help people understand the current status in terms of how thoroughly the test basis has been tested. If requirements-based testing is part of the strategy, then we should be able to show how many of the requirements have been tested and, of those, how many are known to have problems. The coverage of supported configurations, code, data, user types, use cases, and user stories is also sometimes tracked. The best practice is to measure more than one type of coverage, especially if you are measuring only requirements coverage since requirements specifications are notoriously gappy.

- Confidence. While clearly connected to a major objective for testing in most cases, confidence is a tricky one to measure. One approach is to use a survey to measure it, asking people to react to a statement like, "I am confident that the product can be released to users now," gauging the reaction on a five-point Likert scale from "strongly agree" to "strongly disagree." However, the easier approach is to use the collective information from the other metrics, especially coverage, quality risks, and defect metrics, as a surrogate metric for confidence. Of course, the easiest approach is to do this purely subjectively, based on the test team's opinion, but my experience with that approach is that it puts at risk too much of the test team's credibility.

In addition to having these metrics and reporting, it's best to have them linked to explicit exit criteria in the test plan. This allows a truly objective assessment of how close we are to "done testing" based on the plan.

Let's look at some of the measurable metrics of test progress in the first four dimensions of quality risks, defects, tests, and coverage.

Quality Risk and Defect Metrics

For quality risk, one of the ways that I have measured and reported status is using a histogram or a pie chart that shows the quality risks in three categories: passed, failed, and pending. A quality risk is classified as passed, or mitigated, when all tests traceable to the quality risk have been run and currently classified as passed. Assuming that the depth of coverage is appropriate for those quality risks, as was discussed in a previous section, then the residual risk for those quality risks is very low. A quality risk is classified as failed when one or more tests traceable to the quality risk is currently classified as failed or when one or more must-fix bugs traceable to the quality risk is still active. A quality risk is classified as pending, or unmitigated, if no failures or must-fix bugs are traceable to it but some tests still remain to be run.

I particularly like the pie chart format for organizing this information. As an added step, you can use the risk priority number associated with each quality risk to weight how much area in the pie chart is allocated to quality risks based on their level of risk. If you do this weighting, the relative sizes of the three areas in the pie chart give a true measure of the residual level of overall quality risk.

Another approach that I have used, when more detail is needed, is to show quality risk coverage by category. The categories can be organized by the quality risk categories themselves—for example, functionality, reliability, usability, and so on—or by the physical or logical structure of the application, such as the different major subsystems or major functional areas. Coverage within each category can then be broken down as passed, failed, and pending. I've created these types of reports using stack-column charts, with quite effective results in terms of understandability for the stakeholders.

Both of these metrics, the aggregate risk pie chart and the detailed categorized risk histogram, are effective project and product metrics. They tell us about the level of quality risk remaining in the product, and they tell us how close the project is to reaching its quality risk mitigation targets.

Another metric that you can look at is the percentage of quality risks that were identified after the initial quality risk analysis. This is primarily a process metric in that a very high number (say, greater than 25 percent) could indicate a problem with identifying sufficient risks during the quality risk analysis process. It is also a project metric because it indicates moving quality risk mitigation targets, and as the number goes above a certain threshold (which would depend on how tightly the estimation had been performed), it indicates the need to revisit the budget and schedule to see how to best accommodate these new quality risks. I haven't had to use this metric personally, but if your organization tends to have trouble managing change and its impact, this metric might help you tell a convincing story about the need to do a better job in that regard.

For defect metrics, the old stand-by metric, which I have used for much of my career as a test manager and consultant, is a trend chart that shows the cumulative number of defects reported and the cumulative number of defects resolved. As the project proceeds successfully, the defect discovery rate should achieve its maximum as early as possible during test execution, producing a steep line for the cumulative number of defects reported. On a successful project, developers fix defects quickly, resulting in a similarly steep line for the cumulative number of defects resolved that parallels, rather than deviates away from, the cumulative number of defects reported. As the project reaches a successful conclusion, the cumulative number of defects reported line should go flat as the defect discovery rate goes to zero, and the cumulative number of defects resolved line ultimately intercepts it. This is sometimes referred to as "achieving convergence."

This way of presenting defect measurements is quite intuitive and effective for many stakeholders. However, it can exhibit some puzzling and even misleading characteristics. For example, if testing becomes blocked, the defect discovery rate may fall to zero, creating an optical illusion that the product's quality is stabilizing when in fact the very opposite is true. It's important that, as a test manager, you are ready to provide some context and explanation if this metric tells a misleading story.

I consider this metric to be both a product and a project metric. It is a product metric in that the rate of defect discovery and the backlog of unresolved defects both tell us about the quality—or lack of quality—in the product. It is a project metric when we compare how close we are to achieving convergence to how close we are to the planned project end date.

Another classic defect metric, used especially during reliability tests, is mean time between failure (MTBF). When software reliability growth models are being used, this metric may be shown on a trend graph. In hardware testing, the reliability of a system is sometimes calculated from the reliability of the components that make up the system, though I have some doubts as to the validity of those figures because they ignore the possibility of integration issues leading to overall system failure. During accelerated life tests or highly accelerated life tests (sometimes referred to as HALT tests), the mean time between failure is calculated based on the observed time to failure. In the more traditional reliability tests, a target mean time between failure is set during system design or even requirements specification, and then a reliability demonstration test is run during system test or system integration test. Some people would also run a reliability demonstration test during acceptance test, but I would only recommend that if such a reliability demonstration test had already been run and passed during a previous level of testing.

Mean time between failure is both a product and a project metric. It is a product metric because it measures the reliability of the application. It is a project metric because reaching—or failing to reach—reliability targets is a strong influence on readiness to release.

As with quality risks, defects can be categorized. I have done so in a number of ways. One way is to group defects by severity, which can be useful and interesting when compared to the expected distribution. Another way is to group defects by quality risk category, which can be useful and interesting when they are placed side by side in a histogram with the quality risk status. This type of chart is called a stacked column histogram, and while it's difficult to create, it can be very informative. A similar type of chart can be created using the logical or physical structure of the application as the basis for the categorization. These types of metrics give us insight into the relative quality of the product as well as, in comparison with targets for completion, where we stand on the project.

Another metric that I like to use is closure period, which is a measure of the quickness of defect repair. The Advanced syllabus refers to this as "the lag time from defect reporting to resolution." For any given defect report, its closure period is the date on which it was resolved minus the date on which it was opened. This can be calculated and shown on a trend chart. I like to show both the rolling closure period, which is the average closure period for all defects closed on or before a given date, and the daily closure period, which is the average closure period for all defects closed on a given date. Closure period is a process metric that shows the defect repair capability of the software development process. It is also a project metric that allows us to compare actual lag time for repair to targets or expectations.

Finally, another useful defect metric is the percentage of bad defect fixes. A bad defect fix can happen in two ways. One is when the fix doesn't resolve the problem and the defect report fails its confirmation test. Another is when the fix resolves the problem but introduces a new problem, a regression, either locally or in some remote area of the application. (This is what's referred to in the syllabus as "daughter bugs.") Ideally both numbers would be small, around 5 percent or less. If either is above 5 percent, something is broken in the bug fixing process or in the maintainability of the code or both. In addition, the larger each number gets, the more inefficient the project.

Test and Coverage Metrics

For test metrics, the standard metric I have used for years—in fact, my whole career as a test manager—is a breakdown of the test status either in relative terms (by percentage) or in absolute terms (in raw numbers). The status breakdown can be coarse—just pass and fail—or more fine-grained, as I prefer, with planned, implemented, executed, passed, failed, blocked, and skipped. For a number of years, I used tables to give the raw numbers or percentages, and I still think those tables are useful for the test team to provide a detailed view of status. For reporting to outside stakeholders, I've come to believe that a trend chart that shows these breakdowns progressing over time is easier to understand and to explain.

No matter how you report the test status metric, it is a project metric and not a product metric. In other words, we can use it to measure how close we are to our project test design, implementation, and execution targets, but we shouldn't use it to try to measure the quality of the software under test. If you have run 95 percent of the tests and 80 percent pass and 15 percent fail, that could be either good news or bad news, depending on the 15 percent that fail and the 5 percent that haven't yet been run.

One test metric can also be used to complement a defect metric discussed previously, bad defect fixes. If a test fails that previously passed, it can be classified as a regression failure. If a test is reexecuted to confirm a fix and that test fails again, it can be classified as a confirmation test failure. We can count both and report them, for the same purposes as with the bad defect fix metric.

A useful metric is to compare the number of test hours planned versus the number actually achieved. While this can be reported in a table showing cumulative values, I think it's more interesting to show a trend graph on a daily or weekly basis. This is a useful project metric, because if we are hitting our planned test hour targets, that is a positive sign for the successful completion of testing. It is also a useful process metric because deviation from planned targets would indicate some type of breakdown in the test process that would introduce inefficiencies.

Another test metric mentioned in the syllabus is the hours that the test environment is available. This can be shown as absolute numbers—for example,

"37 hours of availability versus 45 hours of planned testing"—or as a percentage of the planned hours. I've not used this metric personally; instead, what I've done is log the number of test hours and person-hours lost when test-blocking incidents occur. Some of these incidents will typically be test environment problems, but other stuff happens to interfere with our ability to get our testing work done.

For coverage metrics, the classic metric for system test, system integration test, and acceptance test is the percentage of requirements specification elements covered. I think requirements coverage is sufficient for acceptance testing. However, for system testing and system integration testing, since requirements are often gappy, especially with respect to error handling and nonfunctional behaviors, I prefer to expand the coverage metric to include quality risk items and, where appropriate, design specification elements, supported environments, supported configurations, and other possible dimensions of test coverage.[28] I've seen too many incidents where people had false confidence in a system based on achieving 100 percent requirements coverage.

Coverage during test design and implementation refers to the creation of the tests themselves and sometimes also their associated test data. During test execution, coverage refers to the execution of the tests and can also involve further classifying the executed tests as passed or failed.

These coverage metrics are both project and product metrics. They are project metrics in that we measure the extent to which coverage targets are being met. They are product metrics in that they tell us, indirectly, how much confidence we can have in the thoroughness of the product's testing and in its quality.

At the component test and component integration test level, when people use the word *coverage* they are typically talking about code coverage, though they might also mean interface coverage during component integration test. As a general rule, I like to see 100 percent decision coverage as the target for component testing and 100 percent interface coverage as the target for component integration testing. Boris Beizer said that when developers are component testing their own new or changed code, achieving anything less than 100 percent statement coverage should be illegal, and I've used enough bad software to agree with him.[29]

---

28. See my webinar "Dimensions of Test Coverage" (presented March 12, 2013) at http://www.rbcs-us.com/software-testing-resources/library/digital-library.
29. This can be found in Beizer's *Software Testing Techniques*.

At the higher levels of testing, structural coverage metrics are useful to test managers to measure the completeness of their testing. I have used these periodically as a test manager to get a sense of how much of the code my team was testing and to identify important areas of the code that we were missing. In one case, I found that an automated test system that people had great confidence in was achieving only 20 percent function coverage and much lower statement coverage. This led to us having to figure out what wasn't being tested and add new tests for those areas, some of which had to be manual tests.

However, in most cases that I have seen, measuring code coverage is something that is done to assess and report the completeness of the tests rather than as a way of reporting test results. I can think of only one exception, where a client used a requirement for 100 percent statement coverage by the end of a year-long system test execution period as a way of making sure it had a low risk of regression in its large, complex, and high-risk application. While this made sense for the client, it also introduced the risk of probe-effect problems because all of the tests were run against instrumented code. I think that, on balance, it's better to use code coverage sparingly, as a periodic check on the tests when running higher-level tests, and leave the heavy reliance on code coverage to lower-level tests.

Product Risk Metrics

Figure 2–23 shows a quick way to report residual quality risk. Let's review how it works.

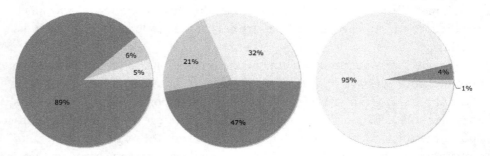

Figure 2–23   *Residual quality risk over time*

The region in green represents risks for which all tests were run and passed and no must-fix bugs were found. The region in red represents risks for which at least one test has failed or at least one must-fix bug is known. The region in black represents other risks, which have no known must-fix bugs but still have tests pending to run.

As you can see from the timeline at the bottom, when we start testing, the pie chart is all black. Over time, as test execution continues, we should see the red region eat into the black region and the green region eat into the red region. As we get toward the end of test execution, most of the black and red should be gone.

At any time, for the green region, we can produce a detailed list of risks that are tested, are known to pass the tests, and are not known to have any must-fix bugs. For the red region, we can produce a detailed list of risks against which known failed tests and must-fix bugs exist. We can list the tests and the bugs. For the black region, we can produce a detailed list of risks and the tests still remaining to be run against them. This gives a clear picture of the risk reduction achieved and the residual level of risk.

This type of metric is not commonly encountered, but it is exactly the kind of strategic, critical information that senior managers, executives, and those outside of testing want to receive from testing.

Cumulative Defects Reported/Resolved

Figure 2–24 shows a data-rich variant of the common bug tracking trend chart. This chart has five main data sets, two of which are plotted on the right-side axis and three of which are plotted on the left-side axis.

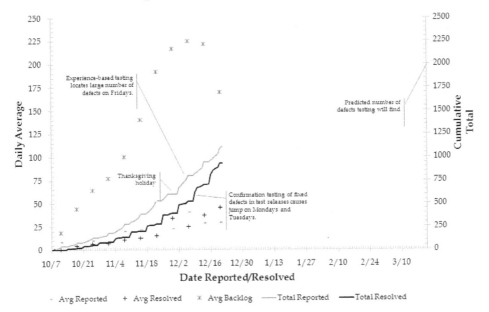

Figure 2–24 *Cumulative defects reported/resolved*

The first data set, shown by the red solid line, is the cumulative number of defects reported. It is graphed against the right-side axis. The second, shown by the green solid line, is the cumulative number of defects resolved, also graphed against the right-side axis. That includes both fixed and deferred defects because the point of this chart is to show whether the defect status is trending toward readiness for delivery.

The third data set, shown by the red minus signs, is the average number of defects reported in a given calendar week. It is graphed against the left-side axis. The fourth, shown by the green plus signs, is the average number of defects resolved in a given calendar week, also graphed against the left-side axis.

The fifth data set, shown by the yellow asterisks, is the average backlog in a given calendar week. The backlog for any day is the total number of defects found minus the number resolved.

Since trend charts show trends in time, not causality, this chart includes notations to explain various shapes of curves, such as the flattening of the cumulative defects reported line during the Thanksgiving holiday. Without such notations, viewers can mistake echoes of the process as the information we are trying to understand, which in this case is our current situation with respect to product quality problems.

Closure Period Trends

Figure 2–25 shows the closure period trend chart.

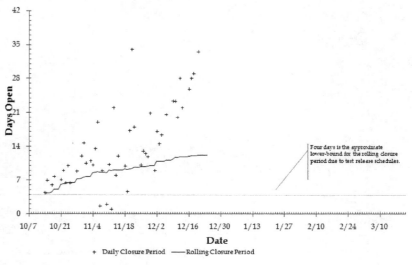

Figure 2–25   *Closure period trends*

The rolling closure period value for any given date is the average number of calendar days from the date reported to the date resolved for all defects resolved *on and before* that given date.

The daily closure period value for any given date is the average number of calendar days from the date reported to the date resolved for all defects resolved *on* that given date.

So, we would want the rolling closure period to stabilize at some number that is acceptable in terms of the turnaround time. Note that, as shown in the figure, the test release process puts a lower bound on how fast this turnaround time can be.

Once the rolling closure period stabilizes at an acceptable value, we would want the daily closure period to bounce around randomly right above and below the rolling closure period. A daily closure period that is consistently above the rolling closure period indicates something happening in the project that is causing it to take longer and longer to resolve defects.

Test Case Completion

Figure 2–26 shows an example of a trend chart for test status.

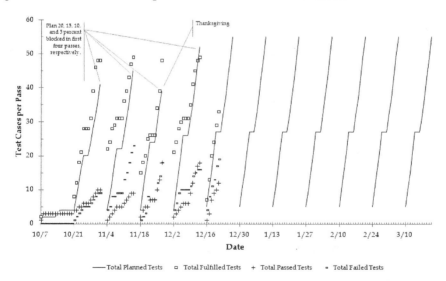

Figure 2–26   *Test case completion*

This chart has four main data sets, all plotted against a single axis on the left side. The first data set is the planned number of tests to be completed in a given pass of testing, shown by the lines that look like lightning bolts. The flat section in the middle of the lightning bolt occurs due to weekends, when no tests are scheduled. The reset of the test completion—in other words, why each lightning bolt starts over near zero—is due to the fact that we are running a sequence of similar test passes, using test repetition to manage regression risks.

The second data set is the actual number of tests completed for the pass at the end of each day, shown as boxes.

The third data set is the number of completed tests that have passed as of the end of each day, shown as plus signs.

The fourth data set is the number of completed tests that have failed as of the end of each day, shown as minus signs.

Again, see that I've used notations to indicate interesting aspects of the data sets, especially why particular test passes are shorter than others.

Test Hours

Figure 2–27 is another chart for test metrics, this one showing test hours progress.

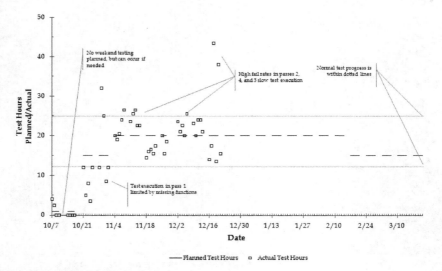

Figure 2–27   *Test hours*

This chart has two main data sets, both plotted against a single axis on the left side. The first data set is the planned test execution hours per day, indicated by the dashed line. Note that the planned hours change first upward and then downward during the project, indicating a differing planned intensity of testing.

The second data set is the actual test execution hours achieved per day, indicated by the boxes.

Two light-gray lines above and below the dashed lines indicate where we think normal weekday progress is. In other words, the boxes can bounce around randomly above and below the dashed lines, provided they stay within the gray lines. For those boxes outside the gray lines, we've provided an explanation of why.

Improving HELLOCARMS Testing Exercise

Figure 2–28, Figure 2–29, Figure 2–30, and Figure 2–31 show defect and test metrics charts at the end of iteration one of HELLOCARMS testing.

Based on what these charts are telling you about the HELLOCARMS testing, outline a list of three to five improvements for the subsequent iterations. How would the charts look at the end of iteration two if the improvements work?

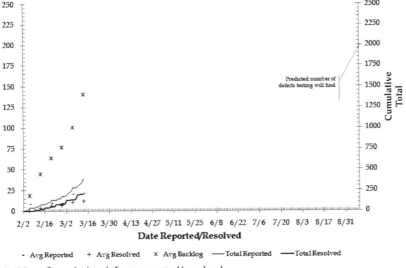

Figure 2–28   *Cumulative defects reported/resolved*

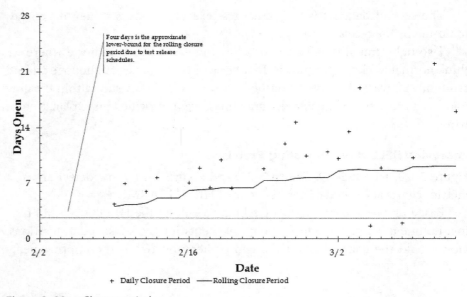

Figure 2–29   *Closure period*

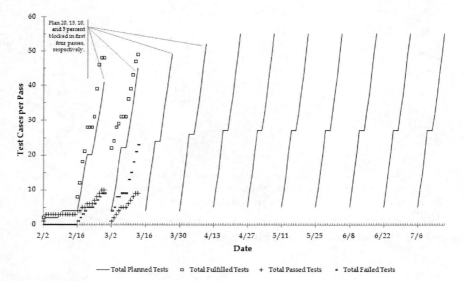

Figure 2–30   *Test case completion*

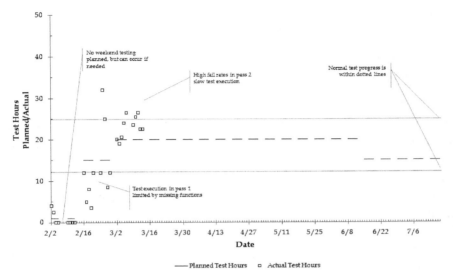

Figure 2–31   *Test hours*

Improving HELLOCARMS Testing Debrief

Looking at the charts, I noticed four areas for further investigation and possible improvement:

- The cumulative defects reported/resolved chart shows a large jump in defects right at the end of the test period. Possible improvement:
Stabilize the product earlier in the iteration, say around week 3, and focus on bug fixing in the last half of testing for that iteration.
- The closure period chart shows a steady upward trend in the closure period throughout the test period.
Possible improvement: Limit the size of subsequent iterations in terms of new functionality and focus on quick elimination of bugs.
- The test case completion chart shows a large number of tests added in the second and third passes (i.e., the last two passes) of this iteration, with a large number of tests failing during the final pass.
Possible improvement: Try to run all tests in the first pass to identify as many problems as possible, and then focus on resolution of defects so that most tests pass by the end of the last pass of the iteration.
- The test hours chart shows limited traction for testing during the first pass of testing, with a late push in testing in the third and final pass.

Possible improvement: Remove any obstacles to efficient testing and completion of test hours during the first pass.

You might have noticed additional possible improvements based on these charts as well as further research to do to understand the reasons for the problems.

Metrics in the Test Process

So far, we've been focusing primarily on test metrics that allow us to understand project or product status; that is, the use of test metrics to promote insight and guide decision making about the development or maintenance effort as a whole. However, testing work is like any other work being done on a project in that you need insight and decision making related to the testing itself. You can embed test metrics into the fundamental test process to manage our testing better. In the next few pages, let's look at how to do that.

You can use the following metrics to monitor and manage the test management activities associated with test planning, monitoring, and control:

- Coverage of the test basis: Earlier, we looked at coverage metrics as a way of measuring the product and project. However, you can also use them to measure how well you are managing the test effort. For example, you can compare the level of coverage achieved during design, implementation, and execution against what you had planned.
- Defect discovery: Defect metrics also have multiple purposes, including as a metric of test management. For example, in risk-based testing, you want to find most of the high-severity defects early in the test execution period, with the more serious problems being found later. So, during test control, you can monitor defect discovery to see if that pattern holds. If not, then control actions must be taken to resolve the problem, which generally will be a failure to identify or to properly assess particular quality risks.
- Resource deviation from plan: The syllabus refers to looking at planned effort versus actual effort during test monitoring and control, but really this can go beyond deviations in actual effort from what was planned. Test managers can and should watch carefully for signs of such deviations because the quicker those are detected, the sooner appropriate steps can be taken to resolve the underlying problem and get back on course. The longer a deviation from plan exists, the greater the risk posed to the project. A common way to monitor for such deviations is for you as the test manager to regularly update your work breakdown structure and budget and compare it against the baseline. I recommend doing this weekly.

ISTQB Glossary

test monitoring: A test management task that deals with the activities related to periodically checking the status of a test project. Reports are prepared that compare the actuals to that which was planned.

You can use the following metrics to monitor and manage the test analyst and technical test analyst activities associated with test analysis:

- Number of identified test conditions: This metric is likely to be most useful if you have a way of comparing it against an expected value. For example, if you have historical data that shows that on average you identify five test conditions for each test basis element (e.g., individual requirements, quality risks, etc.), then you can check to see whether you are finding fewer or more test conditions than expected as the work proceeds. A deviation from expectation does not necessarily indicate a problem, but it is something to be checked.
- Defects found: One value of analytical testing strategies is that they facilitate early testing. Reviewing requirements and analyzing risks tends to identify defects in input work products such as requirements specifications, design specifications, product plans, marketing documents, project plans, and so forth. These defects are a definite contribution from testing and one that you should measure and report to management. You should also compare the defects found against expectations, again using historical data such as the typical number of defects found per page in various types of work products.

You can use the following metrics to monitor and manage the test analyst and technical test analyst activities associated with test design:

- Coverage of test conditions: As mentioned previously, coverage metrics should be gathered during test design and compared to expected levels given the time and effort expended. Deviations should be identified and corrective actions taken if the desired levels of coverage will not be achieved before the test design activities are scheduled to end.
- Defects found: As with test analysis, test design can identify defects in the various test basis documents used to create tests, and the defects should be tracked, reported, and compared to expectations for the same reason.

You can use the following metrics to monitor and manage the test analyst and technical test analyst activities associated with test implementation:

- Test environment readiness: The syllabus refers to monitoring the percentage of test environments configured, and this will work for relatively simple situations. For example, if you need to test a mobile application on 25 separate configurations, then each configuration set up represents a progress of 4 percent. However, I have worked on projects where complex, interdependent systems of systems were involved. In that case, I used a simple but powerful Access database to track and report environmental readiness.[30]

- Test data readiness: Again, the syllabus refers to monitoring the percentage of test data records loaded, and this will also work for relatively simple situations. For example, if you have existing production data that needs to go through a process of anonymization that occurs as the data is being loaded, and once the data is loaded the test data is ready for test execution, then the percentage of records loaded will be a valid metric of test data readiness. However, if disparate data records must be assembled, generated, amalgamated, loaded, evaluated for adequacy, adjusted to correct errors, and possibly expanded to fill test coverage gaps, the percentage of loaded records alone will not adequately capture the true state of test data readiness.

- Percentage of tests automated: This is a common and useful metric, especially when it focuses on the percentage of regression tests automated. However, use it with care because a misguided attempt to achieve 100 percent automation has created problems for many test teams.

You can use the following metrics to monitor and manage the test analyst and technical test analyst activities associated with test execution:

- Test status: As mentioned earlier, looking at the percentage of test conditions or test cases executed, passed, and failed, especially in comparison to expected status given the current schedule, is useful as a project metric. It can also result in the test manager making decisions about course corrections to the testing itself.

- Test coverage: Just as with test status, comparing actual and expected coverage during test execution can result in course corrections to the testing effort as well as to the wider project.

---

30. The database is described in my book *Managing the Testing Process, 3rd Edition,* and can be downloaded from the RBCS Advanced Library.

▨ Defect status: Here again, the same metrics used for the wider project can give the test manager insights into necessary course corrections. For example, if you are one-third through the scheduled test execution period but have found less than one-third of the expected number of defects, this can indicate a number of things, one of which is a breakdown or blockage in the testing process.

You can use the following metrics to monitor and manage the activities associated with test closure:

▨ Test status: Ideally, at the end of test execution, all tests would have been executed and ultimately passed. However, that's often not the case. As part of checking for test completion, you need to ensure that the project team has accepted all tests that remain failed, blocked, or skipped at the end of test execution. As part of the test retrospective, you need to look at the percentage of tests that failed, were blocked, or were skipped throughout test execution to see if you can organize testing to avoid inefficiencies.

▨ Defect status: Also at the end of the ideal test execution period, all defects would be repaired and confirmation tested. However, that doesn't always happen either. As part of checking for test completion, you need to ensure that any defects which were not repaired and confirmation tested are accepted as temporary or permanent product restrictions. As part of the test retrospective, you need to evaluate the effectiveness of your test strategy. For example, in risk-based testing, it is a goal to find a disproportionately higher number of high-severity defects, so you should check during the testing retrospective to ensure that you have.

▨ Test archiving: Considerable time and effort can be spent creating test cases and other work products. As a test manager, you should monitor what percentage of those work products have been checked into a repository for reuse. You should also check to be sure that those are being organized in such a way that people will be able to find them in the future because these repositories can easily become a write-only memory if you're not careful.

▨ Regression test set: When working on a product that will go through many releases, it is wise to have a strategy for the careful growth and management of the regression test set. I had one client tell me that as each project completed, every new test written was put into the regression test set. Unsurprisingly, they were finding that their test execution periods had ballooned and were creating problems for timely releases. The usual solution to this problem is to automate tests, and looking at the percentage of automated tests created can help monitor that. If tests are not entirely automatable, or not even automatable at all, then you'll need to have a careful strategy for creating a regression test set from which you can extract the appropriate subset of tests for each release.

When using metrics to monitor and manage test progress and completion, a good practice is to either derive those metrics from, or link the metrics to, scheduled testing and project milestones, test plan entry criteria, and test plan exit criteria. The following metrics are commonly used in this regard:

- Status of test conditions or cases: Testing milestones, and especially exit criteria, will often specify a certain percentage of tests to be executed and passed or provide limits on how many tests can fail and under what circumstances. Personally, my preference is to state 100 percent execution, 100 percent passed, and 0 percent failed and then use a test exit review meeting to discuss waiver of that criterion if appropriate.

- Defects: Exit criteria often put limits on how many defects of a given severity or priority can be unresolved at the end of testing. As above, my preference is to say no defects should be unresolved at all and then discuss the pros and cons of waivers in a test exit review meeting.

- Changes: In sequential lifecycles, there's often a sort of "cooling off" period at the end of test execution, when the code is supposed to be stable and unchanging. In this case, establish an exit criterion that specifies the number of changes allowed in a given time period and the last date for any changes. These change deadlines will typically be different for requirements, features, code, and the project plan.

- Cost, duration, schedule, and milestones: These metrics should be checked at test entry, at major milestones during test execution, and at test exit.

- Quality risk: When doing risk-based testing, an exit criterion—and possibly some intra-execution milestones—should address the status of the identified quality risks, as mentioned previously.

- Lost effort, cost, or time: As I've mentioned, it's a good practice to track incidents that delay testing or waste testing resources, including effort. My preference is to report this periodically as well as after any significant incident. Reporting this at the end of test execution is sometimes appropriate as well, but it can come across as raining on a parade if you bring up negative incidents during a successful product launch meeting.

▦   Confirmation and regression test status: In terms of exit criteria, it's a good practice to have one criterion that involves checking that all defect fixes have been appropriately confirmation tested and that all necessary regression tests have been completed following changes.

As I've worked through the various metrics that can be used to monitor and manage the project, the product, and the test process, you've probably noticed significant overlaps. Yes, one metric can often be used for multiple purposes. However, you may have to modify the way you analyze, track, present, and report the metric, depending on its purpose.

In addition to the metrics I've just discussed, it's often a good practice, especially on larger, more complex, or longer projects, to use a work breakdown structure to track the test effort. I discussed the construction of these work breakdown structures in section 2.5, on test estimation. Setting aside an hour or so every week to review test status against the work breakdown structure and taking appropriate control steps if deviations have occurred is a practice that has worked well for me over the years.

For teams following agile practices, a work breakdown structure is not common, at least for individual iterations. Instead, the testing is part of a how a user story gets done, and test progress is tracked on a burn-down chart. Some teams prefer to use lean management techniques. In this case, there will be a Kanban board that each user story moves through. Testing would be a column on that board, and each story would move through that column to get done.

Reporting and Using Metrics

Now that we've reviewed some common metrics, let's discuss how to use metrics and how to report status with them.

As a test manager and as a consultant, I regularly use project, process, and product metrics to analyze past, current, and future situations. By looking at trends over time, I can see what has been happening and get a sense of what will happen in the future, especially when I have reliable historical data. By using histograms, pie charts, and scatterplots, I can evaluate possible reasons why things happen. For example, a histogram of defect analysis by subsystem can show me where bug clusters are and thus where I can expect to find more or fewer bugs in future testing. I have used a scatterplot that evaluated defect report rejection rates versus a tester's years of experience to assess whether tester ignorance of product capabilities was leading to a higher rejection rate—which it was not, to the astonishment of everyone on the project team.

I also use these metrics to report findings. When I manage test projects, I'll use metrics to give other project team members insight into what has happened and what I expect will happen. Again, reliable historical data helps with the projection of future outcomes. When I consult with clients, I often use metrics as part of my assessment reports to give my clients insight into what has happened and why.

Metrics are also useful for control. This can be project control, where I've used metrics to course-correct the testing effort and recommend course corrections for the project as a whole to support better outcomes for the project. This can also be process control, where I've used metrics to give recommendations for improvements and targets for what the metrics should show if the recommendations succeed in making the suggested improvements. As these control measures go into effect, the same metrics can (and should) be used to monitor the degree of success achieved and perhaps to adjust the existing control measures or introduce additional control measures if necessary.

I often report these metrics verbally at first, as part of a conversation about what has happened, what will happen without changes, and what can happen if we course-correct. However, in more formal settings such as project status meetings or client assessment reports, I will report the metrics either in tables or in graphs.

It is important to tailor the metrics, and the way you present them, according to the needs, goals, and abilities of the people to whom you will deliver them and according to the objectives that you are trying to achieve. As I've mentioned, a common mistake is to spray project team members with a fire hose of data, much of it irrelevant to their interests or beyond their ability to understand. Unless your goal is to confuse or distract your audience—which by the way makes you either an evil or incompetent test manager—you should work with your stakeholders to give them the exact information they need—no more and no less—when they need it. For example, project managers will need details about your status on a frequent basis, often daily, especially in terms of tactical metrics such as defect and test status. Senior business managers will need information less frequently, and the information should give them a strategic view of the current status and trends in terms of quality risks and requirements to support their ability to make decisions.

Metrics-Based Test Control

I have found metrics absolutely essential to my ability to control test processes and projects. The achievement of test objectives, the fulfillment of the test mission, the successful completion of the test strategy—I have seen these supported by the proper use of metrics and thwarted when metrics were not used properly. The proper use of metrics means that we use them to guide the testing work, and we also respond appropriately to our test results and to project changes.

Proper use of metrics during test control relies on proper test planning. Unless the right data is gathered from the start of a project, you will find yourself without the information you need when critical test control decisions must be made. At the same time, you and your team cannot spend all your time gathering metrics because otherwise you will do nothing but that. In general, as the size, complexity, and risk of a project increases, the volume of information you need and the work required to gather the information will increase. Small, simple, low-risk projects have a greater inherent transparency that makes heavyweight metrics unnecessary.

It's important to remember that test control does not mean working to get the testing work or the project as a whole back on plan. Circumstances change, and project success may be better served by modifying the plan. However, when a situation is discovered where the plan is not being met—which can happen during extraordinary or ordinary project reporting—this is a sign that control actions are needed.

A wide variety of control options are available when such divergence is noted, and your judgment and wisdom are required to select the right ones. However, there are some common options:

- Revising the quality risk analysis, the priorities of tests, and the test plan. For example, if test results indicate serious defects in an area thought to be low risk in terms of impact, then you might need to reevaluate the impact ratings for the relevant risks. This can result in reprioritizing the remaining test effort and perhaps adjusting the test plan to add more testing time or resources if possible.
- Delaying release. In some cases, the test results make it clear that the current planned release date will result in failure to achieve product quality goals. In that case, as painful as it usually is, delaying the release may be the best bad option. Contrary to popular belief, the sooner this decision is made, the less damaging it is because more options remain in terms of

containing the damage. The passage of time without action after project disaster is perceived inexorably reduces options and increases risk.

- Modifying exit criteria. You and the project management team might decide that schedule or budget goals outweigh quality goals and relax exit criteria. Or, you might collectively decide the converse and tighten exit criteria. As a test manager, you should approach this discussion as a business professional, not as an inflexible advocate of higher quality. Yes, you should advocate higher quality, but only with a solid business case. We'll discuss this topic further in the next section.

- Changing scope. In addition to expanding schedule or budget targets, project teams may also choose to reduce scope in response to quality problems. Alternatively, in the happy event that quality is better than expected at some point during test execution, scope may be expanded to include features or nonfunctional attributes that were seen as out of reach during test planning.

All of these test control actions typically require review and approval by project, operation, and product managers. The same people who approved the original test plan must be aware of the control actions proposed and be willing to accept those actions. As painful as these renegotiations may be, it is preferable to creating a set of discontented and unsatisfied stakeholders who may well act to frustrate your plans on future projects or sullenly refuse to collaborate during the planning process.

HELLOCARMS Test Progress Report Exercise

The graphics shown in Figure 2–32, Figure 2–33, Figure 2–34, and Figure 2–35 show the same defect and test charts as the previous exercise, but this time at start of the last week of testing for iteration two. Analyze these results to answer two questions:

1. Do they show evidence for or against the improvements you outlined in the previous exercise?
2. Do you believe the test results for iteration two show HELLOCARMS on track for deployment at the end of this iteration?

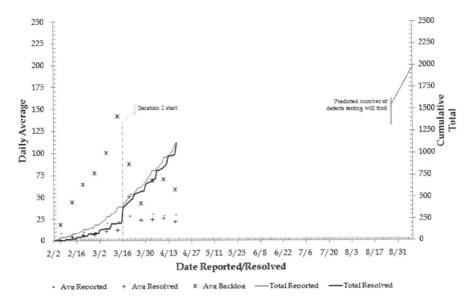

Figure 2-32   *Cumulative defects reported/resolved*

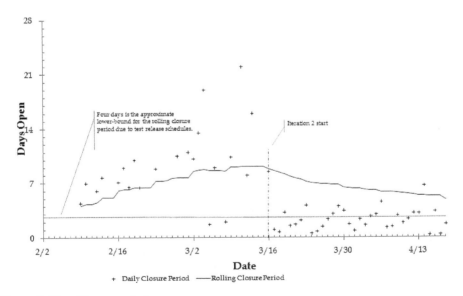

Figure 2-33   *Closure period*

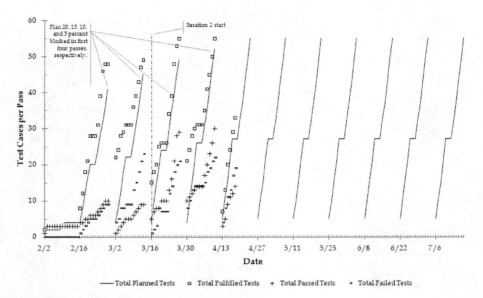

Figure 2–34   Test case completion

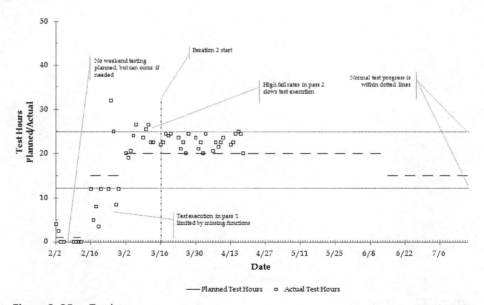

Figure 2–35   Test hours

HELLOCARMS Test Progress Report Debrief

Let's start by assessing progress in terms of the four improvements I suggested in the last exercise.

1. The cumulative defects reported/resolved chart for iteration one showed a large jump in defects right at the end of the test period.
    a. Possible improvement: Stabilize the product earlier in the iteration, say around week 3, and focus on bug fixing in the last half of testing for that iteration.
    b. Status for iteration two: While development has done an excellent job of resolving defects—indeed, achieving convergence with the reported defect count multiple times during the iteration—the defect reporting rate remains extremely high throughout the entire test execution period for iteration two. The test manager and the project management team as a whole should carry out further investigation to discover the root causes of this disturbing outcome. Here are five possible explanations:
        i.   High regression rate of the features in iteration one due to the high rate of defect repair during iteration two.
        ii. High rate of discovery of new bugs in features from iterations one and two due to an expansion of test scope.
        iii. High rate of new feature addition during iteration two.
        iv. Large number of features added in iteration two brought with them a large number of defects.
        v.   Insufficient upstream quality control activities, such as requirements and design reviews, code reviews and static analysis, and unit testing.
2. The closure period chart for iteration one showed a steady upward trend in the closure period throughout the test period.
    a. Possible improvement: Limit the size of subsequent iterations in terms of new functionality and focus on quick elimination of bugs.
    b. Status for iteration two: We cannot conclude that the size of iteration two was limited because that remains a possible explanation of the high rate of bug discovery throughout iteration two. However, the development team has certainly done an excellent job of reversing the negative trend in backlog and closure period. That said, it is possible, as mentioned previously, that the development team is working too quickly

and with insufficient attention to detail to resolve defects, resulting in a high regression rate.

3. The test case completion chart for iteration one shows a large number of tests added in the second and third passes (i.e., the last two passes) of this iteration, with a large number of tests failing during the final pass.

    a. Possible improvement: Try to run all tests in the first pass to identify as many problems as possible; then focus on resolution of defects so that most tests pass by the end of the last pass of the iteration.

    b. Status for iteration two: The test team did a fine job of accelerating the rate of test completion and the total number of tests completed in each pass. However, we still see a large number of tests failing. This problem is especially acute during the last pass, where more tests have so far failed than passed. This is, of course, consistent with the results shown for iteration two in the cumulative defects reported/resolved chart.

4. The test hours chart for iteration one showed limited traction for testing during the first pass of testing, with a late push in testing in the third and final pass.

    a. Possible improvement: Remove any obstacles to efficient testing and completion of test hours during the first pass.

    b. Status for iteration two: Again, the test team did a fine job of ensuring complete traction and engagement with the testing immediately at the start of iteration two test execution. The hours are a bit higher than planned throughout the iteration. This is consistent with the results shown for iteration two in the test case completion chart and the cumulative defects reported/resolved chart because an unexpectedly high rate of failing tests and reporting defects will increase required test effort.

So, based on this analysis, we can conclude that HELLOCARMS is not on track for deployment at the end of iteration two. The cumulative defects reported/resolved chart indicates that a large number of latent defects remain in the system. The test case completion chart indicates that a large number of features are failing.

2.7 Business Value of Testing

Learning objectives

(K2) Give examples for each of the four categories determining the cost of quality.

(K3) Estimate the value of testing based on cost of quality, along with other quantitative and qualitative considerations, and communicate the estimated value to testing stakeholders.

Optimizing Test Value

There is a sort of Goldilocks aspect to testing. If you test too much, the cost of testing exceeds the value received by the business, and testing too much will usually result in delays. If you test too little, ill-informed release decisions are made and buggy products are delivered to customers. You want to test just right, not too much, not too little. To some extent, defining test objectives and their associated goals for the test process and team, selecting proper test strategies, and setting the exit criteria for testing on a project are all about achieving this ideal level of testing. However, there is also a need to understand and communicate the business value of testing.

There are some people in the testing business—even some that I respect, like Boris Beizer—who have said, "Don't try to build a business case for testing." They think it is a waste of time, an exercise the results of which won't be accepted by managers anyway.

That has not been my experience. I have found that a conservative, well-explained business case can be quite persuasive and influential. I also have found that it's essential to changing the way testing is viewed.

Those of us in the testing world have a problem something like that of organized religion in the United States. In the United States, according to sociological surveys, there are very few atheists; that is, people who will say, often and with conviction, that there is *no* God. There are agnostics, of course, people who aren't sure, but for the most part people will say that they believe in some God or other.

However, if you then were to ask them, "Okay, great, when was the last time you were in a mosque, a synagogue, a church, a temple, or other place of worship?" you would frequently get answers like "my cousin's wedding," "my uncle's funeral," and "my nephew's bar mitzvah," but less frequently would you hear,

"Oh, I'm there every week," and even less frequently, "I go three or four times a week." In other words, attendance at organized religious ceremonies is not a priority for many people. The financial situations of many religious organizations in the United States are correspondingly bleak. Most people in the United States are only vaguely religious.

Testing has the same problem. There are very few testing atheists, those who would say that testing has no value. Most would say that testing has some value. However, when you ask them what they are willing to spend, how much delay they are willing to incur, what features they might be willing to forgo, to have the reduced risk, confidence, long-term savings, and information that testing can provide, you find very quickly that most people in IT are vaguely religious about testing.

I believe this problem arises from two main causes. First, very few managers, even seasoned test managers, can quantify, describe, or articulate the value of testing to peer managers, senior managers, or executives. Second, many testers are happy to spend time in their comfort zone, their zone of competence, dealing with tactical issues like finding bugs, writing test cases, setting up test environments, and the like, and so they avoid the broader strategic issues that would allow them to connect what they do as testers to things that are important and valued by the organization.

So, I suggest that we, as testers, start to internalize the following three principles of testing business value:

- First, what gets measured gets done.
- Second, what gets valued gets funded.
- Third, testing has a value that can be measured.

If you can accept those three things as true, you are on a track toward attaching what you do as a tester to what organizations care about and thus having fewer funding difficulties.

The Values of Testing

By itself, running tests has no value. It might sound like I'm contradicting something I said a moment ago, but I'm not. What I mean is that executing tests—pounding away on keyboards and databases, observing screens, checking reports, and so forth—has no intrinsic value. Testing has value when it connects with, it supports, some other goal or objective of the organization.

Some of these goals are quantitative and quantifiable:

- If the organization wants to reduce long-term defect-related costs, we can do that by finding must-fix defects before release.
- If the tech support or help desk staff are tired of being surprised by unknown issues, we can fix that by finding less critical, deferrable defects before release.
- If the organization is concerned about the risk associated with releasing software, we can reduce the risk by running tests, whether those tests find bugs or not.
- If the organization wants to make confident, informed release decisions, we can help it do that by delivering information.

Some of these goals are qualitative but nevertheless very real to those who hold them:

- If the organization wants to enjoy the marketing and sales advantages of an improved reputation for quality, we can help throughout the lifecycle.
- If the organization wants to have smoother, more predictable release cycles, we can help—again, by being involved throughout the lifecycle.
- If the management team wants to have increased confidence upon release, we can help by working with them to ensure that what really matters gets tested—for example, by using risk-based testing.
- If the organization wants protection from legal liability, due to regulations or contractual obligations, we can help by ensuring compliant, defensible testing.
- If the organization is in the safety-critical or mission-critical business, and wants to ensure the lowest possible chance of lost missions or lives, we can work with the project team throughout the lifecycle to filter out as many problems as we can prior to release.

What matters to your organization, on your project, right now? If you can't answer that question, you're probably not focusing on the right things. Test managers should understand which of the quantitative and qualitative values apply and be able to communicate about these values.

Cost of Quality

There are techniques available to quantify most of the quantitative values of testing.[31] However, the Advanced syllabus—and thus this book—focuses on

---

31. Quantifying test value is discussed extensively in my book *Critical Testing Processes*.

cost of quality to measure the quantitative value and efficiency of testing. Cost of quality is sometimes called cost of poor quality, to remind people that it is an analysis that shows that poor quality costs money and good quality saves money.

At its core, cost of quality is an accounting technique that classifies project or operation costs into four categories.

The first category is costs of prevention. Costs of prevention are expenses we incur to prevent bugs from happening. Expenditures for training developers are costs of prevention.

The second category is costs of detection. Costs of detection are expenses we incur *to detect bugs* that we would have to incur even if we didn't *detect any bugs*. Expenditures for test planning, analysis, design, and implementation are costs of detection, as are some of the costs of test execution (for tests that pass) and test closure.

The third category is costs of internal failure. Costs of internal failure are expenses we incur because we did detect bugs. The remaining expenditures for test execution, specifically rerunning tests, confirmation testing fixes, installing the second and all subsequent test releases, and the like, are costs of internal failure incurred by testing. Other project participants also incur costs of internal failure, such as programmers fixing bugs and release engineers creating test releases.

The fourth category is costs of external failure. Costs of external failure are expenses we incur because we didn't detect and remove all the bugs before release. Fifty percent or more of technical support or help desk costs are often external failure costs. Programmers who spend time fixing field failures are incurring external failure costs. In some cases, there are tangible punitive or lost-business costs associated with external failure too. For example, some organizations have service-level-agreements with customers, with penalties associated with failures. Some organizations have to worry about potential customers choosing not to do business with them, such as when an e-commerce site goes down.

When RBCS does testing assessments, we typically measure the efficiency of testing as a bug-finding operation by using cost of quality. In every case I have looked at as a consultant, the costs of detection and internal failure were much cheaper than external failure. Testing is thus an excellent value. I have yet to find a case where testing was not saving the company money on potential costs of external failure, which were avoided by the prerelease detection and removal of defects.

Example: Cost of Quality ROI

Figure 2–36 shows cost of quality analysis applied to the Internet appliance project I've used as a case study a few times. We'll start at the upper left of the table and then work our way down, across to the upper right, and down again to see how the calculations work.

Detection Costs		External Failure Costs	
Test Budget	$1,000,000	Sustaining Costs	$3,000,000
Future Value of Assets	$100,000	Percentage Bug-Related	50%
Re-test Costs	$500,000		
Net Detection Costs	**$400,000**	**Net Ext. Failure Costs**	**$1,500,000**
Must-Fix Test Bugs	**1,500**	**Must-Fix Released Bugs**	**500**
Detection Cost per Bug	**$267**	**Ext. Failure Cost per Bug**	**$3,000**
Internal Failure Costs		Return on Investment	
Test Bug Fix Costs	750,000	Must-Fix Test Bugs	1,500
Re-test Costs	500,000	Money Saved Per Bug	$1,900
Net Int. Failure Costs	**$1,250,000**	**Net Benefit of Testing**	**$2,850,000**
Must-Fix Test Bugs	**1,500**	**Net Detection Costs**	**$400,000**
Int. Failure Cost per Bug	**$833**	**Test ROI**	**713%**

Figure 2–36   *Example: Cost of quality ROI*

We first want to calculate the costs of detection. As I mentioned, a portion of the test budget forms the cost of detection. So, I start with the test budget of $1,000,000. Next, I deduct from that the time to create and capture assets of value for subsequent projects (basically, costs of test closure). Finally, I remove the retest costs—the costs of confirmation testing bug fixes and regression testing features that might have been affected by a bug fix—since those are costs of internal failure. That leaves $400,000. As there were 1,500 must-fix test bugs, that means our average cost of detection was $267.

Next, we calculate the costs of internal failure. This includes the remainder of the test budget, the costs of retesting, which you see added back here. There is also the developer effort spent fixing the bugs, which I estimate based on the three months of system test during which the product was feature complete. Our net internal failure costs are $1.25 million, with an average cost of internal failure of $833. Thus, our average prerelease cost per bug—both detection and internal failure—is $1,100. Provided that a bug found after release costs more than $1,100, testing is saving the organization money.

Let's move to the right side of the table to see if we are saving the organization money, and, if so, how much. We first calculate the external failure costs. The sustaining costs—including developers, testers, and technical support—during the first six months of release were $3,000,000. I estimate that about 50 percent of that cost was due to bugs. (I actually think the true percentage might have been much higher, but as I said, we want to keep these business cases conservative.) Our net external failure costs were $1.5 million, with 500 bugs found after release. That gives us an average post-release bug cost of $3,000, meaning each bug found by test saved $1,900.

Finally, let's calculate our return on investment (ROI). Since each bug found saved $1,900, and 1,500 bugs were found, testing saved the organization $2.85 million. To put that in percentage terms, our cost of testing for this project—if we deduct closure costs and bug-related retesting costs—was the cost of detection, $400,000. If we divide $2.85 million—the net benefit of testing—by $400,000, we get 713 percent. Not too shabby.

Example: Other Values for Testing

While the Advanced syllabus focuses on cost of quality, let's briefly discuss some of the other quantitative and qualitative values delivered by testing.

Based on some further analysis, we found the following additional quantitative values for testing on the Internet appliance project:

- $150,000 in saved support-call time due to known bugs (often with test-identified workarounds).
- $250,000 in risk-reduction value from passed tests, based on the cost of a failure in the field and the likelihood and frequency of tests failing the first time they were run.
- $200,000 in information value, based on the reduced risk of project failure due to bad project tracking.[32]

These values and the analysis behind them are detailed in my article "What IT Managers Should Know about Testing ROI."[33]

---

32. For these figures, see *Estimating Software Costs, 2nd Edition*, by Capers Jones.
33. You can find this article at http://www.rbcs-us.com/images/documents/What-IT-Managers-Should-Know-about-Testing-ROI.pdf.

There were also some additional qualitative values delivered on that project. For one thing, the organization was able to have some confidence on release, particularly in areas we had managed to successfully clean up, such as performance and reliability. (There remained a fair number of bugs, as you can see, because our defect detection percentage was only 75 percent.)

For another thing, thanks in part to our thorough testing of the hardware and of the software update process, there were no recalls and few returns due to boxes being rendered dead by failed software updates.

Value of HELLOCARMS Testing Exercise

Consider the HELLOCARMS project toward the end of iteration two (as shown in the exercise "HELLOCARMS Test Progress Report" in section 2.6 earlier in this chapter). List the quantitative and qualitative values delivered by testing at this point.

Value of HELLOCARMS Testing Debrief

Let's look at the values of testing mentioned in the book to see which apply:

Quantitative values:

- Finding must-fix defects: This is clearly demonstrated by the charts shown in the previous exercise (see Figure 2–32, Figure 2–33, Figure 2–34, and Figure 2–35).
  Finding deferrable defects: We don't have an exact breakdown of the deferrable defects, but we can assume that some defects are being deferred, given the rate of defect resolution.
  Reducing risk by running tests: Again, clearly demonstrated by the charts shown in the previous exercise. Given the large number of test failures, though, this value is less than one might like.
  Delivering information: In the previous exercise, we could make a strong case based on just four charts that the test results did not support deployment. This information, if properly delivered to and received by the project management team, gave Globobank the opportunity to avoid a very embarrassing and costly premature release.

Qualitative values:

- Improving reputation for quality: Again, if the findings of the previous exercise influenced project management to not deploy at the end of iteration two, then we have certainly delivered value here.

Smoothing releases: We certainly have tried to smooth the release process, and based on improvements from iteration two, we continue to make this better. However, we need to perform further investigation as to the causes of high defect discovery rates and high test failure rates at the end of iteration two to increase the value we can deliver here.

Increasing confidence: We have not examined the coverage metrics for HELLOCARMS testing, so we cannot say whether we are doing an adequate job here.

Protecting from legal liability: Since testing does cover security and regulatory compliance characteristics—two key areas of potential legal exposure for banks—we are adding value here.

Reducing risk of loss of missions or lives: This is not a safety-critical application, but it is business critical. Banks that cannot issue home equity loans, lines of credit, and reverse mortgages are missing a major revenue stream.

You might have found other quantitative and qualitative values that apply to this project.

2.8 Distributed, Outsourced, and Insourced Testing

Learning objectives

(K2) Understand the factors required for successful use of distributed, outsourced, and insourced test team staffing strategies.

Not too long ago, a single team carried out most projects. The test team was part of the same company. They all were in the same building. Those days are now over.

Now, in many cases, the test effort might be spread across multiple teams. Perhaps only one or two of these teams are actually employed by the same company as the organization developing the software. The testing, development, and other work might be happening at two, three, five, or more locations. What happened?

Well, it's not just that one thing happened, it's that three different kinds of things are happening, which can be overlapping. Let's look at the variants:

- If the test effort occurs at multiple locations, that test effort is distributed. For example, suppose your company has one test team in Bangalore and another in Prague and those two test teams collaborate on the testing of a single project. Distribution introduces a number of new management issues, such as coordination of the work.

- If people who are not fellow employees of the rest of the project team, and not co-located with the project team, carry out the test effort at one or more locations, that test effort is outsourced. If more than one location is involved, it is distributed-outsourced testing. For example, if you hire a test team in Kuala Lumpur to do all of your testing for you, you have outsourced your testing, but if you retain some of the testing in your team and outsource the rest to the team in Kuala Lumpur, you have distributed-outsourced testing happening. Outsourcing introduces a number of new management issues too, some of which are exacerbated by the distance (both in kilometers and time zones) between the various entities and the number of entities involved.

- If people who are co-located with the project team carry out the test effort but those people are not fellow employees with the rest of the project team, that test effort is insourced. For example, if you hire an RBCS consultant to come work as part of your test team for a project, you have insourced some of your testing. Insourcing introduces a number of new management issues as well, such as ensuring that the people you bring into your team are bringing in the skills you need.

We can apply the same classifications for development and other project roles. The potential combinations of test, development, project management, release engineering, and other project roles across these three classifications can become quite overwhelming—and can provide a great fog cloud in which culpable parties can hide accountability if an organization is not careful.

You'll notice that I'm leaving aside the terms *offshore*, *nearshore*, and so forth. I consider these mostly ways in which marketers try to differentiate their services. To the extent that these terms have any meaning, the meaning is relative—Offshore from whom? Nearshore to whom?—and thus not easy to deal with generally.

In this section, we'll look at how distribution, outsourcing, and insourcing affect testing, particularly test management.

Common Issues

There are common issues that apply to distributed, outsourced, and insourced testing.

We want to make sure everyone starts in the right direction, so well-defined expectations are important. In all the cases we are considering here, we have two or more groups involved. If those groups think they are doing—or are trying to do—something different, don't be surprised when failure, either partial or total, ensues.

If everything always went perfectly on projects, we could spray chunks of work around the globe and gather up the finished work products at the end. However, the realities are that people need to discuss, coordinate, collaborate, learn, and course-correct during projects, which means that clear channels of communication are required.

The channels of communication cannot be informal, like the coffee-maker, cigarette-break, and company gym channels that exist in a company of fellow employees.

As a test manager, you need to realize that a number of things that could happen almost automatically within the project team with minimal effort must be carefully coordinated in these situations. You must carefully plan for and manage test logistics related to hardware, software, tools licenses, information flows, test data access, and a number of other issues.

You will need to manage the various location, time zone, cultural, and language differences that can exist. The location and time zone differences are obvious, but don't underestimate two key things:

- The first is the power of traveling, by plane or if possible train, to the remote location to solve problems. I have solved tricky testing coordination and collaboration issues in one-hour face-to-face meetings in cities around the world, issues that bedeviled the project for weeks before I finally said, "I'm going over there," and got on an airplane.

- The second is the compounding difficulty of managing multiple time zones. Yes, you can find a mutually convenient—or perhaps a mutually inconvenient—time for a phone conference, videoconference, live chat, webinar, or other group information channel, at least when there are only two time zones. And if the time is mutually convenient, you shouldn't have too much trouble as a manager getting people to attend this as a standing meeting. Try having a standing meeting at 7:00 a.m. once a week and see how your non-morning people (such as me) respond. Now, just for grins, try to find a time for a phone conference in the following cities: Sydney, Australia; Austin, Texas; and Berlin, Germany. How about London, Tokyo, and San Diego? How about all six? And when does daylight savings time happen in each time zone?

The cultural and language differences are a lot less obvious, which surprises people. Yes, culture in part refers to things like food, religion, holidays, taboos, and the like, which do exhibit astounding variability around the world and provide endless opportunities for you to do or say something completely inappropriate in a social or business situation. Reading a book on the cultures and histories involved before you start working on projects with a group of people can prove quite useful and help you deal with issues that could arise.

But culture also refers to business culture, which can vary tremendously within a single country. For example, as a rule, in East Asia, business dealings tend to be polite and nonconfrontational. Businesspeople often exhibit a strong bias for consensus and, when presented with a problem, tend to work indirectly toward that problem's solution. Therefore, things tend to move more slowly. However, I remember sitting in a meeting in Tokyo with a business associate, delivering our assessment of a test situation to a client and being dumbfounded when the client tore into my business associate, attacking him on every point and assertion. I have done a lot of business in Israel, where businesspeople have a reputation for very direct and frank discussions in meetings, and even there I had not seen anything similar to what happened in Tokyo.

As for things tending to move slowly due to the consensus building and indirect problem solving, yes, that can be true as a rule too. However, one of the largest courseware development and delivery deals RBCS has ever done was with a company in East Asia, and that deal went from discussions to contract in a few short weeks. In parallel, a similar deal with a US company took three years to complete. So it's hard to generalize about cultures, and as we should all realize by now in this globalized, diverse world, stereotypes can sometimes lead you astray.

Regarding the issue of languages, here are two simple things to remember that have many subtle connotations and interactions:

- First, understanding a language is not a binary state; for example, it's not either you do understand Japanese or you don't. I can read Spanish, and write it reasonably well if I have a dictionary handy, but in terms of speaking and listening, I find that very, very difficult. So if someone says to you,

"Oh, yes, all our testers understand English," don't accept that statement as the end of the matter.

▪ Second, when understanding and expressing yourself in a language—any language, including the one you grew up speaking—on their way to your mouth or to your fingers, all your thoughts and ideas pass through a complex filter composed of your past experiences, your culture, your biases, your personal feelings, and so forth. The fewer of these things you have in common with the person with whom you're trying to communicate, the easier it is to miscommunicate.

Another issue is the alignment of methodologies across the groups. How are bugs reported? How are requirements gathered and documented? What types of reviews occur? For example, if you think of all the activities in the ISTQB fundamental test process and all the tasks within each activity, both groups could carry out many of those tasks properly, but each group could carry out the tasks in slightly or even completely different ways. You have to first identify these methodological misalignments—ideally during test planning, not during test execution—and then decide which ones will affect your testing and only then take steps to deal with them.

Similarly, be sure to manage the lifecycle implications. If one group is using an agile methodology and another is using a sequential one, that's an obvious misalignment. However, two groups could, again, be following the same lifecycle but simply not have thought through the issues associated with scaling that across multiple groups.

Finally, in case this extended discussion didn't already open your eyes to the fact, understand that you will have to deal with more and different project risks than if everything were happening at one place, by one team. Be sure to plan for and manage the increased project risks.

Distributed Issues

What issues are specifically related to distributed test work?

The most important one is the need to divide the test work across the multiple locations. This division must be done explicitly and in some detail. You cannot rely on people to "just figure this out" based on some vague statements about what types of testing go where. The mission, tasks, deliverables, and channels of communication for various types of communication must all be clearly defined.

This organization of the work must be done intelligently. Be sure to consider the skills and qualifications of the various groups, and put the work in the right place. On all sides of the organization, make sure that all groups and individuals understand what they are to do as well as what other groups and individuals are to do. Otherwise, failures to deliver within the team will occur, and disappointments will accumulate, breeding dissatisfaction, lack of trust, and ill will.

Remember that informal communication channels will be much weaker and random conversations between coworkers in the hallways or at the gym are less likely, so self-organization of work will not occur as readily. When defining communication channels, remember that different types of information require different ways of communicating and different audiences. Escalation of problems is different than reporting of results, and reporting of results is different depending on the audience, as noted previously. A "one size fits all" approach to communication is a common mistake in outsourced, distributed, and insourced work, as is the failure to define a comprehensive and complete set of communication processes and channels.

Organizing the work and setting up effective communication channels are made more difficult when geographical separation and time zone separation are in play. When you can drive across town to visit colleagues and brainstorm solutions, problems are much less daunting than when a 12-hour time zone difference and 36 hours of door-to-door travel separate you from your coworkers. Cultural and language differences contribute to misunderstandings too. Make sure your plan realistically addresses these potential obstacles.

During test planning and throughout the test effort, be alert for signs of gaps and overlaps between the groups. Gaps are situations where every group and manager assumes some test condition is getting covered somewhere else but really no one owns it. Gaps lead to false confidence during the test effort, potentially unpleasant surprises during test execution, and usually an increase in the residual quality risk on delivery.

Overlaps are situations where two or more groups and managers assume some test condition is covered by their group and their group alone but it ends up being covered two or more times. Overlaps lead to inefficiency, potential rework during test execution, and confusion about the meaning of the test results if the results for similar tests disagree.

Finally, ensure a single, unified test dashboard. All of the test results should funnel into some single set of reports. Producing these reports should not be a

Herculean labor either. Ideally, everyone is putting information into a central testing repository from which all the reports are automatically generated.

Insourced and Outsourced Issues

What issues are specifically related to outsourced and insourced test work? First, a little history to introduce some of the issues.

In the 1980s and 1990s, the computer hardware business underwent a powerful trend toward outsourcing development and production of laptops, desktops, servers, hard drives, CD-ROMs, and other components to remote vendors, particularly in East Asia. In the late 1990s and 2000s, the software business began to follow the same path along the same powerful trend, this time with a more global distribution of work that includes not only East Asia but also South Asia, Southeast Asia, Africa, South America, East Europe, and Eurasia. Now, as we move toward the end of the 2010s, this trend continues to evolve, while at the same time the processes have matured.

In both cases, hardware and then software, the main driver has been cost savings. A perception of a possible quality gap between low-cost outsource vendors and local developers drove many vendors to pursue accreditation according to ISO 9000, in the case of hardware, or ISO 15504 or Capability Maturity Model Integration (CMMI), in the case of software. However, such accreditation serves primarily as a marketing mechanism, to overcome a potential objection to sales. Even if the vendor sincerely and completely implements CMMI or ISO 15504, that doesn't necessarily help you from a testing point of view. These software development process improvement standards don't say much about software testing.

Similarly, vendors developed slogans like "right-shoring" and "follow the sun" to deal with two other possible objections to sales. Right-shoring addresses the perceived skills issues that can exist in rapidly growing, emerging high-tech economies, particularly in terms of the ratio of senior to junior people. For example, oftentimes, I will hear testers from emerging markets describe themselves as "senior," because they have two or three years experience on three or four projects. In most seasoned high-tech economies, seniority begins with at least five years of experience, and certainly more in the case of management. Indeed, the general rule is that mastery of a complex subject requires 10,000 hours of experience, which requires five years at least to accumulate.[34]

---

34. This rule of thumb is cited in Malcolm Gladwell's book *Outliers*.

Follow-the-sun addresses both the very real and problematic time zone differences that exist in many cases and the very real and problematic project risks that arise from trying to marshal and manage efforts that are happening thousands of kilometers *and* 5 or 10 time zones away.

I've been able to participate in both sides of this entire arc of outsourcing. I've worked in US-based outsource test labs. I've helped clients use emerging-market outsourced test labs. RBCS provides insource and outsource testing services around the globe. This stuff works. It can save you a lot of money and you can manage the risks, but you do need to disabuse yourself of the marketing spin and sales slogans.

First, make sure you are organized for success. This refers to the methodology and lifecycle alignment issues I mentioned earlier as well as communication channels and logistics. But it also refers to contracts and understandings. If you expect to be able to scrutinize a development vendor's test results, you'd better make sure that's in the contract. Otherwise, you're in for a rude surprise when you ask for their test data, test cases, test tools, bug reports, and test case tracking information.

Second, think carefully about whether you should use a separate test partner, and if so, select the partner. Of course, since RBCS provides outsource test services, we believe that having an independent test partner on outsource projects is a smart way to go. Otherwise, no matter how the development vendor structures its organization, you are going to have test independence issues, with all the self-editing and management editing of the test results that goes with them.

Third, whether for outsourced or insourced testing, ensure adequate personal interaction between your key players and their key players. It's harder for outsource testing, of course, because you can't see them as frequently. However, isolation of insourced testers happens remarkably often too.

As mentioned, you'll need to adapt to the cultures. In the case of outsource and insource, an additional cultural issue is the issue of company cultures. Notice I said adapt, not change. If you've hired the outsource or insource vendor, there's no reason for you to change to accommodate its culture, but don't be naïve and expect that it will change its culture to accommodate yours, either. Adaptation on both sides is the best outcome here.

Finally, make sure you maintain focus on the need to get work done. As much as petty bickering can erupt in distributed work when everyone's part of the same company, it can get nasty when outsource or insource companies are involved. This is especially true if people see the outsource or insource company as a threat to their job. Don't get caught up in smokescreens or diversionary issues as a manager. Maintain focus on getting the test work done.

Make sure your outsource or insource vendor maintains focus too. One not-so-nice trick some services companies use is to have a "senior consultant" or someone like that on a project, possibly on-site, who spends their time exploring ways to increase the size of the account. And, yes, that person is billing you for their time when they're doing that.

Watch for that trick and don't tolerate it. Yes, services companies should be able to propose additional services when they see them. Having them do so is helpful to you because they might be able to solve other problems, some that you didn't even know you had. However, if you're paying a test consultant to be working on your project, that person should be working on your project, not billing you to look for new projects.

Trust

Now, it might sound mushy and softhearted to say, but these approaches require trust. Distributed, outsourced, and insourced testing are all collaborative approaches to getting work done. Trust is critical because it's hard to collaborate with someone and gather evidence against them at the same time.

Given all the issues I've mentioned, including those related to organizational, cultural, language, and geographical boundaries, it's easy to be skeptical of the efficacy of these approaches. However, I mention the issues to help you manage them, not to argue against using this technique. If you manage distributed, outsourced, and insourced testing carefully, each of the test teams will carry out their roles properly.

At that point, the only things that continued skepticism and a lack of trust will cause are inefficiencies and delays. In low-trust situations, I have seen people spend an immense amount of time verifying that activities were happening, apportioning blame every time some minor problem arose, and playing organizational politics.

If you have planned and are managing the distributed outsourced or insourced testing properly, you can be confident that the groups are doing the right things. In this situation, the presence of trust helps everyone maintain proper focus.

Trust must be earned and re-earned, from both sides. Certainly, I am not suggesting blind, naïve trust in vendors. That's a good way to get robbed. What I am saying is that, if you can put common expectations in place, with clear metrics for performance attached to them, you should be able to determine that everyone is doing their job properly. If someone is not, then you have a clear set of numbers you can use to address the performance problem and guide the way toward improvement.

Example: Successful Distributed Testing

Let's close this section with two examples of distributed, outsourced testing. For the first example, one of successful distributed testing, consider the Internet appliance project I've used as one of the running case studies in this book.

In that project, the vendor's test team did most of the hardware testing. We had a few of the most critical tests repeated by a third-party hardware test lab. I don't recall any situations where the vendor's testing proved insufficient. During subsequent software testing, with the vendor's production hardware integrated into our overall system, we did not encounter an unusual number of hardware problems in the production hardware units.

So, we have a completely outsourced and doubly distributed hardware testing effort. We can say that distributing testing to this vendor's test team worked.

Example: Unsuccessful Distributed Testing

For the second example, one of unsuccessful distributed testing, consider again the Internet appliance project.

On that project, my client bought a mail server component from a vendor, much as they bought hardware from a vendor. And, again, the vendor's test team tested the component before delivery—at least they said they had. However, when we tried to integrate their software component into our system, unlike our hardware experience, matters did not go well. There were many mail-related problems discovered, including functionality, performance, and reliability; many of those problems were serious.

So, here we have a situation where distributing testing to this vendor's test team failed. Same project, same people in charge (namely, me and my team), so why did that happen?

One key difference is that we were able to engage with and manage the hardware testing. I spent time in Taiwan, working with the hardware test manager directly, and he was very honest and forthright with me. Conversely, the mail server vendor hid its test results from us, refused to deliver a test tool it had promised, and, once forced to deliver the tool, insisted on charging for a "consultant" (at about $1,500 per day).

You could say that my client got lucky in its choice of hardware vendor and unlucky in its choice of software vendor. However, I'd say the underlying problem was that the hardware vendor went into the relationship knowing my client contact and me, and knowing that we would want to be involved in its testing. The hardware vendor had nothing to hide. The software vendor was chosen by another manager, one I hadn't worked with before, and I don't believe he set their expectations properly in advance.

So, as with many matters of testing success and failure, it comes back to properly aligned, realistic expectations.

2.9   Managing the Application of Industry Standards

Learning objectives

(K2) Summarize sources and uses of standards for software testing.

Standards and Testing

Let's start with a quick overview of standards.

First, standards can cover a variety of topics of direct or indirect interest to us as test managers:

- Software development lifecycles
- Software testing and methodologies
- Software configuration management
- Software maintenance
- Quality assurance
- Project management
- Requirements
- Software languages
- Software interfaces
- Defect management

These standards can come from a variety of sources. There are international standards developed by international standards committees. There are national standards, which can be developed by national standards committees or adapted by national standards committees from international standards. And, there are domain-specific standards, where an international or national standard has been adapted to a particular domain or developed specifically for that domain.

It's important to select and adapt standards appropriately. Be sure to understand the history and source of the standards you are considering as well as the proper application of the standard.

Test-Relevant Standards

Important international standards bodies include those organized by ISO and IEEE.

ISO until recently stood for International Standards Organization, but it changed its name to International Organization for Standardization. Analogous to the structure of the ISTQB, it is composed of representatives of national standards boards. It promulgates the following standards that are of interest to testers:

- ISO 9126 covers software engineering aspects of product quality. It is now being replaced by ISO 25000, which refines the quality model, external quality metrics, internal quality metrics, and quality in use metrics introduced in 9126.
- ISO 12207 covers software lifecycle processes.
- ISO 15504 covers process assessment and replaces Software Process Improvement and Capability Determination (SPICE). It is similar to CMMI.

IEEE is the Institute of Electrical and Electronics Engineers. It is a professional organization based in the United States. However, it has national representatives from over 100 countries. It promulgates the following standards that are of interest to testers:

- IEEE 610 is the IEEE standard computer dictionary. It compiles definitions from across the standards. Note that conflicts exist between the IEEE 610 glossary and the ISTQB glossary.
- IEEE 829 is the standard for software test documentation, which was covered extensively in the Foundation syllabus.
- IEEE 1028 is the standard for software reviews, covered at the Foundation level.

For both ISO and IEEE, please note that additional standards exist that might prove useful to you.

National standards, as you might expect, vary from country to country but can have international applicability. As an example of this, consider the UK's British Standard 7925. It covers a number of test design techniques, including many discussed in the Foundation, Advanced Test Analyst, and Advanced Technical Test Analyst syllabi.

Other standards can be business-domain or technical-domain specific. Some of these standards address testing and quality. Let's look at some examples.

In the avionics industry, we find the DO-178B standard, Software Considerations in Airborne Systems and Equipment Certification. In Europe, it is called the ED-12B standard. It applies to civilian aircraft, but I've also seen it used on military systems. It covers software issues, including embedded systems in aircraft and software used to test the embedded systems in aircraft.

For medical systems, we can look at the United States Food and Drug Administration (FDA) standard Title 21 CFR Part 820 as an example. We'll take a closer look at this in a moment.

There are also other standards—indeed, many other standards—that can apply. Some might be company specific. In some cases, a company or a group might adopt a broader industry standard.

As a test manager, you have to ensure appropriate compliance with any applicable standard.

FDA Regulatory Testing Principles

As an example, what does FDA Title 21 CFR Part 820 tell us about testing?

First, it lays out a set of testing principles, including the following:

- The expected test result should be predefined. There must be a test oracle.
- Testing is a search for defects, not just a trip down the happy path to build confidence. The mindset of "look for bugs" is confirmed by adopting the principles that a good test case has a high probability of exposing an error and that a successful test is one that finds an error. Further, examining only the usual, typically correct case is insufficient.
- To deal with author bias and possible vendor problems, the standard calls for tester independence from coding.
- The standard recognizes the multidisciplinary nature of testing skills, calling for both application and software expertise.
- The standard calls for the use of tools and recognizes that testers use different tools from coders.

Finally, the standard calls for test documentation that permits its reuse. It also calls for possible auditing and independent confirmation of the test status, either periodically or in response to some issues in the field.

The principles in the previous section would help us define a test policy. However, what specific tasks should we address in our test plans if we are subject to FDA Title 21 CFR Part 820? The standard calls for the following:

- Test planning, covering the topics addressed earlier in this chapter.
- Structural test design, including statement, branch, condition/multi-condition, loop, path, and dataflow. These techniques are covered in *Advanced Software Testing: Volume 3.*
- Functional test design, including normal case, all outputs, robustness, and input combinations. Techniques for these types of tests are covered in *Advanced Software Testing: Volume 1.*
- Traceability between unit tests and detailed design, integration tests and high level design, and system tests and requirements.
- A number of test levels, including unit test, integration test, functional test, system test, and acceptance test.
- Bug triage that includes the proper set of stakeholders.
- Results evaluation and final report.

Other Standards

In some cases, you may need to adapt to standards that have very little do to with software testing but change the software process in which you operate. CMMI, the Project Management Body of Knowledge (PMBOK, from the Project Management Institute, or PMI), Projects in Controlled Environments, version 2 (PRINCE2), and the Information Technology Infrastructure Library (ITIL) are all examples of such standards that have a profound influence on testing. In the case of CMMI, it has two defined key process areas, verification and validation, that are directly relevant for testing. Some of our clients have interpreted verification, which requires 100 percent coverage of specified requirements, as referring to system testing, and validation, which requires 100 percent coverage of use cases and supported configurations, as referring to forms of acceptance testing such as beta testing and user acceptance testing. Notice that this implies that an analytical test strategy will be part of the larger test approach.

PMBOK and PRINCE2 are important from a project management perspective. If you are in an organization that follows either standard—and it will need to be one or the other because they are not compatible—then you'll benefit from at least learning what they are about, so you can better communicate with project managers and align your test plans with their project plans. The situation with ITIL is similar, but ITIL addresses the broader question of how IT organizations deliver services to the companies in which they exist. In some cases, our clients' test managers pursue certification under these programs to be completely conversant with them as well as to position themselves for career advancement.[35] Because the terminology and activities in these programs are different from the ISTQB's, you must understand them to some extent in order to be effective.

Standards and Templates

Standards can sometimes provide sources of templates. For example, IEEE 829, both the 1998 version and the 2008 version, provides a set of templates for test documentation. The ISTQB decided to stay with the 1998 version, by the way, because the 2008 version of the standard specifies not only templates—which are not in any way improved over the 1998 version—but also processes that are not compatible with the ISTQB approach.

Strictly following the IEEE 829 templates can lead to excessive and redundant documentation in many cases. I've seen this happen with a few clients, and it can be very inefficient. It can also make the teams less effective because excessive documentation can distract testers from their real objectives.

However, the IEEE 829 templates can be tailored to fit a number of different situations. I have done that for my own projects and for projects with clients. There are plenty of other good sources of test templates, too.[36] The best practice is to tailor any templates you obtain to fit your specific needs.

Why not just create your own templates? Well, the better question is, Why create your own templates? Why do extra work?

Why do you need templates? While flexibility in documentation should be allowed, standardization in documentation will promote efficiency. Having a

35. RBCS's webinar series can assist with career advancement by providing relevant information, experiences, and Q & A on various industry topics and opportunities for attendees to earn PMI professional development units (PDUs) when applicable. You can find a listing of the upcoming webinars at www.rbcs-us.com.
36. Test templates are available in the RBCS libraries: the Basic Library is at http://www.rbcs-us.com/software-testing-resources/library/basic-library and the Advanced Library is at http://www.rbcs-us.com/software-testing-resources/library/advanced-library.

> **ISTQB Glossary**
>
> **test approach:** The implementation of the test strategy for a specific project. It typically includes the decisions made that follow based on the (test) project's goal and the risk assessment carried out, starting points regarding the test process, the test design techniques to be applied, exit criteria and test types to be performed.

tailored set of templates that spans all the test teams reduces the amount of training, unifies process, and builds consistency.

Applying Standards

Here are some general aspects to keep in mind about standards.

As mentioned, standards come from various international, national, and domain-specific standards bodies. Ultimately, a standards body is a group of recognized professionals. Unlike physical laws, such as gravity, standards are created and assembled by these professionals based on their collective wisdom, experience, empirical evidence, preferences, and biases. So a standard's credibility and value ultimately should arise from the people who create it. Not all mandatory standards are necessarily valuable, and some voluntary standards are valuable.

Because they are developed by people, standards evolve and change over time. Thus, when evaluating a standard, make sure you know which version you're evaluating. If the standard is under revision, you should at least review the information available on that revision as part of your evaluation. Better yet, if draft copies are available, review those.

Will standards prove useful to you? Well, if you are subject to a mandatory testing standard, it will prove quite useful, probably in at least three important ways. First, you can't do your job properly without referring to the standard, so it's your handbook for testing in a way. Second, you will probably find that the standard serves as a source and valuable reference for your test policy, test strategy, and test plan documents and might provide guidance for all documentation work products. Third, you might find that the standard helps create support for testing and unlocks funding you might not otherwise have gotten. After all, how can management question a particular testing activity if it's mandated by a standard to which you must comply?

Whether or not standards are mandatory, they can still prove useful. For one thing, standards can promote a preventive testing strategy. For another, they can provide adaptable process checklists, ideas on test techniques, potential objectives for testing, and other types of reference frameworks. In a nonmandatory setting, a standard can be a useful starting point for putting some structure around your testing.

It is also true that standards can hinder you. As I mentioned in my earlier discussion about types of test strategies, a standards-driven test strategy has the weakness that, should the standard be derived for situations vastly different than yours, you'll find it a poor fit. You'll end up not doing things you should do and doing things you really don't need to do. You can't afford to make either of these two mistakes—the first dulls your effectiveness and the second dulls your efficiency—but you will make these mistakes if you fail to apply or to tailor the standards appropriately.

Another potential pitfall with standards arises when you are subject to or are adapting multiple standards. Just as laws are developed by people and thus vary from country to country and even from town to town, so too do standards. In some cases, they are simply inconsistent, but in other cases, they are conflicting. In a situation where two or more standards are in play, be watchful for such conflicts and incoherence and be sure to adapt the standards to resolve these problems.

2.10 Sample Exam Questions

To end each chapter, you can try one or more sample exam questions to reinforce your knowledge and understanding of the material and to prepare for the ISTQB Advanced Level Test Manager exam.

1. Which of the following is a project risk mitigation step that you might take as a test manager?

    A. Testing for performance problems

    B. Hiring a contractor after a key test analyst quits

    C. Procuring extra test environments in case one fails during testing

    D. Performing a project retrospective using test results

2. You are planning the testing for an integrated system that will use three off-the-shelf components to manage a bank's accounts-receivable system. You are conducting an informal quality risk analysis session with project and system stakeholders to determine what test conditions should be tested and how much each test condition should be tested. Which of the following is a quality risk item that you might identify in this quality risk analysis session?

    A. Failure of a component vendor to conduct adequate component testing

    B. Calculation of excessive late-payment penalties for invoices

    C. On-time payment of all invoices for international vendors

    D. Calculation of risk priority using likelihood and impact

3. During a formalized quality risk analysis session following the failure mode and effect analysis technique, you are calculating risk priorities. Which of the following are major factors in this calculation?

    A. Severity and priority

    B. Functionality, reliability, usability, efficiency, maintainability, and portability

    C. Loss of a key contributor on the test team

    D. Loss of a key contributor on the development team

4. Assume you are a test manager in charge of integration testing, system testing, and acceptance testing for a bank. You are working on a project to upgrade an existing automated teller machine system to allow customers to obtain cash advances from supported credit cards. The system should allow cash advances from $20 to $500, inclusively, for all supported credit cards. The supported credit cards are American Express, Visa, Japan Credit Bureau, Eurocard, and MasterCard.

    Which of the following statements best associates a key stakeholder with the kind of input that stakeholder can provide during a quality risk analysis?

    A. A tester can provide input on the likelihood of a risk item.

    B. A developer can provide input on the impact of a risk item.

    C. A business analyst can provide input on the likelihood of a risk item.

    D. A help desk staffer can provide input on the impact of a risk item.

5. Which of the following is a situation in which you would expect an iterative quality risk analysis to result in the largest number of new or changed risk items and risk levels?

    A. You perform a risk analysis on the final requirements specification and subsequently receive a draft design specification.

    B. A tester leaves after test design is complete, and you hire a new tester to replace her.

    C. The development manager hires two additional programmers after the quality risk analysis is complete.

    D. You perform a risk analysis on the final requirements specification and then that document is placed under formal configuration management.

6. Assume you are a test manager working on a project to create a programmable thermostat for home use to control central heating, ventilation, and air conditioning (HVAC) systems. In addition to the normal HVAC control functions, the thermostat has the ability to download data to a browser-based application that runs on PCs, tablets, and smartphones for further analysis..

    During quality risk analysis, you identify compatibility problems between the browser-based application and the different PC configurations that can host that application as a quality risk item with a high level of likelihood. You plan to perform compatibility testing to address this risk.

    Which of the following is a way in which you might monitor the effect of testing on the reduction of this risk during test execution?

    A. Reduce the number of supported PC configurations.

    B. Assign more testers to cover compatibility than testers to cover functionality.

    C. Analyze the number of defects found that relate to this risk item.

    D. Plan to test the most common PC configurations.

7. Which of the following is an example of a project where failure mode and effect analysis could be a good choice for risk analysis?

    A. It is the project team's first application of risk-based testing.

    B. The system under test is both complex and safety critical.

    C. The system under test is a simple e-commerce application.

    D. Minimizing the amount of documentation is a priority.

8. Assume you are a test manager in charge of integration testing, system testing, and acceptance testing for a bank. You are working on a project to upgrade an existing automated teller machine system to allow customers to obtain cash advances from supported credit cards. The system should allow cash advances from $20 to $500, inclusively, for all supported credit cards. The supported credit cards are American Express, Visa, Japan Credit Bureau, Eurocard, and MasterCard.

In the master test plan, the Features to Be Tested section lists the following:

I. All supported credit cards
II. Language localization
III. Valid and invalid advances
IV. Usability
V. Response time

Relying only on the information given above, select the features to be tested for which sufficient information is available to proceed with test design.

A. I
B. II
C. III
D. IV
E. V

9. Continue with the scenario described in the previous question. Which of the following topics would you need to address in detail in the master test plan?

A. A strategy for regression testing
B. A list of advance amount boundary values
C. A description of intercase dependencies
D. A logical collection of test cases

10. Assume you are a test manager working on a project to create a programmable thermostat for home use to control central heating, ventilation, and air conditioning (HVAC) systems. In addition to the normal HVAC control functions, the thermostat has the ability to download data to a browser-based application that runs on PCs, tablets, and smartphones for further analysis.

    The company test strategy calls for each test case to be run on all combinations of configuration options. For this system, you identify the following factors and, for each factor, the following options:

    > Supported PC/thermostat connections: USB and Bluetooth

    > Supported operating systems: Windows XP, Windows 7, Windows 8, Mac OS X, Linux

    > Supported browsers: Internet Explorer, Firefox, Opera

Since there are 10 test cases that involve downloading data, this would require running 300 test cases, each of which requires an hour to run.

    With management approval, you decide to test five configurations, covering each option but not all the possible pairs and triples of options. Which of the following statements describes the best option for documenting this deviation from the test strategy?

A. In the test cases, explain the alternate approach planned for this project and how to set up the test configurations.

B. In the project plan, explain which test cases should be run against which configurations.

C. In the master test plan, explain the alternate approach planned for this project and why this approach is sufficient.

D. In the test item transmittal report, explain the alternate approach planned for this project and which test items were tested against which configuration.

11. Continue with the scenario described in the previous question. You are writing a master test plan to cover integration testing and system testing of the programmable thermostat. Select all of the following statements that are true.

    A. The approach section should describe how to test the integration of the thermostat with other parts of the HVAC system.

    B. The schedule section should describe the entry and exit criteria for integration testing and system testing.

    C. The environmental needs section should address who is responsible for each level of testing.

    D. The test items section should describe the equipment required for each level of testing.

    E. The test deliverables section should describe results reporting for each level of testing.

12. Continue with the scenario described in the previous questions, where you are a test manager working on a project to create a programmable thermostat for home use to control central heating, ventilation, and air conditioning (HVAC) systems. One critical quality risk identified for this system is the possibility of damage to the HVAC system caused by excessive cycling of the compressor (i.e., turning the unit on and off repeatedly in short intervals). Which of the following is a reasonable way to use test planning to direct appropriate testing for this risk?

    A. Write a separate test plan for this level of testing.

    B. List the feature that prevents excessive cycling as a feature to be tested.

    C. Detail all of the requirements of the programmable thermostat in the introduction of the test plan.

    D. Include a fully functioning compressor as one of the test items.

13. Continue with the scenario from the previous question.

Historically, on seven past projects, the test team has found approximately 12 bugs during system test for each person-month of development team effort. Five developers are assigned to work on a new project that is scheduled to last six months. Assume that the cumulative number of bugs found has leveled off at 351 defects.

Based on this information only, which of the following statements is most likely to be true?

A. You would expect to find exactly 20 more defects before the end of system test.

B. You have omitted tests for at least one critical quality risk category.

C. You needed a test team of at least three testers for optimum testing.

D. You have found roughly the number of defects you would expect to find during system test.

14. Continue with the scenario from the previous question.

Assume that this project is following an iterative lifecycle, while the previous projects for which you have bug metrics followed a sequential lifecycle. Assuming no other dissimilarities between this project and the previous projects, which of the following might be a reason to question the accuracy of the predicted number of defects?

A. People factors

B. Material factors

C. Process factors

D. Quality factors

15. You are a test manager in charge of system testing on a project to update a cruise-control module for a new model of a car. The goal of the cruise-control software update is to make the car more fuel efficient.

You have written a first release of the system test plan based on the final requirements specification. You receive an early draft of the design specification. Identify which *two* of the following statements are true.

A. Publish a list of all past defects found in design specifications to the team.

B. Produce a draft update of the system test plan based on this version of the design specification.

C. Check this version of the design specification for inconsistencies with the requirements specification.

D. Participate in the final review of the design specification but not any preliminary reviews of the design specification.

E. Review the quality risk analysis to see if the design specification has identified additional risk items.

16. Which of the following is the best example of a technique for controlling test progress in terms of the residual level of quality risk?

A. Counting the number of defects found and the number of defects resolved

B. Counting the number of test cases passed and the number of test cases failed

C. Counting the number of requirements that work properly and the number of requirements with known defects

D. Counting the number of tested risk items without known defects and the number of tested risk items with known defects

17. You are a test manager in charge of system testing on a project to update a cruise-control module for a new model of a car. The goal of the cruise-control software update is to make the car more fuel efficient.

Halfway through test execution, you find that the test results do not conclusively determine whether fuel efficiency has improved. Identify *two* of the following actions that you might direct the test analysts to take to help to resolve this problem.

A. Remove the fuel efficiency tests from the test plan.

B. Revise the quality risk analysis.

C. Modify the test environment to gather more detailed actual results.

D. Check for consistency in tested fuel mixtures.

E. Report fuel efficiency as apparently unchanged.

18. Assume you are a test manager in charge of integration testing, system testing, and acceptance testing for a bank. You are working on a project to upgrade an existing automated teller machine system to allow customers to obtain cash advances from supported credit cards. The system should allow cash advances from $20 to $500, inclusively, for all supported credit cards.

The supported credit cards are American Express, Visa, Japan Credit Bureau, Eurocard, and MasterCard.

During test execution, you find five defects, each reported by a different tester, that involve the same problem with cash advances, with the only difference between these reports being the credit card tested. Which of the following is an improvement to the test process that you might suggest?

A. Revise all cash advance test cases to test with only one credit card.

B. Review all reports filed subsequently and close any duplicate defect reports before assignment to development.

C. Change the requirements to delete support for American Express cards.

D. Have testers check for similar problems with other cards and report their findings in defect reports.

19. You are the manager of a bank's quality assessment group, in charge of independent testing for banking applications. You are working on a project to implement an integrated system that will use three off-the-shelf systems to manage a bank's accounts-receivable system. You are currently managing the execution of system integration testing.

Consider the following bug open/closed or convergence chart.

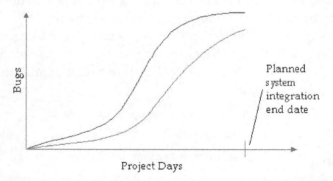

Which of the following interpretations of this chart provides a reason to not declare the system integration testing complete?

A. The bug find rate has not leveled off.

B. Developers aren't fixing bugs fast enough.

C. The complete set of tests has not yet been run.

D. A number of unresolved bugs remain in the backlog.

20. Which of the following is an example of a cost of internal failure?

    A. Finding a bug during testing

    B. Training developers in secure coding practices

    C. Designing test cases

    D. Fixing a customer-detected bug

    A is the correct answer

21. You are the manager of a bank's quality assessment group, in charge of independent testing for banking applications. You are in charge of testing for a project to implement an integrated system that uses three off-the-shelf components to manage a bank's accounts-receivable system.

    Which of the following is most likely to be a major business motivation for testing this system?

    A. Avoiding loss of life

    B. Having confidence in correct customer billing

    C. Finding as many bugs as possible before release

    D. Gathering evidence to sue the component vendors

22. Which of the following is a risk of outsourced testing that might not apply to distributed testing?

    A. Selection of an improper test partner

    B. Communication problems created by time zone differences

    C. Insufficient skills in some of the test team members

    D. Inconsistent test processes across the testing locations

23. You are the manager of a bank's quality assessment group, in charge of independent testing for banking applications. You used quality risk analysis to allocate effort and prioritize your tests during test preparation. You are currently executing the system integration test.

    You have finished running each test case once. You are not certain how much time the project management team will allow for additional test execution because regulatory changes might require the system to be activated ahead of schedule.

    Based on the severity and priority of the bugs found by each test case, you have calculated weighted failure for each test case. You also know the risk priority number for each test case based on the quality risk item(s) the test case covers. Considering both the weighted failure and the risk priority number, you have reprioritized your test cases for the final days or weeks of testing.

Which of the following is a benefit this reprioritization will provide?

A. If testing is curtailed, you will have expended the minimum amount of effort possible.

B. If testing is extended, you will have time to run all of your tests.

C. If testing is curtailed, you will have run the most important tests.

D. If testing is extended, you will have covered all of the requirements.

24. Which of the following is a benefit of exploratory testing and other reactive test strategies that would not apply to an analytical requirements-based test strategy?

A. The ability to utilize a very experienced test team

B. The ability to accurately predict the residual risk prior to delivery

C. The ability to prevent defects during requirements analysis

D. The ability to test effectively without a complete test basis

3 Reviews

NASA lost a $125 million Mars orbiter because a Lockheed Martin engineering team used English units of measurement while the agency's team used the more conventional metric system for a key spacecraft operation, according to a review finding released Thursday. The units mismatch prevented navigation information from transferring between the Mars Climate Orbiter spacecraft team at Lockheed Martin in Denver and the flight team at NASA's Jet Propulsion Laboratory in Pasadena, California.

From CNN, a news story on a bug
that could have been found by a good set of design reviews.

Chapter 3, Reviews, of the Advanced syllabus contains the following five sections:

1. Introduction
2. Management Reviews and Audits
3. Managing Reviews
4. Metrics for Reviews
5. Managing Formal Reviews

3.1 Introduction

Learning objectives
Recall of content only

As discussed in the ISTQB Foundation syllabus, a review is a form of static testing where a group of people (the reviewers), led by a moderator, work separately and together to identify defects, reach consensus, and build understanding of the work product being reviewed. In some cases—specifically audits and management reviews, which I'll discuss in a moment—reviews are not focused on a work product but rather on the process or the project.

Testers should participate in reviews because they have a special outlook based on their role in finding defects throughout the lifecycle, they have unique insights into how the software behaves under various conditions, and they understand functional and nonfunctional characteristics of the product. In some cases, test managers are responsible for the review process and its success, especially when the target of the review is a testing work product or the testing process. In other cases the responsible party is a quality assurance manager or a specialized, trained review coordinator. Because of the variation in ownership that often exists, I'll refer to the responsible person as the review leader in this chapter.

Whoever the review leader is, that person plays a vital role in ensuring proper reviews. Industry studies have shown that such reviews create an enormous opportunity in terms of avoiding downstream costs of failure and delivering high-quality software.[1] A review leader must commit to supporting success in the review process. The degree of success, and business value delivered, can and should be measured. It must also be communicated effectively to decision makers so that the process is strengthened and continued.

In addition to proper leadership, proper training is necessary to ensure review success. Simply showing up and grousing about some aspect of a work product one disagrees with is hardly constructive behavior and will not result in significant quality improvements. In fact, it usually leads to dissension and ill-will between the author and the reviewers. Instead, all review participants, in every role in the process, must have a good understanding of how to contribute to the success of the process. In addition, they must be personally committed to taking the process seriously and helping their project reap the benefits of good reviews.

Because this chapter builds on the Foundation syllabus to a great degree, I encourage you to review Chapter 3 of the syllabus, especially section 2. That chapter describes the process, the roles, and the benefits of reviews.

---

1. For example, see *Estimating Software Costs, 2nd Edition*, and *The Economics of Software Quality*, both by Capers Jones.

ISTQB Glossary

audit: An independent evaluation of software products or processes to ascertain compliance to standards, guidelines, specifications, and/or procedures based on objective criteria, including documents that specify the following:

(1) the form or content of the products to be produced
(2) the process by which the products shall be produced
(3) how compliance to standards or guidelines shall be measured.

management review: A systematic evaluation of software acquisition, supply, development, operation, or maintenance process performed by or on behalf of management that monitors progress, determines the status of plans and schedules, confirms requirements and their system allocation, or evaluates the effectiveness of management approaches to achieve fitness for purpose.

moderator: The leader and main person responsible for an inspection or other review process.

review: An evaluation of a product or project status to ascertain discrepancies from planned results and to recommend improvements. Examples include management review, informal review, technical review, inspection, and walk-through.

reviewer: The person involved in the review that identifies and describes anomalies in the product or project under review. Reviewers can be chosen to represent different viewpoints and roles in the review process.

Project Reviews and Review Types

One way to classify reviews is used at the Foundation level, based on the review process and the level of formality applied to the review. The Foundation level classification follows the IEEE 1028 standard and adds another type of review that is very common, the informal review:

- Informal reviews have no formal process, with results that might or might not be documented and that vary greatly in usefulness depending on the reviewers. While not always especially effective, they are cheap and provide some benefit in terms of defect removal.
- Walk-throughs are meetings led by the author, with varying degrees of formality and with various agendas depending on the goal. They allow attendees to learn more about the system and gain understanding of why choices were made as well as to find defects.

- Technical reviews follow an expansively defined process that includes a meeting, with a defined procedure for defect detection that includes peers and technical experts, which results in a report of the findings and recommendations. They can serve various purposes, such as discussing the work product, deciding what to do based on various alternatives, finding defects and possibly resolving them, and checking conformance to applicable standards, regulations, and guidelines.

- Inspections are the most formal of the reviews, characterized by precisely defined roles and processes, careful preparation, entry and exit criteria, a final report, and a formal follow-up process. The main purpose is finding defects.

At the Advanced level, test managers are also concerned with, and often involved in, management reviews and audits. I'll discuss these in the next section.

In addition to classifying reviews based on the process and the level of formality, we can classify them based on the objective:

- A contractual review is designed to ensure both initial and ongoing alignment of the contract with the needs of the project. It often involves evaluation of cost and schedule, deliverable status, and other important management considerations. Contractual reviews are typically management reviews but are sometimes audits. They usually occur at the start of a project and at major project milestones.

- A requirements review can be informal, a walk-through, a technical review, or an inspection with the associated goals and objectives. Sometimes, a requirements review can be a management review with the objective of approving the requirements as the basis for further work. Requirements reviews can take place using draft documents as an input, though reviews that are intended to provide approval should occur based on proposed final documents. A requirements review should address functional and non-functional requirements, and a checklist such as ISO 9126 can help detect and remove gaps.

- Top-level design reviews and detailed design reviews, like requirements reviews, can follow any of the four work product review types and can also involve a management review that approves these documents as the basis for further work. Technical reviews are particularly effective when the design documents are in draft form because discussions of possible design alternatives can be conducted among experts and peers using this type of review.

- Code reviews can also follow any of the four work product review types. They typically do not involve management reviews because they are focused on individual units of code. In my experience, the best practice is for code reviews to address not only the code but also unit tests run against the code and the unit test results. According to Capers Jones, formal inspections of code have the highest possible defect removal effectiveness of all reviews, up to 85 percent.[2]

- Test work products can and should be reviewed too. When the objectives are improving the test work product, building consensus about the testing to be done, or increasing the understanding of the testing work, any of the four work product review techniques may be used, though I have found that inspections are relatively rare for test work products. These work products can include test plans, test conditions, quality risk analysis results, tests, test data, and test environments. In the case of test results reviews, test plan reviews, test condition reviews, and quality risk analysis results, management reviews may be used to obtain approval, and audits are sometimes used when independent verification and validation is involved.

- Test entry and exit criteria are often reviewed as part of the test plan review. During management reviews, these criteria are often re-reviewed to check whether the test team is ready to start or conclude a level of testing.

- At the end of a project, upon proposed delivery of the system, customers or stakeholders may be involved in acceptance reviews. These are typically management reviews.

If you are serving as the review leader on a project—or just for the test work products—remember that a work product can be put through multiple rounds of different types of reviews. For example, a test plan can go through an informal review with the test team first. Once the review is complete and any defects are resolved, you can then plan and carry out a management review to approve the test plan. Similarly, early drafts of a requirements specification can be subjected to informal reviews and perhaps a technical review, with a walk-through on the final version of the requirements.

In addition, reviews are only one form of static testing that can occur. For example, a requirements specification, a design specification, and a test plan can

---

2. This figure can be found in his book *Estimating Software Costs, 2nd Edition.*

> **ISTQB Glossary**
>
> **informal review:** A review not based on a formal (documented) procedure.
>
> **inspection:** A type of peer review that relies on visual examination of documents to detect defects, e.g., violations of development standards and non-conformance to higher-level documentation. The most formal review technique and therefore always based on a documented procedure.
>
> **peer review:** A review of a software work product by colleagues of the producer of the product for the purpose of identifying defects and improvements. Examples are inspection, technical review, and walk-through.
>
> **technical review:** A peer group discussion activity that focuses on achieving consensus on the technical approach to be taken.
>
> **walk-through:** A step-by-step presentation by the author of a document in order to gather information and to establish a common understanding of its content.

be given a static analysis using a tool like Microsoft Word. Word's spelling and grammar checker can find simple mistakes that might cause confusion when someone is reading the document, and it can check readability to ensure that all recipients of the document—especially those who did not grow up reading and speaking English—will be able to comprehend it. Code can be reviewed by sophisticated tools that will identify maintainability and coding standards problems. Such a comprehensive approach to static testing, which is subsequently augmented by behavioral, structural, experience-based, and defect-based dynamic testing, will tend to cover most aspects of the product and find the maximum number of defects since these static and dynamic techniques are complementary in terms of their bug-finding abilities.

In addition to the defect-finding capabilities of static testing, reviews especially can serve an educational and consensus-building purpose. If patterns emerge in the defects found by static testing, the review leader can propose—and if approved, plan for—internal and external training courses to help reduce the incidence of such defects. This type of process improvement can also be done based on patterns in dynamic testing, of course, but the cost of finding these defects and introducing the appropriate process changes will be lower for static testing.

3.2 Management Reviews and Audits

Learning objectives

(K2) Understand the key characteristics of management reviews and audits.

While they are not discussed at the Foundation level, at the Advanced Test Manager level we need to discuss management reviews because they are relevant to test managers. Most test managers involved in active test projects will attend management reviews at least weekly. In the case of agile projects, test managers or even test leads might well attend daily management reviews, in the form of daily stand-up meetings.

The attendees of these management reviews vary depending on the scope and the agenda of the review. Some reviews, such as agile stand-up meetings, tend to be very tactical, focused on how to successfully achieve the goals of the current sprint or iteration, with the attendees making immediate, short-term decisions. Other reviews, especially those conducted at major milestones on large projects, will have a more strategic view and attendees will make long-term decisions.

In management reviews, the project team will check progress against the plan. If the current status indicates that all is going well, then the team may decide to proceed as currently planned. Evaluating status includes checking whether you are proceeding according to the plan as originally set down or as modified based on project changes over time. The actions taken so far on the project, and the results obtained, should be considered, ideally using measurements to determine status as well as informed opinions about how things are going. Evaluating status also includes assessing project risks and whether those risks are becoming events. The adequacy of the project management activities and procedures should also be considered, in case something important is being missed.

If the current status is not good, then corrective actions might be initiated and ultimately managed by the project management team. These actions could include modifying the scope of the project, adding or removing resources, increasing or decreasing the amount of testing being done, revising the quality risk analysis, and triggering contingencies for project risks. In this case, action items should be clearly identified and assigned, decisions documented, and subsequent check-points decided. If the current status is troubling but not such that immediate actions are appropriate, the issues should be identified and documented, with follow-up actions set for subsequent management reviews.

An important form of management review is the retrospective. As discussed in Chapter 1, retrospectives can cover the entire project or just a portion of the project. Test managers are typically responsible for test retrospectives, which they will lead with their test teams. Test managers or their designees should also attend project retrospectives to ensure that test-related process observations and improvements are represented in those meetings.

Audits

An audit is a particular type of review where the objective is to check for compliance. The compliance check can be against a regulatory requirement, as with FDA regulated software, where the auditor will check whether the requirements for the project and testing are fulfilled. The compliance check can be against a mandatory or voluntary standard, as with testing in an agile project, where a consultant will evaluate whether the team is following agile best practices. The compliance check can also be against a contract, based on requirements that the project team follows certain practices or achieves certain measures of effectiveness, efficiency, or satisfaction.

A key characteristic of an audit is that someone (or a collection of someones) is playing a formal or informal auditing role. The auditor should be independent, in that they should have no interest in whether the audit shows compliance or lack of compliance. In practice, pure objectivity is often difficult to obtain, and managers should be aware of this possibility of bias. The auditors will typically interview project participants and other stakeholders, watch processes being carried out properly (or not), and examine evidence such as documents and metrics.

The result of an audit varies. It can typically include observations by the auditor about what they found. If improvements are needed or simply suggested, recommendations are often included. If specific deviations from required behaviors are found, then corrective actions will be stated as requirements for a successful re-audit. In many cases, the audit includes an assessment of whether the audit passed or failed. A conditional pass based on implementation of corrective action within a given time frame is also possible.

As a test consulting company, RBCS performs assessments of test teams and their processes. Other organizations do the same. We don't refer to these as audits but rather as assessments, in a deliberate fashion. Our objective is not to adopt an adversarial relationship but rather a coaching relationship. Our assessments include recommendations, with the suggested order of implementing those recommendations based on business value. I'll return to this topic of test process improvement in Chapter 5.

Example: Formal Management Review

In Figure 3–1?, you see an outline of the formal change management process used by one client. These change control board (CCB) meetings were recurring, formal management review meetings.

Change Control Board Process

Scope: The Change Control Board will facilitate change requests...for initial release and changes to production released products.

Submit Change Request: Change requests should be submitted through Development or Program Management. A change request must...include... the following: Definition of the change... Areas impacted... Documentation to be updated... Priority... Dependencies... Estimated impact... Requested date

CCB Review:

Team Members: ...Development... Test... Support... Network Operations... Supply Chain...Program Management/Release Management... Finance... Marketing

Signature Criteria: ...

Attachment Requirements:...

Approved?:...

Implement Change:...

Figure 3–1   *Formal change management process*

Let me point out some key areas of the document shown in Figure 3–1?.

First, notice that we have a well-defined scope. The change control board is there to facilitate change requests in terms of the definition of the initial release as well as subsequent changes to production released products.

There is a requirement that before the meeting, the proposer or proposers of the change must adequately prepare their request. There are rules laid down about how to submit a change request. Those rules address both the channel through which the request should be submitted and the content that must be included.

The document then goes on to describe how the CCB should review these requests.

It starts by defining the team members of the CCB. This includes a complete cross section of the project team and all stakeholders.

Each member group plays a defined role. The Signature Criteria subsection describes that role. The document also defines here what it means when a team member signs a change request. It did not necessarily indicate approval of the request. In some cases, signature meant, "Yes, I understand and will support this change, but I don't think this is a good idea." The signature by the test team specifically means that we will test or have tested the change but not that we feel that the test results support its release.

In addition to the change request itself, in many cases there were attachments required for the document to be considered complete.

In the Approved? section, the document talks about how to note the disposition of the change request.

Finally, the Implement Change section describes the requirements for each group to play their part once the change is approved and going into production.

3.3   Managing Reviews

Learning objectives

(K4) Analyze a project to select the appropriate review type and to define a plan for conducting reviews, in order to ensure proper execution, follow-up, and accountability

(K2) Understand the factors, skills, and time required for participation in reviews.

Reviews have their own natural point of occurrence and should be planned to occur at those points. You probably know this from your own experience. When writing a test plan, there comes a point when you are ready for feedback on your ideas. That's the time to have a review, if only an informal review of an early draft. Ultimately, you'll reach a point where you believe the document is done and ready for approval. That's the time to schedule a management review with the test stakeholders.

It's similar with requirements and design specifications. Business analysts and system architects often need to get some feedback on their ideas as they

ISTQB Glossary

review plan: A document describing the approach, resources, and schedule of intended review activities. It identifies, amongst others: documents and code to be reviewed, review types to be used, and participants, as well as entry and exit criteria to be applied in case of formal reviews, and the rationale for their choice. It is a record of the review planning.

proceed, and informal reviews and technical reviews are good ways to do this. Once the documents are in a more mature state, a walk-through or inspection might be in order. As mentioned previously, multiple reviews of different types can ensure the highest quality deliverables, though of course there is a balance between getting too little feedback and getting too much.

Management reviews likewise have their own rhythm. Major project milestones are points at which project status should be reviewed. Management reviews should usually be scheduled regularly during the project to monitor progress. The meaning of "regularly" is based on the lifecycle being followed. On medium- to long-term projects following sequential lifecycles, weekly project status meetings are common. On agile projects, daily stand-up meetings to review status often occur.

Test managers must manage reviews on their own testing efforts, and sometimes they are responsible for managing reviews across the entire project. Even if another manager is in charge of reviews, reviews are part of the process by which organizations improve quality, just as testing is, and therefore the strategy for reviews should be aligned with the testing policy and strategy. So, in this section, we'll look at how to develop a successful plan for reviews.

Specifically, a review plan should consider the following topics:

- What work product reviews and other types of reviews to conduct and what review processes to use for those reviews
- What metrics should be gathered during reviews and how those should be used
- What benefits the organization should receive, in terms of return on investment
- Who should be involved in the reviews, based on work product and role
- What the relevant quality and project risks are and how to best manage those
- What the review leader needs to do as part of these reviews

Let's examine the various questions raised about review planning on the next few pages.

What Should We Review and How?

During the initial project planning period, the review leader must consider the work products that will be produced, including getting some rough idea of when these items should be available in draft and in final form. If the review leader is also in charge of process and project reviews, they should also consider when these reviews will take place. Of course, it's quite possible that these dates will be fluid and changeable at this point, so the plan should retain flexibility about the exact dates for specific reviews.

For work products needing review, the review leader should select the type of work product review to apply. As mentioned earlier, multiple review types may apply to these work products, so the review leader might consider such multiple reviews for applicable work products as well. In addition, the level of formality for each review should be selected. This means determining the extent to which a documented process will be followed, entry and exit criteria will be applied to each step of the process, metrics will be gathered and analyzed, and so forth. In some cases, the organization will have standards that determine the answers to these questions of type and formality, but it's possible that exceptions to these standards will be appropriate.

Since review meetings should be limited to at most two hours, it may be necessary to plan multiple review sessions to avoid going over that time limit by trying to inspect a long document. This is especially true of inspections since the rate of inspections, on a minutes-per-page basis, tends to be considerably slower than for other review types. However, this issue of review meeting duration should be considered for all reviews, and if necessary, reviews should be divided based on subsystems or individual elements.

For process and project reviews, the review leader—if responsible for such reviews—should also consider the proper process to follow. Sometimes, though, the project manager is responsible for such reviews. In that case, the review leader should coordinate with the project manager to make sure there are no mistaken assumptions about who is responsible for what. A surefire way to have important things fall through the cracks in a project is to have misunderstandings as to responsibility.

With the types of reviews and their formality determined, the review leader should consider whether training is necessary for review participants. Reviews are something that most people seem to consider themselves qualified to attend and participate in, based simply on the understanding of the subject matter or technology involved. While this is true for informal reviews to some extent, the more formal review types, especially inspections, are quite specific in terms of their processes and rules. Next to proper preparation of the review participants prior to the review, proper training in review methods is probably the most important factor in review effectiveness. As a test manager, I have seen instances where improper behavior in review meetings seriously degraded the results, and I have heard many accounts of such instances in my work as a consultant.

With the reviews determined and the training needs identified, a training review budget can be created. This budget should specify the time (i.e., person-hours of effort) and the resources (i.e., facilities, training funds, etc.) required. Again, if responsibility for reviews is shared across multiple parties, such as the test manager, QA manager, project manager, and so forth, creating this budget ideally would be a coordinated effort involving all responsible parties. The coordinated budget will prevent misunderstandings and perhaps underfunding that can occur if approving managers think that one of the party's budgets represents the entire investment.

As with any plan, it's a good idea to identify project risks associated with the reviews along with appropriate mitigation and contingency actions for the important risks. Important risks I've seen with reviews include review training problems with participants, lack of adequate preparation, the tendency to curtail reviews when schedule pressures intrude, and the misuse of review defect metrics. Other risks may well exist for your project.

As you are doing this planning work, keep in mind the project size and complexity and the overall risks to the quality of the system. You don't want to plan for a top-heavy, excessively formalized set of reviews in small, simple, low-risk projects. At the same time, you don't want to rely on a few informal reviews when the project is large, complex, and risky. I've personally seen a number of cases where large, complex, and risky projects were seriously impacted by the failure to institute adequately rigorous reviews during the requirements, design, and implementation processes. In two cases I can think of, these omissions were significant contributors to the ultimate failure of the projects as a whole, and when large projects fail, there is typically significant impact to the careers of the managers involved.

What Should We Measure?

A continuing theme in this book is the need for defined objectives. Unless all stakeholders agree on what is to be accomplished, different opinions about the success or failure of an activity are hard to avoid. Reviews are the same. The review leader should define objectives for the reviews.

This applies even if the test manager is responsible only for reviews of test work products and test management reviews. For example, during a walk-through or informal review of the results of a quality risk analysis, a test manager should not say that the objective is to talk about the results of the risk analysis. Rather, they should clearly state that the objective of the review is to detect any missing risk items or improperly rated risk items and, based on agreed-upon additions or changes to the risk analysis, to build consensus that the risk analysis results represent the correct list of what to test, in what order, and how much. A clear decision is being made in a review.

Another theme in this book is that the definition of successfully achieving objectives should be measurable. Reviews should have defined metrics for their objectives, just as with other objectives for testing. Consider the following examples:

- For effectiveness, we can measure the defect detection effectiveness of the review process. Of the defects present in the work product during the review, what percentage did we find?
- For efficiency, we can measure the cost of finding and removing defects in the review. Of the defects found and removed in the work product during the review, how do those costs compare with the costs of finding and removing such defects later, such as in testing or in production?
- In terms of building consensus or educating participants about the work product, we can measure the degree to which participants are satisfied with the process. As mentioned in Chapter 2, you can use surveys on a Likert scale to determine whether people agree with the proposition that the review process helped them achieve consensus and understanding.

As a way of setting goals for these metrics, the metrics can be compared against historical values within the organization to gauge success. In some cases, these metrics can also be compared with industry averages. The metrics, traceable to objectives, along with their goals should be part of the review plan.

What's the ROI?

I mentioned a budget for reviews earlier. To win approval of the budget, it's a good idea to include an estimate of the return on investment (ROI). The ROI estimate can be rough, in most cases. For example, if you can estimate that a defect found and removed in a review costs on average $100 while a defect found and removed in system testing costs on average $1,000, and if you can estimate that 100 defects total will be found in reviews of 10 work products (which is certainly a conservative estimate), then at least $90,000 will be saved. If a defect found and removed in production costs on average $10,000, since some of the defects found in reviews would probably have escaped into production, you can add some additional ROI based on the typical percentage of defects that escape from system testing into production. That benefit, set against the cost of training participants and holding the reviews, will probably show a positive return on investment. You can use the cost of quality technique, discussed in Chapter 2, to structure this ROI estimate.

To obtain the ideal ROI, though, the reviews must be conducted at the proper time. If a review is conducted too early against a work product not sufficiently complete in content or format, the defect detection effectiveness will be significantly reduced. The right participants must be involved in the review and given adequate time to prepare and participate.

Who Should Review?

So, who are the proper participants for these reviews? Partly, it's a matter of knowledge. Ideally, each reviewer brings unique perspectives, experiences, and insights. This knowledge can be technical, in terms of how the system is to be built. It can be business oriented, in terms of the problem that the system is to solve. And it can be test related.

However, some of the attributes of a good reviewer are similar to those for a good tester. A good reviewer, like a good tester, must be thorough in their review. They must pay close attention to the details of the work product or project status that they are reviewing. They must be able to express their findings clearly, and if a reviewer is playing the role of secretary, they must be able to capture the findings of the review team. Good reviewers must have a sense of perspective, and the ability to see which findings are more important than other findings, and they must not let their ego become involved in whether "their" findings get fixed.

In addition, good reviewers must know how to be good reviewers. They must understand the proper way to operate in reviews, both in terms of the preparation and the review meeting itself. Authors must understand how to properly follow up on review comments. Review leaders must understand how to handle the planning, kick-off, and follow-up associated with reviews as well as how to assign roles that each participant can properly carry out. Since very few people are born knowing how to be good reviewers—many of the behaviors are not intuitive—training is typically required to ensure that the reviewers do a good job.

How Do We Manage the Risks?

Reviews, like any other project undertaking, are subject to risks that can reduce, eliminate, or even reverse the benefits associated with them. In other words, it's possible for reviews to return zero or less than zero value if risks are not properly managed. The risks can arise from technical, organizational, and people factors. Let's examine some of these risks and how you can include proper management of these risks in your review plan.

First, as mentioned a moment ago, we need to have the right people involved. People without sufficient knowledge or without proper focus can make the review process less efficient to the extent that they participate—and thus expend time and effort—but contribute very little. People can be disruptive influences if they don't understand how to participate as a member of a team. Therefore, the review plan should address how to ensure that the right people are involved and the wrong people are not involved. While a strong moderator can help manage the participants—and a strong moderator is also certainly one of the "right people" to have involved—you don't need a situation where the moderator must devote all their energy to preventing disruptive influences from derailing the progress of the review team.

Sometimes, some people are the wrong people due to attitude or understanding of review processes but the right people in terms of their skills and knowledge with respect to the item being reviewed. In most cases, training is required to make sure people are able to participate. This is especially true of those who are more introverted, too aggressively extroverted, or otherwise socially awkward or socially challenged. After all, reviews are social events, like any other meeting.

The shoe can be on the other foot, too. In some cases, there are people who should be involved in the review process who have the right attitude and outlook but are missing key facts about the technical aspects of the system under test. In this case, the training they require might well be technical rather than process related.

Now, part of being effective and efficient at any task is being committed. As a consultant and a manager, I've found that you can educate people who are subject matter experts until you get blue in the face, but if those people are not motivated to do a proper job, they won't. In fact, while this is a false choice that you shouldn't have to make, you're better off having people committed to doing good work without all of the skills needed to do the work than having people who know how to do the work but can't be bothered to do it or, worse yet, are actually opposed to doing it. So, the review plan should address the matter of how to ensure that participants are properly motivated and how to deal with those who are not.

In the Advanced Test Manager syllabus, there is a concept of "backup reviewers." These are people who fill in for preferred participants, assuming the preferred participant has a personal or business priority that makes attending the review impossible. While I understand the concept, I have to say that I'm less than enthusiastic about this kind of substitution. I'd have a number of questions about such reviewers. Have they prepared adequately? Are they committed to the review process? Why is the review so unimportant to the primary reviewer that they want to shunt this responsibility to an alternate? The review plan should manage these risks.

Another important risk is the possibility that important stakeholders and potential participants will not be involved in the reviews. This can happen because the review leader failed to invite them or because these participants refused to get involved.

To manage the risk of failing to invite all the relevant people, the review leader needs to carefully consider all the possible invitees to ensure that no one is omitted. To manage the risk that relevant people refuse to be involved, the review leader must understand what benefits from reviews accrue to each possible participant. When inviting someone to participate in an activity, you'll get much better results if you appeal to each participant's own interests rather than a general urge to do right by the great needs of the organization.

Tools for reviews are often simpler than those required for dynamic testing, but they are sometimes required. Defects found in reviews should be tracked, and while this may be less complex than tracking defects from dynamic testing, the information gathered should be compatible for purposes of consistency and process improvement (see Chapter 4 for more on this topic of defect management). The review plan should compare and contrast information gathered about defects with information gathered later in the process, and the planning process should deal with this question of how to ensure comparability.

As mentioned, sufficient time for preparation and participation is important for successful reviews. An important risk is the possibility that a key participant won't spend the time required in either activity. Now, the key question, from my perspective, is, Why? Why is the participant unable or unwilling to spend the necessary time? Is it a matter of commitment? If so, then see the previous discussion. Or is it—as in my experience is more likely the case—that management is denying the participant the time required or creating a situation where the participant must choose between their "real job" and their review responsibilities. In this situation, you are dealing with classic suboptimization, where someone is being made to feel that their immediate tactical responsibilities are more important than an activity that is essential to the delivery of a quality product.

The review process itself is important. The different types of reviews were discussed earlier. It's important that the proper review process be selected. Excessive formality will result in delays and a feeling of ennui or frustration among the participants. Excessive informality will result in too many defects escaping to the next step in the use of the work product being reviewed. Not only must the right process be selected, it must also be properly executed. The review leader must ensure that both are true.

Finally, the review leader should ensure that not only are review objectives clearly defined but also that post-review metrics can be used to measure and appraise the achievement of those objectives. For example, if we say that a key objective of reviews is to detect defects, then we should measure the number of defects detected in each review. This metric can be expressed in terms of defect density (i.e., defects per page reviewed, categorized by type of item reviewed). These metrics can—and should—then be compared against expectations, ideally expectations derived from historical averages.

What Must the Review Leader Do?

As mentioned in the Foundation syllabus and earlier in the Advanced Test Manager syllabus, the review leader plays a critical role in review success. This role starts with the planning, as just discussed, but also continues through the reviews themselves and beyond.

During the review meeting itself, the review leader must ensure that adequate measurements are taken. Otherwise, the success or failure of the reviews, on an objective standard, cannot be determined. Of course, planning for proper measurements must occur first, but even with proper planning, participants often fail to gather the measurements properly unless adequate review leader oversight occurs.

Since many of these metrics involve defects detected by the review, proper classification of these defects is critical. We'll revisit this topic in detail in Chapter 4. However, for the moment I'll mention that the review leader needs to ensure that the defect metrics gathered during the reviews are completely accurate in terms of their classifications, especially severity and priority.

Another review meeting issue is the creation and maintenance of checklists. For each type of work product reviewed by the review team, the best practice is to have a specific checklist. For example, requirements reviews would involve a requirements checklist, design reviews a design checklist, code reviews a code checklist, and so forth. Plenty of examples of good starting-point checklists can be found in books and on the Internet, and the review leader should ensure the selection of the right ones. The review leader should also make sure issues discovered in reviews that were not on the checklist get added to the checklist in an appropriate fashion.

The review leader's responsibilities continue beyond the end of the review. First, the metrics mentioned earlier must be collected and calculated. Success or failure of each review should be determined. If a failure has occurred, the review leader must take remedial steps to correct the failure. Successes, of course, should be appropriately publicized. Review metrics should measure effectiveness against these objectives and also efficiency. Since effectiveness and efficiency can be in tension at a certain level, the relative importance of each must be considered when determining the success of a review. For example, when thorough defect removal is more critical, spending a higher number of person-hours per page (one possible review efficiency metric) is perfectly acceptable.

A successful review—even a marginally successful review—will detect defects. The value of this defect detection can be realized only when the important defects are fixed, so review leaders must ensure that proper follow-up occurs. Not every defect found in a review needs to be fixed, of course. I've been involved in reviews where as many as half of the defects were deferred, and justly so, I thought, based on schedule priorities and other considerations. However, these choices—fix or defer—must always be made intelligently, including during reviews.

In most cases, the return on the review investment is measured based on the defects found in a review. The review leader should make this measurement because it's another metric of success.

Once the success or failure of a review has been determined—at least based on the immediate results—the review leader should provide feedback to the stakeholders and participants. In the case of success, of course, this should be proclaimed as loudly as decorum will permit, as should any successful testing effort. In the case of failure, as with any other failure, the message must include the steps that will be taken as result. These steps must include the immediate remediation of the failure and its consequences as well as how to prevent such failures in the future.

Ultimately, the final success of the review process on a project can be measured only in retrospectives. How many defects were found in reviews, how many defects were found in the reviewed work products during test execution, and how many defects were eventually found in production? As mentioned earlier, not every defect found in a review must be fixed, but certainly very few important defects should escape. The retrospective team must consider the reasons for any defect escapes to later stages of the software engineering process. The review leader must work with the review team to determine how to improve the review process so that such escapes don't occur in the future.

Retrospectives should evaluate defect escapes not only for the current project but also in terms of past projects. Is our escape rate going down? If so, that's good, even if we've not yet hit our targets (provided the decrease is statistically significant). If our escape rate is staying steady or going up, and it is unacceptably high, then urgent action is needed. This kind of "death spiral" is commonly associated with general process failure and abandonment. Organizations that abandon previously successful review processes due to temporary setbacks often never pick the habit back up again, under the motto of, "Oh, well, we tried that and it just didn't work out for us." (A common lament sung to the itinerant consultant by managers and individual contributors around the world, that line is.)

Why do defects escape from reviews? Well, first of all, we must recognize that reviews are a human process, and all human processes are fallible. Anyone with the expectation that reviews will find 100 percent of the defects is bound to be disappointed. Realistic expectations must be established, based on the review type and the work product being reviewed, and we'll look at some examples of such realistic expectations shortly. When those expectations are not achieved, then the review leader should consider various possible causes. The review process itself might have been incorrectly selected or incorrectly executed. The review team might have consisted of the wrong people, in terms of their skills, or their attitudes, or their training, or their experience with reviews or the system under test, or their behaviors in the review, or their commitment level, or their availability, or their understanding of proper review processes, or any of the other myriad reasons that members of a team can be wrong together.

While it's an uncomfortable reality, review leaders should understand that suboptimal results from a review can also be your fault, as the review leader. If insufficient review preparation or review time was allocated, or if sufficient time was allocated but then not allowed in practice, then the results will fail to meet expectations.

Review Plan Exercise

Let's travel backward in time for a moment, to the beginning of the HELLO-CARMS project, prior to the start of iteration one.

Assume that, due to your expertise with quality assurance, management has assigned you the job of planning a review of the HELLOCARMS system requirements specification.

Identify the following:

- Which review technique(s) would you apply and why?
- What level of formality would you apply and why?
- What defects would you expect to find?
- What skills would you need in the review team?

Review Plan Debrief

Here are my answers to each of the four questions.

- *Which review technique(s) would you apply and why?*
  - My experience with doing reviews on documents like these and on projects like this one would lead me to use a walk-through. I find it the most accessible form of a review, the one least likely to get sidetracked, and reasonably effective. It also has a strong side-effect of building consensus and educating the project team, assuming you invite the right people. However, since it is not as effective as techniques like an inspection, I would also use static analysis and quality risk analysis (based on the requirements) to detect and remove additional problems.

■ *What level of formality would you apply and why?*
  ● Unless the Globobank project team has experience with highly formal reviews, I would keep the level of formality low and rely more on the multiple-filter approach discussed in the previous paragraph to ensure a high rate of defect removal for this critical document.

■ *What defects would you expect to find?*
  ● I would hope to find a large number of ambiguities, contradictions, and untestable requirements, because just a quick read of the document reveals such problems. If the review resulted in few of these and a disproportionate number of grammar, spelling, formatting, and other cosmetic defects, I would try to schedule a new review after cleaning up the document first.

■ *What skills would you need in the review team?*
  ● Basically, the same cross-functional team that participated in the quality risk analysis should participate here.

Example: Review Types and Effectiveness

Early in this chapter, I mentioned the differences between various review types, including differences in formality, and how those differences influence defect removal effectiveness. I specifically cited some figures from Capers Jones. Let's look at the data behind Jones's observations a bit more closely for a moment.

Capers Jones, in his studies of thousands of projects across hundreds of clients, has found some interesting data on reviews, their applications, and the effectiveness of various types of reviews. Jones mentions that the informal reviews are the least effective, while reviews that have some but not all elements of formality are about average, and the most effective are the highly formalized inspections. Of course, to be effective at any level of formality, you have to do the reviews well and you have to have organizational support for the process.

Table 3–1   *Range of defect removal effectiveness*

	Least	Average	Most
Requirements	20%	30%	50%
High-level design	30%	40%	60%
Functional design	30%	45%	65%
Detailed design	35%	55%	75%
Code	35%	60%	85%

In Table 3–1, I show the range of defect removal effectiveness that Jones has observed for various types of reviews.[3] Defect removal effectiveness is the percentage of defects present at the time of some static or dynamic testing activity that were successfully detected and removed by that testing activity.

He analyzes reviews based on two factors. The first factor is the type of work product being reviewed. The second factor is the level of formality used for the review. As you can see, both factors have a strong influence on the defect removal effectiveness. If you think of the reviews as a series of filters, here's a quick mathematical demonstration of how effective reviews can be.

First, imagine that you started with 1,000 defects. You follow worst practices in reviews, but at least you review all types of items. In this case, you would enter testing with about 166 defects.

Now, imagine that you started with 1,000 defects again. However, this time you follow best practices (and again you review all types of items). This time, you go into testing with 3 defects.

Of course, this is a simplification, because defects are actually introduced throughout the software lifecycle, not just in requirements. However, the basic point stands: By aggressively using reviews through the work-product-creation stages of the lifecycle, the number of defects that must be removed in testing is greatly decreased, which reduces test costs and schedule risks.

Example: Defects Found in MRD Review

In Figure 3–2?, you see a list of ambiguous areas found in the marketing requirements document (or MRD) for the client-side system on the Internet appliance project I've mentioned a few times in this book. This shows part of a six-page-long list. Each page described about a dozen or so ambiguities that we had found in this document during review.

Example: Reaction to MRD Review

Figure 3–2? showed some of the myriad issues identified during a review of the client-side marketing requirements document on the Internet appliance project.

Interestingly, not all of the questions and issues the test team identified in its review of that document were resolved prior to—or even during—implementation. Of course, I guess you could say, "Well, Rex, ultimately some programmer made a decision and that resolved the question or issue."

---

3. This table was derived from figures found in Capers Jones's book *Software Assessments, Benchmarks, and Best Practices.*

> Mail
>
> 1. When users lose their mailboxes automatically when their 30-day-intro expires, do they get a warning?
>
> *No longer a test problem, since the user must call to change service level. The telemarketer can give the warning. [CLOSED]*
>
> 2. If an account drops from Premium to Basic, and then decides to go back to Premium, can the sub-account mailboxes be recovered, or are they gone for good?
>
> [TBD]
>
> 3. Is email access from the web a requirement? A previous reply said that it was out of R1, but a subsequent email…indicates that it's still under consideration.
>
> [TBD]

Figure 3–2   *Defects found in MRD review*

I would agree with that—ultimately, the system *does* something in every given situation, and that something is generally what the programmer told it to do. However, I would suggest that this is not the best way to solve serious questions about how a system should behave.

What happened was that Development and Marketing decided to proceed with open questions. We were told to stop pestering them with these questions and to proceed with developing and ultimately executing tests.

We did some estimating of where we were in test design and implementation versus where we needed to be and how hard it would be to get there without additional information. We concluded we would incur about a 20 to 25 percent test inefficiency due to the lack of clearly defined product requirements.

To this, our client contact memorably responded, "I would rather pay RBCS the extra money than have to teach these guys how to write requirements right now."

To which I responded, "Well, as long as your checks don't bounce, that is your decision to make."

During test execution, this inefficiency manifested itself in part in a high rate of false positives and false negatives. It also reduced test coverage since we had to spend time during test execution documenting what the system actually did, what we thought it should do, and the differences between the two.

So, what we have here is a classic example of failing to plan and estimate for adequate time for reviews and the resolution of the issues they reveal under deadline pressures.

3.4 Metrics for Reviews

Learning objectives

(K3) Define process and product metrics to be used in reviews.

I emphasized the need for proper metrics in the previous section, but I was rather vague about what kinds of metrics you could use. In this section, I'll be specific.

Let's start, as we always should with metrics, by defining what we're trying to accomplish with the metrics. First, of course, we want to be able to measure the quality of the work product being reviewed, both during the review and after the review is completed. These measurements should show significant quality improvements due to the reviews. The measurements feed into the determination of overall review benefits. By also measuring the review costs, we can then calculate the return on the review investment and its overall efficiency.

These metrics can be used for two general purposes. As an immediate need, they are used to report on the success—we hope—of the review process on our projects or, failing that desirable state, to guide immediate course corrections on the project to achieve better results. In the longer term, these metrics can be used to make process improvement decisions. We'll cover the topic of process improvement in Chapter 5, but for the moment I'll mention that this would include improving the defect detection effectiveness and the review process efficiency.

Review Product Metrics

What metrics should we measure to get a sense of the status of the work product being reviewed? Here are some typical metrics:

- Product size. This would be the number of pages or lines of code or function points or whatever. This metric by itself isn't good for much, but it's an essential element of calculating defect density (part of measuring effectiveness) and review rates (part of measuring efficiency).

▨ Expended effort. Ideally, the review leader should ensure that this is measured for each step of the review process, from planning and kick-off to rework and follow-up. These metrics are an important part of measuring and improving efficiency and return on investment.

▨ Duration. Efficiency is usually considered primarily in terms of effort, but a review process that consumes little effort but also lasts forever is hardly a success. Therefore, measuring duration is also important.

▨ Defect counts and classifications. This metric is the kingpin of many other product and process metrics as well as being central to understanding and improving effectiveness and efficiency for reviews. Defect metrics should show the relative severity and priority distribution. They should also support defect cluster analysis.

▨ Review type. As you saw earlier in this chapter, the review type is usually correlated with review effectiveness. We should capture this information for reviews so that we can calculate relative review effectiveness and make smarter review process selection decisions.

▨ Residual defects. Based on the defects found and the size of the reviewed item, we can estimate the number of defects remaining from historical averages. This will help us make good decisions about whether to declare the review process complete for a given work product.

Some of these metrics are also useful as part of calculating process metrics, which I'll now address.

Review Process Metrics

Here are some typical process metrics:

▨ Defect detection effectiveness. We should understand how effectively reviews remove defects. The complement of this metric is the defect escape rate. This usually can be fully measured only during the project retrospective.

▨ Process improvement. This metric involves measuring the effort and duration invested in improving the review process.

▨ Review progress. This can be measured a number of ways, but perhaps the easiest is to determine the number of work products that will be reviewed and then measure the percentage of reviews that have been completed.

▨ Defects. As with product metrics, defect metrics are important. For process metrics, it usually makes sense to break the defects down by type as well as severity and location, as mentioned previously.

- Participant satisfaction. Perception is a reality that must be managed just as reality must be. You should survey the review participants to see how they feel about the effectiveness and efficiency of the review process.
- Cost of quality. This approach for calculating benefits and return on investment is just as useful for reviews as for testing. However, when doing this for reviews, be sure to compare the cost of defects found in reviews with the cost of defects found in dynamic testing and with the cost of defects found in production.
- Effectiveness by type. By using the review type classification mentioned earlier, along with calculating defect detection effectiveness on a per-review basis, you can then determine which types of reviews are the most effective.
- Reviewers. These metrics should include the number of reviewers, their skills and backgrounds, the number of hours spent by each reviewer, and so forth.
- Defect detection rate. This can be calculated by effort (which is typical, often as part of a cost of quality measurement) or by day.
- Savings. Using cost of quality, this would be the comparison of the effort associated with dynamic testing or production defects with the effort associated with review defects. Cost of quality can also be used to derive the schedule savings by figuring out how many additional days of test execution would have been associated with removing the defects during dynamic testing.

It's important to keep in mind that these are process and product metrics we're talking about here. They are not people metrics. As I've said earlier, it's a classic management worst practice to assign rewards and punishments to people based on metrics that are often outside of their individual control, as these metrics are.

Review Metrics Exercise

Enhance your plan for the HELLOCARMS requirements review.

Identify the following:

- Product metrics you will gather during the review
- Process metrics you will gather during the review
- The process you will use to measure them
- How you will report them

Review Metrics Debrief

The following are the product metrics discussed in the syllabus, along with the process I would use to measure and report each one.

Work-product size	Count the number of pages in the requirements document. I would not report this separately but would use it to calculate other metrics that I would report.
Preparation time	Have each participant count the number of person-hours spent preparing for the review. I would not report this separately but would use it to calculate other metrics that I would report.
Time to conduct the review	Have each participant count the number of person-hours spent participating in the review meeting. I would not report this separately but would use it to calculate other metrics that I would report.
Rework time to fix defects	Have the author of the requirements document count the number of person-hours spent fixing defects found in the review. I would not report this separately but would use it to calculate other metrics that I would report.
Duration of the review process	Count the number of days from initially distributing the requirements document until the requirements document was finally approved. I would not report this separately but might use it to calculate other metrics that I would report.
Number of defects found and their severity and defect clusters	For each defect found, I would note the following: defect type (using the same classifications as in the defect tracking system), location (in this case, where in the requirements document), severity (using the same scale as in the defect tracking system), and phase of introduction (probably the requirements phase, but perhaps project initiation). I would report an analysis (e.g., via histograms, Pareto charts, etc.) of this information for each review as well as aggregate it across all reviews on a project (if possible, depending on how the other reviews were done).
Review type	Capture the type of review used and the type of work product reviewed. I would not report these separately but would use them to calculate other metrics that I would report.
Defect density	Divide number of defects found by pages in the HELLOCARMS requirements document. I would include this in the individual review and aggregate review analysis metrics mentioned previously.
Estimated residual defects	Use historical data to estimate the defect removal effectiveness of the review (probably by review type and work product reviewed), then calculate the number of defects that probably escaped. I would include this in the individual review and aggregate review analysis metrics mentioned previously.

The following are the process metrics discussed in the syllabus, along with the process I would use to measure and report each one.

Defect detection effectiveness	After product release, count the defects found in the requirements reviews, requirements defects found in dynamic testing, and requirements defects found in production, and use these three numbers to calculate the defect detection effectiveness. Note that the phase of introduction must be captured for each defect reported in dynamic testing and in production to do this calculation. I would include this in the aggregate review analysis metrics mentioned previously.
Review process improvement	Use a project plan, budget, and/or work breakdown structure for any review process improvement plans. I would include this in a retrospective report after the project, assuming that improving the review process was my responsibility.
Percent coverage of planned work products	During the project, keep track of the planned work products and which of them have been reviewed. At the end of the project, if the percentage reviewed is less than 100 percent, research why. I would include this in a retrospective report after the project.
Defect type and severity	I discussed the capture of this information, and its reporting, in the previous table (with the "number of defects found and their severity and defect clusters" product metric).
Participant surveys	I would create a simple survey (perhaps using a tool) to ask people about how effective and efficient they felt the review was, as well as their overall satisfaction with the review, and send that to people immediately after the review process for each work product reviewed. I would include this in the individual review and aggregate review analysis metrics mentioned previously.
Cost of quality metrics	I would use the effort and defect metrics mentioned earlier to calculate the average cost of detection, the average cost of removal, and the average cost of detection and removal for defects. I would include this in the individual review and aggregate review analysis metrics mentioned previously.
Correlation of review effectiveness	By categorizing the review type and the work products reviewed, I would calculate average defect detection effectiveness. I would include this in the aggregate review analysis metrics mentioned previously.
Number of reviewers	Count the number of people who participated. I would include this in the individual review and aggregate review analysis metrics mentioned previously.
Defects found per hour	This would be included in the cost of quality metrics.
Estimated project time saved	Based on the effort and duration associated with defect removal later in the lifecycle, I would estimate effort and time saved. I would include this in the individual review and aggregate review analysis metrics mentioned previously.
Average defect effort	This would be included in the cost of quality metrics.

As I mentioned, it's important to remember that these are process metrics, not people metrics!

3.5   Managing Formal Reviews

Learning objectives

(K2) Explain, using examples, the characteristics of a formal review.

Let's take a look at a generic review process. It consists of six steps:

1. Planning, which includes defining the review criteria, selecting the personnel, allocating roles, defining the entry and exit criteria for more formal review types (e.g., inspections), selecting which parts of documents to review, and checking entry criteria (for more formal review types).
2. Kick-off, which includes distributing documents and explaining the objectives, process, and documents to the participants.
3. Individual preparation, which includes preparing for the review meeting by reviewing the documents and noting potential defects, questions, and comments.
4. The review meeting itself, which includes activities related to examining, evaluating, and recording the results. These activities include discussing and logging the results or minutes (for more formal review types), noting defects, making recommendations for how to handle the defects, making decisions about the defects, and examining, evaluating, and recording issues during any physical meetings or tracking any group electronic communications.
5. Rework, which includes fixing defects found (typically done by the author) and recording updated status of defects (in formal reviews).
6. Follow-up, which includes checking that defects have been addressed, gathering metrics, and checking on exit criteria (for more formal review types).

Planning, defining entry and exit criteria, and kick-off activities include work for the entire project and for each item to be reviewed.

The checking of entry criteria, individual preparation, noting of findings, the review meeting, analysis of the meeting, rework, fixing defects, and follow-up activities repeat per each item reviewed. The preparation work is usually one to two hours alone. The meeting is one to two hours alone. The rework and fixing of bugs is done by the author.

However, the follow-up does not only include work on individual items. Follow-up also includes overall process improvement analysis, evaluation of defect (or bug) removal at phase exit reviews (exit meetings), and so on.

Notice that the details of the review process depend on the specific review type used on the project, as well as the review type used for each particular kind of item.

This material is a summary of what is explained in the Foundation syllabus section 3.2.1. It would be a good idea to review that section before you take the exam.

Formal Review Characteristics

Formal reviews follow the process presented a moment ago. However, they also have a number of other characteristics:

- Entry and exit criteria. These can be as simple as ways of determining when to start and end the review process as a whole or as sophisticated as specific measurements associated with each step in the process.
- Checklists. As I mentioned before, having work-product-specific checklists is a good way to promote effectiveness of reviews.
- Metrics. Formal reviews should use the various metrics mentioned earlier to demonstrate effectiveness, efficiency, and overall progress.
- Reporting. Formal reviews should involve not only measuring effectiveness, efficiency, and progress, but also reporting it.

This material is a summary of what is explained, in more detail, in the Foundation syllabus, sections 3.2.2 to 3.2.4. It would be a good idea to review those sections before you take the exam.

Managing Formal Reviews

I discussed earlier what the review leader should do during reviews. During formal reviews, the review leader must also make sure that all proper steps are followed, including adherence to the entry and exit criteria. All of the characteristics of formal reviews just discussed should be present, and the review leader should ensure that they are.

- What if these characteristics are not present? Usually, it's not the review leader's decision to make, but the review leader can make a recommendation. If the impact of the deviations is minimal, then perhaps redefining the review objectives makes sense. If it's possible to correct the deviations without interfering with the planned review or reviews, then that might be the smart way to go. If the impact is high and correction is impossible, though, delaying the review process is often the best move. All too often, we see situations with clients where avoidable problems occurred due to inappropriate relaxation of the review process.

- The management of formal reviews should be an ongoing activity by the review leader. In addition, the review leader should coordinate this management process with program needs and the larger overall project quality assurance strategy. Finally, the product and process metrics mentioned earlier should be a key part of managing these formal reviews.

Review Exercise

Select a review type and apply that review type to the HELLOCARMS system requirements document. Focus on serious problems rather than superficial ones. Capture metrics for effort, defects, and severity, according to your plan from the review metrics exercise in section 4.

Review Debrief

Here is one possible solution:

Senior RBCS Associate Jose Mata reviewed the HELLOCARMS system requirements document. He used a checklist from Karl Wiegers, which is discussed in the book on the Advanced Test Analyst syllabus (*Advanced Software Testing: Volume 1*). He provided the following feedback:

- Are internal cross-references correct? If we reference another document or within this document, is that reference valid?
  - No. Section 010-010-040 states, "Field validation details are described in a separate document," but that document is not identified anywhere in the requirements document.

- Is the level of detail consistent and appropriate?
  - No. As an example, see section 010-010-180: "Provide features and screens that support the operations of the Globobank's retail branches." That is too vague to be actionable.
  - Section 010-010-170 states, "Support the submission of applications via the Internet, which includes the capability of untrained users to properly enter applications." This is a huge, and vague, requirement.
  - Sections 010-010-180 through 010-010-240 start with "Support the marketing, sales, and processing of…," which is so vague that important functionality can be missed.

- Do the requirements provide an adequate basis for design?
    - No. Section 010-010-070 states, "Ask each applicant whether there is an existing relationship with Globobank; e.g., any checking or savings accounts," but the list is not complete, and it should be.
    - Section 010-010-080 states, "Maintain application status from initiation through to rejection, decline, or acceptance…," but we don't know if these states are a subset or if they are comprehensive.
    - Section 010-010-150 states, "Provide inbound and outbound telemarketing support for all States, Provinces, and Countries in which Globobank operates," but the list is not defined.
    - Section 010-010-160 states, "Support brokers and other business partners by providing limited partner-specific screens, logos, interfaces, and branding," yet screens, or areas of the interface, are not identified.
    - Section 010-010-250 states, "Support flexible pricing schemes, including introductory pricing, short term pricing, and others," but the "and others" needs to be defined.
- Is the priority of each requirement included?
    - Yes.
- Are all external interfaces defined?
    - No. We don't know how complete the information is. Data structures are hinted at, but not defined. The implied interfaces are with:
        - LoDoPS: 010-010-050, 010-010-100, 010-020-050, 010-030-040, 010-030-060, 010-030-070, 010-030-080, 010-030-120, 010-030-103, 010-030-140, 010-030-150
        - GLADS: 010-010-070
        - Scoring Mainframe: 010-020-020, 010-030-020
        - GloboRainBQW: 010-030-010
- Is there any missing information? If so, is it clearly marked as TBD, "to be determined"?
    - Yes.
- Is the expected behavior documented?
    - No. For example, section 010-010-080 states, "Maintain application status from initiation through to rejection…," but how and where the status is maintained is not stated.

- Is each requirement clear, concise, and unambiguous?
  - No. For example, section 010-010-070 states, "Ask each applicant whether there is an existing relationship with Globobank," but it is unclear how the applicant is asked.
  - Sections 010-010-100, 010-030-040, and 010-030-070 state, "Allow user to indicate on a separate screen which, if any, are existing debts that the customer will retire…" but it's not clear what the screen is supposed to be separate from.
  - Section 010-040-010 states, "Support agreed-upon security requirements (encryption, firewalls, etc.)," which is vague.
  - Section 010-040-060 states, "Support fraud detection for processing of all financial applications." This is vague, which is especially bad for a priority 1 requirement.

- Is each requirement verifiable? Could you design a test to show that this requirement was met or not met?
  - No. Section 010-010-150 states, "Provide inbound and outbound telemarketing support for…," which is vague and thus not verifiable.
  - Sections 010-010-180 through 010-010-240 start with "Support the marketing, sales, and processing of…" and the marketing part is not verifiable.
  - Section 010-010-250 states, "Support flexible pricing schemes, including introductory pricing, short term pricing, and others," and the "and others" part is not verifiable.
  - Section 010-030-150 states, "Support computer-telephony integration to provide customized marketing and sales support for inbound telemarketing campaigns and branded business partners," which is vague and thus not verifiable.

- Is each requirement in scope?
  - No. For example, section 010-010-170 states, "Support the submission of applications via the Internet, which includes the capability of untrained users to properly enter applications." This is beyond the scope of section 003 because allowing Internet-based customers is slated for subsequent releases.
  - Section 010-040-030 states, "Allow outsourced telemarketers to see the credit tier but disallow them from seeing the actual credit score of applicants." This is beyond the scope of section 003.

- Section 010-040-050 states, "Allow Internet users to browse potential loans without requiring such users to divulge…" This is beyond the scope of section 003.

- Is each requirement free from content and grammar errors?
  - Yes.

- Can the requirements be implemented within constraints?
  - Possibly not. Section 010-040-060 states, "Support fraud detection for processing of all financial applications." This might not be able to be implemented. Specific checks would need to be defined.

- Are all security and safety considerations properly specified?
  - No. Specific types of users, and their permissions, are not defined. User name and password strength are not addressed. Encryption of specific data is not addressed. Maintenance and purging requirements are not addressed. Server physical security requirements are not addressed.

- Is each requirement uniquely and correctly identified? Is the granularity of the requirements such that it will be possible to have traceability from tests to requirements?
  - No. For example, section 010-010-180 through 010-010-240 start with "Support the marketing, sales, and processing of…" The granularity of these requirements is too large.
  - Section 010-010-250 states, "Support flexible pricing schemes, including introductory pricing, short-term pricing, and others." This and several other compound requirements would be clearer if they were separately numbered requirements. It may be somewhat repetitious, but the requirements would be clearer and there would be more balance in scoping development and test efforts.

- Have we stayed in the proper realm of requirements, not design? In other words, are all requirements actually requirements and not design or implementation solutions?
  - No. Sections 010-010-100, 010-030-040, and 010-030-070 state, "Allow user to indicate on a separate screen which, if any, are existing debts that the customer will retire…" Specifying a separate screen appears to be a design detail.

3.6   Sample Exam Questions

To end each chapter, you can try one or more sample exam questions to reinforce your knowledge and understanding of the material and to prepare for the ISTQB Advanced Level Test Manager exam.

1. Which of the following is a type of defect that you can detect more easily in a review than by a dynamic test?

    A. Regression

    B. Maintainability

    C. Performance

    D. Reliability

2. Which of the following is a type of review that you would expect to detect the greatest percentage of defects present in the item under review?

    A. Informal

    B. Static analysis

    C. Simulation

    D. Inspection

3. Assume you are a test manager working on a project to create a programmable thermostat for home use to control central heating, ventilation, and air conditioning (HVAC) systems. In addition to the normal HVAC control functions, the thermostat has the ability to download data to a browser-based application that runs on PCs, tablets, and smartphones for further analysis.

    During quality risk analysis, you identify compatibility problems between the browser-based application and the different PC configurations that can host that application as a quality risk item with a high level of likelihood.

    Select *two* of the following actions that should occur in the quality and test plans to best ensure that the project team will minimize this risk upon release.

    A. Carefully select the list of supported configurations.

    B. Review the list of supported configurations with project stakeholders.

C. Support only a single browser based on technical attributes.

D. Downgrade the likelihood of the risk based on available test resources.

E. Test the supported PC configurations at the end of test execution.

4. Assume you are a test manager in charge of integration testing, system testing, and acceptance testing for a bank. You are working on a project to upgrade an existing automated teller machine system to allow customers to obtain cash advances from supported credit cards. You have received a requirements specification that states that the system should allow cash advances from $20 to $500, inclusively, for all supported credit cards. Assume that the bank is required contractually to support the following credit cards: American Express, Visa, Japan Credit Bureau, Eurocard, and MasterCard.

The bank has given you the responsibility of organizing a review of the requirements specification. Which of the following is a risk for this review?

A. You do not know the supported credit cards.

B. You do not include the proper stakeholders in the review.

C. You do not know which test levels to address.

D. You do not receive the requirements specification.

4 Defect Management

"If I extrapolate the current trend, then 100% of the 2017 release budget
will be spent on contemplating changes, with 0% actual change.
On the positive side, this means testing the 2017 release will cost nothing."

V.V.L., European test engineer.

Chapter 4, Defect Management, of the Advanced syllabus contains the following four sections:

1. Introduction
2. The Defect Lifecycle and the Software Development Lifecycle
3. Defect Report Information
4. Assessing Process Capability with Defect Report Information

4.1 Introduction

Learning objectives
Recall of content only

When some people think of defect management processes and tools, they think, "Oh, well, those are just things for the test team to worry about." While it's true that the test team is often responsible for the defect management tools and much of the defect management process, proper management of defects is critical for the entire team, and failure to properly manage defects is a common cause of problems for organizations.

Properly managed, defect information has both immediate and long-term benefits. On an immediate basis, defect information will help us understand the current status of the product that we're working on and make smarter decisions about how to move the project forward. On a long-term basis, we can use

> **ISTQB Glossary**
>
> **defect:** A flaw in a component or system that can cause the component or system to fail to perform its required function—for example, an incorrect statement or data definition. A defect, if encountered during execution, may cause a failure of the component or system.
>
> **failure:** Deviation of the component or system from its expected delivery, service, or result.
>
> **phase containment:** The percentage of defects that are removed in the same phase of the software lifecycle in which they were introduced.
>
> **priority:** The level of (business) importance assigned to an item such as, for example, a defect.
>
> **root cause:** A source of a defect such that if it is removed, the occurrence of the defect type is decreased or removed.
>
> **severity:** The degree of impact that a defect has on the development or operation of a component or system.

patterns in the collective defect information, gathered in a single project and across multiple projects, to see where our testing and development processes are weak. This will allow the implementation of improvements.

However, it is true that the test management process and tools are things that the testers, especially the test manager, must master. The defect lifecycle, and what happens along each state in the defect lifecycle, should be fully understood by the entire test team, especially the test manager. In particular, they should fully understand the data and classifications that should be captured by testers (among other project participants) using the test tool.

With a proper understanding of the tool and the process comes an ability to advocate their proper usage. Since test managers should know the benefits from proper usage, along with the harm possible from improper usage, they should also be able to advocate—via a detailed explanation of the benefits and harms, not just through exhortation.

Since this material draws heavily on the Foundation syllabus, I recommend that you review Chapter 5, section 6 of the syllabus.

4.2 The Defect Lifecycle and the Software Development Lifecycle

Learning objectives

(K3) Develop a defect management process for a testing organization, including the defect report workflow, that can be used to monitor and control a project's defects throughout the testing lifecycle.

(K2) Explain the process and participants required for effective defect management.

You should remember from the Foundation syllabus that mistakes (also called errors) lead to the introduction of defects (also called bugs or faults). As I personally am aware, like all human beings I can make mistakes at any point in time, no matter what I might be working on. So it is on projects, where the business analyst can put a defect into a requirements specification, a tester can put a defect into a test case, a programmer can put a defect into the code, a technical writer can put a defect into the user guide, and so forth. Any work product can and often will have defects because any worker can and will make mistakes!

Now, I like to drink good wine, and I've collected bottles from around the world on my travels. Some I've stashed away for years, waiting for the right time to drink them, which always comes sooner or later. Some of these bottles have gotten a lot more valuable over the years. Odd as this will sound, in just a few ways, bugs are like wine. They definitely get more expensive with age, taking more effort and thus incurring more cost the longer they are in the system. Also, sooner or later most bugs need to be fixed. However, it's definitely not a good idea to leave bugs lying around—or perhaps crawling around—in a cellar, and they're certainly not appetizing!

Because defects can be introduced anywhere in the lifecycle, in any work product, and because the cost of removing them increases the longer they are around, we should try to remove them throughout the lifecycle, as close as possible to the point of introduction. When all defects are removed in the same phase in which they were introduced, this is referred to as perfect phase containment. Perfect phase containment minimizes the cost of quality for a system with a given level of quality. Of course, cost of quality can also be reduced through defect prevention, which can be promoted through process improvements, a topic I'll return to later in this chapter.

So, by using static techniques such as reviews and static analysis on work products during the process of creating those work products, we can contain many—in fact, with the right processes, most—of the defects to their exact phase of introduction. This minimizes the damage those defects can do, especially since defects are found directly during static testing, thus avoiding the costly and slow debugging process.

Of course, debugging defects revealed as failures during dynamic testing is more expensive than fixing defects found in static testing, but it's still much cheaper than debugging defects found in production. To minimize the cost of debugging, we need to avoid false positives. I'll discuss ways to do so later. For the moment, though, let me mention that removing bugs found in dynamic testing requires a solid process for investigating failures, usually via a defined bug management process.

Let's review the chain of events associated with dynamic test failures a bit more closely. The author of a work product introduces a defect. These defects may be introduced in the code itself, or they can be introduced in requirements specifications, design specifications, user stories, use cases, or other precursor work products, but they eventually end up as defects in the code. (If defects in precursor work products were removed before they ended up in the code, they were perforce removed by static testing because only the code can be subjected to dynamic testing.)

Now, a defect in code is a somewhat passive and shy thing. It is passive in the sense that it will not display symptoms unless someone executes the code in which it exists. It is shy in the sense that it can be seen only through the symptoms of its presence, and often those symptoms can be seen only by executing the code with particular types of inputs and preconditions. Those symptoms take the form of an anomaly, a case where the actual results don't match the expected results. Sometimes, the anomaly is sufficiently subtle—or the tester sufficiently inattentive or the test poorly defined—that the tester misses it, which is referred to as a false negative in ISTQB terminology.

When the tester observes the anomaly, the defect management process can be said to begin. After some efforts to avoid a false positive (again, more on that shortly), having been satisfied that the anomaly is truly a failure—that is, not a false positive but rather an anomaly due to a defect—the tester files a defect report. The defect lifecycle begins now.

Before we go further though, here's a riddle for you: When is a bona fide test failure not the result of a defect? Give up? How about now? The answer is, When the failure is the result of an automated unit test used in test-driven

> **ISTQB Glossary**
>
> **anomaly:** Any condition that deviates from expectation based on requirements specifications, design documents, user documents, standards, and so on or from someone's perception or experience. Anomalies may be found during, but not limited to, reviewing, testing, analysis, compilation, or use of software products or applicable documentation.
>
> **error:** A human action that produces an incorrect result.
>
> **incident:** Any event occurring that requires investigation.

development. In test-driven development, the tests are written before the code and are basically executable design specifications, in that the code is written and refined until the tests pass. Usually the process is iterative, in that a few tests are written to start with, then some code is written and revised until the tests pass, and then more tests are written and the cycle resumes. Because the failure of the tests is by design—in other words, it's inherent in the process—the failure is not the result of a defect because a defect is introduced by mistake rather than by the nature of the process. Since these test-driven development failures are not defects, they should not be reported, though there's little risk that they would ever be, given developers' hesitancy to report any defects found in unit testing of any sort.

Defect Workflow

Once surfaced as a failure in dynamic testing, each defect goes through a lifecycle from discovery to some sort of ultimate resolution. Without a well-defined workflow, though, it's quite possible for the lifecycle of some defects to suffer from unnecessary delays or even to get lost and never actually fixed. Even with a well-defined workflow, there is potentially a lot of overhead associated with managing all the defect reports on a project, so most mature organizations use a defect management tool to automate the defect workflow. Let's look at how to make this work.

First, you need a clearly defined set of states for defect reports from discovery to resolution, along with allowed transitions between those states. This is the defect workflow. Many defect management tools include such a workflow for the defect reports by default, but it's a good idea to use this workflow as a starting point rather than accepting it without question. It may be that the "out of the box" workflow is fine for your organization, but that's not always the case.

Any good defect management tool will allow you to customize the workflow to fit your organization's needs. We'll look at an example of a workflow with a more detailed discussion of the states in the workflow later.

Part of understanding the proper workflow for your organization is to understand the roles involved in the workflow. A fairly typical workflow involves the following states and roles:

1. The defect finder, often a tester, reports the defect. The underlying report is in an initial state, which may also be called a new or open state.

2. The defect report is triaged by a cross-functional team, often including representatives of the test team, the development team, project management, and other business and technical stakeholders. Triage involves deciding whether the defect report actually describes a failure at all; if not, the defect report is put into a canceled state or placed into a closed state with the reason that the report was invalid. For actual failures, triage also involves deciding whether to fix the defect at all and, if so, when to fix it. If the defect is not to be fixed in this release, the defect report may be placed in a deferred state, either deferred to a subsequent release or deferred indefinitely. If the defect is not to be fixed at all, then the defect may be placed in an accepted state as a permanent limitation.

3. If the defect is to be fixed, it is placed in an assigned state for a particular fixer, often a developer. In some cases, the fixer needs more information or disagrees about whether the behavior is incorrect. In the former situation, the defect report is placed in a returned (or clarification) state and routed back to the defect finder in step 1; in the latter situation, the defect report is placed in a rejected state and returned to the triage team in step 2. In other cases, the fixer has no problem with the report but simply cannot reproduce the failure and may return the defect report to the triage team. The triage team may place the defect report in an irreproducible state, which might involve no further action on the report until the failure is observed again. Alternatively, the triage team may reassign the defect report to the fixer, returning to the start of this step, or they may reassign the defect report to the finder to gather further information, returning to the start of step 1.

4. If there is no problem (either with the defect report or the failure itself) detected in step 3, the developer fixes the underlying defect. Once the developer believes the defect is fixed, the defect fix is routed to configuration management for inclusion in a test release. The defect report is usually placed in a build state.

5. Once the test release is installed in the test environment, someone—often, but not always, the original finder of the defect—is assigned to verify the repair of the defect described in the report, which is in a confirmation test (or simply test) state.

6. If the confirmation test passes, the defect report is placed in a closed state. If a new defect is discovered during the confirmation test, a new report is originated and the cycle for that report begins at step 1.

7. If the confirmation test fails, the defect report is placed in a reopened state and returned to step 3. If a new defect is also discovered during the confirmation test, a new report is originated for that defect and the cycle for that report begins at step 1.

Note that, in each state, the report has an owner who is responsible for taking action to move that report into an appropriate next state, unless the report is in a terminal state. The terminal states mentioned in the syllabus are closed, canceled, irreproducible, or deferred. I added the terminal state of accepted in the preceding list because that is also a possibility.

Notice that the finder, who is often a tester during dynamic testing, owns the defect report at the beginning and the end of the workflow. Let's look more closely at what the tester must do during these states.

Tester Defect Report States

In the workflow outlined previously, the finder of the defect—who I'll refer to as the tester for convenience and familiarity for now—had certain states in which actions are—or may be—required.

In the initial state, the tester needs to collect information about the failure and the underlying defect. There are limits as to how much information is possible and practical to gather, but in general, the more information collected in the report, the easier it is for the fixer to reproduce the failure and repair the underlying defect.

In the returned state, the fixer either has asserted that no problem exists or wants the tester to provide more information. If possible, the tester must either substantiate their assertion of a problem or gather additional information about the problem. The test manager should run regular reports to check the number of defect reports that enter this state because it's a potential source of inefficiency and delay in the entire defect workflow. My usual rule of thumb is that no more than 5 percent of defect reports should be returned; if the number is higher than 5 percent, then a problem exists that the test manager should address.

In the confirmation test state, the tester should repeat the steps to reproduce the failure from the defect report. In some cases, the test strategy will call for a complete repeat of the test or tests that originally identified the failure; while this is the most risk-averse approach, it is more expensive than just repeating the steps to reproduce the failure. As noted, the confirmation test may pass or fail, which results in different actions, and in addition a new failure might be observed as part of that confirmation test.

Whenever defect reports are owned by testers, the test manager should make sure that prompt and proper actions occur. It's a common problem for test managers to lose track of which reports their testers must act upon. Such problems can cause delays and inefficiencies in the defect workflow and in some cases reputational damage for the test team.

Invalid and Duplicate Defect Reports

As much as the test team might try to avoid it, some defect reports are invalid in that the anomaly does not result from a defect. Such invalid defect reports are referred to as false positives in the ISTQB nomenclature. A false positive can occur when the test environment is set up incorrectly. It can also occur when the test data is wrong or just improperly loaded. It can occur when there are problems with the test steps, the test inputs, or the test's expected results or when the automated test script is wrong. It can also occur when the tester is mistaken in their expectations of the proper results or behavior.

Test teams should also try to avoid filing duplicate defect reports. Duplicate defect reports exist when two or more reports describe behavior that is due to a single underlying defect. This can happen because multiple testers detected a related failure at the same time; either the testers might have not communicated about the failure or the symptoms might have been different enough that they thought different defects were in play. It can also happen because the number of active defect reports becomes so large that it is impossible for testers to keep track of what has already been reported. When duplicate reports are detected, the best practice is to keep the better of the reports open as the main report and to close the other report or reports as duplicates (while retaining a link to the active report to help searches). Duplicate reports should not be canceled or closed as invalid because the problem described is real.

As I said earlier, we should try to avoid invalid and duplicate defect reports. Inefficiency is invariably associated with such reports, due to the extra effort associated with managing them through their workflow from discovery to resolution. In large numbers, the associated effort can be significant. However, the test manager's dilemma is that pressure put on testers to eliminate such reports will result in hesitancy by testers to report defects at all. This leads to an increase in the number of real defects that are not reported at all, which drags down the test team's defect detection effectiveness. Since defect detection is a central objective for most test teams, such a problem is worse than the usually minor inefficiency caused by a small percentage of invalid and duplicate defect reports. As a general rule, I feel that as long as the number of invalid and duplicate defect reports is no more than 5 percent in each category, the situation is acceptable.

Cross-Functional Defect Management

Let's return to a topic I introduced earlier, which is the bug triage team, also called the defect management committee. As I said, this is a cross-functional team that includes representatives from various business and technical stakeholder groups, such as development, project management, product management, and other stakeholders. The test manager might be the moderator of the meeting, or the moderator might be a project manager or sponsor. I have seen many variations in terms of leadership and composition of these teams.

The triage team should meet regularly during periods of active testing, when defect reports are being entered into the defect management tool. This might include periods when reviews are happening, if defect reports from those reviews are being entered into the defect management tool, but my experience is that more frequently review defects are managed by the review team rather than by a defect triage committee.

As I mentioned earlier when I outlined the defect management process, the triage committee decides whether the defect report describes a failure. If the defect report doesn't, the report is canceled or closed as invalid. If the defect report does describe a failure, the triage committee decides whether to fix the defect or to defer it. There are benefits of fixing defects, of course, such as increased quality, but there are also costs, because resources are always limited, and there are risks associated with changing code to fix a bug. If the costs and risks outweigh the benefits temporarily, then repair of the defect should be deferred until later in the project, until the next project, or until some yet-to-be-determined project in the future. If the costs and risks outweigh the benefits permanently, then the defect may be deferred in perpetuity, accepted as a permanent limitation of the product.

If the defect is to be fixed, then the triage committee must consider priority. Many other project tasks are going on during test execution, including fixing defects that were previously discovered. While you as the test manager might

ISTQB Glossary

defect management committee: A cross-functional team of stakeholders who manage reported defects from initial detection to ultimate resolution (defect removal, defect deferral, or report cancellation). In some cases, the same team as the configuration control board.

defect triage committee: A cross-functional team of stakeholders who manage reported defects from initial detection to ultimate resolution (defect removal, defect deferral, or report cancellation). In some cases, the same team as the configuration control board.

want every bug your team finds fixed, and fixed immediately, that is not possible on most projects. Some bugs will be deferred, and there will be some delay associated with the repair of all but the most critical bugs. It behooves you to be realistic in your approach to and participation in the bug triage committee. Remember that the best possible project outcome must be achieved within the constraints of the project, including limits on the number of bugs that can be fixed. You—and perhaps other testers—should participate constructively, give good (not strident or angry) advice, and provide the information the bug triage team needs to make smart decisions.

The goal of defect management is to effectively and efficiently manage the known quality problems on a project up to the point of product release. No single element of defect management by itself can achieve this goal, but all elements—good communication, good defect management tools, and a proper defect workflow, guided by a professional, thorough, and committed defect management committee—must work together to reach it.

Example: IEEE 1044 Process

We've looked at the defect workflow and the participants in it. However, we haven't looked at the main force behind what moves defect reports through the workflow or what is happening to the participants as defect reports move through the workflow. The answer is that each owner, or the triage team collectively, learns more about the defect and what it means. This knowledge drives the decisions that are made. To be effectively utilized, the knowledge gained must be captured. Let's look an example of how that knowledge can be captured throughout the defect workflow, using IEEE 1044 as an example.

Table 4–1 shows how the gathering of classifications and data for defect reports works throughout the defect lifecycle within the IEEE 1044 standard. In each step—and indeed, embedded in each state—are three information capture activities:

- Recording
- Classifying
- Identifying impact

Table 4–1   Example: IEEE 1044 process

Step	Activities		
	Record...	*Classify...*	*Identify impact...*
1. Recognition	Include supporting data	Based on important attributes	Based on perceived impact
2. Investigation	Update and add supporting data	Update and add classification on important attributes	Update based on investigation
3. Action	Add data based on the action taken	Add data based on the action taken	Update based on action
4. Disposition	Add data based on disposition	Based on disposition	Update based on disposition

During the recognition step, we will record supporting data. We will classify based on important attributes that we have observed. We will identify impact based on perceived impact, which might differ from the final impact assessment.

During the investigation step, we will update and record more supporting data. We will update and add classification information on importance based on attributes uncovered during the investigation. We will update the impact based on investigation too.

During the action step, we will record new supporting data based on the action taken. We will also add classification data based on the action taken. We will update the impact based on the action too.

Finally, during the disposition step, we will record final data based on the disposition. The classifications will be adjusted and finalized based on the disposition. The final impact assessment will be captured.

Notice that I've been talking about data and classifications. The IEEE 1044 standard includes mandatory and optional supporting data and classifications for each activity in each step. When I say "mandatory supporting data and classifications," I mean mandatory for IEEE standards compliance.

Each of these data items and classifications is associated with a step or activity. The IEEE has assigned a two-character code in the standard: RR (recognition), IV (investigation), AC (action), IM (impact identification), and DP (disposition).

Example: IEEE 1044 Lifecycle

In Figure 4–1?, you see a diagram that shows the IEEE 1044 incident management lifecycle, including a mapping from IEEE 1044 that shows how typical incident report states in an incident tracking system would fit into this lifecycle.

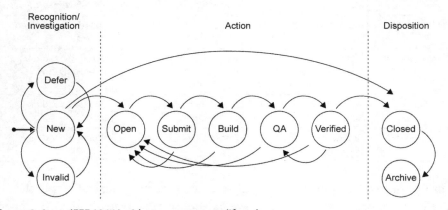

Figure 4–1   *IEEE 1044 incident management lifecycle*

We assume that all incidents will follow some sequence of states in their lifecycle, from initial recognition to ultimate disposition. Not all incidents will travel through the exact same sequence of states, as you can see from the figure. The IEEE 1044 defect lifecycle consists of four steps:

- Step 1: Recognition. Recognition occurs when we observe an anomaly, that observation being an incident. If the cause of the anomaly is a defect, then this incident is a failure. This can occur in any phase of the software lifecycle.
- Step 2: Investigation. After recognition, investigation of the incident occurs. Investigation can reveal related issues. Investigation can propose solutions. One solution is to conclude that the incident does not arise from an actual defect; for example, it might be a problem in the test data.

- Step 3: Action. The results of the investigation trigger the action step. We might decide to resolve the defect. We might want to take action to prevent future similar defects. If the defect is resolved, regression testing and confirmation testing must occur. Any tests that were blocked by the defect can now progress.

- Step 4: Disposition. With action concluded, the incident moves to the disposition step. Here we are principally interested in capturing further information and moving the incident into a terminal state.

Example: Defect Lifecycle

In Figure 4–2?, you see the lifecycle used on a defect tracking system we implemented for the IVR system of systems project I've used as a case study throughout this book. We created this defect tracking application for the client, using Microsoft Access. This was before widely available freeware defect tracking systems like Bugzilla became available, so we felt this was a cost-effective option.

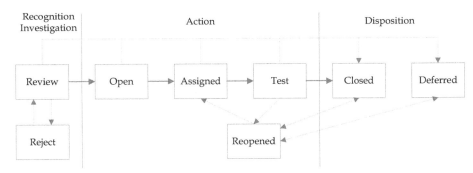

Figure 4–2   *Example: Defect lifecycle*

If you refer back to Figure 4–1, you can see that the states and step mappings are quite similar. There are a few differences.

For one thing, we considered deferred a final disposition. We did not have an invalid state, but we would close a report as invalid if we decided to permanently reject it. That is also a final disposition.

In addition, we used a single combined assigned state rather than separate submit and build states because we didn't track build time separate from fix time. We used a single combined test state rather than separate QA and verified states because my test team was empowered to determine if the problem was fixed.

Finally, we did not have an archive state because we assumed the reports would remain indefinitely in their final state.

Defining a Workflow Exercise

Assume that a select group of Telephone Bankers will participate in HELLO-CARMS testing as a beta test. The bankers will enter live applications from customers, but they will also capture the information and enter it into the current system afterward to ensure that no HELLOCARMS defects affect the customers. However, the bankers are not trained testers and are unwilling to spend time learning testing fundamentals.

Define a process whereby any defects found by Telephone Bankers can be properly entered into the defect tracking tool.

Defining a Workflow Debrief

Here is the process I would use:

- Each Telephone Banker will be assigned a "tester buddy" from the test team. Each tester buddy will support the banker's beta testing.
- When a Telephone Banker observes an anomaly, the banker will capture as much information as they can about the problem and send it via email to their tester buddy.
- Twice a day, each tester buddy will spend up to an hour processing failures reported by their Telephone Banker(s), starting with an attempt to reproduce the failure.
  - If the tester buddy can reproduce the failure, the tester will report the defect, including the information from the Telephone Banker as well as any additional information the tester gathered.
  - If the tester buddy cannot reproduce the failure based on the email, the tester buddy will contact the Telephone Banker by phone to discuss the failure. Based on that discussion, the tester buddy will try to reproduce the failure again.
  - If the tester buddy now can reproduce the failure, the tester buddy will report the defect, including the information from the Telephone Banker as well as any additional information they gathered.
  - If the tester buddy still cannot reproduce the failure, the defect will be reported as irreproducible.
  - If some tester buddies find they are spending more than two hours a day on reporting defects found during beta testing, the test manager will review tester buddy assignments and the information being sent to them to determine whether adjustments are needed.

This process should avoid a situation where Telephone Bankers enter poorly written defect reports and introduce inefficiency into the defect management process and noise into the defect report metrics.

4.3 Defect Report Information

Learning objectives

(K3) Define the data and classification information that should be gathered during the defect management process.

I said earlier that an essential part of managing a defect from discovery to resolution is to gather and report the proper information. Without such information, the wrong decisions are likely to be made about how to move the defect forward and about what is the appropriate resolution. This information can be based on a static test that detects a defect or on a dynamic test that reveals a failure, though as I mentioned earlier, it's less common for static testing defects to be managed using defect management tools.

However the defect is managed in terms of the tool, the information provided serves similar purposes for the project and the organization. First, the immediate tactical need is that the information must allow the project team to move the defect efficiently from discovery to resolution. Efficiency here implies effort, cost, and duration. Second, the defect information should allow us to assess our project status, as discussed in Chapter 2. The information should shed light on the project status and the test progress. Third, the defect information should help us assess the capability of our processes. We'll cover this further in section 4.4, later in this chapter.

For the first purpose, there is no real need for consistency of the information, provided the information serves the tactical need sufficiently in terms of giving information to the participants. However, for the second and especially the third purpose—assessment of status and process capability—we need the ability to see patterns across multiple defect reports. This requires that a core set of information be defined in the tool and the defect management process, and collected for each defect report, so that we have comparable information for all defects on the project and, for process assessment, across all projects.

We'll discuss the specific information to be gathered shortly. However, let me start by mentioning that the information is of two basic types. First, we have data, by which I mean free-form text fields (such as defect report history), attachments (such as screen shots and video captures), and other such entries that are unrestricted other than by type. Second, we have classifications, where a prescribed list of possible values is available, and one value must be selected from that list.

Defect data and classification information is not gathered just because it can be gathered. It should be gathered to support specific needs. Some of the test progress monitoring metrics you saw in Chapter 2 grew out of analysis of defect data. For example, defect discovery and resolution trends are used to monitor test status. Some of the test control metrics you saw in Chapter 1 were based on defect data. For example, discovery of defect clusters can result in a change in risk prioritization, and a negative trend in closure period can lead to measures to improve the turnaround time for defect reports. The evaluation of exit criteria often includes one or more metrics that are based on defect data. For example, if reliability is an important quality characteristic for a product, the exit criteria may include one that addresses mean time between failure.

Defect Data and Classifications to Collect

Let's look at some of the defect classifications and data that the defect management process—via the defect management tool—may collect:

- Submitter name and role. Knowing the name allows people to direct questions to the submitter, and knowing the role provides insight into the submitter's perspective. Most defect management tools can automatically populate this information based on the finder's login credentials.
- Test type. The type of test being run when the failure was observed can be used to do analysis of various types, such as which test types are finding the most defects. This should be a basic pull-down menu from which the finder selects.
- Failure summary. The finder should describe, in brief text, the failure that occurred and how it might affect the users, customers, or other stakeholders.
- Detailed description. In some defect management tools, the finder also includes a more in-depth text description of the failure. In some tools, this is included in the steps to reproduce field.
- Step to reproduce. The finder should describe the steps they used to cause the failure to occur, usually in a numbered list text format. Where appropriate in these steps, the finder should contrast the actual results observed at

that step with the expected results; in other words, the finder should draw the reader's attention to the anomalies where they occurred. Screen shots, database dumps, logs, and other sources of supporting information can be attached for most defect management tools.

- Phase of introduction, phase of detection, and phase of removal. The finder should select the phase of detection when initially reporting the defect. The fixer should select the phase of introduction after determining the root cause of the defect. The finder—or whoever does the confirmation testing—should select the phase of removal after the confirmation test is successfully concluded. Each of these three fields should use the same pull-down classification menu.

- Work product. The fixer should select the work product in which the defect was originally introduced after determining the root cause of the defect. In some cases, this is a pull-down menu restricted to the work products created for the project, while in other cases it is a pull-down menu with generic work product names such as requirements specification, code, and so on. Free-form text fields will not be useful for analysis due to the unlikelihood that consistent information will be entered by disparate individuals.

- Severity. The finder should select an initial severity from a simple pull-down menu, often a one-to-five scale with defined criteria for each selection. The severity is often based on the technical implications and problems associated with the failure. The triage team can adjust the severity rating when the defect report is reviewed.

- Priority. The finder should select an initial priority from a simple pull-down menu, often a one-to-five scale with defined criteria for each selection. Priority is often based on business considerations, in contrast to severity. The triage team can adjust the priority rating when the defect report is reviewed.

- Subsystem. The finder should select, from a predefined menu, the subsystem in which the defect exists or the one affected by the defect. This can be adjusted by the fixer in some situations. This classification will allow for defect cluster analysis.

- Project activity. The finder should select, from a predefined menu, the project activity that was underway when the failure was observed. This is not the same as the phase of detection, because different activities can be underway during a given phase.

- Identification method. The finder should select a classification based on the specific way in which the failure or defect was found. One possible way to populate the menu is to use the ISTQB classification: review, static analysis, structural test, behavioral test, experience-based test, defect-based test, or dynamic analysis.

- Defect type. The finder should select a classification based on a defect taxonomy. The best practice is for the defect taxonomy to be common across all projects, though in some cases product differences can lead to the use of different taxonomies. This use of different taxonomies can reduce comparability of results and analytical value for process improvement.

- Affected quality characteristic. The finder should select a classification based on some quality characteristic breakdown, such as ISO 9126. The triage team might adjust this classification during the review of the report.

- Test environment. The finder should describe the test environment. Sometimes, this is a text field, but a customized classification based on the project is also possible.

- Affected project and product. Typically, these will be classifications selected by the finder.

- Owner. This is a classification based on project participants and is usually managed by the tool, with the triage team able to make direct selections at certain points in the process.

- Current state. As with owner, this is a classification that is managed by the tool, with the triage team able to make direct selections at certain points in the process.

- Version information. This is typically a text field, though sometimes it's a classification, that allows the finder to specify the particular test items and release numbers associated with the problem. Later, when the confirmation test is successfully passed, the same information is entered for the particular test items and release numbers associated with the fix.

- Impact. This is typically a text field assessment of how the defect will affect the project and product stakeholders. It's initially done by the finder but potentially updated by the triage team and possibly also the fixer.

- Conclusions, recommendations, and approvals. These are various text fields and, in the case of approvals, possibly sign-off fields via pull-down lists of project participants. These fields should document what was and wasn't done to resolve the defect.

- Risks, costs, opportunities, and benefits. This is a text field (or a collection of text fields) that captures the triage team's decision-making criteria as they decided whether to fix or defer the defect.
- Defect lifecycle history. This includes the dates when the defect report entered the various states in which it has been, who owned the report in each state, and what the owner did during that period. Some of this information is automatically captured by the tool, while other elements are entered by the owner.
- Description of resolution. This is text information entered by the fixer of the defect or, if the defect is deferred or accepted as a permanent limitation, a description of the way in which the consequences of doing so will be handled.
- Confirmation and regression test recommendations. This is text information entered by the fixer of the defect that gives advice to the finder of the defect on what confirmation tests and regression tests should be run.
- Test in progress. This is usually text information that the finder enters to list the test or tests that were able to locate the failure or, if the test was not a predesigned test (e.g., an exploratory test), to describe what elements of that test caused the failure. It should be helpful information for the fixer primarily, though the triage team may also consider it when determining whether to fix the defect.
- Test basis. This is usually text information entered by the finder that references the risk, requirement, design element, supported configuration, or other aspect of the system that the test was verifying. It might also include a reference to the test oracle upon which the tester relied when concluding that the test failed.

This list of data and classifications is not exhaustive. Different organizations and different tools capture other information.

Consistency and Criticality of Information

The level of information gathered about a defect, and the level of detail in that information, tends to vary depending on where the defect is found in the lifecycle. Typically, less information (and less-detailed information) is gathered in earlier activities such as requirements reviews, design reviews, static code analysis, and unit testing. In later activities such as system test, system integration test, and user acceptance test, more information that's more detailed is gathered.

These variations can be acceptable, but they can also cause problems. When no information is gathered, such as in static code analysis and unit testing, this can create blind spots that make it difficult to understand the true quality capability of the software engineering process, or even to make smart decisions about the project, because insight into where and when defects are being introduced, detected, and removed is lost. This is especially true of classification information, which can be important when you're trying to aggregate findings across the project and across multiple projects. The best practice is to keep the classifications consistent and to gather those classifications across all testing activities. This will allow meaningful project and process assessment.

As I mentioned, the list of defect data and classifications given in the ISTQB syllabi is neither universal nor exhaustive. You can refer to other sources for ideas, such as ISO 9126, IEEE 829, IEEE 1044, Orthogonal Defect Classification (ODC), and more.

When deciding whether to include more information, make sure you determine whether the value of gathering the information justifies the effort associated with training people to do so and the effort associated with gathering the information. I've seen plenty of situations where too much information was required of the finder when submitting a defect report. This can result in information overload for the triage team when a defect is evaluated and can also result in a sort of "reporting fatigue" on the part of the finders, the triage team, and the fixers. If people feel the information-gathering process is excessive, they will start to take shortcuts that will reduce the quality of the information. It's better to concentrate on a few fields that give essential information and make sure the information is being used properly.

Consider the following criteria for determining what information to gather and how to gather it:

- Completeness. The information gathered should give the various participants in the defect management process all the facts they need to carry out their roles. In addition, each participant should know how to gather all the information needed.
- Conciseness. As I said previously, it's better to gather only and exactly the information needed than to subject the participants to a bewildering thicket of data-gathering requirements and the recipients to an overwhelming set of facts. Psychological studies have shown that, at a certain point, people actually make worse decisions when confronted by an excessive amount of information.[1]

---

1. A great discussion of this can be found in Daniel Kahneman's book *Thinking, Fast and Slow*.

- Accuracy. This is related to the issue of conciseness and completeness. The people gathering the information must know how to accurately gather what is requested from them. Otherwise, they are likely to start guessing at what to enter. Inaccuracy is particularly problematic for classifications because classification information is used to discern patterns in defects that will support process improvements. With inaccurate classification information, wrong decisions will be made, resulting in inefficient process improvements at best and sometimes process degradation.

- Objectivity. Accuracy of information is in part a function of knowing what the right entry is. It's also a function of having no personal or financial stake in the entry of inaccurate information. If incentives or disincentives are tied to the entry of certain information or selection of certain classification values, bad data is sure to follow. People must be educated and motivated to provide purely objective information.

- Relevance. For each piece of information to be gathered, we should ask ourselves, "Who is going to be able to do their job better based on this information?" If the answer is that the information is of no use to anyone, or that the information will not support better decision making, then you should question whether that information should be gathered.

- Timeliness. Especially for information that enables the project to move forward, timeliness is an important factor.

Keep in mind that problems with defect report information can have both immediate and long-term effects. In the immediate term, problems with defect reports can slow down the resolution process for individual defects. Such situations can be addressed through manual intervention and direct communication between the finder, the triage team, and the fixer, though such actions are less efficient than properly functioning information flows between these participants. In the long term, the situation created by bad defect reports is worse because noise in the data results in confusing or misleading assessments of the current situation with the project, the status of test progress, and the true capabilities of the testing and software process.

Example: Classification

Figure 4–3? shows an example of using classification information to learn something interesting about a project. This Pareto chart analyzes the number and percentage of bugs associated with each major subsystem—system, really—in the IVR system-of-systems project I've mentioned a number of times. This project, called the NOP project, tied together 10 systems via a wide area network, a local area network, and the phone system to implement a large distributed entertainment application.

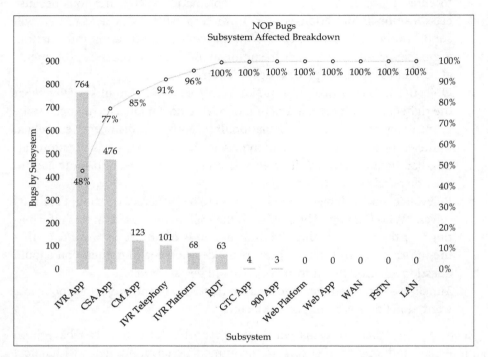

Figure 4–3   *Example: Classification*

As you can see in the graph in Figure 4–3?, the interactive voice response (or IVR) application is responsible for about half of the bugs. The customer service application (or CSA) adds about 30 percent more. The rest of the applications are relatively solid. The content management (or CM) application is less than 10 percent of the bugs. The interactive voice response server's telephony and OS/hardware layers each are around 5 percent, with the remaining applications and infrastructure accounting for the other 4 percent.

This tells us that the technical risk—the likelihood of finding bugs—is highest for the IVR application. If we wanted to use this information to reallocate the test effort, we could update our risk analysis based on this information, then see how that updated risk analysis would affect our testing. If we wanted to use this for a project retrospective, we might do further analysis to see why so many bugs were in that application. What changes can we make in subsequent projects to reduce the incidence of bugs in the IVR application?

HELLOCARMS Defect Information Exercise

Using the data and classifications discussed in this course, select information to gather for HELLOCARMS defects. Assign the role responsible for gathering the information. Briefly explain the source and use of each piece of information.

HELLOCARMS Defect Information Debrief

Table 4–2 shows the information presented in the syllabus along with the responsible role for gathering the information, the source of the information, and its use. In Table 4–2, there are three roles:

- Finder: This is the person who found the defect or observed the failure. It's often a tester.
- Fixer: This is the person who is repairing the defect. It's often a developer, but it can also be a system architect, a business analyst, or a marketing person in the case of a specification defect.
- Triagers: These are the people on the defect triage committee (or defect management committee), the cross-functional team discussed in the previous section.

The other entry in the role column, tool, indicates that the defect management tool will typically handle this field automatically as part of the defect lifecycle.

Table 4–2   Information by role, source, and use

Information	Gatherer Role	Source and Use
Submitter name and role	Finder	S: The person who found the defect. U: Reporting by submitter (but not for people metrics); connecting submitter with fixer.
Test type	Tester	S: A list of test types. U: Test type effectiveness analysis.
Failure summary	Finder	S: Observed test results. U: Prioritize defect repair; give a short name to the defect.
Detailed description	Finder	S: Observed test results. U: Prioritize defect repair; inform fixer.
Steps to reproduce	Finder	S: Observed test results. U: Prioritize defect repair; inform fixer.

Information	Gatherer Role	Source and Use
Actual and expected results	Finder	S: Observed test results and test oracle (often as documented in the test). U: Prioritize defect repair; inform fixer.
Screen shots, logs, and database dumps	Finder	S: Observed test results and submitter research. U: Prioritize defect repair; inform fixer.
Introduction phase	Fixer (usually)	S: Fixer's location of the underlying defect and therefore the point in time where it was introduced. U: Process assessment.
Detection phase	Finder (often tester)	S: Current phase when defect is discovered. U: Process assessment.
Removal phase	Fixer (usually)	S: Current phase when defect is removed. U: Process assessment.
Work product	Fixer (usually)	S: The work product in which the fixer locates the defect. U: Defect density analysis.
Severity (technical)	Finder, then triagers	S: Observed test results. U: Prioritize defect; project and process assessment.
Priority (business)	Finder (sometimes), then triagers	S: Observed test results. U: Prioritize defect; project and process assessment.
Subsystem	Finder (often), then fixer	S: The work product in which the fixer locates the defect. U: Defect density analysis
Project activity	Finder	S: The project activity that was underway when the defect was found. U: Defect detection effectiveness assessment.
Identification method	Finder	S: The method used to identify the failure or defect. U: Defect detection effectiveness assessment.
Defect type	Fixer	S: The specific repair made to the work product. U: Process assessment.
Affected quality characteristic	Finder	S: Observed test results. U: Process and project assessment.
Test environment	Finder	S: Test environment in use when failure was observed. U: Informing the fixer; prioritizing the defect (sometimes).
Affected project	Finder	S: Observed test results. U: Project and process assessment.
Affected product	Finder	S: Observed test results. U: Project, product, and process assessment.

Table continues

Information	Gatherer Role	Source and Use
Current owner	Tool (in some states), triagers	S: The defect lifecycle. U: Assignment of work; reporting defect status (but not for people metrics).
Current state	Tool (in some states), triagers.	S: The defect lifecycle. U: Reporting defect status (but not for people metrics).
Observed version	Finder	S: The version installed in the test environment when the failure was observed. U: Inform the fixer.
Fixed version	Finder	S: The version installed in the test environment when the defect fix passes the confirmation test. U: Process assessment; proof of closure.
Impact	Finder (in some cases), then triagers	S: The observed test results. U: Prioritize the defect; inform the fixer.
Conclusions, recommendations, and approvals	Varies	S: Depends on the workflow and process for managing defects. U: Documents root cause analysis, lessons learned.
Fix/don't fix risks, opportunities, costs, and benefits	Triagers	S: Analysis of the failure and the defect. U: Determine whether to fix and, if so, the priority.
Defect lifecycle history	Tool, finder, fixer, and triagers	S: Date, actor, state change, and status information gathered by tool from defect lifecycle participants. U: Audit trail; process assessment.
Description of resolution	Fixer	S: A textual discussion of how the defect was fixed. U: Knowledge transfer among the project team.
Confirmation/ regression test recommendations	Fixer	S: Analysis of the changes made to implement the fix and how these changes will affect the system. U: Inform finder's confirmation and regression testing.
Test in progress	Finder	S: The ID number of the test being run. U: Inform finder's confirmation and regression testing; defect detection effectiveness analysis.
Relevant test basis element(s)	Finder	S: The requirement, design, risk, configuration, or other item impacted by the defect. U: Product, project, and process assessment.

Let me provide some more details for each row in the table:

- Submitter name and role is gathered by the finder. The source is the person who found the defect. The use is for reporting grouped by submitter (but not for people metrics); connecting submitter with fixer.

- Test type is gathered by the tester. The source is a list of test types. The use is analyzing test type effectiveness.
- Failure summary is gathered by the finder. The source is observed test results. The use is to prioritize defect repair and give a short name to the defect.
- Detailed description is gathered by the finder. The source is observed test results. The use is to prioritize defect repair and inform the fixer.
- Steps to reproduce are gathered by the finder. The source is observed test results. The use is to prioritize defect repair and inform the fixer.
- Actual and expected results are gathered by the finder The source is observed test results and the test oracle (often as documented in the test). The use is to prioritize defect repair and inform the fixer.
- Screen shots, logs, and database dumps are gathered by the finder. The source is observed test results and submitter research. The use is to prioritize defect repair and inform fixer.
- The introduction phase is gathered by the fixer (usually). The source is the fixer's location of the underlying defect and therefore the point in time where it was introduced. The use is process assessment.
- The detection phase is gathered by the finder (often the tester). The source is the current phase when the defect is discovered. The use is process assessment.
- The removal phase is gathered by the fixer (usually). The source is the current phase when the defect is removed. The use is process assessment.
- The work product is gathered by the fixer (usually). The source is the work product in which the fixer locates the defect. The use is defect density analysis.
- Severity is determined by the finder, then triagers, based on technical considerations. The source is observed test results. The use is to prioritize defects and make project and process assessments.
- Priority is determined by the finder (sometimes), then triagers, based on business considerations. The source is observed test results. The use is to prioritize defects and make project and process assessments.
- Subsystem is gathered by the finder (often), then the fixer. The source is the work product in which the fixer locates the defect. The use is defect density analysis.
- Project activity is gathered by the finder. The source is the project activity that was underway when the defect was found. The use is defect detection effectiveness assessment.

- Identification method is gathered by the finder. The source is the method used to identify the failure or defect. The use is defect detection effectiveness assessment.
- Defect type is gathered by the fixer. The source is the specific repair made to the work product. The use is process assessment.
- Affected quality characteristic is gathered by the finder. The source is observed test results. The use is process and project assessment.
- Test environment is gathered by the finder. The source is the test environment in use when the failure was observed. The use is informing the fixer and sometimes prioritizing the defect.
- Affected project is gathered by the finder. The source is observed test results. The use is project and process assessment.
- Affected product is gathered by the finder. The source is observed test results. The use is project, product, and process assessment.
- Current owner is assigned by the tool (in some defect report states) or by triagers. The source is the defect lifecycle. The use is the assignment of work and reporting defect status (but not for people metrics).
- Current state is assigned by the tool (in some defect report states) or by triagers. The source is the defect lifecycle. The use is reporting defect status (but not for people metrics).
- Observed version is gathered by the finder. The source is the version installed in the test environment when the failure was observed. The use is to inform the fixer.
- Fixed version is gathered by the finder. The source is the version installed in the test environment when the defect fix passes the confirmation test. The use is process assessment and proof of closure.
- Impact is gathered by the finder (in some cases), then triagers. The source is the observed test results. The use is to prioritize the defect and inform the fixer.
- Conclusions, recommendations, and approvals are set by various parties. The source depends on the workflow and the process for managing the defects. The use is to document root cause analysis and lessons learned.
- Fix/don't fix risks, opportunities, costs, and benefits are assigned by the triagers. The source is an analysis of the failure and the defect. The use is to determine whether to fix and, if so, the priority.
- Defect lifecycle history is captured by the tool based on input from the finder, the fixer, and triagers. The source is the date, actor, state change, and

status information gathered by tool from defect lifecycle participants. The use is as an audit trail and process assessment.

- Description of resolution is gathered by the fixer. The source is a textual discussion of how the defect was fixed. The use is to promote knowledge transfer among the project team.
- The confirmation and regression test recommendations come from the fixer. The source is an analysis of the changes made to implement the fix and how these changes will affect the system. The use is to inform the finder's confirmation and regression testing.
- Test in progress is gathered by the finder. The source is the ID number of the test being run. The use is to inform the finder's confirmation and regression testing and to be analyzed for defect detection effectiveness.
- Relevant test basis elements are gathered by the finder. The source is the requirement, design, risk, configuration, or other item impacted by the defect. The use is product, project, and process assessment.

It's important to keep in mind that not all of this information will be required in every situation. When recently doing an assessment for a client, I found that about half of these items would be relevant for their projects.

4.4   Assessing Process Capability with Defect Report Information

Learning objectives

(K2) Explain how defect report statistics can be used to evaluate the process capability of the testing and software development processes.

In section 2.6, we looked at various metrics that can be derived from defect information to evaluate where we are on a project and to report our test results. Earlier in this chapter, I mentioned that accurate defect information is essential to gaining insights in terms of where a project is and where it's going. I also mentioned the importance of defect information in terms of understanding the capabilities of our software processes.

In my work as a consultant, one of the things we do with clients is to assess their processes and how to improve them. Defect information plays an important role in this assessment. I have gained powerful insights and been able to propose highly beneficial process improvements for clients based on what their defect information has told me. The classification information is especially useful for these purposes.

However, I have also been confronted with situations where the defect information confounded my efforts at understanding what was happening. These situations typically arose where the defect data had issues with completeness, accuracy, objectivity, relevance, and timeliness, the criteria I mentioned earlier as quality criteria for defect report information.

It is not necessary for all the reports to be bad for these problems to arise. I've seen situations where just 10 or 20 percent of the defect reports had bad classification information, and that was enough to make it impossible to determine what exactly was going on in the process.

As a test manager, you are responsible for the quality of the work done by your team. This includes the quality of the information captured for defects. You should remember that, even if the defects being reported are moving from discovery to resolution, it's possible that you are missing important classification information that would allow smart process improvements.

Here are some examples of process assessment that depend on proper defect reports:

- Phase containment. When a defect escapes from one phase to a later phase, the cost increases. Many organizations have millions of dollars in avoidable defect costs associated with such escapes. By accurately measuring the phase of defect introduction, detection, and removal, as well as the cost of quality associated with defects in each phase, we can expose these true costs. With this information in hand, a business case for increasing the defect detection effectiveness of each phase can be proposed and the resulting improvements measured.

- Reducing defects at their phase of introduction. With accurate phase of defect introduction information, we can not only improve phase containment, we can also improve quality overall. The phase of introduction information can be used to determine when most defects are introduced, using Pareto analysis to focus on the vital few origins of defects. Then, steps to improve processes can be taken to reduce the total number of defects that are introduced, by focusing on the most important points of defect introduction.

- Root cause analysis. In addition to when defects are introduced, good defect information should allow us to understand why defects are introduced. As with the previous item, we can use Pareto analysis to identify the most important reasons we have defects in our products. We can then make process improvements to eliminate these reasons for defect introduction.

- Cost of quality. As discussed in Chapter 2, cost of quality is a useful way to assess the efficiency of testing. However, it can also be used to examine phase containment to determine the avoidable defect costs. When the particularly expensive avoidable defect costs are identified, process improvements can be put in place.

- Defect clusters. As mentioned in the Foundation syllabus and earlier in this chapter, defects are not uniformly and randomly distributed through the product. By using good defect information to identify defect clusters, we can do better risk analysis because we'll have a better understanding of where defects are likely. In addition, developers can rework these buggy elements of the system, removing the clusters entirely.

These are only a few examples of how you can use defect metrics to assess the effectiveness and efficiency of the testing and software engineering processes.[2]

As I mentioned earlier, the amount of information gathered for defects tends to vary depending on the stage of the lifecycle in which the defects are found. Some teams don't capture any information at all for defects found in reviews and unit tests. Some teams following agile processes don't even capture information for defects found during an iteration, provided that defect is fixed before the next iteration starts.

Usually, the justification for this lack of information gathering is that capturing the defect information is unnecessary because the defects will get fixed anyway. Why capture information that is not needed to move the defect from discovery to resolution?

While that makes sense from a tactical perspective, it leaves out the larger strategic issue of how we go about getting better in the long run if we don't know what mistakes are being made. Without insight into the defects being introduced throughout the lifecycle, we don't have a true grasp of the quality (or lack of it), process capability, and cost of quality associated with our current process. We cannot assess, not to mention improve, our software processes without complete and reliable data about defects. Since many organizations waste as much as 10 to 25 percent of their software budgets on avoidable costs of

---

2. See my books *Testing Metrics* and *Improving the Testing Process* for more information.

> **ISTQB Glossary**
>
> **false-negative result:** A test result that fails to identify the presence of a defect that is actually present in the test object.
>
> **false-positive result:** A test result in which a defect is reported although no such defect actually exists in the test object.

failure, the savings associated with avoiding defect reporting during some parts of the software process are illusory.[3]

Example: Defect Closure over Time

Figure 4–4? shows an example of the closure period chart for the Internet appliance project I've mentioned a number of times. Closure period charts analyze defect trends over time.

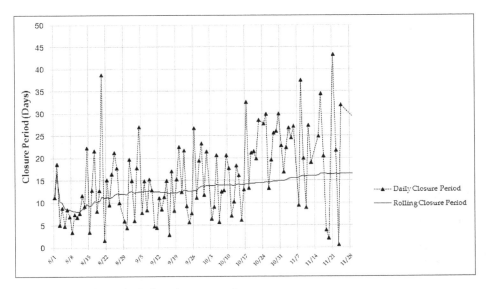

Figure 4–4   *Example: Defect closure over time*

Figure 4–4? shows something interesting. During the first 12 weeks—from August 1 to about October 17—the rolling closure period gradually trended

---

3. A good discussion of this topic can be found in Capers Jones's book *The Economics of Software Quality.*

upward. After a brief unstable period right at the start, it had settled at around 11 days but then over a two-month period moved to about 14 days.

However, on October 17, some discontinuity must have occurred. In the month from October 17 to November 17, the rolling closure period moved up another 3 days to around 17 days. Previously in the project it had taken two months to creep up by 3 days, but now it has jumped up 3 days in just one month, a rate twice as fast before. Remember too that the rolling closure period becomes harder to pull up or down as the project continues because the set of bug reports already closed becomes larger and thus the rolling closure period is anchored by the past numbers.

You can see there were over 20 daily closure periods above the rolling closure period during that month, while only 4 daily closure periods were below the rolling closure period. In addition, the daily closure periods that were above the rolling closure period were more significantly above the rolling closure period than the daily closure periods that were below the rolling closure period were below it. Thus, you can think of the daily closure period as acting to sharply pull up the rolling closure period.

What happened? It's not possible to say for sure, based on a trend chart. Trend charts show trends in time, not causality. To find the answer in such a situation, I would start with two avenues of investigation. First, I would check to see if some major project milestone occurred on October 17. That could be entry into a new level of testing, especially a more formal level of testing that would tend to have slower-moving processes. Alternatively, the introduction of a large chunk of new functionality could lead to tricky problems being discovered. Or, perhaps the development team was in part redeployed to another project.

The second avenue lies in the bug taxonomy. I would run three analyses:

- Percentage distribution of bugs by affected subsystem for the entire project
- Percentage distribution of bugs by affected subsystem for the period from August 1 to October 17
- Percentage distribution of bugs by affected subsystem for the period from October 17 to November 17

I showed this type of graph in the chapter on test management, Chapter 2, when discussing metrics for test progress monitoring and control.

This analysis might reveal a change in where the bugs are. That in turn would lead to the next round of investigation. Finally, we might adjust the defect taxonomy, our risk analysis, and our plan for the rest of the testing based on this information.

4.5 Sample Exam Questions

To end each chapter, you can try one or more sample exam questions to reinforce your knowledge and understanding of the material and to prepare for the ISTQB Advanced Level Test Manager exam.

1. Assume you are a test manager working on a project to create a programmable thermostat for home use to control central heating, ventilation, and air conditioning (HVAC) systems. In addition to the normal HVAC control functions, the thermostat has the ability to download data to a browser-based application that runs on PCs, tablets, and smartphones for further analysis.

    During quality risk analysis, you identify compatibility problems between the browser-based application and the different PC configurations that can host that application as a quality risk item with a high level of likelihood.

    Your test team is currently executing compatibility tests. Consider the following excerpt from the failure description of a compatibility bug report:

    1. Connect the thermostat to a Windows 8 PC.
    2. Start the thermostat analysis application on the PC. Application starts normally and recognizes connected thermostat.
    3. Attempt to download the data from the thermostat.
    4. Data does not download.
    5. Attempt to download the data three times. Data will not download.

    Based on this information alone, which of the following is a problem that exists with this bug report?

    A. Lack of structured testing

    B. Inadequate classification information

    C. Insufficient isolation

    D. Poorly documented steps to reproduce

2. Continue with the previous scenario. Your test team is still executing compatibility tests. Consider the following excerpt from the failure description of a compatibility bug report:

    1. Install the thermostat analysis application on an iPad.
    2. Attempt to start the thermostat analysis application.
    3. Thermostat analysis application does not start.
    4. Reinstall the thermostat analysis application three times. Thermostat analysis application does not start after any reinstallation.
    5. This test passed on the previous test release.

    Based on this information alone, which of the following is the most reasonable hypothesis about this bug?

    A. The bug might be a regression.

    B. The bug might be intermittent.

    C. The application didn't install on iPads before.

    D. The bug might be a duplicate.

5 Improving the Testing Process

Bridgekeeper: Stop! Who approaches the Bridge of Death must answer me these questions three, 'ere the other side he see.

Sir Robin: Ask me the questions, bridgekeeper. I'm not afraid.

Bridgekeeper: What is your name?

Sir Robin: Sir Robin of Camelot.

Bridgekeeper: What is your quest?

Sir Robin: To seek the Holy Grail.

Bridgekeeper: What is the capital of Assyria?

Sir Robin: I don't know that! [Flies screaming from the bridge.]

Bridgekeeper: Stop! What is your name?

Sir Galahad: Sir Galahad of Camelot.

Bridgekeeper: What is your quest?

Sir Galahad: I seek the Holy Grail.

Bridgekeeper: What is your favorite color?

Sir Galahad: Blue. No yel [Flies screaming from the bridge.]

Bridgekeeper: [Laughs.] Stop! What is your name?

King Arthur: It is Arthur, King of the Britons.

Bridgekeeper: What is your quest?

King Arthur: To seek the Holy Grail.

Bridgekeeper: What is the air-speed velocity of an unladen swallow?

King Arthur: What do you mean? An African or European swallow?

Bridgekeeper: What? I don't know that! [Flies screaming from the bridge.]

Squire Bedemir: How do you know so much about swallows?

King Arthur: Well, you have to know these things when you're a king, you know.

> King Arthur demonstrates his mastery of the flying process, in the geek-classic movie, *Monty Python and the Holy Grail*, written by the British comedy troupe Monty Python.

Chapter 5, Improving the Testing Process, of the Advanced syllabus contains the following seven sections:

1. Introduction
2. Test Improvement Process
3. Improving the Testing Process
4. Improving the Testing Process with TMMi
5. Improving the Testing Process with TPI Next
6. Improving the Testing Process with CTP
7. Improving the Testing Process with STEP

5.1 Introduction

Learning objectives

Recall of content only

Much of this syllabus is about how to establish and operate good test processes in your organization. However, as a test manager, you should also look for ways to improve your test processes. Continuous improvement results in ever-greater measures of effectiveness and efficiency for your test processes and greater satisfaction of your testing stakeholders.

So, in this chapter, I'll share some ideas on how to do that. I'll start with reviewing some general ideas related to process improvement, including how software process improvement and test process improvement result in better-quality software. We'll then look at a generic process improvement framework that can be used for any process, the IDEAL model. After that, we'll quickly review four industry-standard test process improvement models: Testing Maturity Model integration (TMMi), Test Process Improvement Next (TPI Next), Critical Testing Processes (CTP), and Systematic Test and Evaluation Process (STEP).

ISTQB Glossary

content-based model: A process model that provides a detailed description of good engineering practices, such as, for example, test practices.

Critical Testing Processes (CTP): A content-based model for test process improvement built around 12 critical processes. These include highly visible processes, by which peers and management judge competence, and mission-critical processes, in which performance affects the company's profits and reputation.

Systematic Test and Evaluation (STEP): A structured testing methodology, also used as a content-based model for improving the testing process. Systematic Test and Evaluation Process (STEP) does not require that improvements occur in a specific order.

Test Maturity Model integration (TMMi): A five-level staged framework for test process improvement that is related to the Capability Maturity Model Integration (CMMI) and describes the key elements of an effective test process.

TPI Next: A continuous business-driven framework for test process improvement that describes the key elements of an effective and efficient test process.

If the test processes at your organization are to improve, you're probably the one who will make that happen. Therefore, you should be familiar with the techniques discussed in this chapter. You can also refer to the Expert Level Improving the Test Process syllabus for more information.[1]

5.2 Test Improvement Process

Learning objectives

(K2) Explain, using examples, why it is important to improve the test process.

When conducted with the objective of finding defects, testing is typically about improving software because the point of finding defects is usually to select the most important ones and remove them. While testing doesn't directly improve the software, it provides the information needed to do so.

---

1. In addition to the ISTQB document, you might want to read my book (with Judy McKay) *Improving the Testing Process*.

Another way to improve software quality is to improve the processes used to develop and deliver the software. This too has an indirect effect, in that improved software processes reduce the likelihood of mistakes during the software development and maintenance processes and thus decrease the rate of defect introduction.

Since software testing is part of the software process, software testing processes can and should be improved. As I mentioned, we'll look at five techniques for doing so in this chapter. We'll start with a generic process improvement model, then look at the four test-specific models I mentioned earlier.

While testing has a positive return on investment, as I demonstrated earlier using cost of quality analysis in Chapter 2, the size of the investment can nevertheless be significant. In spite of this, software process improvement models such as Capability Maturity Model Integration (CMMI) and ISO 15504 have very little to say directly about testing.

So, various software testing figures, myself among them, created process improvement models focused specifically on testing, including Testing Maturity Model integration (TMMi), Test Process Improvement Next (TPI Next), Critical Testing Processes (CTP), Systematic Test and Evaluation Process (STEP), and others. In addition to providing a means for identifying test process improvement opportunities, the standard nature of each model allows comparisons across organizations that have used the same model. That's especially true when the model includes—or is augmented with—metrics that provide for an objective measurement.

Please keep in mind that the ISTQB does not endorse or recommend any specific test improvement models. The purpose of including these models in the Advanced Test Manager and Expert Improving the Testing Process syllabi is to provide you with some idea of the models available, how they work, and what the models consider.

I mentioned earlier that process improvement can and should apply to the entire software process, including testing. A simple way to think of process improvement is as a form of learning from mistakes. We can improve any process, from cooking a meal to developing software and testing it, because all human activities are prone to error. Sometimes the mistakes and their consequences are obvious; sometimes they are not so obvious. A good process improvement model should help us see the mistakes that matter most, no matter how subtle those mistakes may be. To be less pejorative, we can discover and subsequently exploit opportunities to do better next time every time we do something, if we look for those opportunities.

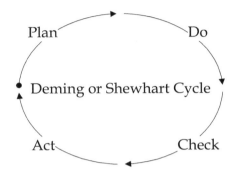

Figure 5–1   *The Deming cycle or the Shewhart improvement cycle*

The quality control expert Walter A. Shewhart put a process in place for process improvement, as shown in Figure 5–1?. Another quality expert, W.E. Deming, popularized this approach, so it is referred to variously as the Deming cycle or the Shewhart improvement cycle. The basic idea is that process improvement consists of four sequential but iterative steps:

- Plan. Think about how to do a process better.
- Do. Carry out the process.
- Check. Evaluate the improvements.
- Act. Take action based on the evaluation, which might lead to further planning for the next iteration.

This same approach can be used to improve test processes.

Now, Deming's cycle provides us with a framework for assessing and improving a process with reference to itself and its context. In other words, we can start with whatever processes we have, apply plan-do-check-act to one or all of them, and over time, get very good at those processes.

However, this approach provides incremental improvement in most cases. In addition, you can only improve a process you have, so if you are not doing something you should be doing, this approach has trouble detecting that. Further, while you know that Deming's cycle will lead to you doing better over time, at any given time how do you know if you're doing well or poorly?

Types of Process Improvement

Externally developed process assessment models can provide a starting point, a standard framework, and a way of measuring your processes. You can perform a process assessment using a process model and identify opportunities to improve your current process. Process assessments may be performed iteratively, after each improvement effort is completed, to gauge its effects and to plan the next round of improvements.

In some cases, assessment using the process model will result in the assignment of some maturity rating to your current process. Because the maturity ratings are one-dimensional—or in some cases, one-dimensional on a process-by-process basis—I consider such models prescriptive models. I call them prescriptive because they prescribe the order in which specific processes should be improved. The syllabus refers to these as process reference models.

My problem with prescriptive models is that as a consultant, I believe that businesses should make improvements based on the business value of the improvement and the organizational pain that the improvement will alleviate. A one-dimensional maturity rating might lead a business to start making improvements in parts of the overall software process or test process that are actually less problematic or less important than other parts of the process, simply because the model listed them in order.

My preference is for process models to be nonprescriptive. The process model should describe the important software processes and what should happen in them, but it shouldn't put them in any order of improvement.

Now that doesn't mean that assessment via a nonprescriptive process model doesn't result in recommendations and an order in which to implement them. When we do an assessment for clients, our report definitely includes both. The key is that, if you look at any two of our assessment reports, you might see two very similar recommendations but in the opposite order. Why? Because each client has a different level of opportunity associated with the recommendation. In some cases, constraints or preconditions can influence the order. Those constraints and levels of opportunity tend to be unique from one organization to another, and a nonprescriptive model adapts to those unique organizational needs.

By the way, the syllabus refers to nonprescriptive models such as these as content models.

Whichever approach you use, don't use process assessments as a one-time activity. Having done an assessment and found opportunities to improve, you should—of course—improve. At some point in the future, you should reassess to see the effect of the changes and course-correct your process improvement. This is simply the application of the Deming cycle to the chosen process model.

In addition, you should not feel constrained by any chosen process model framework. If you want to augment—or even replace—the model by analyzing results and metrics and by tapping project retrospective meetings, you certainly can explore doing so.

What you see in Figure 5–2? is an example of a failing project. As you can see, runaway defect discovery began in mid-November and shows no sign of abating four months later. In fact, just a couple months after this chart was produced, the project did indeed die.

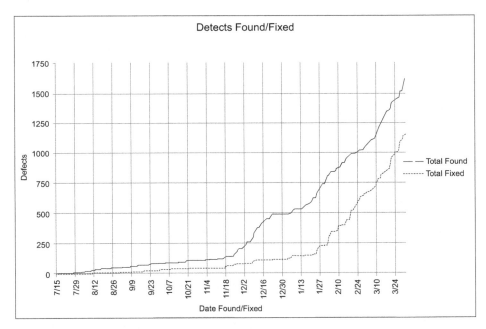

Figure 5–2   *A troubled project's defect metrics*

What killed this project? In general, it was a lack of software process maturity, especially in terms of early testing levels such as unit testing and component integration testing. Shortcuts in these processes—which were supposed to be happening July through November—left a large number of undiscovered and very expensive defects lurking in the product. Once system test started in mid-November, followed by system integration test in January, a deluge of defects came to light, overwhelming the development team.

5.3   Improving the Testing Process

Learning objectives

(K3) Define a test process improvement plan using the IDEAL model.

In the Advanced Test Manager syllabus, we discuss four leading test improvement models. While careful not to make any endorsement of any or all of these models, the Advanced Working Group recognized them as useful examples of how organizations can apply industry-standard test process improvement models. The proper application of these models leads to increased capability (i.e., effectiveness and efficiency) as well as a higher level of testing professionalism.

Being industry-standard models, the use of one or more of them also allows comparability with other organizations following the same model. Comparability is enhanced when the model involves using metrics to evaluate process capabilities rather than relying entirely on interviewee responses to questions about whether a particular process is carried out.

In the syllabus, there is a discussion about staged and continuous models that I think requires some clarification. TMMi and CMMI are mentioned as examples of staged models, and that is certainly correct. They are staged in that there is a single maturity number assigned, based on an assessment of whether certain processes are being carried out. All of the processes within a certain maturity level grouping must be achieved before that maturity level can be claimed, which naturally leads to the staging of process improvements using these models.

CTP and STEP are mentioned as continuous models, and that is certainly correct too. They are continuous in that each model leaves the organization free to implement process improvements in the order of the business value that will be delivered by each improvement rather than pushing an organization to improve processes based on predetermined maturity groupings that might not reflect a particular organization's needs. In the case of CTP, metrics are provided to evaluate the business value of the process improvements.

However, the syllabus includes a mistake because it cites TPI Next as a continuous model. That is incorrect. TPI Next also has maturity levels, but those are multidimensional. In other words, processes fall into multiple maturity level groupings in that each process has multiple levels of maturity associated with it. This is somewhat similar to CTP in that assessment of each process area in CTP

> **ISTQB Glossary**
>
> **Capability Maturity Model Integration (CMMI):** A framework that describes the key elements of an effective product development and maintenance process. The Capability Maturity Model Integration model covers best practices for planning, engineering, and managing product development and maintenance.

can result in different findings ranging from entirely missing to excellent. However, TPI Next assigns specific maturity ratings to each process and then aggregates those maturity ratings to derive an overall maturity rating. This means that TPI Next is actually staged too because particular groups of processes are to be taken to a particular level of maturity as part of improving the test process.

Whichever model you use, the end result is an assessment. This assessment will include recommendations on what to do next. For TMMi and TPI Next, the assessment effectively puts a test organization on a one-dimensional scale (TMMi) or a two-dimensional scale (TPI Next), and the road map involves moving toward the higher-maturity end of the scale. For STEP and CTP, the recommendations will be based on return on investment, and thus the resulting road map is more organization focused.

IDEAL

When you're improving the test process, the assessment is only a piece of the puzzle. Various generic process improvement frameworks exist. In the Advanced Test Manager syllabus, the IDEAL model is used.[2] This model consists of five steps, which may be performed iteratively:

1. Initiate: This step includes the decision to pursue process improvements, based on the objectives and goals that the stakeholders have for the improvement. The stakeholders must consider the scope of the process improvement; for example, focused on a few of the testing processes, on all of the test processes carried out by the independent test team, or on all processes carried out by the organization that affect quality. They must also consider the extent of coverage for each process. Based on these decisions, the test process improvement team can choose the most appropriate of the standard test process improvement models or can decide to develop their own model. At that point, specific success criteria can be defined, often by

---

2. For more information, see Bob McFeeley's *IDEAL: A User's Guide for Software Process Improvement*.

deriving them from the objectives and goals captured earlier. Finally, metrics for each success criteria should be determined so that objective decisions about whether the improvements have succeeded are possible.

2. Diagnose: This step is where the assessment of the test processes occurs, using either an industry-standard model or the internally developed model. Out of this assessment comes a report. The specific content of the report depends on the model used, but most models will deliver an evaluation of the current capability of the processes that were assessed and improvements that could be made for each process.

3. Establish: This step transforms the assessment report into a concrete plan for test process improvement. Since not everything can usually be done, and not everything can ever be done all at once, the process improvements that were included in the assessment must be selected and prioritized. Organizations have various reasons behind their selection and prioritization decisions, but generally four factors figure prominently: (a) the financial return on investment that will result from the improvement (i.e., how does the net benefit of this improvement compare with the cost of the process of making the improvement?); (b) the risks that are associated with doing or not doing the improvement, which is sort of a balance of fear between allowing the current practices to persist on the one hand and putting in the effort to make the changes on the other hand; (c) alignment of each improvement with the broader test and organizational strategies and policies, because those changes that are consistent with what we're currently doing elsewhere are usually easier; and (d) any other quantitative (i.e., hard) or qualitative (i.e., soft) benefits that will accrue from making the improvement.

4. Act: In this step, the test process improvement plan is put into action. The plan should include some training or mentoring of those who have to change the way they work in order to increase the odds of success. The plan should also include piloting of the process changes, along with assessment of the success of the pilot and course-correction from that assessment, before full-scale deployment occurs.

5. Learn: After the process improvements are deployed, we return to the success criteria established earlier and measure our success with the metrics defined there. In addition, depending on the factors considered during the selection and prioritization of improvements, measurement of the return on investment, evaluation of the benefits (expected and unexpected), and an assessment of the risk may occur.

If the organization is following a staged model, the processes selected for improvement may be those that move the organization to the next level of maturity. In that case, there would be a decision at this point—having completed the IDEAL steps—as to whether to repeat the IDEAL steps to move to the next level of maturity. When continuous models are used, improvements are often grouped by priority, so repeating the IDEAL steps would allow the next set of improvements to be undertaken.

Example: Recommendations for Improvement

At RBCS, we do many assessments for clients. We typically use the Critical Testing Process (CTP) framework, which we'll discuss shortly.

Figure 5–3? shows an extract from an RBCS assessment report for a client with operations in both the United States and India. This initial section of the report listed a dozen or so prioritized recommendations. These are from the high-priority group of recommendations.

Problem: Excessive reliance on late removal of bugs during System Test wastes money, delays releases, and exacerbates end-of-project time crunches.

Recommendations:

Ensure that every development task has an associated code review task and unit testing task, as code reviews and unit testing account for the largest number of bugs escaping into System Test.

Continue to formalize the requirements and design processes, including ensuring proper reviews.

Focus on prevention of bugs via requirement reviews or early removal of bugs during Unit Test.

Gather metrics on the percentage of bugs introduced and removed in each major project phase, and take action to drive the percentage of bugs escaping from one phase to the next as close to zero as possible.

Adopt a uniform process and phase of formal bug tracking across all projects.

Figure 5–3   *Example: Recommendations for improvement*

As you can see, this client was overly reliant on system test as the sole filter for defect detection and removal. Consequently, many bugs were found during that period. These bugs were removed at a cost cheaper than in production—as discussed in Chapter 2—but more expensively than had they been removed during early phases of the lifecycle. The inability to deal with all the bugs led to both delays in release and excessive overtime.

I made five recommendations to address this:

1. Ensure that every development task has an associated code review task and unit testing task. Metrics showed that code reviews and unit testing, while they were performed, were not removing the same number of defects as we saw in those companies that followed industry best practices. Root cause analysis found that underperforming code reviews and unit testing together accounted for the largest number of bugs escaping into system test.

2. Continue to formalize the requirements and design processes. A major source of defects was the requirements specification process. Holes in the requirements and design specifications, especially in the area of nonfunctional requirements, led to holes in the tests. So, a better process, including ensuring proper reviews, was needed to reduce the total number of bugs introduced in the lifecycle.

3. Focus on prevention of bugs via requirement reviews or early removal of bugs during unit test. By this I meant that it was not enough just to do requirements reviews and unit tests but also that these activities explicitly focus on finding and removing bugs.

4. Gather metrics on the percentage of bugs introduced and removed in each major project phase, and take action to drive the percentage of bugs escaping from one phase to the next as close to zero as possible. Here I am calling for a measured process of defect management, one that leads to an awareness of where quality problems are introduced and where they are not found in sufficient numbers.

5. Adopt a uniform process of formal bug tracking across all projects and a consistent phase at which formal bug tracking is introduced. Formalized bug tracking processes like those described in Chapter 4 are not necessary to gather all bug metrics. Early bug-detecting activities in the lifecycle, like requirements and design reviews and unit testing, can often include informal techniques to track bugs and gather metrics, while formal test phases like system test and acceptance test require more formal techniques.

I wrote additional supporting details behind these recommendations, including the business case for them.

5.4   **Improving the Testing Process with TMMi**

Learning objectives

(K2) Summarize the background, scope, and objectives of the
TMMi test process improvement model.

The first model we're going to look at is Testing Maturity Model integration
(TMMi). It has been designed to be a good fit for organizations that use CMMI.
There are five maturity levels, as in CMMI. And as with CMMI, TMMi has process areas, with goals and practices defined for each process area. In addition,
the test process areas defined in levels two through five are meant to build on
broader software development process areas defined in CMMI.

TMMi's five maturity levels are as follows:

1. Initial. As with CMMI, the initial level of TMMi is one where chaos reigns.
    Testing is done without any process, other than whatever occurs on the spur
    of the moment to those doing the testing. Test activities don't start until
    code has been written, and the tests are created on the fly, often without
    writing anything down and without applying any of the techniques dis-
    cussed in the Foundation and Advanced syllabi. Testing is seen as a way to
    help developers debug their code. Once the testing is complete, people often
    assume that testing has proven that the software works—at least until pro-
    duction failures occur, at which point testing is blamed.
2. Managed. To achieve this level, testing must become its own entity, not just
    an adjunct activity that helps developers debug their code. A test process is
    put in place, usually along the lines of that described in the Foundation syl-
    labus. A test policy and strategy, similar to what was discussed in Chapter 2,
    are defined in collaboration with test stakeholders. Basic test techniques
    such as those discussed in Chapter 4 of the Foundation syllabus are intro-
    duced. Informally, most RBCS clients operate at this level of maturity but
    often without much of the formalized documentation that is required by
    TMMi.
3. Defined. At this level, the test processes that were defined at level two are
    aligned with the larger software development lifecycle, activities, and pro-
    cesses, as discussed in Chapter 2. The test processes are also formalized,
    meaning that standards are adopted and procedures for the main activities
    are documented. Testing is done by a test team, which is fully professional-

ized at this level, including training and skills development. This test team is also professionally managed, including proper test monitoring and control as discussed in Chapter 1. Moving beyond the realm of dynamic testing, reviews of requirements specifications and other work products are required at this level, but the full integration of the review process into the test process is not required. Most RBCS clients also have many of the attributes of teams at this level, but again without a lot of the documentation.

4. Measured. At the measured level, the test team focuses on achieving a level of consistency and a maturity of metrics that allows test managers to manage testing across individual projects. For example, the test team has the kind of standardized project, product, and process metrics defined in Chapter 2. Test managers tailor the test process to the needs of individual projects while maintaining consistency and standardization where it matters, including creating comparable metrics. Some RBCS clients qualify qualitatively for parts of this level, but TMMi requires a level of documentation that most omit.

5. Optimized. At this point, testing becomes not only about tactical goals (e.g., helping projects get to completion) but also about strategic goals (e.g., helping the organization learn how to prevent defects from happening). Testing results and process metrics are used as an input for continuous test process and software process improvement. I can think of a few RBCS clients that operate in this way, but again from a TMMi perspective these clients might not even qualify for level two because of their lightweight documentation.

To achieve a given a maturity level, 85 percent of the specific and generic goals for the process areas associated with that level must be completed. For example, to achieve level two, the following process areas and goals apply:

-   Test policy and strategy: Establish a test policy, and establish test performance indicators.
-   Test planning: Perform a product risk assessment, establish a test approach, establish test estimates, develop a test plan, and obtain commitment to the test plan.
-   Test monitoring and control: Monitor test progress against plan, monitor product quality against plan and expectations, and manage corrective action to closure.

- Test design and execution: Perform test analysis and design using test design techniques, perform test implementation, perform test execution, and manage test incidents to closure.
- Test environment: Develop test environment requirements, perform test environment implementation, and manage and control test environments.

There are practices within each goal that must be defined to achieve the goal.[3]

The staged improvement models such as TMMi are often used as part of advertising and promoting testing services, as you can see in the example shown in Figure 5–4?, taken from a testing services provider website (with identifying information redacted). Note the claim to TMMi certification, though oddly without a level being given. According to the Software Engineering Institute (the creators of CMM and CMMI), when maturity models are used primarily for advertising and marketing, the process improvement benefits are often limited.

> Some quick facts on [redacted]:
>
> - Founded in [redacted] by [redacted] in [redacted]
> - Rated as the largest independent testing company in the world (source [redacted]
> - 2,500 test professionals worldwide
> - Served over 300 customers since inception with around 120 currently active customers
> - Key verticals are financial services, insurance, technology, healthcare and life sciences, retail, and travel
> - Primary operations in [redacted] and [redacted]
> - Delivery centers in [redacted] and [redacted]
> - Service offerings include every type of software testing including functional, test automation, performance, security, usability, mobile, and technology certification
> - Certifications: CMMI Level 5, TMMi, ISO9001, ISO 13485:2003 and ISO27001:2005
> - Acquisitions: [redacted] [redacted] and [redacted] spread across 3 different geographies
> - Backed by [redacted], the largest venture capital company in the world
>
> [redacted] culture is one where innovation is respected. The environment is open and collaboration is encouraged. We pride ourselves as being the best in the world at what we do.

Figure 5–4 *Example: TMMi in advertisement*

Let's summarize TMMi. In terms of its background, it was derived from Testing Maturity Model (TMM), which was originally proposed by Ilene Burnstein in the 1990s. The TMMi Foundation, a consortium primarily of European test consultancies and various testing service providers, continues to develop TMMi in a way that complements CMMI.

3. For more information on TMMi. visit http://www.tmmi.org/.

TMMi is broad in scope. It includes all testing activities, even those typically outside the purview of an independent testing team, such as reviews, static analysis, and unit testing. This can make achieving high levels of maturity difficult because testing maturity on this scale can be held back by poor quality processes in other parts of the organization.

TMMi lays out a set of process areas, with goals and practices associated with each process area. The process areas are grouped by maturity level. The objectives are to improve these process areas through the achievement of these goals and thus make testing more effective and efficient.

5.5   Improving the Testing Process with TPI Next

Learning objectives

(K2) Summarize the background, scope, and objectives of the TPI-Next test process improvement model.

Like TMMi, TPI Next has defined process areas and maturity levels associated with those process areas. However, TPI Next is more focused, in that there are only 16 key process areas:

1. Stakeholder commitment
2. Degree of involvement
3. Test strategy
4. Test organization
5. Communication
6. Reporting
7. Test process management
8. Estimating and planning
9. Metrics
10. Defect management
11. Testware management
12. Methodology practice
13. Tester professionalism
14. Test case design
15. Test tools
16. Test environment.

In addition, TPI Next provides for multiple levels of maturity for each process area, as opposed to TMMi, which rates a process area as completed once most of the goals are achieved within it.[4]

As each process area achieves a specific level of maturity, those levels of maturity are combined to determine the overall level of maturity. If sufficient process areas have achieved a sufficient level of maturity, then the overall level of test process maturity can advance. TPI Next's test process maturity levels are as follows:

- Initial
- Controlled
- Efficient
- Optimizing

The overall level of maturity is determined by examining a maturity matrix that shows the minimum required level of maturity—referred to as *checkpoints*—for each process area to reach a given level of overall maturity. Failure of just one process area to achieve the required level of maturity will hold back the overall level of maturity. However, tailoring is allow to limit, expand, or modify the objectives required to meet a particular level of maturity for any given process area, which thus allows organizational constraints in terms of individual process areas to be worked around to avoid limiting overall process maturity.

TPI Next does not attempt to fit into any other process improvement model. This can be seen as a disadvantage if an organization is heavily invested in improving via a particular software process model and the test team is attempting to leverage that larger investment to spur improvements in testing. That said, I've not encountered any clients that told me that they rejected TPI Next (or any other test process improvement model) because of the lack of alignment with CMMI (or any other software process improvement model). Sometimes, there are advantages to being seen as the red-headed stepchild[5] of the software process, and this freedom to choose the test process improvement model that best fits your needs—be it TPI Next or any other model—can be one of those advantages.

TPI Next is more focused on the typical domains of the independent test team, which are proper test engineering and test management of test levels such as system test and system integration test. This is in contrast to TMMi, which

---

4. For more details on this maturity model, see *TPI Next* by Gerrit de Vries, et al.

5. In case you're not familiar with this expression, red-headed stepchild as defined by *Oxford Dictionaries* is "a person or thing that is neglected, unwanted, or mistreated."

requires a certain level of broader process maturity in areas such as reviews and the use of defect metrics for software process improvement. Don't get me wrong: reviews and defect metrics are great things, and I'm all for them. However, limiting the maturity of the test team, and thus making the test team accountable for areas outside its actual responsibilities, can lead to dysfunctions such as test managers inserting themselves into management decisions outside their scope. Such well-meaning but misguided attempts to tell other people in other groups what they should do can lead to real political problems for test managers, especially when the perception is that the test team has a way to go before achieving excellence it its own processes.[6]

In Figure 5–5? you see another example of testing maturity levels being used for advertisement. The quote from the TPI assessor is—well, rather hyperbolic. It's worth pointing out the mistake here, too, in that TMMi is not an American "certification" but rather primarily a European test process framework.

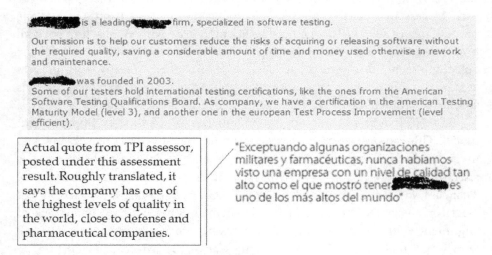

Figure 5–5   *Example: TPI assessment and claim*

Let's summarize TPI Next. TPI Next is a test process improvement model that relates to TMap Next. TPI Next builds on TPI, the progenitor model, which built on TMap, the Test Management Approach method. The original TMap and TPI were developed in the mid- to late 1990s, with the new version of each coming in the mid 2000s. TMap, TMap Next, TPI, and TPI Next were all developed by Sogeti, a test consulting company originally from Europe. Sogeti has since been

---

6. For more information on TPI Next, visit http://www.tmap.net/en/tpi-next.

purchased by Cap Gemini, a worldwide consulting and outsourcing company that has maintained these two frameworks. TMMi assessments can be officially performed only by one of the small group of test consultancies involved with the TMMi Foundation, and TPI Next assessments can be officially performed only by Sogeti or its authorized consultants. That makes both forms of assessment effectively closed in that an assessment done with either model by an outside party would not be recognized by the owner of the assessment model.

As I mentioned previously, the scope of TPI Next is focused on higher levels of testing, such as system test and system integration test. This aligns TPI Next well with the areas of responsibility for a typical independent test team.

Finally, while TPI Next is a prescriptive maturity model, it does allow something unavailable in TMMi, which is that process areas are improved in parallel. In other words, rather than trying to achieve some ideal level of maturity for a process area in one effort and then leaving that area alone for the rest of the test process improvement project, TPI Next encourages the organization to make incremental steps in all of the process areas in parallel. The improvements should make the testing more effective and efficient overall rather than making just part of the testing better at any one time.

5.6   Improving the Testing Process with CTP

Learning objectives

(K2) Summarize the background, scope, and objectives of the CTP test process improvement model.

When I created the Critical Testing Processes test assessment model, it was based on my observation that some test processes are critical to the success of the test organization. I've seen that talented test teams that carry out these 12 processes well will be—and be seen as—successful. I've also seen a number of test teams that were composed of highly skilled people but, because they failed at one or more of these processes, were not successful, in terms of either objective reality or stakeholder perception or both.[7] Properly executed critical test

---

7. I originally wrote the book *Critical Testing Processes* in 2003. This framework is now supported by a complete assessment guidebook, *Improving the Testing Process*, which includes definitions of each process, metrics, assessment questions, and, for organizations using outsourcing, special considerations.

processes, performed by a team with the right skills—the creation of which is itself a critical test process—lead to the delivery of effective, efficient, and satisfying test services to their stakeholders.

I also observed that test processes must be modified to accommodate the specific needs of the stakeholders, the project, the product, the organization, the software lifecycle, and other important contextual variables, as described in Chapter 2. So, I made the model as flexible as possible to these considerations and explicitly defined adaptation and tailoring of the test processes to relevant context as one of the critical testing processes.

Since the complex context of the situation changes the way each test process must be performed, and changes the relative importance of each test process, I did not include prescriptive maturity model measurements within the model. In other words, I made no attempt to ascribe a single number to the maturity of the overall test process. Instead, the assessment process weighs the cumulative success of the critical test processes to give a qualitative rating to the overall test process. Because of this nuanced approach, the Advanced Test Manager syllabus refers to the CTP model as a content reference model.

Rather than rate each test process on a simple yes/no scale for adequacy, as TMMi does, or on a linear maturity scale, as TPI Next does, the CTP model defines the following for each process:

- The major challenges that exist to carrying out each process properly. For example, the fact that most people have difficulty evaluating risk in a completely rational fashion affects the critical testing process of analyzing quality risks.
- The common attributes that exist, across many different contextual situations, for properly executed test processes. For example, understanding the factors that affect the estimate is essential for test estimation, regardless of the context.
- General guidelines for implementing process improvements. For example, introducing skills assessment and management is an important part of developing the test team.

While general guidelines for improvement are provided for each process, as mentioned previously, the model is nonprescriptive. The specific improvements needed, and the order in which those improvements should occur, is based on the business value offered by each improvement.

Unlike other models discussed in this chapter, the CTP model includes metrics for each process. These are provided in the e-book *Improving the Testing Process*, which is the companion to the original book that publicized the framework, *Critical Testing Processes*. The status of each process, and the business value available from improving each process, is measured by interview responses to specific questions (as in the other models) but also by the use of objective metrics. The metrics can be used to compare the test organization's performance, for each of the 12 processes, against past performance, industry averages, and best practices.

You can find more information about the CTP model, including complete checklists for each process, on the RBCS website, www.rbcs-us.com.

In Figure 5–6?, you see the summary results of a CTP assessment for a client.

---

1. Value of the Test Team and Process: Good.
2. Alignment of the Test Team with the Organization: Needs improvement.
3. Alignment of Test with Quality: Opportunity to improve.
4. Test Estimation: Opportunity to improve.
5. Test Planning: Generally strong, but regression strategy needs improvement.
6. Test Team Development: Evolving positively; optimize with direction.
7. Test System Development: Improving.
8. Test Releases Management: Excellent.
9. Running Tests: Improving.
10. Reporting Bugs: Inconsistent; presents opportunities to improve.
11. Test Results Reporting: Incomplete; inadequate for many stakeholders.
12. Change Management and Bug Triage Process: Needs improvement.

Figure 5–6   *Example: CTP assessment summary*

As you can see, our evaluation is fine-grained, much like TPI Next's, in that we don't rate the process areas fulfilled or unfulfilled but rather give them a qualitative evaluation. We specifically identify opportunities to improve, sometimes in fine-grained, specific areas of the process. The assessment is not only a snapshot in time, but it captures the momentum of the organization in a specific process.

In Figure 5–7?, you see a specific quantitative metric used to measure the test system development process.

$$detail\ density = \frac{\#\ of\ words}{\#\ of\ minutes}$$

Figure 5–7   *Test development process quantitative metric*

The metric looks at test case detail. You can substitute *test procedure* for test case if that's the term used for the actual unit of work assigned to a tester executing a manual test. We can assume that the more words per unit of execution time in the written test case or procedure, the more explicitly specified the test is, and thus the more instruction and guidance we are giving the tester.

The point is to evaluate whether the level of detail in the test cases is suitable for needs. You see, CTP prescribes neither a lightweight documentation regime nor a heavyweight one but instead measures to see the actual current state of documentation and then evaluates that against the business needs. For this specific metric, we are looking at test cases or test procedures.

To calculate this metric, we take a sample of at least 10 test cases. We count the number of words in each test case and the number of minutes required to execute it. We also calculate the average and standard deviation. What we often see during assessments is an order-of-magnitude variation between tests, or sometimes even two or three orders-of-magnitude variation. That's fine if the variation is carefully considered and managed, but generally it arises from the lack of clear management direction on this topic as well as the lack of any understanding by the individual contributors as to what drives documentation density needs in one direction or another.

A couple of additional points: For one thing, we want to measure across multiple testers and applications, and the larger the sample the better. For another, this metric applies to manual tests only because we use other metrics for automated test cases.

There are some 5 or 10 metrics for each critical testing process, along with some qualitative evaluations. Now, we don't typically look at every metric for every process on every single assessment because the selected metrics, like the model itself, are tunable.

Let's summarize CTP. The model was introduced in the early 2000s in the book *Critical Testing Processes* and expanded in the early 2010s with the e-book

Improving the Testing Process. In the model, 12 critical testing processes are identified and described:

1. Testing. The overall process, viewed at a macro, strategic level. It consists of 11 constituent critical testing processes.

2. Establishing context. This process aligns testing within the project and the organization. It clarifies expectations on all sides. It establishes the ground-work for tailoring all other testing processes. As you can see, when appropriate, the creation of test policy and test strategy documents would fit into this process. However, those are not prescribed because some situations might need them and some might not.

3. Quality risk analysis. This process identifies the key risks to system quality. It aligns testing with the key risks to system quality. It builds quality and test stakeholder consensus around what is to be tested (and how much) and what is not to be tested (and why). As you can see, this process requires tailoring to accommodate a strategy other than risk-based testing.

4. Test estimation. This process balances the costs and time required for testing against project needs and risks. It accurately and actionably forecasts the tasks and duration of testing. It demonstrates the return on the testing investment to justify the amount of test work requested.

5. Test planning. This process builds consensus and commitment among test team and broader project team participants. It creates a detailed map for all test participants. It captures information for retrospectives and future projects.

6. Test team development. Since testing is only as good as the team that does it, this process matches test team skills to the critical test tasks. It assures competence in the critical skills areas. It continuously aligns team capabilities with what the organization values from testing.

7. Test system development. This process ensures coverage of the critical risks to system quality. It creates tests that reproduce the customers' and users' experiences of quality. It balances resource and time requirements against criticality of risk. It includes test cases, test data, test procedures, test environments, and other supporting materiel.

8. Test release management. If we don't have the test object, we can't test it. If the test items don't work in the test environment, we can't test them. If each test release is not better than the one before, we're not on a path for success. So, this process focuses on how to get solid, reliable test releases into the test environment.

9. Test execution. This process, the running of test cases and comparison of test results against expected results, generates information about bugs, what works, and what doesn't. In other words, this is where the value of testing is created. This process consumes significant resources. It occurs at the end of the project and gates project completion.

10. Bug reporting. This process creates an opportunity to improve the system (and thus to save money). While test execution generates the value of testing, this process delivers part of the value of testing to the project team, specifically the individual contributors and line managers. It builds tester credibility with programmers.

11. Results reporting. This process provides management with the information needed to guide the project. It delivers another part of the value of testing to the project team, particularly line managers, senior managers, and executives. Since test results are often bad news, it separates the message from messenger. It builds tester credibility with managers.

12. Change management. This process allows the test team and the project team to respond to what they've learned so far. It selects the right changes in the right order. It focuses efforts on the highest return-on-investment activities.

You might notice that I've described each of these processes in terms of what an optimal process will achieve. If the process does not achieve those standards—and more—then it is not optimal and has room for improvement.

The CTP model is narrower in scope than the other models. It covers the test levels and activities that are the responsibility of the independent test team. It acknowledges the influence on delivered product quality of other processes, such as reviews and unit testing, but also acknowledges that the influence of the test organization on these processes is often limited.

The CTP model has as its objective the identification and implementation of test process improvements. It is unique among the models in that it evaluates these improvements on both qualitative and quantitative criteria. It is also unique in that the improvements are explicitly targeted at improving stakeholder satisfaction in the test process along with the effectiveness and efficiency of the test process.

5.7   **Improving the Testing Process with STEP**

Learning objectives

(K2) Summarize the background, scope, and objectives of the STEP test process improvement model.

STEP, which stands for Systematic Test and Evaluation Process, is a nonprescriptive model. Improvements recommended by a STEP evaluation need not be implemented in a predefined order but rather based on business value, perceived priority, ease of implementation, or any other decision criteria.

STEP's main premise is that testing should start in parallel with the requirements specification process and that designing and creating tests from the requirements—before design or coding starts—should be used as a way of verifying that the requirements are correct and testable. The resulting tests are also to be used as usage models to help people—including developers—better understand how the system is to be used, augmenting the requirements. Similar concepts are included in the V-model (which is part of STEP and assumed to the relevant lifecycle) with respect to higher-level testing such as system test and system integration test and in the ISTQB syllabi, such as in the principle of early testing and QA introduced in the Foundation syllabus. The rationale is the same as in the ISTQB syllabi: that we can detect defects in requirements specifications, remove those defects, and thus prevent corresponding defects from being introduced into the code.

Under STEP, after commencing during requirements specification, testing activities should continue throughout the lifecycle. Those activities would closely correspond to the fundamental test process defined in the ISTQB syllabi. This makes sense because both STEP and the ISTQB syllabi draw heavily from the IEEE 829 standard. However, STEP talks about doing testware design before starting software design, while these would be parallel activities in the ISTQB fundamental test process. As a practical matter, it's unlikely that projects would delay the start of software design by waiting for the conclusion of test design.

When defects are detected—whether in requirements during test design or subsequently during test implementation or execution—those defects should be studied. Root cause, phase of introduction, location of the defect, and other information discussed in Chapter 4 should be determined. This information should then be used to reduce the number of defects introduced in the first place.

Throughout this process, STEP assumes that testers and developers collaborate to release the highest quality software possible. Any adversarial relationships with developers or other stakeholders are to be avoided. In this area, STEP echoes CTP, which talks about identification of testing stakeholders and their needs as a first step to good testing.

As mentioned, STEP is nonprescriptive, as is CTP, but it is proprietary, which CTP is not. In other words, only an SQE consultant can perform a STEP assessment, while no such restrictions exist for CTP assessments. TPI Next is also proprietary, though sufficient public information exists that organizations can self-assess using that information. (In fairness, it would probably also be possible for an organization to self-assess using Rick Craig's book *Systematic Software Testing*, which describes STEP.) Interestingly, SQE sometimes partners with Sogeti consultants to blend STEP and TPI Next assessments. This would have the effect of making the resulting assessment prescriptive, of course.

Let's summarize STEP. STEP was originally developed by Dave Gelperin in the 1980s. Gelperin was part of the team that defined the IEEE 829 standard, which originally addressed only documentation. (The 2008 version of the standard also includes a defined process, which is not compatible with either STEP or the ISTQB.) Gelperin wanted to put a process around the standard, and STEP was the result. It was used as the basis for not only assessments but also a training course delivered by SQE.

The scope of STEP includes higher levels of testing throughout the entire lifecycle. As I mentioned, it defines a process, similar to the ISTQB fundamental test process, that starts during requirements specification and continues to the retirement of the system. STEP assumes that multiple levels of testing will occur but that some of those levels will be handled by other groups, such as, for example, developers and users.

The objectives of STEP are twofold. First, testing activities should start as early as possible in order to detect and remove defects when they are cheapest. Second, testing of requirements and systematic analysis of all defects should be used to prevent defects in the future.

HELLOCARMS Test Improvement Exercise

As HELLOCARMS test manager, you have asked management for a budget to improve your test process during the current project. The budget and plan have been approved, so the "initiating" stage of the IDEAL improvement model is complete. You have now entered the "diagnosing" stage of the IDEAL improvement model.

Refer to the exercises completed so far for data, and reflect on what you have learned about the HELLOCARMS project so far. Assume you are at the end of iteration two and the project will last about five more months.

Outline test process improvements you would like to implement, related to one or more process areas. You may use any of the four process models as a framework or make up your own.

HELLOCARMS Test Improvement Debrief

I will use the Critical Testing Processes framework to outline what I would do in terms of improvement.

- Testing
  - Because one concern toward the end of iteration two related to the number of bugs, I would want to measure the defect detection percentage for testing done in iteration one. I would select a sample of 100 bugs found in iteration two and determine the percentage of bugs that were present during testing of iteration one. I would use that to estimate the total number of bugs that escaped detection in iteration one and thus the defect detection percentage for iteration one.
  - Based on that analysis, I would then take appropriate steps if warranted to improve the defect detection effectiveness of testing for subsequent iterations.

- Establishing context
  - To confirm the business values I identified in a previous exercise, I would survey the test stakeholders to confirm their perception of the value of testing. If I found that any stakeholders questioned the value of testing, I would address that promptly.
  - I would use cost of quality to attempt to quantify the value of testing so far, based on a predicted or actual historical cost of a field failure. I would then look at ways to reduce the cost per defect found—for example, introducing some easy test automation or using test outsourcing—to further increase the quantified value of testing.
  - I would also check to see if we had high regression of features from iteration one during testing of iteration two. If so, I would discuss with the development manager the possibility of an automated unit test harness, say using J-Unit or a similar facility, to try to reduce regression risk earlier in the lifecycle.

- In general, I would check for insufficient upstream quality control activities, such as requirements and design reviews, code reviews and static analysis, and unit testing, that result in a large number of defects delivered into system test for each iteration. Such a large number of defects makes it difficult to complete testing during an iteration of fixed length and reduces the likelihood of having a deployable system at the end of that iteration.

- Quality risk analysis
  - To check correctness of the quality risk analysis, I would evaluate the defects found so far. I would look especially for the following:
    - High number of defects in areas we had assessed as unlikely to contain defects
    - Low number of defects in areas we had assessed as likely to contain defects
    - Disproportionately large number of high-impact defects compared to low-impact defects in areas we had assessed as low impact
    - Disproportionately large number of low-impact defects compared to high-impact defects in areas we had assessed as high impact

    Based on this evaluation, I would correct the quality risk analysis, reallocate test effort, and reprioritize the test cases.

- Test estimation
  - I would analyze the actual effort and completion dates for all tasks against the estimated effort and completion dates in the Gantt chart. If the variance indicated an unachievable plan for the remaining three iterations, I would adjust the estimate and reobtain management approval.

- Test planning
  - I would analyze variances from the test plan to date, particularly in the area of any unanticipated or unmanageable test project risks. If the variance indicated an unachievable plan or other major risks for completing testing for the remaining three iterations, I would adjust the plan and reobtain management approval.

- Test team development
  - I would perform a skills inventory for my test team (as discussed in Chapter 7). If this assessment revealed gaps in test team skills, I would look for ways to make immediate improvements in the most urgent areas during the remaining three iterations.

- Test system development
  - I would check to see what proportion of test cases were blocked during iterations one or two. I would then investigate whether those blockages were due to test case, test tool, or test environment design decisions. If so, I would resolve those to improve the ability to run tests without delay when needed.
  - I would also reassess test coverage on three dimensions: risks, requirements, and code. I would check to see if we had a large expansion of test scope from iteration one to iteration two. If so, I would then try to identify the cause of that expansion and the project risks posed by it and put a plan in place to manage the growth in test scope over the next three iterations.

- Test release management
  - I would check to see if the large number of bugs found in iteration two had anything to do with build or installation problems. If so, I would recommend changes in those processes to the release engineering team, based on a business analysis of the cost of those problems during iteration two.

- Test execution
  - The test completion and test hours charts indicated efficient, effective execution of test cases during iteration two. I would check to see if the defects were being found in order of priority. Ideally, a test team should find defects in the exact order of priority. If that is approximately true, then the quality risk analysis prioritization is correct and the test team is running the tests without encountering excessive blockage. However, if the test team is finding defects in an order that is inconsistent with their priority, a root cause analysis as to why is necessary, with improvements needed to correct that. Finding bugs in the proper order is particularly urgent when the defect find rate remains very high through a test execution period, as it has on this project.

- Bug reporting
  - I would check for an excessively high rate of the following bug reporting dysfunctions:
    - Bug reports rejected by the bug triage committee as not describing failures but rather describing correct behaviors (false positives)

- Bug reports returned to the test team for further clarifying information (bug report ping-pong)
- Bug reports closed as duplicates by the development team
- Bug reports deferred by the bug triage committee
  - I would target a rate of less than 5 percent for each of these types of noise or inefficiency. I would investigate causes for any dysfunctions that exceeded that rate. Given the quality of the requirements—or lack of quality, more accurately—it's likely that 10 percent or more of the first two of these dysfunctions could occur. We have seen very high false positive rates and significant ping-pong impacts on efficiency in such situations.

- Results reporting
  - I would survey the various project stakeholders as to whether they found the information coming from the test team complete, pertinent, timely, and concise. If they had any suggestions for improvement of test results reporting, I would implement those.

- Change management
  - I would check for a large rate of feature addition during past and future iterations. I would then assess whether that exceeded the capacity of my test team to handle the testing of such a volume of features. If so, I would adjust my resource plan and discuss with management.

5.8 Sample Exam Questions

To end each chapter, you can try one or more sample exam questions to reinforce your knowledge and understanding of the material and to prepare for the ISTQB Advanced Level Test Manager exam.

1. Which of the following is a best practice for retrospective meetings that will lead to process improvement?

    A. Ensuring management commitment to implement improvements

    B. Allowing retrospective participants to rely exclusively on subjective assessment

    C. Requiring that every project include a retrospective meeting in its closure activities

D. Prohibiting any management staff from attending the retrospective meeting

2. Assume you are a test manager and you have just concluded a project to create a programmable thermostat for home use to control central heating, ventilation, and air conditioning (HVAC) systems. After release, you find that quality risk analysis failed to identify certain significant risk items, resulting in defects escaping to customers.

   Assume you are using TPI Next to improve the test process. Which of the following is a TPI Next process area that you would look at to address this problem?

   A. Life cycle model

   B. Test policy and goals

   C. Moment of involvement

   D. Estimating and planning

3. Which of the following statements accurately captures the distinction between evaluation criteria for the four test improvement models discussed in the Advanced syllabus?

   A. TMMi and TPI next use a maturity model to guide the order of improvement, while CTP and STEP provide a means for assessing the effects of certain improvements.

   B. CTP and STEP use a maturity model to guide the order of improvement, while TMMi and TPI next provide a means for assessing the effects of certain improvements.

   C. CTP and TMMi use a maturity model to guide the order of improvement, while STEP and TPI next provide a means for assessing the effects of certain improvements.

   D. STEP and TMMi use a maturity model to guide the order of improvement, while CTP and TPI next provide a means for assessing the effects of certain improvements.

6 Test Tools and Automation

"What is the business case for automation?"

A question posed by the author to a team of consultants
who had been working for a client for four years
without making significant progress in the percentage
of test cases automated.
They were unable to answer the question
in any meaningful fashion.

Chapter 6, Test Tools and Automation, of the Advanced syllabus contains the following four sections:

1. Introduction
2. Tool Selection
3. Tool Lifecycle
4. Tool Metrics

6.1 Introduction

Learning objectives
Recall of content only

In this chapter, we'll expand on the discussion of test tools and automation that is in the Foundation syllabus. We'll focus on the test manager's responsibilities in terms of selecting, deploying, using, refining, and adapting test tools and test automation. It would be good to review Chapter 6 of the Foundation syllabus prior to reading this chapter.

6.2 Tool Selection

Learning objectives

(K2) Describe management issues when selecting an open-source tool.

(K2) Describe management issues when deciding on a custom tool.

(K4) Assess a given situation in order to devise a plan for tool selection, including risks, costs and benefits.

Test tool selection? How hard could it be? Just pick any available tool because they all work the same, right? Wrong! Selecting the wrong test tool is one of the main hidden rocks upon which many test automation efforts founder. As a test manager, you should take this complex and difficult task very seriously, to avoid problems in the future. In this section, we'll look at the various issues you'll need to consider during this process.

As you go through these issues, it's important to keep in mind that you have various options for tools. What you hear about most frequently—because of history and marketing money—are the commercial tools. For certain situations, you might find that commercial tools are the only ones available, or the only ones that meet your requirements, including timeliness of availability. However, there are many open-source tools available. A number of our clients have used these tools quite successfully. We have used these tools on our own projects successfully as well.

There is also the possibility of building your own tool. My associates and I have built custom test tools for a number of clients. I've also worked with many clients who have built their own tools, or built extensions to open-source and commercial tools. There's really no magic to building test tools, provided you have the right software development skills within your team and follow development best practices.

Another important thing to keep in mind, regardless of what type of tool is used, is that any test tool put into place should deliver positive benefits relative to the initial and recurring costs. All too often we've seen situations where clients engaged in long-term test automation projects without any cost-benefit or return-on-investment (ROI) analysis. Not surprisingly, when we've encountered these situations during assessments and done our own ROI analysis, the return

> **ISTQB Glossary**
>
> **custom tool:** A software tool developed specifically for a set of users or customers.
>
> **open-source tool:** A software tool that is available to all potential users in source code form, usually via the Internet; its users are permitted, usually under license, to study, change, improve, and, at times, distribute the software.

is almost always negative. This topic is critical enough that we'll return to it in detail later in this section.

First, let's examine your options in terms of tools and what considerations apply for each option.

Open-Source Tools

Open-source test tools are, for many testers, the most popular test tools they've never heard of. Often when I'm consulting or doing training sessions for clients, they are surprised to learn that they can simply download free source code or even a free installable application that might solve some testing problem they have, whether that problem is managing a library of manual tests, managing defects reports (as discussed in Chapter 4), or automating the execution of tests. However, such tools are widely available, and various volunteer professional communities exist to develop and maintain them. Let's look at some of the attributes of these open-source tools.

First, as mentioned, any open-source test tool is freely downloadable from one or more websites. There is no cost associated with downloading the software, though that doesn't mean there are no initial costs, as you'll see later in this section. Usually, the volunteer community maintains such sites. The downloadable content will include at least the source code that constitutes the tool, which leads to the name "open-source." However, it's often the case that you can also find precompiled, installable packages for major operating systems, such as Windows, Mac OS, and Linux. In addition, various types of user documentation are often available for the tools, and some documentation packages are quite sophisticated. For example, the "man" (for "user manual") pages provided with Linux are extensive and professional.

The "freely downloadable" attribute of these tools is not without its own perils. I have heard numerous stories from test managers about people within their teams running amok, each downloading their own tool to solve their own testing problem, even when the problems were similar and could be solved by the same tool. The resulting "Tower of Babel"[1] meant that no one could read anyone else's test scripts and utilities. As a test manager, you should retain control over the specific mix of open-source tools that are used.

The volunteer community might provide informal support for the tools. In some cases—for example, Linux comes to mind—various commercial entities have arisen that provide support too. With commercial support for an open-source tool, you'll pay much as you do for commercial tool support and will receive support of similar (or in some cases better) quality. If you rely on the volunteer community, the responsiveness and completeness of the support will depend on who chooses to respond to your question and request for help. However, some of these volunteers are quite dedicated and will devote a great deal of their time to solving your problem for you.

Of course, you might, and can, decide to solve your own problem with an open-source tool, especially if what you need is to change the way it works or to add new features to it. In this case, you'll typically need the source code itself, unless the tool is highly customizable through table-driven modifications or other similar mechanisms. Given the source code, and a competent set of developers (ideally within the test team and with testing experience), you can make any changes or additions you like. Of course, you'll have to remember to test those changes, just as you would test any changes to the system under test.

One good reason to extend an open-source tool is because you intend to use it with various other test tools that you're already using, or that you intend to use. In contrast to commercial tools, which either integrate without modification or will need often-cumbersome integration utilities to make them work together, two or more open-source tools that don't work together in their default configurations can be extended to do so. In many cases, this can result in a highly customized solution that goes well beyond anything available commercially. As before, though, be careful of creating a Tower of Babel situation by introducing excessive complexity and overhead.

That said, you might find that the open-source tools don't always include all of the facilities that commercial tools do. Don't assume that the community that created the tool was trying to solve the specific testing problems that the com-

---

1. According to Genesis 11: 1–9, people decided to build a tower to heaven so they could ask God why things are the way they are on Earth. God didn't like that idea, and he "confused their tongues"—created different languages—so that they couldn't continue the project because no one could understand anyone else. That happens on plenty of projects without any divine intervention.

mercial tool vendors addressed. Now, this might be a nonissue for you; if the tool has the capabilities you need, then who cares what's missing? However, if one or more of the specific capabilities you need is missing, then you have to consider whether the zero price of acquisition makes up for the effort you'll need to expend to expand the capabilities to include what you need. Further, is expanding the capabilities of the tool even within the ability of your team, from either a bandwidth or skills perspective? Just because something is free doesn't mean it's what you need. So be sure to carefully evaluate your needs and the capabilities of any tool—open source or commercial—before you select it.

Before you decide to modify and extend any open-source tools, you need to check the licensing agreements that cover them. In some cases, you'll find that these agreements require that any changes and extensions be released to the broader volunteer community. This can create problems for you or people on your team, since typical employee agreements—at least in North America—include provisions that make all intellectual property created during the term of employment the property of the employer. This means that, without advanced arrangements, someone on your team could find themselves in a situation where modifications that they made to an open-source tool legally belong to two entities: your employer and the open-source community.

Before you think, "Oh, pshaw, who is possibly going to find out?" consider this cautionary tale. A client of ours modified a popular bug tracking tool without releasing the changes. I was told that they received a threatening letter from an attorney with the Free Software Foundation, claiming the right to seize not only the changes but in fact all of their company software. This incident led to some hefty legal bills and some nasty consequences for the test manager who had approved the use and modification of the open-source tool.

If you plan to use an open-source tool to test regulated systems, you should also check to see what the rules are regarding such situations. For example, our clients who build FDA-regulated medical devices need to certify the tools as fit for use in such settings before they can use them. This entails running a set of tests against the tools to ensure that they do what is necessary to support the testing that the regulated system will require. This must also be done for custom tools or for commercial tools that are not already certified for their intended use in regulated environments.

Example: Integrated Test Architecture

Let's look at an example, shown in Figure 6–1, of an integrated test system architecture. This is an automated test system for an insurance company. The system
under test—or, more properly, the system of systems under test—is shown in
the middle.

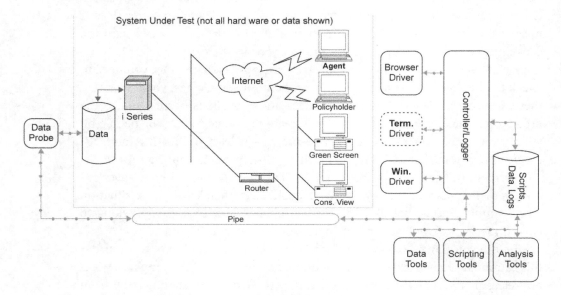

Figure 6–1   *Example: Integrated test architecture*

On the front end are three main interface types: browsers, legacy Unix-based
green screen applications, and a newer Windows-based application called Con-
solidated View. The front-end applications communicate through the insurance
company's network infrastructure, and through the Internet, to the iSeries
server at the back end. The iSeries server, as you might imagine for a well-established regional insurance company, manages a very large repository of customers, policies, claim history, accounts payable and receivable, and the like.

On the right side of the figure, you see the main elements of the test automation system. For each of the three interface types, we need a driver that will
allow us to submit inputs and observe responses. The terminal driver is shown
in a dotted line because there was some question initially about whether that
would be needed. The controller/logger piece uses the drivers to make tests

happen, based on a repository of scripts, and it logs results of the tests. The test data and scripts are created using tools as well, and the test log analysis is performed with a tool.

Notice that all of these elements on the right side of the figure could be present in a single, integrated tool. However, this is a test system design figure, so we leave out the question of implementation details now. It is a good practice to design what you need first, then find tools that can support it rather than letting the tools dictate how you design your tests. Trust me on this one; I have the scars to prove it! If you let the tools drive the testing, you can end up not testing important things.

This brings us to the left side and bottom of the figure. In many complex applications, the action on the screens is just a small piece of what goes on. What really matters is data transformations, data storage, data deletion, and other data operations. To know whether a test passed or failed, we need to check the data. The data probe allows us to do this.

The pipe is a construct for passing requests to the data probe from the controller and for the data probe to return the results. For example, if starting a particular transaction should add 100 records to a table, then the controller uses one of the applications to start the transaction—through a Windows interface via the Windows driver, say—and then has the data probe watch for 100 records being added. See, it could be that the screen messages report success, but only 90 records are added. We need a way to catch those kinds of bugs, and this design does that for us.

In all likelihood, the tool or tools used to implement the right-hand side of this figure would be one or two commercial or freeware tools, integrated together. The data probe and pipe would probably be custom developed.

Custom Tools

In some cases, such as those just mentioned, open-source and/or commercial tools can be used to fulfill some of the test tool needs, while custom development is only required for some portions of the solution. In other cases, you might find that you need to develop the entire solution, creating your own custom tool. Now, fortunately, open-source components are often available to provide building blocks for these custom tools, but the amount of development can be significant.

It's not just about effort; it's also about skills. You need to have the same types of abilities within your team that a development group would have. I've been involved in plenty of successful custom test tool development projects in my career. I was always careful to have highly technical testers on my teams in these projects, people who understood software development and software testing, with years of experience in both fields across the team. Not everyone needs to be an expert at both development and testing—I've had plenty of highly specialized teams on these kinds of projects—but collectively the team needs expertise in both areas.

And it's not just about skills; it's also about development best practices. Custom tools need to be developed according to a software lifecycle. You get to pick the lifecycle, as a test manager, but you should pick one and follow the rules carefully. Just muddling through will only work for very short, very small, very simple projects, and it's not always possible to predict whether that's what you're dealing with. I have found iterative lifecycles such as agile particularly suited to test tool development. However, you should make sure you create sufficient documentation for the tool to ensure that long-term maintenance will not be an issue. I've seen multiple situations where clients relied on a single technical developer to create a tool, which then could not be maintained when that person left the test team. You should also make sure careful design work precedes the development of the tool and testing is thoroughly integrated into the process.

Custom tool development is often needed when unusual, heavily customized, or proprietary hardware or software is involved. For example, my colleagues and I found that we needed to create our own automation tool to provide functional, performance, reliability, and load testing capabilities for an interactive voice response server on one project because the commercial tools were too limited in their capabilities, far too expensive, and unable to do the specific menu-navigation tasks that we needed done.

It's also the case that legacy platforms are often abandoned or poorly supported by the commercial tool vendors. For example, some of our clients are trying to automate applications that were developed almost two decades ago, using platforms and processes that were popular at the time but have since fallen into disfavor. In these cases, you might be able to find some open-source tools to support the platforms, as our clients have, though they are often not complete solutions. If you develop your own custom tools for these environments, be very careful of the issue of obsolescence. I have had situations where clients invested time and money in creating automation solutions for such legacy platforms, only to discover—sometimes to their late-breaking surprise—that the organization had decided to transition away from the platform.

Why would you want to create a custom tool? One of the motivations is that a custom tool can meet your specific requirements exactly. When you are doing something that is very typical—for example, building a browser-based application for e-commerce—then you might find that commercial tools and open-source tools do everything that you want, but if you get off the beaten path a bit, you start to find that workarounds are needed. Eventually those workarounds can become a significant obstacle to the use of the tools, and a custom tool becomes increasingly attractive. You might have very specific needs in terms of interfacing with other testing or development tools, and you might find that the open-source and commercial tools don't do this well. You might find that you have complex test data needs that no commercial or open-source tool can satisfy. You might also find that you can create a tool that has uses beyond just testing or beyond just the current project, though you need to be careful not to confuse grandiose thinking with planning for broad reuse.

As an example of custom tool development, one of our clients has an application that runs on handheld and tablet devices that have unique platforms. It is built using a precisely formatted set of machine-readable requirements. The data is unique to the application, so they decided to build their own test tool to do reliability, user interface, and functionality testing. They were able to assemble this tool using open-source components in the space of a month. It's worth noting that the people involved in this effort were extremely skilled and experienced software developers and not everyone could replicate their achievement.[2]

Example: IVR Testing Tool

Here is a graphic that shows the architecture of the end-to-end, system integration testing harness we built for the IVR system of systems project.

We used a commercial tool, SilkTest, to interface with the Windows GUI on the customer service application host PCs. However, we also had two custom-created tools.

One was the IVR interface test tool. It could send phone signals (called DTMF tones) into the phone lines, simulating a user interacting with the IVR input interface. By use of special branded voice messages, it could also recognize whether the correct message was played. We had to build this tool from scratch, using some open-source components like the scripting language TCL. No commercial tool of the appropriate scale (or within our budget) existed.

---

2. For more details, see "Quality Goes Bananas" at http://www.rbcs-us.com/images/documents/engineering-quality-goes-bananas.pdf.

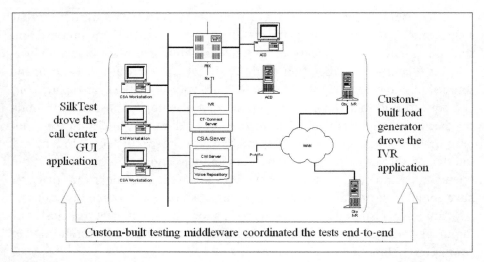

Figure 6–2   *Example: IVR testing tool*

Another custom-created tool was the middleware that tied together the IVR interface tool with the GUI tool. We called this a "fake pipe." It allowed each side of the overall test system to send messages to the other. In that way, they could coordinate tests, including end-to-end functional and performance tests.

Tool Cost-Benefit Analysis

A common mistake that test teams—and, by extension, their managers—make is automation for automation's sake. Testers often want to automate tests because it's fun, or easy, or interesting, and this is all well and good, but an organization will only fund—and continue to fund—automation projects that are seen as valuable. Often, a positive, quantifiable return on investment is necessary to demonstrate this value, but such an ROI calculation is only part of the way by which a test manager can promote and defend an automation effort. Remember to consider the qualitative values that might be delivered, such as a reduced risk of regression. As a test manager, you should ensure (and insist) that all automation efforts deliver value for the organization.

We'll now look at the factors you must consider to prepare a proper cost-benefit analysis when you are selecting a tool and proposing test automation. This analysis should show significant, measurable, meaningful, and long-term benefits.

If you perform a cost-benefit analysis and find that the proposed effort will not deliver such benefits, you should first revisit the factors discussed here; if, after careful consideration, the benefits are still not forthcoming, then the automation effort should be scrapped. I have seen a number of situations where clients rushed into automation without such careful analysis and wasted literally hundreds of thousands of dollars. Such precipitous and rash decisions can have significant career impacts on a manager.

In this analysis, you'll need to consider the following factors:

- Nonrecurring costs that will occur at the start of the automation effort
- Recurring costs that will occur periodically during the automation effort
- Risks that could endanger the automation effort at various points
- Opportunity costs that result from resources invested in automation that could otherwise be spent on other testing activities

Be careful to consider all the tools and all the automation efforts underway. Typically, you'll want to have a long-term, comprehensive test tool and automation strategy rather than a piecemeal approach that addresses one tool at a time. Also, remember that costs include both expenditures (i.e., money spent) as well as resources and time spent on the automation effort.

Tool Costs

Let's start our discussion of tool costs with nonrecurring costs. It's important to keep in mind that efforts to minimize nonrecurring costs will often increase recurring costs or risks, so you should avoid scrimping on these items.

To start with, you should always know what you are trying to accomplish with any endeavor, and automation is no exception to that rule. I have seen so many failed test automation efforts where the root cause was a solution in search of a problem, a problem no one could define or for which they could not state the criteria for its solution. To build upon the test policy concepts discussed in Chapter 2, you should define objectives for your test automation effort, define metrics for those objectives, and then define goals for each metric.

With clearly defined objectives, you can then define what your requirements are for the tools that you might use. Again, be careful about skipping this step. If you feel that you must proceed in an experimental mode, you can, as part of defining the requirements, try to play around with some different tools to see what can be done. However, avoid making a serious, irrevocable, expensive decision if you are in a "let's try different tools and see what they can do" mode. If you are experimenting, make that a separate step in your process, and then define requirements after the experimentation is over and before you commit to a tool.

With requirements defined—and only at this point—you can start to make serious decisions about which tool to select. Your requirements should address both the tool itself and the vendor. A good tool offered by a vendor that is about to go out of business is not a good selection. A bad tool (i.e., one that does not satisfy your requirements), no matter how reputable the vendor, is not a good selection either. You should go through a careful process to evaluate the various tool options—open-source, commercial, and custom developed—against your requirements. Be careful about settling for a tool and a vendor (or open-source community) that doesn't make the grade because you're going to live with this decision for a while, ideally for years.

Now comes the obvious nonrecurring cost. You'll buy a commercial tool, adapt an open-source tool to your needs, develop a tool, or some combination of these options. If you are buying a commercial tool, this is where your negotiating skills come into play. In many cases, the sticker price and the actual price are not necessarily the same, especially if your plan is for large-scale automation across many testers. You'll want to work with the vendor—or perhaps you have an acquisitions team within your company—to try to get the best possible price for the full intended use. Beware of low-price "introductory offers" or various forms of bait-and-switch that can occur here.

Once you select a tool, you incur three additional nonrecurring costs. One of these is also obvious, being the need to get the hardware and software required to support the use of the tool. In most cases, you'll be aware of this cost as part of selecting the tool, but it's best to avoid surprises. A budget for these items is essential, of course, because otherwise you can't use the tool.

The two other costs are not always obvious. One cost involves integrating the tool with other tools that you already use; for example, getting your requirements management tool to share information with your test management tool. People do forget about this cost, which can include add-on modules for one or both integrating tools or, if such modules are not available, work to create integration utilities as discussed previously. Over the long term, you'll want to avoid the recurring effort that would otherwise be expended, so address this issue up front.

The other cost involves initial training for people to properly use the tool. No matter what any tool vendor might say, most tools are not self-explanatory. Even if the tool itself is simple to use, the proper use of the tool in your particular context is probably not. You should therefore consider this issue carefully. Do not attempt to save money by assuming people will teach themselves and figure things out as they go along; by this path lies sorrow, wailing, and gnashing of teeth, based on my own experience and those of our clients. Even if the tool vendor offers training, remember that your team's use of the tool is specific to your context, and additional training will be required for that. As my colleague, Jamie Mitchell, pointed out while reviewing this material, a lot of tool vendor training is focused on entry-level learning objectives, such as what each menu does. He said, "I have yet to see effective vendor training on what really matters: how to really use the tool in earnest."

So, with the tool in place and integrated, and people trained in its use, that's the end of the costs, right? Well, unfortunately, no. There are always recurring costs, some of which can be substantial. Let's review what those costs are.

First, the costs of owning the tool. Wait, you say, I just bought the tool. What recurring costs? Well, it's sometimes the case that the tool vendor didn't tell you about the recurring costs, but one or more of these costs is always applicable, and always significant. One such cost is the maintenance of the tests, test data, traceability information, and whatever work products you create with the tool itself.

As the system under test evolves, as your coverage of the system under test expands, and as your understanding of the tool and its abilities expands, your team will need to modify and grow this set of work products. As you expand the use of the tool, you'll find that new people are using the tool, that existing people are using it in new ways, or that people did not understand the tool training the first time around,[3] so we're back to the need for training and mentoring. Failure to address this skills-growth need will result in divergence of usage, incompatibilities of work products, and another Tower of Babel problem as I mentioned earlier, so make sure you address this need properly.

Now, in terms of the tool itself, most commercial tools will involve licensing and support fees. Licensing fees will usually expand as the pool of users expands. There's no ethical way around paying these fees, and in most cases no practical way either. Most tools that require per-user licensing fees or floating fees based on the number of concurrent users also include some sort of enforcement capability, and we've had a number of clients that have incurred significant inefficiencies in an attempt to stay within some predetermined limit on these fees. It's better to be realistic about what you need immediately, and what you'll need as the tool deployment continues, in order to use the tool efficiently.

---

3. This is a point raised by my colleague, Jamie Mitchell, during review of this material.

Support fees and support quality vary from one commercial tool vendor to another. There can be annual fees, which can be flat fees, graduated fees based on the number of licenses, as-needed fees for updates, or some combination of these fees. These fees are often very irksome to the budgetary decision makers because they are essentially fees paid to a software vendor to deal with the bugs that the vendor itself put into the software. However, attempts to minimize expenditures on these fees often result in inefficiencies in the use of the tool. Again, be realistic and budget for these costs. At the same time, you should also plan to use these support fee invoices as an opportunity to revisit your return on the automation investment and decide whether to continue the use of the tool. Don't pay support fees for a tool that you're not using, that is of poor quality, or that is resulting in a negative return on investment.

It's often the case that commercial tools also include fees to expand the use to new environments. This is another source of frustration and pain for those paying the bills, but in the tool vendors' defense on this topic, these costs involve increasing the ability of the tool beyond what was originally purchased. That is not to say that some tool vendors' new environment support charges are not exorbitant. All the more reason to make sure you understand these fees before you commit to buying a particular tool.

Sometimes you'll find that you discover new potential uses for the tool. That's always a good thing, but it usually does involve some additional costs. In some cases, the features you want to use are already included in the tool as originally purchased, so there's no acquisition cost, though there will be training and potentially integration costs. In other cases, the features are part of some add-on module that you'll need to purchase. Either way, these costs are usually proportional to the expansion of the tool's usage, or at least they should be. These types of costs are difficult to anticipate and thus to include in the initial budget, but some effort should be made. Otherwise, if you discover a new application of the tool, you might be met with a response along the lines of, "That's very nice, but it's not in the test budget this year, so please come back and ask again next year."

In any case, as you continue to use the tool, you'll find better ways to use it. Making these changes could be as cheap and simple as some internal training of the team. Or, it could involve significant changes to work already done. Either way, it's better to get better over time than to accept limitations that were put into place in the early days of tool adoption. Again, this is difficult to anticipate, but try to put some sort of buffer into your budget to allow for it.

The last few paragraphs probably sounded like an argument for open-source or custom tools, but these tools will have ownership costs as well. If you develop a custom tool, then you have to expand the tool, improve its abilities, fix its bugs, figure out how best to use it, and port it to new environments at your own expense. If you are using an open-source tool, then you might benefit from the largesse of the open-source community. However, if luck does not favor you, you'll need to invest your team's time in doing the work itself, and depending on the license, you'll need to submit these changes to the open-source community—which might include your competitors. That's not an argument against open-source tools, because they will usually save time and money over commercial tools or custom development, but you should apprise your managers of the conditions of the license agreement and how that could result in this very bind.

Finally, whatever type of tool you decide to use, remember that your budget and resources are limited. You'll spend time and money on the tool. That's time your team won't spend on doing other testing activities. Now, if you've been careful in your business case analysis, you know that you'll get that time and money back manyfold, over time. However, consider this: If you have $100 in your pocket and you give $20 to someone on the promise of getting back $50 in a year, the fact remains that you have only $80 in your pocket right now. If you come across an opportunity to spend $100 on something you want, you don't have it and can buy only $80 of whatever that thing is. The point is that automation efforts have opportunity costs. Either the organization will choose to invest more in testing to make up for the nonrecurring and recurring tool costs until the break-even point is reached or you will choose to do less testing.

Tool Risks

Not only do tools have costs, but tool selection, implementation, and usage projects also have risks. Some of these risks were discussed in the Foundation syllabus, and include the following:

- Unrealistic expectations. This is the biggest one. People expect automated test tools to solve all their testing problems, including time and money issues. That won't happen.
- Underestimating the time, cost, and effort of development, execution, and maintenance. It's expensive to get to a point of significant automation of tests. Most organizations that try to do so have a lot of trouble achieving that. Many of these organizations give up before they get there because they

didn't budget enough for it. In other cases, the initial introduction is achieved, but the long-term costs of running and maintaining the tests are underestimated, leading to abandonment of the automated tests. Yet another possibility is that the implications of changes in the testing process and the need for continuous improvement in the use of the tool are underestimated, which can lead either to abandonment or to suboptimal returns from the use of the automated tests.

- Use of the tool for unsuitable tests. Some tests simply aren't automatable. Some would be better done in a manual fashion. Some testers consider automated test tools as a substitute for good test design, which is not the right way to think of automated test tools.

We've also seen clients have problems with improper version control and configuration management, tool integration, and orphaned or neglected tools.

These risks identified in the Foundation syllabus are ones that concern both test analysts and test managers. At the Advanced level, test managers should expand their scope to include some additional management risks:

- Organization immaturity. In some cases, the organization as a whole, or the test team itself, is not ready to implement test automation or to reap sustainable benefits from it. To give you an example, we built a custom test tool for a client to allow automated test execution across dozens of similar security-related API modules (called agents). The tool itself was a great success, but because the client was never able to stabilize the process for building, testing, and releasing these agents to their clients, they achieved very little payoff from it.

- Unmaintainable artifacts. Some test teams adopt tools that promise shortcuts to automation or fail to implement proper, maintainable architectures for their automation. Eventually, these test teams end up in a cul-de-sac where the cost of maintaining the existing artifacts—which usually give depressingly low regression risk coverage—eats up the entire automation budget, precluding any expansion of the coverage. The best thing to do at this point is junk the entire approach and start over—right back at the tool evaluation step—but the more frequent outcome, at least that I have seen, is for the team to persevere with the failed approach until some fiscal crisis or change of management brings down the curtain.

- Distraction. For some test teams, automation becomes a fetish, a totem, a goal in and of itself rather than a means to manage regression risks or other kinds of quality risks. I've heard testers and test managers say things such as, "We should have 100 percent of our regression tests automated," "We should always automate every test we run if we intend to re-run it," "We should have an automated test for every defect detected in production," and "The only really valuable way to run a test is to run an automated test." Now, automated testing is a key component of the testing effort for many successful test teams, but it's also the case that successful test teams integrate automated and manual tests to optimize their coverage. Focusing too much on test automation will result in a reduced level of defect detection effectiveness as well as the failure to achieve other broader test policy goals (see Chapter 2). It's important to remember, as my colleague Jamie Mitchell pointed out, "Manual testers find bugs that no automated test will; often ones that the test was not defined to find."

This list of risks is not exhaustive, so remain aware of the possibility of additional risks for your automation effort.

Tool Benefits

So, the last two pages have been kind of a bummer, huh? Lots of focus on costs and risks of various kinds. Well, when the right investments are made and the risks are managed, tools can bring benefits, in many cases with a positive return on the investment. These benefits can include the following:

- Reduced repetition. Regression testing is a boring, repetitive chore, and people—being bad at most rote activities that are not mentally or physically challenging—don't do a good job of repeating tests. But computers don't get bored and they don't mind doing the same thing over and over again. So automating many of the regression tests is a smart move in most cases.
- Accelerated test cycles. Not only do computers not get bored, they go very fast. A set of tests that could take a large number of people a couple weeks to run can be done by automated tests overnight. Automated tests are also very useful for smoke testing builds, which avoids costly and delaying incidents associated with untestable builds.
- Reduced test execution costs. Automated tests are not only fast, when properly designed, they require very little babysitting from people. Proper design also reduces the number of false positives reported by the tool, which decreases tests results analysis time. I've personally managed an automated test system where over 15,000 tests (each corresponding to a database query yielding one or more screens of data or pages of reports) could be run mostly unattended over the weekend with a negligible false

positive rate and a total execution cost of about five person-hours, excluding the costs of internal failure (to use cost of quality parlance) associated with diagnosing and reporting defects detected by the tests.

- Increased coverage of test types. Because of resource limitations, regression testing, when done manually, usually doesn't achieve good coverage, no matter what dimension of coverage you might use to measure it—requirements, regression risks, configurations, data, and so on.[4] Automated regression tests, due to the factors mentioned earlier, can cover a substantial number of elements across various coverage dimensions. Some other types of testing, such as performance and reliability, are almost only testable with the use of automation, so proper use of tools can provide essential coverage increases here.

- Reduced human error. As I mentioned, people are really bad at boring, repetitive tasks. This makes them bad at manual regression testing because they have to follow hundreds of rote steps and compare dozens of results in order to ensure unchanging behavior. Similarly, trying to generate large volumes of test data, or simply test data that must meet precise specifications, is not a human strength, and trying to load that data accurately is error prone too. Setting up test environments is a very error-prone process. However, all of these tasks are subject to automation. If the automation is done properly, the accurate repetition of these tasks is assured, no matter how many times they need to be done, no matter how large the volume of information involved, and no matter how complex the environment is. By automating these tasks, you release the testers to spend time on more productive and creative activities.

- Easier generation of reports and metrics. When properly set up, automated tools can help with the collection of metrics, including metrics about test data loaded; test environments checked with smoke tests; test cases run, passed, and failed; and coverage achieved. Such automation often involves the careful integration of multiple test tools, including test execution tools and test management tools. Now, "properly" in this case has a number of implications, including that you are careful not to aggregate data that makes no sense when aggregated, such as different groups of test cases that cover different numbers of conditions. This is an easy mistake to make when

---

4. See my webinar *Dimensions of Test Coverage*, found at http://www.rbcs-us.com/software-testing-resources/library/digital-library.

using automated tools.[5] My personal preference is to use the tools for gathering tactical metrics and then use spreadsheets or business intelligence tools to aggregate that data into meaningful strategic information.

- Reuse of test cases, test scripts, and test data. When properly used, test automation results in a significant number of reusable test work products. This reuse is what makes the low costs of test execution and test maintenance possible.

- Improved tester and test team status. Finally, when done properly and demonstrated to other test stakeholders, the effective and efficient use of test automation changes the way outside groups look at your team. In many organizations, meritocracy is an important force, especially among developers and especially in organizations that are following agile methodologies. Proving that your team has competently handled complex technical tasks will increase the respect accorded to them.

These benefits usually do not come from the use of one tool by itself but rather from multiple tools that are properly integrated. In almost all cases, this proper integration of the tools will increase the benefits delivered. Instead of seeing the benefits as accruing to a single tool, it's better to think about all of the tools that you will use and formulate a good strategy that addresses all of these tools as long as they are used.

Perspectives on Tools

Test tools are generally a long-term investment rather than a quick-win or short-term strategy. Exceptions to this rule occur from time to time, but the safest assumption is that you'll want to carefully select tools for years of valuable service.

Another important perspective is to remember that valuable service means valuable to the organization, not just valuable to the testers. You should perform a thorough return on investment analysis and be able to show that the benefits of the tools exceed the costs (both nonrecurring and recurring). You should also have a plan in place that manages the significant risks for the automation effort.

Interoperability between tools is often necessary to achieve the full benefits of each tool, as mentioned earlier. So, you should work to achieve the highest

---

5. More information can be found in my books *Testing Metrics* and *Managing the Testing Process, 3rd Edition.*

possible level of interoperability, and make sure that your ROI analysis accurately states the benefits achieved based on the interoperability actually in place.

Part of achieving a positive ROI is proper design of the test architecture and test cases. Another part is making sure the tool is used properly and accurately. However, even when the tool is used properly, a positive return on investment will not start on the first day it's used. When the tool is launched, expect that learning curve issues, initial development of the tool work products, debugging of the tool's use, and other overheads will limit the benefits for a while. Eventually, the benefits will begin to accrue and the break-even point will be reached, but patience is necessary. It could take months or even over a year. Rushing the job will often result in shortcuts that undermine the long-term ROI that will be delivered.

Another essential element of achieving positive ROI is making sure the users of the tool get proper support and training. As discussed in the Foundation syllabus, the roll-out plan for a tool must include careful consideration of training, learning curves, and mentoring for the tool users. Otherwise, the usual result of "sink or swim" initiations will prevail, where a few bright and fortunate souls find the tool easy to learn while the rest struggle to a greater or lesser extent before giving up.

Test automation and tool introduction is a project, like any other. A good plan, a solid road map, will make success much more likely. Yes, you will make discoveries along the way, learn new things, and change the path you are on. However, if you have no idea how to address the costs, benefits, risks, and perspectives discussed so far, you can bet that many of the surprises that await you are not good ones.

Tool Selection Process

Let's review the tool selection process. To some extent, this process was introduced in the Foundation syllabus, but we'll expand on it here. In doing so, I'll address the various topics I've been covering in this chapter so far, tying them in with the way in which we want to select tools.

To start with, assess whether your organization and your test team are ready to start doing test automation. Is automation a fit, based on the way you currently work, the kind of testing you do, the maturity of your team and organization, and so forth? Would your team and organization be able exploit the benefits of a set of tests repeated over and over again? If not, what changes would need to occur before you could? You should be honest on these points because plenty of test automation efforts have failed for being good seeds tossed onto rocky and inhospitable soil.

Next, be sure you know exactly what you are trying to accomplish and what the tool will need to be able to do in order to enable those accomplishments. You should be as specific as possible in identifying these requirements. If you are working in an agile environment where for some the word *requirements* has somehow become tainted, think *acceptance criteria*. Just be sure that you think, long and carefully, about what you need the tool to do. Otherwise, the odds are very good that you'll select a suboptimal or even completely improper tool.

With the requirements—or acceptance criteria, if you prefer—defined, you can now evaluate the available commercial and open-source tools. This evaluation should include all of the elements mentioned earlier in the discussion about tools, including options for support. If none of the existing tools fit, then you should consider a custom tool, albeit under the careful constraints given earlier. The automation, programming, and technical skills in the test team currently should be carefully considered as part of the tool evaluation.

It's typically the case that, whatever tool is selected, there will be some gaps between the current team's skills and what will be needed. So as mentioned earlier, make sure that training, coaching, and mentoring are considered as part of the evaluation process. For example, your evaluation should take the form of, "If we choose *tool A*, here is what we'll need to do in terms of training, coaching, and mentoring, and here's what resources are available for that," where *tool A* is replaced by each tool under consideration in turn.

Based on all these considerations, the nonrecurring and recurring costs, the risks, and the benefits, you should estimate the return on investment and the break-even point for the automation. Obviously, if the return on investment is negative, or if the break-even point is too far in the future, that could indicate that your tool selection is improper and you should discard that particular tool. It might also indicate a problem with your analysis, so check your work before deciding that the tool you've picked is unworkable. It will be necessary to show a positive return on investment before going forward with the automation effort, because otherwise your management colleagues will raise serious questions about your competence as a manager when it comes to light that you proceeded with an automation project in spite of the absence of any solid business justification.

At the Advanced level, there are some additional considerations that you should address during tool selection. These issues must be addressed throughout the tool lifecycle.

When analyzing the problem to be solved by the tool, you should consider the inputs that will be available for the tool. This step can help you avoid the use of a tool for an improper purpose. For example, when you're thinking about a performance test, the inputs to the tool are models of system usage. A functional testing tool will not be able to understand these inputs, or create the proper resulting inputs to the system from such models.

As you think about designing the tests, consider the way in which the tool supports test design. In some cases, tools can use existing information to design tests and even create tests; for example, many unit testing frameworks can do a fairly good job of creating test artifacts in an automated fashion, even including test data.

In some cases, the test data is not generated by the tool but can be selected based on the particular tests. Since test data sets can be complicated, it makes sense to consider how much help the tool will give you in this regard. Test selection is also something that can be supported by the tool, or at least an analysis of the coverage achieved based on the test selection.

For tools that execute tests, you should carefully consider how much of the execution will be automated. A test automation tool that requires frequent manual intervention may not deliver a positive ROI, so such a solution should be carefully considered.[6] It should also be relatively easy to start the tests, to stop them if needed, and to restart them where they left off rather than having to run them from the beginning every time.

During test execution, it's often the case that failures can occur. Some of these are simple results mismatches during the evaluation, and resuming the tests is fairly simple in those cases. However, in other cases the failures are more serious, such as an application not displaying an expected screen, displaying an

---

6. It is worth noting the comments of my colleague, Jamie Mitchell, who said, "The real question is whether the tool allows more testing to be done with less effort. I have had some cases where manual intervention was absolutely needed. For example, at Jasc, testing PaintShop Pro, they needed to run thousands of tests to evaluate the transforms done to images. Evaluation had to be human; the rendering engine was tweaked each day by development and the resulting effects on image transforms had to be checked. By automating the steps that made the image changes and then saving off the resulting files for humans to check, they got very good ROI, even though there was heavy manual intervention. What you say in this sentence might stop people from solving an important business case simply because it could not be fully automated."

extraneous screen, experiencing serious delays in accepting inputs or returning outputs, or similar such problems. While it's usually not possible to set up a test execution tool such that it can recover from any arbitrary failure, it's smart to evaluate the ability of the tool to recover from the failures you expect to occur most frequently.

Test execution tools also must be able to reliably evaluate actual versus expected results, using the appropriate test oracle. If the test oracle consists of previously captured and validated baselines, can the tool reliably read these files and determine the pass/fail result? If the test oracle is automated and generates the expected results dynamically, is the oracle properly and reliably integrated with the test tool itself? If the answer to either question is no, then a large number of false positives will occur, detracting from or completely negating the test tool's benefits.

As the evaluation proceeds, the results of the comparisons must be logged, and after the evaluation is complete, reports must be produced. You should evaluate the adequacy of these logs and reports. In many cases, these can be customized. If so, then evaluate the adequacy of the customizations to support your needs rather than the out-of-box logs and reports.

If the tool doesn't execute tests itself but supports the execution of tests, then you'll want to evaluate how well it does that. For example, a test management tool that requires a slow, manually initiated, and error-prone process to update test status based on the latest test results isn't a very useful tool.

Example: Objectives for Unit Test Tool

Let's look at an example. We helped one client implement test execution tools for unit testing. At the start of the project, we identified the objectives for the four main stakeholders in the engagement.

Management has a number of major objectives:

- Reduce regression, both during system testing and after release.
- Increase confidence in changes at release.
- Deliver on time, with acceptable quality.
- Increase test and development efficiency.
- Reduce delays and costs of fixing regressions and other side effects of changes, especially by reducing regression issues during system test.
- Schedule acceleration, especially by reducing the number of bugs in system test.

The development team, being the primary users of the unit test tool, had a number of objectives too:

- Reduce regression via automatic regression testing for individual developers.
- Achieve a uniform standard of unit testing to make sure everyone agreed on what "done" meant for this task.
- Reduce regression test lab resource needs, because the regression testing lab consumed a lot of resources and required a lot of developer support.

The test team, being downstream of the development team, had a few objectives:

- Increase percentage of stable test releases, because bad test releases ate much of their test time.
- Reduce regression bugs.
- Increase tester efficiency.

Finally, our objective was to enable client unit test project success. We wanted a satisfied client. Of course, we also wanted to get paid!

It's always good to start a test automation project—of any sort—with clearly defined objectives like these. A good next step is to define one or more metrics (often referred to as key process indicators in process improvement efforts) for each of these objectives.

In addition to these objectives, a number of important aspects or constraints applied to this project. We needed a tool and a process that were both lightweight and easy to use. Creating and running tests had to be a minor, incremental task compared to the programmers' existing workload. Any sort of paperbound process would not be acceptable.

We needed a tool that would integrate with existing tools and environments. Specifically, this meant the development environment, Visual C++; the developers' Windows desktops; and, the Quality Center database.

Finally, given the nature of the project, we had to support regression testing at the unit level. This meant high availability to developers, as well as multiple regression tests running at the same time, on different "private" versions but with shared customization of the tests.

HELLOCARMS Tool Selection Exercise

Assume that, prior to the first iteration, you have decided to automate the tests for each iteration at the end of each iteration so that these tests can be used as regression tests in the next iteration.

Briefly outline a plan for tool selection, listing the relevant risks, costs, and desired benefits.

HELLOCARMS Tool Selection Debrief

I would follow the process given in the Foundation and Advanced Test Manager syllabi:

- Assess organizational maturity. This could be part of a larger evaluation or could be focused strictly on how organizational maturity affects test automation.
- Identify requirements for tools. In this case, we are looking for a functional regression test automation tool. It could be a tool that works through the GUI (e.g., Selenium) or one that interfaces at a lower level (e.g., Fitnesse).
- Evaluate tools. The tool evaluation process is best done in a two-pass approach. First, develop a list of all possible tools, given the requirements. Second, based on a qualitative or quantitative ranking scheme, select the top three or four tools for an on-site demo using the application you intend to test (not the vendor's demo).
- Evaluate the vendor's support. This should be included in the tool evaluation step and taken into account in the rankings. The weaker the team's automation skills, the more critical this is. If the vendor's support is weak, then you might want to consider whether third-party company support is available and whether that support is acceptable.
- Identify internal requirements for coaching and mentoring in the use of the tools. This should be included in the tool evaluation step and taken into account in the rankings. The weaker the team's automation skills, the more critical this is.
- Evaluate training needs considering the current test team's test automation skills. This should be included in the tool evaluation step and taken into account in the rankings. The weaker the team's automation skills, the more critical this is.
- Estimate ROI. This should take into account the costs and benefits discussed later.

The tool selection and implementation plan must manage risks by addressing the following issues:

- Ensuring that all stakeholders, especially managers, have realistic expectations of what can be accomplished
- Providing a realistic estimate of the time, cost, and effort associated with developing and maintaining the tests
- Accurately estimating the break-even point (where financial benefits exceed financial costs)
- Preventing misuse of the tool on the wrong problem (e.g., in this case, trying to do performance testing with a functional regression tool)
- Balancing the effort spent on automated regression testing so that coverage of new functionality is maintained in each iteration
- Ensuring that the release process and test process will be organized such that automated testing can be effectively used
- Designing a framework that will allow for maintenance of tool artifacts in a reasonable period of time for each iteration

The tool selection and implementation plan must include a budget that incorporates the following nonrecurring costs:

- Defining the requirements associated with functional regression testing within the iterative lifecycle proposed for HELLOCARMS
- Carrying out the tool selection process outlined previously
- Acquiring the tool, which in this case may well be zero, given the open-source options
- Training the team in the use of the tool, which is more expensive the less experienced the team is with automation
- Integrating the functional regression tool with other tools, such as a test management tool, a continuous integration and build tool, developer's unit test tools, and so on.

Since most functional regression test automation tools are intrusive tools (i.e., they run on the same system as the application under test), there usually aren't any hardware or software tool hosting costs.

The tool selection and implementation plan must include a budget that incorporates the following recurring costs:

- Owning the tool, such as licensing fees and upgrade fees, which you can avoid if an open-source tool is selected

- Supporting the tool, such as support fees, which might still apply with an open-source tool if you buy commercial support
- Maintaining the tool, which can be significant for open-source tools
- Maintaining the tests and other artifacts created by the tool, which usually depends on how carefully the framework was designed
- Training and mentoring people as they join the team or advance in their use of the tool
- Expanding the use of the tool to new environments, such as when new browsers are supported for HELLOCARMS or the currently supported browsers are up-versioned
- Adapting the tool to future needs, such as when the capabilities of HELLO-CARMS are expanded
- Improving the use of the tool, through end-of-project retrospectives focused on how to get more value from the tool

The tool selection and implementation plan should call out the following benefits for this effort:

- Reducing the time required to complete the regression tests in each iteration
- Reducing the overall test execution effort (and thus cost) for each iteration
- Increasing the amount of regression test coverage that can occur in each iteration, and thus reducing regression risk

These benefits are quantifiable and should be measured as part of the ROI analysis.

The following additional, albeit less tangible, benefit should also be mentioned. Automated regression testing reduces the boredom and human error inherent in manual regression testing. Trying to quantify and measure this benefit is not advised.

- If the tool integrates with the test management tool, it might make getting reports of regression test status easier. Integration with the project configuration management tool would make reuse easier as well as help link specific versions of tests with the code tested by them.
- Since we are looking at a functional regression test automation tool, it will not allow us to do performance tests, load tests, or reliability tests. Some other tool must be selected for that.

Depending on the current perception of the test team, introducing automation can improve the perceived professionalism of the test team along with overall stakeholder satisfaction with the job the testers do. This can be a priceless intangible benefit in some circumstances.

6.3 Tool Lifecycle

Learning objectives

(K2) Explain the different phases in the lifecycle of a tool.

The selection of the proper tool is the beginning of a long process, at least if you are successful at using the tool. Tools go through a lifecycle, just like other software. As a test manager, you'll need to be able to manage that lifecycle.

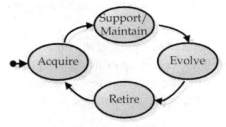

Figure 6–3   *Tool lifecycle*

The lifecycle as shown in Figure 6–3 starts with acquisition. The acquisition process was discussed in a previous section. With the tool selected and acquired, an administrator must be assigned. In some cases, more than one administrator is needed, each focused on different areas. The administrator standardizes the use of the tool, as in setting the way that work products should be created, named, stored, and reused. This standardization must happen in advance, before widespread use of the tool starts. Otherwise, people will make up their own standards as they go along, which of course aren't standards at all. Such divergent usages will significantly retard work product sharing and reuse, which in turn reduces the return on investment. In addition to defining these standards, the administrator should be ready to deliver training on these standards to the tool users.

With the acquisition phase complete, support and maintenance begin. At this point, the planning that you did earlier in terms of support, training, maintenance, and so forth will pay off. (You did do all that kind of planning before you bought the tool, right?) Proper configuration management and work product management practices must be put in place, including backing up and restoring the tool itself and the artifacts produced by it. If your team will not handle support and maintenance, then make sure you coordinate with the tools group that will.

With the tool in place and operational, you might think that the lifecycle has reached a static point. However, it's usually the case that the use of the tool evolves over time. New environments are supported by the application under test. The features of the application change. The vendor changes the tool in a way that enables new uses, affects existing ones, or interferes with other tools that have been integrated with the tool. As you can see, this evolution can be positive or negative in its impact. If the evolution is positive, then you're happy, because new opportunities have arisen. If negative, then you have been impacted by a risk. Hopefully, this is a risk that you anticipated and managed.

Finally, no tool lasts forever. Even the most successful tool will eventually reach the end of its useful lifetime. As a test manager, you'll need to recognize the warning signs as retirement approaches. Trying to flog extra life out of a tool whose ROI has gone negative is a common mistake. Instead, look for ways to smoothly transition to a new tool that will provide benefits and opportunities that exceed the costs and risks of the conversion.

At this point, of course, the lifecycle starts anew, with the conversion being the acquisition of a new tool. From beginning to end of this process, make sure you keep things running smoothly. Any situation where severe disruptions occur in terms of the value gained from test automation indicates a breakdown in your management of the use of tools by your team.

Example: Test Implementation Road Map

A few years ago, we did an assessment for a client that was having trouble with automation. Those involved weren't really aware of how bad it was, but they had large, negative return on their test automation investment. In my report, I made two basic points:

First, I told them that the current test automation approaches had achieved very limited success. Load testing delivered some value but was constrained by test environment issues. Functional regression testing was stuck in an endless maintenance mode and making no progress in automating any of the 99 percent of other data center applications that had big regression risks but zero automation coverage.

Second, I told them that, in spite of a large investment in test automation over the previous four years—an investment in the millions of dollars—they had no demonstrable business value or return on investment. The only company to get a return on test automation at their shop, I told them, was the outsource company that had done a horrible job designing the unmaintainable automated test framework and was now charging them by the hour to maintain tests.

Due to the high regression risks I mentioned, abandoning automation was not an option. So, I proposed the road map shown in Figure 6–4 for revitalizing test automation. Let me walk you through it, starting at the upper left of the figure.

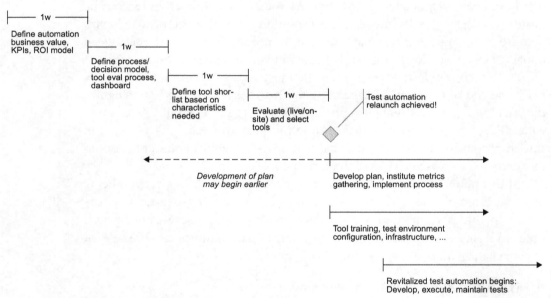

Figure 6–4   *Test implementation road map*

In the first week, define the benefits desired from automation, select key process indicators for automation, and create a model for calculating return on investment.

In the second week, define the processes for deciding which tests to automate, along with a tool evaluation process and a dashboard for measuring the automation benefits.

In the third week, develop a short list of a few candidate tools using the needed characteristics for the tool enumerated in the tool evaluation process.

In the fourth week, using a live, on-site, realistic tool evaluation process, select the appropriate tools.

At this point, I told them, they could consider the test automation effort revitalized. A clear strategy for delivering real, measurable business value exists.

Now, in the fifth week, launch the revitalized test automation effort. Develop a detailed project plan. (Note that I showed on the diagram that they could accelerate this activity and begin as early as the second week.) Put test automation metrics gathering mechanisms in place. Define the processes by which automation will take place and by which automation will fit into the larger test process.

Also in the fifth week, launch the tools. Train the automated test engineers in the use of the tools. (I made clear in my report that they should select only outsource staff involved in test automation that had solid knowledge of and experience with the selected tools because that had been part of their mistake before.) Configure the automated test execution environment. Create any other infrastructure needed for automation.

Shortly after the fifth week, the revitalized test automation effort would begin to produce automated tests. At that point, the work to develop, execute, and maintain tests starts.

6.4   Tool Metrics

Learning objectives

(K2) Describe how metric collection and evaluation can be improved by using tools.

In a number of cases, test tools can be configured to capture various metrics. When the tools are used properly, the metrics can be captured quickly and automatically, with the underlying data being objective and reliable. By setting up the data collection during the initial configuration of the tool, based on the needs of the test metrics program, the metrics can be accumulated in a consistent fashion as the tools are used.

Performance testing tools will capture, for example, response time, throughput, load, and resource utilization metrics as the tests run. Functional test tools will capture metrics on the number of tests run in various test groups, the number of passed and failed tests, the number of blocked or not-run tests, and so forth. Coverage tools gather code coverage metrics. In fact, if anything, test tools can lead to an embarrassment of riches when it comes to metrics, and the challenge for the test manager is ensuring that the right set of metrics is selected.

To do so, make sure you include data and metrics gathering as part of your requirements analysis during the tool selection process. What data do you want to gather? How will you ensure that the data is gathered accurately and the metrics are reported accurately? What metrics will you derive from that data? How will you use those metrics in reporting? How would you recognize and avoid situations where the metrics would give misleading results? How will you educate stakeholders about the use and meaning of the metrics?

You should be able to address each of these questions in your tool requirements. In most cases, the tools will need to be configured to meet these requirements. In other words, the out-of-the-box configuration will typically not satisfy your particular needs.

Types of Tool Metrics

To define the metrics requirements for your tools, you must first understand what the different tools can provide. Let's consider some quick examples for five major types of tools:

- Test management tools: These are perhaps the most versatile of tools in terms of testing metrics, but you also have to be careful not to misuse the metrics in terms of what they can tell you. Many of the test management tools provide traceability between the test basis, the tests themselves, and the test results. Each test can often be reported in terms of which tests are in the repository, which tests are planned, which tests have been run, the status of the previous and current attempts to run the tests, and so forth. The tests can be manual or automated, which is part of what can lead to misuse in terms of aggregation of test results of different sizes. Most test management tools do a good job of reporting tactical results for the test manager to guide the test effort but don't typically provide default reports that are useful to people outside of testing. However, by carefully observing the details discussed in Chapter 2 about results reporting, you can often use the raw data in the test management tools to create informative, compelling, timely, and accurate test dashboards.

- Defect management tools: These tools are also both versatile and potentially dangerous when misused, but like test management tools, they are a good source of raw data to create useful strategic reports. At a tactical level, the test manager can check on the current status of the reports; group and analyze reports by severity, priority, defect clustering, and phase containment; and capture trend and traceability information that may be very useful.

- Static analysis tools: From a metrics perspective, the main focus of the Advanced Test Manager syllabus is on the use of these tools to analyze and report the maintainability, security, and other internal attributes of the code. This can be useful in terms of determining opportunities for development process improvement as well as to identify defect clusters as part of risk analysis.

- Performance tools: I mentioned the various metrics available from performance testing tools a moment ago. In terms of reporting performance testing results, these metrics are valuable. The most important thing, from my experience with performance testing, is to make sure that the person using the tools and creating the metrics from the tools actually understands what they are doing with the tools. It's easy for the inexperienced to misunderstand the results.

- Code coverage tools: At the lower levels of testing, ensuring proper degrees of code coverage is important because otherwise, untested code is delivered to higher levels of testing and to customers. For higher levels of testing, such as system test and system integration test, code coverage tools are best used to periodically check what areas of the application might be missed by the tests.

These are only some examples intended to get you thinking about what the tools can do. You should be careful to evaluate what each specific tool can provide in terms of metrics.

Example: Tool Metrics

Let's end this section with a few examples. I've worked as a consultant with various clients to help them establish metrics programs. This often involved the use of tools. The tools used must handle the various issues associated with the metrics programs and the testing.

I did some consulting with a major defense vendor in a US-allied country. As part of our analysis of the situation, we identified a number of requirements for the vendor's testing. First, because it was building aircraft that might operate in both military and domestic modes, we found that DO-178B compliance was important. Therefore, we needed the testing to collect, evaluate, and report code coverage metrics against the standard. One major challenge was that the target software ran on an embedded system in the avionics of the aircraft, while the development and testing was done on a PC-based host. We had to be careful that the metrics obtained in terms of code coverage were applicable to the target environment. Simply creating test environments that realistically simulated the target environment was quite a challenge. The fact that real-time avionics software is subject to interrupts that can result in abrupt changes in control flow added another challenge.

I have also consulted with a number of FDA-regulated clients. I discussed FDA regulations earlier in this book. FDA regulations impose a number of requirements on testing, such as bidirectional traceability between requirements and test results. The test team must be able to report their test results in a way that will satisfy an FDA auditor. This auditor may have little knowledge of the system under test as well as very high expectations of what information will be provided to them.

6.5   Sample Exam Questions

To end each chapter, you can try one or more sample exam questions to reinforce your knowledge and understanding of the material and to prepare for the ISTQB Advanced Level Test Manager exam.

1.   Which of the following is a risk associated with test management tools?

   A. Untrained staff misuse complex classification fields.

   B. False positives result when inappropriate tests are automated.

   C. Test managers gain insight into trends that span multiple projects.

   D. Programmers introduce new defects when modifying code to comply with coding standards.

2.   Identify *two* of the following topics that you could address in a test tool strategy document.

   A. List of each of the tools that will be purchased

   B. Selection of pilot projects for particular tools

   C. Best practices gleaned from other organizations using similar tools

D. List of the programmers developing the applications under test

E. Specific quality risk items for each application under test

3. Which of the following applications is most likely to *require* a custom-built automated test execution tool?

A. An accounting application running on Windows PCs

B. A spreadsheet application running on a browser

C. An email application running on Linux PCs

D. An embedded application running on an iPod

7 People Skills – Team Composition

Most of us as managers are prone to one particular failing: a tendency to manage people as though they were modular components. It's obvious enough where this tendency comes from. Consider the preparation we had for the task of management: We were judged to be good management material because we performed well as doers, technicians, and developers. That often involved organizing our resources into modular pieces, such as software routines, circuits, or other units of work. The modules we constructed were made to exhibit a black-box characteristic, so that their internal idiosyncrasies could be safely ignored. They were desired to be used with a standard interface.

After years of reliance on these modular methods, small wonder that as newly promoted managers, we try to manage our human resources the same way. Unfortunately, it doesn't work very well.

Tim Lister and Tom DeMarco,
from the introduction to Part I of *Peopleware*

Chapter 7, People Skills – Team Composition, of the Advanced syllabus contains the following six sections:

1. Introduction
2. Individual Skills
3. Test Team Dynamics
4. Fitting Testing within an Organization
5. Motivation
6. Communication

7.1   Introduction

Learning objectives

Recall of content only

Managers get work done through other people, so to be successful as a manager, you must have a successful team. You will recruit and hire some of the people on the team, while others may very well be part of an existing team that you take over or people who transfer into your team from another team. To the extent that these people have the right blend of skills, they can be successful.

The particular blend of skills that you need will change. For an extreme example, consider the use of technology by insurance and banking. In the 1990s, with a few exceptions such as the ATM, IT teams wrote and tested software for use by their fellow employees. Then came interactive voice response (IVR) applications to allow customers limited access to their accounts from their phones. Then came Internet banking, policy changes, insurance claims, and more, as more and more of the functions previously used in-house became accessible to customers directly via phones and Internet browsers. More recently, we see mobile applications and smartphones changing the way customers access their banking and insurance accounts. And I've looked at only the customer-facing side of the IT puzzle; other advances in the use of technology have affected the way software and systems are used inside the banks as well. Over 20 years of rapid change has dramatically shifted the needs of developers and testers in banking and insurance, and in other industries too.

The perfect test team of today could be the perfect dinosaur within five years, unless you continuously adapt the skills of your team to the evolving needs of your organization. The test manager's job is to make sure as-needed hiring, ongoing training and career development, and key-player retention activities all work together to build and maintain a test team that has the skills needed today and is busily acquiring the skills needed tomorrow. To make that even trickier, this skills growth and management must take place in parallel with the urgent tactical needs associated with ongoing projects. Testers and test managers need the right temperament to adapt and flourish under pressure in shifting situations.

In this chapter, we'll examine what you need to know to address the rewarding and challenging management activities associated with building a successful test team. These activities include assessing the skills that you need and that you currently have in your team. They also include hiring and training people to fill the skills gaps in your team while at the same time assembling a group of people who work effectively and collaboratively together and with their organizational colleagues. In addition, since people with the right skills will do the right things only when properly led and motivated, we'll consider motivation. Finally, since communication within the test team and with other colleagues is essential to the successful test team, we'll address that as well.

This material builds on Chapter 1, section 5, and Chapter 5, section 1 of the Foundation syllabus. If you are preparing for the exam, it would be smart to review those sections before reading this material.

7.2 Individual Skills

Learning objectives

(K4) Using a skills assessment spreadsheet, analyze the strengths and weaknesses of team members related to use of software systems, domain and business knowledge, areas of systems development, software testing and interpersonal skills.

(K4) Analyze a given skills assessment for a team in order to define a training and skills development plan.

So what does it mean for a tester to have an appropriate set of skills? A tester should know how software is used. This includes a general understanding of the users of software as well as a specific understanding of the business problem to be solved by the software under test—whether to calculate finances, communicate, diagnose diseases, play video games, create art, or augment other human activities—and how the software can be used to solve that problem. A tester should know the process by which software is developed, and often it is helpful for testers to know how software works internally, at the level of networking, programming languages, operating systems, databases, and so forth. And, of course, a tester should be a talented, inspired, and inspiring software tester, knowing the classic concepts such as those in the Foundation syllabus, the sophisticated concepts in the relevant Advanced syllabus, and more. These skills can be gained through work and other experience, through formal education, through training, or better yet, through some mix of all these means.

The specific skills and experience, and the specific mix of skills and experience, depends on a number of factors, spanning project, product, process, and organizational considerations. In agile organizations, where testers often work closely with developers on tasks like unit testing, code coverage analysis, and test automation, strong technical skills, including knowing programming and test automation details, will be required. In other organizations, such as those where the software being tested solves an especially complex problem, business expertise may be more important. As I mentioned earlier, the skills mix will change over time—sometimes even in the course of a single project—so be watchful for such evolution.

In the next few pages, we'll look at the main skills needed in a test team. However, before we do, I should mention something important. Even when you do a great job of managing the skills of your team, from time to time people will be surprised by something they don't know during a project. A good team is one where people aren't afraid to admit that and seek to learn from their peers. A good team is also one where people don't hoard their knowledge, thinking that doing so makes them essential, but rather where everyone is willing to share their knowledge by teaching their colleagues.

User Skills

Testers should have some level of user skills and domain expertise, which are related but not entirely overlapping. User skills include having an understanding of how the system works from a behavioral perspective; that is, being able to recognize proper workflows, dataflows, screens, reports, and other system inputs, processing, and outputs in different situations. Having such skills also means being able to do a reasonably reliable job of assessing the severity and priority of a defect based on the impact that the associated failure would have on users, customers, and the business.

Some systems are simple in terms of their operations, while other systems can have particularly sophisticated operations. In these cases, domain expertise—a sophisticated understanding of the problem that the software solves and its capabilities—can be necessary in the test team. Domain expertise allows the testers to know what matters most to the business and to know how particular system behaviors will affect the way the business fulfills its objectives and missions. It's not always the case that this level of skill must be as sophisticated as the most expert users, though we have some clients in particularly complex lines of work—for example, oil exploration—where that is the requirement for testers. In most situations, though, there is a level of sufficiency in terms of these skills, provided the tester has access to people in other teams who can fill gaps in their knowledge as needed.

User skills and, where applicable, domain knowledge are important for testers. When testers participate in risk analyses and when they prioritize test tasks, their understanding of what matters to the users, customers, and the business will be important. When testers communicate with business stakeholders, they will need to communicate in terms of usage and domain knowledge if they want to speak the same language as the stakeholders. When testers design, implement, and execute tests, they need tests and data that realistically simulate end-user conditions, especially for higher levels of testing such as system test and system integration test. When testers participate in reviews or even authoring of user stories, use cases, requirements specifications, user guides, owner's manuals, and similar work products, user skills and domain knowledge help to make them particularly effective.

Software Development Knowledge

In addition to user skills, testers need to understand the software development process. The depth of the knowledge needed varies, but testers will be more effective the more they know about the entire process. An understanding of requirements analysis leads to a better understanding of how the software should behave and how mistakes in the analysis of requirements result in defective behaviors when the software is ultimately built. An understanding of system architecture and design leads to a better understanding of how the software is structured and how mistakes in the architecture and design of the system result in internal defects that can cause functional and nonfunctional failures. An understanding of the coding process leads to a better understanding of how software works at a fine-grained level and how programmer errors result in simple and complex interactions within and between code modules that cause failures to occur. An awareness of how these defects are introduced and how they manifest themselves helps testers understand how to detect the defects in reviews and testing and how better software development practices can prevent defects from being introduced or, at least, from escaping to subsequent phases of the process.

This understanding of the software development process can be gained by various routes. One route is through experience as a business analyst, designer, architect, or programmer. I have experience as a programmer, designer, and architect, and this experience has helped me throughout my career in understanding the way in which software works and the way in which it fails. Another route is through training and education as a business analyst, designer, architect, or programmer. I have a degree in computer science and engineering from UCLA, and my education on the software development process has also helped me throughout my career, sometimes in unexpected ways. When I found myself involved in projects that included hardware and software elements, my education as an engineer helped me understand the way hardware reliability, electrical engineering, and software engineering intersected in the creation of quality systems and, in some cases, the introduction of defects.

Another way to gain understanding of the software development process is to have worked in technical support. This experience will give you insight into the users' viewpoint on software, and that viewpoint is often useful for testers. Some very good testers got their start in technical support. However, some testers think that an understanding of the user experience, expectations, and usability requirements is all they need to know—no further skills need be acquired. My experience as a test manager and consultant tells me that viewpoint is at best self-limiting. A background as a technical support person is very useful to testers, but it does not provide an entire picture.

For technical testers, experience as a software developer is not just a good idea, it's critical. Testers who will be involved in automation must understand programming because the successful use of automated tools requires it. For performance and reliability testing, not only must the testers understand how to program the tool, they must also understand the design and architecture defects that cause performance and reliability failures. For testers to participate in static code analysis, code reviews, and unit testing, they must understand the code that they are looking at. To participate in design reviews, architecture reviews, database reviews, and integration testing, testers must understand the underlying structure of the system.

Many of our clients are using agile methodologies. Testers involved in such projects are tightly integrated into the development teams that are creating the software. They are often involved in technical tasks such as code reviews, unit testing, integration testing, and test automation. It's difficult to be successful in these roles without a deep understanding of software development, software design, programming, and the larger process in which these tasks are embedded. I expect that this trend toward greater technical skills for testers will continue in the next decade.

Testing Skills

Finally, of course, testers need to have testing skills. This seems like an obvious thing to say, but it's amazing how often I have encountered people who are working as testers but don't have knowledge of essential testing skills. The very fact that you are reading this right now indicates that you don't manage such a team, of course, because you are studying the ISTQB's Advanced Test Manager syllabus. The ISTQB program stresses the importance of testers having the skills discussed at the Foundation level when entering the field and progressing to the Advanced level (Advanced Test Analyst, Advanced Technical Test Analyst, or Advanced Test Manager) at the appropriate point in their careers.

What are the testing skills that a professional tester has? They can vary depending on the particular position that a tester holds, but often include the following:

- Analyze specifications: Whether specifications are delivered as user stories, use cases, requirements specifications, design specifications, user guides, or other text or graphical descriptions of how the software should behave or work internally, testers need to be able to use these work products as inputs to the test analysis process described in Chapter 1. This process includes identifying test conditions that need to be covered in testing. It also includes identifying defects in these work products as part of early QA and testing.
- Participate in risk analysis: As discussed in Chapter 2, testers have a unique and valuable perspective for risk analysis. They can bridge the viewpoints of technical and business stakeholders, especially if they have the balanced skills in terms of usage and software development discussed earlier.
- Design tests: Testers who fill individual contributor roles (as opposed to test management roles) will often need to design black-box, white-box, experience-based, or defect-based tests. These techniques are not trivial but involve significant skills that can take months or even years to master.
- Execute tests: Testers are often called upon to execute tests. In some cases, concrete tests are handed to junior testers for execution after their creation by more senior testers. The impression sometimes is that executing tests, especially concrete tests, is not a skilled activity. That's incorrect. Whether tests are documented to a logical or concrete level, tests will be executed under changing and challenging circumstances. If junior testers are called on to execute the tests, senior testers should be available to support that process and fill in any skills gaps that may exist.

Log and report test results: When tests are executed, detailed information must be captured about the results, as discussed earlier in this book. From the most junior tester to the most experienced test manager, these testers will need to be able to report test results to various project stakeholders in a way that is meaningful to each audience member.

This list of testing skills is by no means exhaustive, but it certainly includes core skills for all testers.

Test Manager Skills

As test managers, we also have particular skills needs, because after all, we are managers. Testing is an especially challenging part of a project, and so we need to have the project management know-how, proficiency, and experience required to carry out a test manager's duties. It's a common problem for people who are promoted from tester roles into test management roles to underestimate the amount of project management involved. "Hey, I know how to test," they say, "and so I must be able to manage testing." This is almost as wrongheaded as saying, "I was a kid once, therefore I know everything I need to know about being a parent."

I have seen a number of test managers damage their own careers and ill-serve the test teams they were managing by failing to recognize the project management skills they were lacking. Caught up in the details of the test activities themselves, these managers failed at a number of essential test management tasks:

- Properly understanding or carrying out the planning activities necessary to prepare themselves and their teams for the work ahead, and coordinating their plans with project management peers and other project participants
- Correctly identifying the key milestones, touchpoints, and project and product metrics necessary to track progress and escalate blockages when they arise
- Effectively communicating with or delivering value to other stakeholders, especially in terms of reporting results

The individual testers on these teams often see these test managers as geniuses because they are immersed in the daily test activities, providing technical and managerial leadership inward. Only the most perceptive testers see the failure of the manager to engage outward and upward in the organization and understand that the test manager is creating a dangerous situation for everyone.

In some cases, there is no test manager, and the testers report directly to a project manager. This is not a good situation because project managers rarely—in my experience—have enough knowledge of testing to manage it effectively, and testers rarely have the communication skills needed to talk to project managers in terms the project manager can relate to. I have seen some exceptions on both sides of the impasse, but for the most part the obstacles are too large.

The syllabus mentions the possibility of test managers playing a project manager role. Personally, I can't say that I've seen this happen very frequently. I have seen test managers who are effectively backstopping a weak project manager. This doesn't always play out well for the test manager, or for the project, because not all test managers are particularly good at balancing all of the elements of a successful project: features, schedule, budget, and quality. Test managers are inclined to emphasize quality, which is good when that emphasis is balanced by other stakeholders, but it can be a problem if not balanced.

It's important to point out that, while the Foundation syllabus and this book do provide a number of skills essential to—and unique to—test managers, there is no intention to substitute for project management skills. To be a successful test manager, you'll need to learn more about project management as well as other aspects of software engineering, such as business analysis. Well-rounded test managers understand the work done by the groups with which they interact, the better to communicate with these stakeholders and serve their needs.

In addition to project management competence, you need to be good at communicating and handling tricky situations with diplomacy and finesse. I've known some testers and test managers who confuse being a jerk with having integrity or preserving their independence. Don't be a jerk. Know how to pour water, not gasoline, on a fire, especially a fire set by controversy over test results. Use communication media effectively by knowing when to send an email versus when to make a phone call versus when to meet someone in person versus when to deliver information in a group meeting. The exact same message delivered using the wrong media can blow up in your face like an exploding cigar.

It's also important that you build and maintain good relationships with peer managers, testing stakeholders, and managers above you in the organizational structure. A good relationship can smooth the way for a lot of otherwise-difficult conversations. Conversely, the absence of a relationship—or, worse yet, an existing bad relationship—can make even routine conversations more difficult because of the lack of trust and credibility.

Do you need to be a good tester to be a test manager? It's a typical career path into test management from the individual contributor role, so it's probably fair to say that most test managers do have a strong testing background. I do personally. However, I have seen and worked with test managers and directors of test groups that had no background as a tester but had experience as developers, business analysts, or system operators or experience in related fields. These managers had to work a little harder at first to understand the unique attributes of test management, but many of them were successful.

Interpersonal Skills

So far, this discussion has mostly focused on what might be called "hard skills," skills that have more to do with intellect and learning. However, testers and especially test managers need to have "soft skills" as well. Soft skills have to do with perceiving and feeling, with working successfully with colleagues in a positive spirit of collaboration, and with personal work habits and personality traits. Let's look at some of these skills.

First, testing usually identifies defects. Since test results sometimes reflect badly on the product or even project participants, test managers often find themselves in a position of appearing to give criticism. All too often, this is perceived as negative, and sometimes it is meant that way. Instead, successful test managers must master giving constructive criticism so that our findings are used by the project team to support the best possible outcome for the project.

It's also the case that testers and test managers aren't perfect either. We make mistakes too. Sometimes, when test managers are brought face-to-face with evidence of tester mistakes, such as invalid defect reports, false negatives, duplicate defect reports, improper tests, missing quality risks, and the like, they react in a defensive way, personalizing the conflict. Instead, test managers should carefully examine any possible mistakes that have occurred in the testing activities. If the mistakes are unavoidable—such as a certain number of false positives, false negatives, and duplicate defect reports, just as are a certain number of defects in requirements, design, and code—then you should find ways to effectively communicate that to other stakeholders. When the mistakes illustrate opportunities to improve, you should take that feedback and act on it.

Testers and test managers can have all the facts at their fingertips, but if we can't convince our peers, subordinates, superiors, and stakeholders of the validity of those facts and the proper way to respond to those facts, we haven't delivered the full value of testing. Therefore, testers and especially test managers must strive to learn how to influence people. I mean that in the most constructive sense of the word *influence*, that of influencing people to learn something important or to make positive changes in their approach or decisions. For example, when doctors inform their patients of the health consequences of certain behaviors, they are trying to influence those patients to make more healthful choices, choices that will benefit the patients. The tester and test manager should not influence in a self-serving way but rather in a way that serves the needs of the project and the wider organization.

Testers and test managers must also be effective negotiators. Test planning involves activities that interact with and depend on many other activities in the project, and that means we must negotiate those activities with the relevant participants. Test estimates predict duration and request resources that must be approved and provided by the organization, and rarely are initial test estimates approved without some negotiation of test scope reductions for the sake of meeting budget and cost constraints. As described in Chapter 2, risk management is a collaborative activity, where test professionals help negotiate an agreement among all stakeholders regarding what is to be tested, in what order, and how much. Finally, as test control proceeds throughout the project, changes to the test plan and sometimes the larger project must be negotiated to keep testing on track for success.

Part of influencing people is communicating with them effectively. If people don't know what you are trying to tell them or asking them to do, it's unlikely that you'll get your point across. I've spent a lot of time in this book writing about the ways in which testers and test managers communicate, both with written work products and verbal reports. Effective communication is not just a matter of showcasing your incisive analysis and brilliant grasp of details through sharp charts and masterful presentation of test results; it's also a matter of connecting with people, knowing when you have their attention and comprehension, knowing when you've lost them and how to get them back, and knowing how to speak their language. We'll return to this topic at the end of this chapter.

Turning to the inward-focused soft skills, testers and test managers must be able to organize their work. I've seen situations where, in the course of trying to isolate one defect, testers have discovered five or six additional defects. That's a good thing—finding defects, that is—but it requires good organizational skills to keep straight all the information that comes flowing out of such a target-rich test situation. Reactive test techniques require testers to keep track of what they've tested and keep that testing within the scope of the test. Formal test design techniques such as state-based testing require testers to take a very organized approach to test design. Superior organizational skills are required to master and carry out these and other testing activities.

Testing often takes place under conditions of time and resource pressure. Test execution often takes place under conditions that are, at best, changing rapidly and, at worst, highly chaotic and discontinuous. It's easy to squander precious time. The best testers carefully husband their time, and the best test managers know how to enable and support that behavior in their test teams.

Testing also involves details. The best testers and test managers are inherently detail oriented. Sometimes, it can be hard to turn that personality trait off. I was once walking down an aisle in an electronics store, looking for routers, when I saw the following phrase on the side of one box: "Provides the highest level of qaulity of service." If there were one word that shouldn't be misspelled, it's that one, huh? That said, while you probably can't help but notice these details, you should keep your perspective when reporting your results. As a test manager, you want to avoid feeding the industry stereotype of testers as nit-picky, irrelevant, beside-the-point, fountains of negativity.

You might be saying, "Well, I'm not so good at these, but I'm super-talented at the testing stuff, so surely that will carry me." Not in my experience, no, it won't. Plenty of testers and test managers who had excellent hard skills have managed to sabotage their overall effectiveness through a lack of soft skills.

Skills Assessment

I've mentioned skills assessment earlier in this chapter. One practical way to accomplish this is to use a spreadsheet to capture the assessment and its results. Let's see how specifically to carry that out.

The first step of a skills assessment is to do what's called a skills analysis. This involves going through the major tasks and activities associated with testing and determining what skills are important to carrying out those tasks and activities. Be careful to identify only the important skills, and only those associated with important tasks. If you start identifying ordering pizza for the end-of-project party as an important task and understanding of pizza variations as an important skill, you're gone too far.

The next step is to assess the individuals in your team on each skill. The syllabus suggests using a scale of 1 to 5 for this rating. I've always used a scale of 0 to 3, as follows:

0   This person knows nothing about the skill.

1   This person has basic knowledge of the skill and can carry out simple tasks involving the skill if provided with support.

2   This person has good knowledge of the skill and can carry out most tasks involving the skill without any need for support.

3   This person has significant expertise related to the skill and is able to work independently on any task involving the skill.

This assessment then allows you to see where each individual is strong and weak as well as where the team overall is strong and weak. Based on that, you can create training and career development plans for each member of the team that support their individual growth *and* the overall needs of the team too. I'll discuss that a little later in this chapter. You can—and I believe should—use individual skills growth, and meeting the goals set for such growth, as a primary metric for people's performance evaluations.[1]

Skills Inventory and Management

Okay, so it's fine to agree in general about the individual skills required for testers. However, how can you as a test manager measure, manage, and grow these skills?

Figure 7–1?, Figure 7–2?, Figure 7–3?, and Figure 7–4? give an example of how to do it. Together, these figures are an example of a skills inventory. It is based on a hypothetical project to develop a browser-based word processor.

Legend	0 = No Knowledge		1 = Some Knowledge		R = Required		
	2 = Knowledgeable		3 = Expert Knowledge		D = Desirable		
	TM = Test Manager		TA = Test Analyst		TTA = Technical Test Analyst		

Skills and Qualifications	TA Minimum Ratings	TTA Minimum Ratings	TM Irit Kesef	TA Charlotte Wright	TTA James Malone	Team Minimum	Team Average
General Qualifications							
Education							
Bachelor Science Degree (or Advanced)	D	D					
Test Training or Certification	D	D					
Work Experience (Years)							
Test Roles	5R	5R					
Non-Test, Computer	D	D					
Non-Computer, Domain	D	D					
Non-Computer, Non-Domain							
Professionalism							
Oral Communication	2R	2R				0	#DIV/0!
Written Informal Communication	3R	3R				0	#DIV/0!
Written Formal Communication	D	D				0	#DIV/0!
Continuing Education	R	R					
Test Team Building/Cross-training	2R	2R				0	#DIV/0!
Cross-functional Relationship Building	2R	2R				0	#DIV/0!
Reading (Retention, Reasoning, and Analysis)	2R	2R				0	#DIV/0!
Business/Technical Trends	1R	1R				0	#DIV/0!

Figure 7–1   *Skills inventory and management – general professionalism*

---

1. You can find a good discussion of tester skills—and managing testers in general—in Judy McKay's book *Managing the Test People*.

In Figure 7–1?, you see a list of skills down the left column. This first figure shows the skills associated with general professionalism. The next three figures show testing skills, domain skills, and technical skills. Again, this list is an example for a hypothetical project. You'd need to customize the critical skills list based on a task analysis of what your team actually does and what they need to be able to do.

The legend across the top helps explain the entries in the body of the spreadsheet. We are going to rate the skill levels required for various positions, along with the skills of the current team, on the four-point scale described earlier (0 to 3).

Note that R indicates that a skill (at a particular rating, typically) is required to hold a given position. D indicates that the skill is desirable but not required. A lot of confusion happens in the hiring process when people don't distinguish between required and desired skills, so be smart and keep those distinct in your mind.

TM indicates test manager, TA indicates test analyst, and TTA indicates technical test analyst. I am using those position titles in the same sense in which they are meant in the Advanced syllabi.

Okay, so now look down at the skills list again, on the leftmost side. In the two columns immediately to the right of the skills list, we have the test analyst minimum ratings and the technical test analyst minimum ratings. In these columns, for each critical skill, you establish the minimum skill rating required. For most skills, you use the four-point scale from 0 to 3, but the "years of experience" ratings are done, of course, in years.

To use these columns, you review your list of critical skills one by one and ask yourself, "What rating is required to hold this position in this skill area?" The temptation will be to enter the ideal value. That's not realistic. Set the minimum value, the level of skill at which you literally would not hire someone if they didn't reach it. Again, remember to distinguish between required and desired skills.

In addition, during this part of the skills inventory process, be ready to start to suspect that your existing team does not meet the minimum requirements. Don't worry; that doesn't mean you have to fire a bunch of people and start over. What it means is that you'll need to undertake some serious skills growth work with your team.

Now, in the three columns in the middle of the spreadsheet, you'll have exactly one column for each person in your team. Rate each person in your team, again using the scale discussed earlier. Be fair, but be honest. All parents rate their children as above average in some way or another, but this is not the time for wishful thinking.

You'll notice that I have included the test manager in this example. I would suggest that you include yourself as the test manager, if you might be a source of internal team knowledge transfer. In other words, if you have in the recent past done a lot of testing work—actual individual practitioner stuff—and you have strong expertise in that area, you might be able to spend some time teaching people what you know, even if you don't do much hands-on work personally any more. However, don't make a fool of yourself by pretending to know something you don't or by touting obsolete knowledge; you might end up attempting to "train" people in skills that they know or in skills that are no longer pertinent to the job.

With these columns populated, you will now see the two columns on the right side meaningfully populated. The team minimum indicates areas where at least one member of your team is weak. This is interesting if you intend to have a team of test generalists because weaknesses mean that there are one or more tasks that require a particular person, or at least that can't be done by one or more particularly weak people. If you want a team of specialists, you should look at the team maximum because you want at least one person at the "three" (expert knowledge) rating for each skill.

The team average again is a generalist-focused metric that tells you, on average, where your team stands. You'd like an average rating of "two" (knowledgeable) in a generalist team across all skills. For a specialist team, you'd probably prefer a metric like a count of the number of people with a "three" (expert knowledge) rating for each skill. In other words, how many experts do you have in your team?

Having done this assessment, review your team and identify weaknesses. Then, put a plan in place to address those weaknesses via training and job assignments. Periodically reassess your team skills, update this inventory, and revise your plan. This is an ongoing job for a test manager, not a one-off project. Plan to do this at least every six months.

Figure 7–2? shows the skills list for the testing skills.

You should have noticed a couple of errors in this sheet. For example, the technical test analyst is the one who should have test automation skills, not the test analyst. These kinds of mistakes are easy to make in a worksheet like this, but they also tend to be self-correcting. You'll notice them when you do the skills analysis with the team.

Figure 7–3? shows the skills list for the domain skills.

Skills and Qualifications	TA Minimum Ratings	TTA Minimum Ratings	TM Irit Kesef	TA Charlotte Wright	TTA James Malone	Team Minimum	Team Average
Testing Skills							
General							
Testing Standards and Maturity	2R	2R				0	#DIV/0!
Version Control and Config Management	1R	1R				0	#DIV/0!
Planning							
Estimation and Cost of Quality	D	D				0	#DIV/0!
Documentation	D	D				0	#DIV/0!
Quality Risk Analysis/Management	D	D				0	#DIV/0!
Design and Development							
Behavioral (Black-box)	2R	2R				0	#DIV/0!
Structural (White-box)	D	1R				0	#DIV/0!
Static (Reviews and Analysis)	D	2R				0	#DIV/0!
Performance (Modeling/Simulation/Testing)	2R	D				0	#DIV/0!
Test Automation							
COTS Execution Tools	3R	D				0	#DIV/0!
COTS Test Management	D	D				0	#DIV/0!
Test Data Generators	1R	D				0	#DIV/0!
Execution							
Manual (Scripted and Dynamic)	D	3R				0	#DIV/0!
Automated	3R	D				0	#DIV/0!
Test Status Reporting and Metrics	2R	2R				0	#DIV/0!
Average Testing Skills			#DIV/0!	#DIV/0!	#DIV/0!	0.0	#DIV/0!

Figure 7–2   *Skills inventory and management – testing skills*

Skills and Qualifications	TA Minimum Ratings	TTA Minimum Ratings	TM Irit Kesef	TA Charlotte Wright	TTA James Malone	Team Minimum	Team Average
Domain Knowledge							
Word Processing							
Windows Applications	1R	2R				0	#DIV/0!
Linux/Unix Applications	D	D				0	#DIV/0!
Macintosh Applications	D	D				0	#DIV/0!
Graphics, Figures, and Tables	1R	2R				0	#DIV/0!
Document Management							
Windows Applications	D	D				0	#DIV/0!
Linux/Unix Applications	D	D				0	#DIV/0!
Macintosh Applications	D	D				0	#DIV/0!
Document Interchange							
Windows Applications	D	D				0	#DIV/0!
Linux/Unix Applications	D	D				0	#DIV/0!
Macintosh Applications	D	D				0	#DIV/0!
Printing							
Color vs. BW	D	D				0	#DIV/0!
Laser, Inkjet, Other	D	D				0	#DIV/0!
Publishing/Binding	D	D				0	#DIV/0!
Web Publishing							
HTML	D	D				0	#DIV/0!
PDF	D	D				0	#DIV/0!
Average Domain Knowledge			#DIV/0!	#DIV/0!	#DIV/0!	0.0	#DIV/0!

Figure 7–3   *Skills inventory and management – domain skills*

Again, you might find you need to make corrections in this worksheet. For example, the domain knowledge for a test analyst should usually be higher than that of a technical test analyst. You will find and correct these problems when you do the actual skills inventory.

Figure 7–4? shows the skills list for the technical skills.

Skills and Qualifications	TA Minimum Ratings	TTA Minimum Ratings	TM Irit Kesef	TA Charlotte Wright	TTA James Malone	Team Minimum	Team Average
Technical Expertise							
Programming							
C/VB (3GL)	1R	D				0	#DIV/0!
Java/C++ (OO)	1R	D				0	#DIV/0!
Shell Scripting	2R	D				0	#DIV/0!
Code Complexity and Metrics	1R	D				0	#DIV/0!
Operating Systems							
Windows	1R	1R				0	#DIV/0!
Linux/Unix	1R	1R				0	#DIV/0!
Mac OS	D	D				0	#DIV/0!
Networking/Internetworking							
TCP/IP, FTP, RCP (Internet Architecture)	1R	1R				0	#DIV/0!
Browsers (FF IE, etc.)	1R	1R				0	#DIV/0!
Network Application Architecture	1R	1R				0	#DIV/0!
Network Hardware	1R	1R				0	#DIV/0!
Systems and Servers							
Web/Application Servers	1R	1R				0	#DIV/0!
Database Servers	1R	1R				0	#DIV/0!
Average Technical Expertise			#DIV/0!	#DIV/0!	#DIV/0!	0.0	#DIV/0!

Figure 7–4   *Skills inventory and management – technical skills*

Hiring People

Contractors and outsourcing can be used to fill short-term skills and labor shortages, such as a transient need on a single project. If you hire an employee, though, you should be thinking long term. Thinking long term means that you provide ongoing opportunities for learning new skills and applying those skills to solving real testing problems.

Most people—at least most people that you would want to have working for you—will be motivated to learn new skills and take on new tasks. Software engineering is called "knowledge work," and software engineers are called "knowledge workers," for a very good reason. If you find that someone is resistant to learning new skills and trying new tasks, you should put that person on a personal improvement plan as quickly as possible, starting with identifying the reason for this "stuck in their ways" problem. It is quite likely that this person is a drag on overall team morale as well as someone committed to becoming more and more obsolete every day. You should make it clear that those who seize opportunities to learn new skills and apply them will advance in your team, and even more so those who seize opportunities to share those new skills with their colleagues. People who don't learn new skills, or who hoard their skills and knowledge, should be given an opportunity to change their ways, and if they won't, they should be sent on their way.

While you should try to hire people who are a good fit for your team—more on that topic later—you should also recognize that a perfect hire, like a perfect team, is a vanishingly rare find. Even if you could find the perfect hire, or build the perfect team, you should keep in mind that the rapid rate of change in our industry makes this perfection a fleeting thing if ongoing skills growth and career development are not pursued.

So rather than going for perfect, go for perfectible. Look for people who are clearly smart. Look for people who have the tester's curiosity, as well as the curiosity associated with an eagerness to learn. Look for people who will welcome new ways of doing things, new skills, and new tasks and who will adapt themselves as the needs and roles of the test team change. Look for people who will work hard and bring extraordinary focus and diligence to their job. Look for people who are energized by working with others, accomplishing things together, learning from colleagues and teaching colleagues at the same time. By using the skills assessment, you can hire people whose individual weaknesses are complemented by the strengths of the team.

Gap Analysis

On that note, let's return to the skills assessment to discuss gap analysis. The skills assessment spreadsheet will show you the strengths and weakness of the team overall as well as of individuals. As I mentioned, you want to hire *into* the weaknesses of the team, and you want to hire *against* the strengths of the team where you must. In other words, hire people whose strengths lie where the team is weak and whose weaknesses lie where the team is strong.

You should also use the gap analysis to determine where to focus your training and skills development plan. You will want to address the weaknesses in the team by increasing the skills of individuals or of the team as a whole. It's important that you consider your objectives and the goals set for them, as discussed in Chapter 2, when creating this plan. The most important skills gap to address is not the biggest gap but the gap that has the highest impact on effectiveness and efficiency. This direct traceability between the training and skills growth you intend to propose and the objectives of the team is how you are going to sell your manager on the investment you'll be asking them to make. The stronger the business case, the more likely the plan will be approved, the money allocated, and the time freed up on people's schedules, so be sure that you make it compelling.

The plan can and should consist of multiple cross-balancing and reinforcing elements. Four typical elements are as follows:

- Train. If you need to grow skills in a few specific people, you can send them to public training courses. If you need to grow skills in a larger number of people, you can have on-site courses. You can also use e-learning and online virtual classrooms to get training. Keep in mind that the level of dedication required to learn from e-learning and other self-directed types of training is much higher than for instructor-directed training. Training can be part of obtaining certification (whether for testing or for some other skill) or can be simply part of gaining knowledge.

- Self-study. In some cases, self-study can be an effective way of gaining knowledge, or perhaps it is the only way. There might be books or Internet material available on a topic, but no training, or at least no training you can afford. Self-study can and does work, but it is highly self-directed and requires very motivated learners.
- Cross-train. This is where one or two people on your team who already have a skill transfer their knowledge to others. This can be done by formal or informal training or by side-by-side work. It can have some significant efficiency impacts in the short term, but it's a very effective way to teach people because they learn by doing and have help available in real time if they get stuck.
- Mentor. In mentoring, one person with a skill is assigned to serve as a source of information and help for another person who does not have the skill. The person needing the skill can approach the mentor on an as-needed basis for help. This is much more self-directed than cross-training, but it can be effective when the level of knowledge transfer needed is low (e.g., when the person being mentored has a basic level of skill in the skill area already).

The inclusion of opportunities to put the skills to work on real tasks as quickly as possible is key. Nothing cements the learning of new skills like the application of those skills, and nothing assures the forgetting of those skills like the lack of any use of those skills. Most intellectual skills, unlike riding a bicycle, are not things that, once learned, you never forget, and keep in mind that even riding a bicycle requires a strong practical element before the muscle memory is fixed.

Gap Analysis Using Inventory

In Figure 7–5?, Figure 7–6?, Figure 7–7?, and Figure 7–8?, we'll continue the example from the previous section, this time using the skills inventory to do a gap analysis for a hypothetical test team. The team consists of just three people, Irit, Charlotte, and James. However, it's sufficient to demonstrate the technique.

Legend	0 = No Knowledge		1 = Some Knowledge		R = Required		
	2 = Knowledgeable		3 = Expert Knowledge		D = Desirable		
	TM = Test Manager		TA = Test Analyst		TTA = Technical Test Analyst		

Skills and Qualifications	TA Minimum Ratings	TTA Minimum Ratings	TM Irit Kesef	TA Charlotte Wright	TTA James Malone	Team Minimum	Team Average
General Qualifications							
Education							
Bachelor Science Degree (or Advanced)	D	D	BS/MBA	BA	BS		
Test Training or Certification	D	D	ISTQB	ISTQB	ISTQB		
Work Experience (Years)							
Test Roles	5R	5R	12	10	7		
Non-Test, Computer	D	D	2	3	4		
Non-Computer, Domain	D	D	0	2	0		
Non-Computer, Non-Domain			0	0	0		
Professionalism							
Oral Communication	2R	2R	3	2	2	2	2.3
Written Informal Communication	3R	3R	3	3	3	3	3.0
Written Formal Communication	D	D	3	2	2	2	2.3
Continuing Education	R	R	Y	Y	Y		
Test Team Building/Cross-training	2R	2R	2	2	2	2	2.0
Cross-functional Relationship Building	2R	2R	3	3	2	2	2.7
Reading (Retention, Reasoning, and Analysis)	2R	2R	2	2	2	2	2.0
Business/Technical Trends	1R	1R	3	1	1	1	1.7

Figure 7–5   *Example: Gap analysis using inventory – general professionalism*

Remember that the skills listed on the left side of this worksheet are those required to carry out important testing tasks in this team. They are grouped into four categories: general qualifications, testing skills, domain skills, and technical skills. We are going to rate each team member on our four-point, 0 to 3 scale, and use those ratings to identify where we need to improve the team's skills. Remember that the rating of 2 indicates basic, autonomous competence with the skill in question.

Let's assume we're trying to build a team of generalists. In that case, we would want to evaluate closely two specific situations:

- One or more individual scores of less than 2 on the skills rating. The Team Minimum column at the right side of the worksheet will reveal this problem if it exists.
- The team as a whole scores only at or slightly above 2 on the skills rating. The Team Average column at the rightmost side of the worksheet will reveal this problem if it exists.

Let's evaluate those situations on this worksheet.

In Figure 7–5?, you can see that Charlotte, the test analyst, and James, the technical test analyst, are weak on business and technical trends. Some increased time spent studying these trends would help. Perhaps Irit, the test manager, could assign each of them to research and report on a trend affecting this work?

The other areas, where the team average is 2, do not seem troublesome because of the even distribution of skills.

The next three pages will show similar comparisons for the testing skills, domain skills, and technical skills.

Now, what can we do with this skills inventory and gap analysis? For one thing, we can generate job descriptions for hiring directly from these worksheets. We can list the required skills from the worksheets and in particular emphasize the skills where the team is currently the weakest. We can also generate a training and cross-training plan from this worksheet, starting with the weakest areas.

Let's see where we have gaps in terms of test skills.

Skills and Qualifications	TA Minimum Ratings	TTA Minimum Ratings	TM Irit Kesef	TA Charlotte Wright	TTA James Malone	Team Minimum	Team Average
Testing Skills							
General							
Testing Standards and Maturity	2R	2R	3	1	1	1	1.7
Version Control and Config Management	1R	1R	2	1	1	1	1.3
Planning							
Estimation and Cost of Quality	D	D	2	1	1	1	1.3
Documentation	D	D	2	1	1	1	1.3
Quality Risk Analysis/Management	D	D	2	1	1	1	1.3
Design and Development							
Behavioral (Black-box)	2R	2R	1	3	1	1	1.7
Structural (White-box)	D	1R	1	0	2	0	1.0
Static (Reviews and Analysis)	D	2R	1	3	2	1	2.0
Performance (Modeling/Simulation/Testing)	2R	D	1	2	2	1	1.7
Test Automation							
COTS Execution Tools	3R	D	1	1	3	1	1.7
COTS Test Management	D	D	1	3	2	1	2.0
Test Data Generators	1R	D	1	2	1	1	1.3
Execution							
Manual (Scripted and Dynamic)	D	3R	3	2	2	2	2.3
Automated	3R	D	1	1	3	1	1.7
Test Status Reporting and Metrics	2R	2R	2	3	1	1	2.0
Average Testing Skills			1.6	1.7	1.6	1.0	1.6

Figure 7–6   *Gap analysis using inventory – testing skills*

In Figure 7–6?, we can see that the team is quite weak compared to where we'd like it to be. Before she starts having Charlotte and James do research on industry trends, Irit should sort the list of skills on this page by importance and have a plan in place to bring these ratings up, systematically and across the board, over the next six months.

Let's see where we have gaps in terms of domain skills.

In Figure 7–7?, we see what appears at first to be an equally bleak picture. However, notice that many of the skills are ranked as "desirable" rather than "required." So, in terms of domain skills, Irit should plan to address the areas of

Skills and Qualifications	TA Minimum Ratings	TTA Minimum Ratings	TM Irit Kesef	TA Charlotte Wright	TTA James Malone	Team Minimum	Team Average
Domain Knowledge							
Word Processing							
Windows Applications	1R	2R	2	2	1	1	1.7
Linux/Unix Applications	D	D	1	1	1	1	1.0
Macintosh Applications	D	D	0	0	0	0	0.0
Graphics, Figures, and Tables	1R	2R	2	2	0	0	1.3
Document Management							
Windows Applications	D	D	1	0	1	0	0.7
Linux/Unix Applications	D	D	0	2	1	0	1.0
Macintosh Applications	D	D	0	0	0	0	0.0
Document Interchange							
Windows Applications	D	D	0	2	1	0	1.0
Linux/Unix Applications	D	D	0	2	1	0	1.0
Macintosh Applications	D	D	0	1	0	0	0.3
Printing							
Color vs. BW	D	D	1	2	1	1	1.3
Laser, Inkjet, Other	D	D	1	2	1	1	1.3
Publishing/Binding	D	D	1	3	1	1	1.7
Web Publishing							
HTML	D	D	1	3	1	1	1.7
PDF	D	D	1	3	1	1	1.7
Average Domain Knowledge			0.7	1.7	0.7	0.5	1.0

Figure 7–7   *Gap analysis using inventory – domain skills*

serious ignorance (team minimums or, worse yet, averages of 0) or systemic ignorance (team averages around 1) in the coming year and then gradually, over the next couple years, increase the other ratings.

Let's see where we have gaps in terms of technical skills.

Skills and Qualifications	TA Minimum Ratings	TTA Minimum Ratings	TM Irit Kesef	TA Charlotte Wright	TTA James Malone	Team Minimum	Team Average
Technical Expertise							
Programming							
C/VB (3GL)	1R	D	1	0	3	0	1.3
Java/C++ (OO)	1R	D	0	0	2	0	0.7
Shell Scripting	2R	D	1	0	3	0	1.3
Code Complexity and Metrics	1R	D	1	0	2	0	1.0
Operating Systems							
Windows	1R	1R	1	1	2	1	1.3
Linux/Unix	1R	1R	1	1	3	1	1.7
Mac OS	D	D	0	0	0	0	0.0
Networking/Internetworking							
TCP/IP, FTP, RCP (Internet Architecture)	1R	1R	1	1	2	1	1.3
Browsers (FF IE, etc.)	1R	1R	1	1	3	1	1.7
Network Application Architecture	1R	1R	1	1	3	1	1.7
Network Hardware	1R	1R	1	1	1	1	1.0
Systems and Servers							
Web/Application Servers	1R	1R	1	1	3	1	1.7
Database Servers	1R	1R	1	1	2	1	1.3
Average Technical Expertise			0.8	0.6	2.2	0.6	1.2

Figure 7–8   *Gap analysis using inventory – technical skills*

As you can see in Figure 7–8?, the evaluation here is less bleak than for domain knowledge. In fact, it is considerably less so when you see that these requirements fall mostly on James, the technical test analyst. In addition, it's likely the case that Irit, the test manager, can accept basic familiarity (signified by the 1 rating) as opposed to autonomous competence (signified by the 2 rating) because project team stakeholders probably expect a lower level of skill in this area for testers.

Perhaps a plan to gradually infuse better knowledge of the Mac OS into the team, along with giving Charlotte basic familiarity with various programming concepts, will suffice.

HELLOCARMS Team Skills Exercise

As HELLOCARMS test manager, you want to assess your test team. How would you update the skills list shown in the previous example to assess the team for this banking project? Show the skills that would remain on the list and the ones that would change.

Here are the general qualifications skills.

- **Education**
  Bachelor Science Degree (or higher)
  Test Training or Certification

- **Work Experience (Years)**
  Test Roles
  Non-Test, Computer
  Non-Computer, Domain
  Non-Computer, Non-Domain

- **Professionalism**
  Oral Communication
  Written Informal Communication
  Written Formal Communication
  Continuing Education
  Test Team Building/Cross-training
  Cross-functional
  Relationship Building
  Reading
  Business/Technical Trends

Here are the tester qualifications skills.

- **General**
  Testing Standards and Maturity
  Version Control/Config Management

- **Planning**
  Estimation and Cost of Quality
  Documentation
  Quality Risk Analysis/Management

- **Design and Development**
  Behavioral (Black-box)
  Structural (White-box)
  Static (Reviews and Analysis)
  Performance (Modeling/Simulation/Testing)

- **Test Automation**
  COTS Execution Tools
  COTS Test Management
  Test Data Generators

- **Execution**
  Manual (Scripted and Dynamic)
  Automated
  Test Status Reporting and Metrics

Here are the domain knowledge skills.

- **Word Processing**
  Windows Applications
  Linux/Unix Applications
  Macintosh Applications
  Graphics, Figures, Tables

- **Document Management**
  Windows Applications
  Linux/Unix Applications
  Macintosh Applications

- **Document Interchange**
  Windows Applications
  Linux/Unix Applications
  Macintosh Applications

▒ **Printing**
Color vs. BW
Laser, Inkjet, Other
Publishing/Binding

▒ **Web Publishing**
HTML
PDF

Here are the technical qualifications skills.

▒ **Programming**
C/VB (3GL)
Java/C++ (OO)
Shell Scripting
Code Complexity and Metrics

▒ **Operating Systems**
Windows
Linux/Unix
Mac OS

▒ **Networking**
TCP/IP, FTP, RCP (Internet Architecture)
Browsers (FF, IE, etc.)
Network Application Architecture
Network Hardware

▒ **Systems and Servers**
Web/Application Servers
Database Servers

HELLOCARMS Team Skills Debrief

In Figure 7–9?, Figure 7–10?, Figure 7–11?, and Figure 7–12?, I have shown the list of skills in the four major areas.

Skills that I would delete are shown in strikethrough text (like ~~this~~). Skills that I would add are shown in bold text (like **this**). Skills shown in neither bold nor strikethrough text are those that remain unchanged across the teams. I have provided explanatory comments where I felt they were needed.

You'll notice that, outside of the domain expertise area, the changes are minor or nonexistent. This is because the testing skills required to test an application are relatively constant across all applications and because of the common technology behind all browser-based applications, be they word processors or banking applications.

In Figure 7–9?, you see the general qualifications for testers on the HELLO-CARMS project. I would leave this list the same as the original version.

General Qualifications
Skill
Education
Bachelor Science Degree (or Advanced)
Test Training or Certification
Work Experience (Years)
Test Roles
Non-Test, Computer
Non-Computer, Domain
Non-Computer, Non-Domain
Professionalism
Oral Communication
Written Informal Communication
Written Formal Communication
Continuing Education
Test Team Building/Cross-training
Cross-functional Relationship Building
Reading (Retention, Reasoning, and Analysis)
Business/Technical Trends

Figure 7–9   *General qualifications for testers on HELLOCARMS project*

In Figure 7–10?, you see the testing qualifications for testers on the HELLO-CARMS project. I would leave this list the same as the original version too.

Testing Skills
Skill
General
Testing Standards and Maturity
Version Control and Config Management
Planning
Estimation and Cost of Quality
Documentation
Quality Risk Analysis/Management
Design and Development
Behavioral (Black-box)
Structural (White-box)
Static (Reviews and Analysis)
Performance (Modeling/Simulation/Testing)
Test Automation
COTS Execution Tools
COTS Test Management
Test Data Generators
Execution
Manual (Scripted and Dynamic)
Automated
Test Status Reporting and Metrics

Figure 7–10   *Testing qualifications for testers on HELLOCARMS project*

In Figure 7–11?, you see the domain knowledge qualifications for testers on the HELLOCARMS project. This list is substantially changed from the original list, due to the completely different nature of the product. I've shown the old skills list on the left side of the table and the new skills list on the right side.

Domain Knowledge	
Original Skills	New Skills
Word Processing	Banking
Windows Applications	Home equity loans
Linux/Unix Applications	Reverse mortgages
Macintosh Applications	Lines of credit
Graphics, Figures, and Tables	Mortgages
	General branch applications
Document Management	Credit
Windows Applications	Decisioning systems
Linux/Unix Applications	Credit bureau
Macintosh Applications	
Document Interchange	Regulations
Windows Applications	Sarbanes-Oxley
Linux/Unix Applications	Data privacy
Macintosh Applications	State regulations
Printing	
Color vs. BW	
Laser, Inkjet, Other	
Publishing/Binding	
Web Publishing	
HTML	
PDF	

Figure 7–11   *Domain knowledge qualifications for testers on HELLOCARMS project*

In Figure 7–12?, you see the technical qualifications for testers on the HELLO-CARMS project. This list is mostly the same as the original list because the technologies behind browser-based applications are mostly the same. However, some of the technical skills would probably not be relevant. For example, the specific programming language would be selected, Mac OS would not be necessary based on the Windows PCs in the call center, and the specific networking skills would change.

Technical Expertise		
Skill		
Programming		
C/VB (3GL)		
Java/C++ (OO)		
Shell Scripting		
Code Complexity and Metrics		
Operating Systems		
Windows		
Linux/Unix		
~~MacOS~~		
Networking/Internetworking		
TCP/IP, FTP, RCP (Internet Architecture)		
Browsers (Firefox, Internet Explorer, etc.)		
Network Application Architecture		
Network Hardware		
Systems and Servers		
Web/Application Servers		
Database Servers		

Figure 7–12   *Technical qualifications for testers on HELLOCARMS project*

7.3 Test Team Dynamics

Learning objectives

(K2) For a given situation, discuss the necessary hard and soft skills required to lead a testing team.

Staff Selection

While some test managers are lucky and get to hire people frequently, most test managers have limited opportunities to hire people. Therefore, it's critical that you hire the right people when you do get the chance. That's true whether you hire one person this year or one dozen people. As mentioned earlier, you should try to hire into the existing team's weakness and against the existing team's strengths, meaning hiring people who complement your team.

This complementary nature should be determined based on the skills gaps identified in the skills assessment discussed earlier. You should use interviews as part of how you determine a candidate's skills along with exams and skills demonstrations, a review of sample work products, and reference checks (where possible). Let's look at each of these techniques:

- Interviews. You should ask direct questions about the skills you need. These questions will usually be in a sequence as you zero in on whether the candidate has the requisite skill at the required level. For example, you can start the sequence by asking the candidate, "Tell me about the bug classification system you use in your current company." The next question might be, "Okay, so tell me about a defect you reported recently and how you went about selecting the right values for each classification." Assuming the questioning is still going well—in other words, the person has not demonstrated a lack of skill in this area—you might progress to a more sophisticated question such as, "Tell me about a time when you misclassified a defect report, and how did you resolve that situation."

- Exams. You can use exams (such as the ones used by the ISTQB) to evaluate candidates. We have, for some clients, developed and delivered such exams for use in their hiring processes. These exams can be targeted at the specific skills you need to evaluate, at the level of mastery (roughly the same as the K-levels of ISTQB learning objectives) you need. You should be careful that you make the questions properly universal; in other words, make sure they are not dependent on quirks, unique attributes, or terminological oddities of your organization. You should also be careful not to ask low-level questions when you need high-level skills. It's very easy to write K1 types of questions that focus on memorization and terms and hard to write K3 and K4 questions, but for most of the skills you'll be evaluating, application and analysis is what you are trying to measure. Note that a few good exam questions will be much more useful than a larger number of poor questions.

- Skills demonstrations. This is also known as "audition interviewing," and it involves the candidate demonstrating the particular skills required to carry out a task For example, we have in the past assigned candidates test cases to execute against the system under test. We select tests we know will fail and ask the candidates to note the final status of the test and to write up any defects that they happen to see. You'd be surprised how many candidates—ones who were previously doing well in the interview process—we had to drop abruptly when they said, "Oh, the test passed, there aren't any bugs." For more senior positions, you might ask the candidate to design a test from a requirements specification excerpt or use case.

- Sample work products. If someone can provide samples of test plans, test cases, risk analyses, bug reports, test status reports, and other work products they've created, these can be worth evaluating. I've certainly learned a lot about organizations and the people in them by evaluating such work products as part of doing assessments. One obstacle here can be that non-disclosure agreements and employment contracts may forbid candidates from providing such samples. If you seem to be requiring them as a condition of being interviewed, that may inspire less-than-ethical behavior in some candidates.

- Reference checks. In theory, reference checks should be useful. You call the candidate's former manager, have a nice chat with the person about the candidate, get lots of useful details about what it's actually like to work with the person, and use that information in making your decision. Sometimes it works that way, but often there are problems on both sides. On the former manager's side, company policy may forbid confirming anything other than dates of employment (if that), for fear of being sued if the candidate doesn't get the job based on something the former manager said. On your side, you might be required to use a human resources person or an outside contractor to do the reference check, again in the interests of insulating the company from lawsuits.

You also need to consider personality types and team dynamics. A test team consisting entirely of introverts or extroverts would not be ideal because the overall test process includes solitary, introspective activities as well as group, collaborative activities. Test teams need to have soft skills as well as hard skills because testers must be able to work effectively with a variety of project participants and stakeholders. Different projects have different challenges and levels of complexity, and the team must be flexible enough to accommodate these variations. You should consider the types of projects your team must handle, along with the personalities of the testers, project participants, and stakeholders, as you assess whether someone will work effectively within your team.

Assessing Skills, Hard and Soft

Let's look at some of the hard skills that you might need to evaluate as part of the hiring process.

- Creating tests. You can evaluate this skill through interviews, exam questions, skills demonstrations, sample work products, and reference checks. However, actually giving someone the same kind of documentation they'll receive in your company and asking them to derive a test from it is the gold standard, in my opinion. For more junior-level people, you can tell them which technique to apply. For more senior-level people, you should let them select the technique and then explain why they selected it. You should evaluate both the application of the technique and the quality of the test created.

- Participating in reviews. This can be evaluated through interviews, exam questions, and skills demonstrations. My personal preference would be to provide an actual requirements specification or design specification excerpt, a code module, a test plan, a test case, a risk analysis, or some other work product that the candidate might need to review. Ask them to identify defects in the item and write those down. Next, role-play a review process where you take on the role of the author. Evaluate both their written notes and the way they handled the interaction for clarity, objectivity, and comprehensibility.

- Reporting failures. This can be evaluated through interviews, exam questions, skills demonstrations, sample work products, and reference checks. Your evaluation should include describing the failure and the steps to reproduce it, the proper use of the defect classifications in use in your organization, and at least some level of understanding about how developers determine and select root cause. I like the approach of having someone run a test with known failures, asking them to report the failures they see.

- Tool use. This can be evaluated through interviews, skills demonstrations, and sample work products, with exam questions and reference checks a possible source of information but hardly ideal or complete by themselves. The particular skills you are looking for can include white-box testing of APIs or code, gray-box testing involving database access as part of a functional test, designing test automation frameworks that can execute tests and report results, or executing existing tests and troubleshooting any failures. You should use someone who is an expert at these matters to conduct the interview, oversee the demonstration, or evaluate the work product.

- Lead or manager activities. This can be evaluated through interviews, exam questions, skills demonstrations, sample work products, and reference checks, ideally a mix of all. You can have someone write a portion of a test plan, such as entry and exit criteria, based on a scenario you describe. Exam questions can check the candidate's ability to detect problems with some portion of a plan or some management scenario. Role-playing during an interview can be a good way to assess someone's ability to present and defend test results.

This list is by no means exhaustive, but it should get you thinking about the hard skills required and how you can assess them.

Let's look at some of the soft, interpersonal skills that you might need to evaluate as part of the hiring process. These skills are best assessed through some combination of interview and demonstration as well as—if you can get reliable input this way—from reference checks.

- Present test results to stakeholders. I have an exercise that we do in some of our training on test management. It involves presenting the test results for three projects in serious trouble to the rest of the class. There aren't really any right answers to this exercise, but it is always interesting and informative to see how people approach doing so. If you use this approach in an interview, ask yourself, as you listen to the person's response, "Will this approach to presenting bad news work for us here?"

- Communicate effectively with developers. Another interesting exercise that we like to do is to have people critique and improve a defective bug report. In this approach, you could take the side of the skeptical developer and ask the tester to explain exactly what the report means. The syllabus also recommends having candidates participate in a role-playing scenario in which they compliment a developer. I'm not sure how to arrange this in an interview setting, but I would try to get information on how people worked with developers in past jobs through behavioral interview questions and reference checks.

- Train. As mentioned earlier, cross-training and mentoring are important elements of any well-rounded skills development and team growth plan. So, especially for senior positions of technical or team leadership, you should ask someone to demonstrate how they would train someone in a skill they claim to have. It's important that the person who evaluates their training ability already knows the skill so they can be sure they are being told the right things.

- Report on a process problem. You can use a demonstration or behavioral interview questions to see how someone might describe a process breakdown to management. The process breakdown can be either in testing (in which case the explanation can be relatively simple and focused on how to solve the problem within the team) or in some other part of the development process (in which case there's also a sales job required to convince the owner of that part of the process that a problem exists).

- Participate in a review. You can pick various types of work products for someone to review, but to emphasize the soft skills, having the candidate review a test case and give feedback to the tester who wrote it will give you a good idea how they'll do. The test case should contain some real, honest-to-God problems, which might need to be seeded deliberately. The person getting the feedback should be the author of the test (and perhaps also the author of the purpose-built defects in the test). Pick someone who can accept honest feedback, objectively presented, without reacting defensively.

- Interview. If you are hiring someone who will participate in the hiring process, having them do a mock interview makes sense. Reference checks can be useful in discovering how former managers do in terms of interviewing.

The preceding lists of hard and soft skills are not intended to be exhaustive, but they should give you some ideas to consider when you are planning your interviewing process. During this process, it's a best practice to consider the unique organizational, project, and product attributes that you need testers to understand and handle effectively. Coming up with a "one size fits all" plan for interviewing testers is not smart, but having a typical framework and a playbook of interview questions, skills demonstrations, exam questions, rubrics for the review of sample work products, and questions for references is smart because it ensures consistency and fairness. You should tune this framework and playbook over time to ensure that it does a good job of assessing the important skills (which should of course be aligned with your skills analysis) and determining each candidate's strengths and weaknesses. This hiring process playbook can also become part of how you perform your skills assessments.

Onboarding New Hires

When you do hire someone, you should already know how you intend to onboard them. I remember being hired as a contractor once, showing up my first day and having no place to sit, no computer, no phone, no nothing. It turned out that the person who had hired me had been let go the week before, and no one had picked up the pieces on his new hires. Once that got straightened out, I did end up working for one of the better managers I've had in my career, but it was a bumpy start to a job.

When you bring new hires onboard, you should consider how you intend to give them appropriate job assignments immediately, with proper guidance, supervision, and support. You want to avoid the two extremes of "sink or swim" on the one hand (no guidance at all) and "helicopter manager" on the other hand (micromanaging the poor tester to the point of codependence and learned helplessness).

During the interview process, you should have determined the strengths, weaknesses, and personality type of the new hire. You also should have your team's skills assessment, so you should know how the new hire fills gaps in your existing team. Based on these insights, you can clearly define a role and an initial job assignment for each new hire. This assignment should allow the new hire to exercise their existing strengths while at the same time giving them opportunities to grow.

It's important to remember that the most successful teams usually consist entirely of successful individuals. People who are failing on a team create a multitude of problems. Failing people are usually aware of the fact they're failing—even if they are almost entirely clueless, as was the case with the last person I had to fire—meaning that their morale is poor. Bad morale is contagious to the rest of the team. Failing people require frequent management intervention, with the general rule of thumb being that a single problem employee can consume 50 percent of a manager's discretionary time. This means there's little time left to manage the rest of the team. Failing people also don't carry their own weight, of course, which reduces the effective headcount and usually sloughs off work onto others who already are carrying their own share and perhaps more. This combination of creeping bad morale, a lack of management guidance, and workload dysfunction is toxic; avoid exposing your team to it.

Dealing with Pressure

Another reason you want a team consisting entirely of successful, high-morale achievers is that, well, testing is hard. There's a lot of pressure on test teams, especially during test execution. No matter how well you do your estimating, you will often find that you are forced to work within a context of too little time and too few resources. At that same time, some stakeholders will expect your team to cover every risk, test every configuration combination, verify every requirement, validate every use case, find every bug, and know the future quality of your product. So you and your team must do a great job of managing your time, your resources, and your stakeholders' expectations, all at the same time.

Yes, you need to take the lead in terms of managing these challenges, but the pressure will drip down onto the testers, no matter how good a manager you are. Even when you do a good job of managing these pressures upward and outward, you'll need the team's help managing the internal testing dynamics that these pressures create. Each member of the team will need to be able to work effectively, efficiently, and gracefully with their colleagues (inside and outside the test team) no matter what the pressure level is.

I had a test lead working for me once who had been in combat situations. He was good at restoring a sense of balance, because whenever anyone—including sometimes me—would complain about the pressure or a tough meeting or some other triviality, he would ask with a smile, "Did anyone shoot at you today?"

A good tester has a sense of humor, and can find ways to defuse tension with a friendly joke. Sarcasm and gallows humor can also have a place in these situations, though you have to be careful that it doesn't turn into barbs or resentment directed at other people on the project team. Other ways of deflecting and managing frustration can be useful too, such as exercising with colleagues and having team lunches and social events to inject fun and stress relief into the team.

In some cases, there's nothing wrong with some team outings to a bar or other alcohol-related events, depending on the culture. However, consider the feelings of those who don't drink and ensure that matters don't get out of hand. I've seen a couple instances where "alcohol as stress relief" became, instead, "alcohol as pressure creator." In these cases, both collective and individual drinking behavior started to contribute to the problems the team already had rather than being a fun way to blow off steam. This is especially true if you're working with a relatively young team, where some people may be predisposed to alcohol problems and not yet aware of that.

Impossible schedules, looming deadlines, or a seemingly endless load of work can contribute to a sense of dread, helplessness, being overwhelmed, and even getting depressed. If you can get people to remember the management aphorism about how to eat an elephant—one bite at a time—you can help people think about the importance of effectively and efficiently taking on the tasks at hand, day by day. Celebrate the progress and the milestones achieved with the team to help them keep this attitude.

Organizations are different in terms of pressure and acceptable ways of dealing with it. You should keep in mind the kind of pressure you'll face and the ways that pressure is managed in your organization and in your team. When you are making hiring decisions, keep these factors in mind. I've hired one or two testers in my career who were just too emotionally brittle for the environment we had to work in. Not only did they not work out well in their positions, but I also realize, looking back on these incidents, that I certainly hadn't done them any favors by putting them into those situations.

Building a Self-Directing Team

The most successful managers I know are the ones who know how to create the preconditions for team success. They effectively deal with the skills growth, hiring, organizational, and pressure-management issues we've discussed. They also create a team where people see that their work is valuable, that they are an essential part of the team, not just a replaceable cog in a machine. Such a manager communicates and manages in a way that gives the team the whole picture, from the objectives and strategy to the tactics and tasks, and helps each person see how they contribute to the achievement of those objectives through their daily work.

If you manage in this way, you'll find that you are building a self-directing team. Testers will work together to share knowledge and work. Testers will foresee problems and solve them without your intervention in many cases. Testers will escalate problems to you when necessary, and you'll see that they've already thought of the obvious things to try. Having a team like this creates a powerful positive feedback loop because you can focus on managing outward and upward in order to clear external obstacles from the team's path.

Example: Friends and Family Beta Test

On the Internet appliance project that I've mentioned a few times, we had a beta testing level. You should recall that the Foundation syllabus classifies beta testing as a form of acceptance testing.

The product marketing team instituted this beta testing effort. In Figure 7–13?, you can see the objectives as defined by the marketing staff for this program.

Objective

Have 500…employee sponsored people test the stability of [the product] and our network and provide constant, detailed feedback on the product and service. This feedback will help us make improvements to our product before we go nationwide. The [Beta test] marks our product launch into the market – therefore it is extremely important that every [employee] participate to the max! The results and feedback from this program **will define** our success in the market.

Figure 7–13   *Example: Friends and family beta test*

Since the product was designed for non–computer users, it was a challenge to find such people using typical beta program methods. So, to try to replicate the approximate skill and computer experience level of the target market, employees were encouraged to recruit their friends and family as the beta testers.

This effort was a bit Janus-faced in its objectives, as you can see if you read the excerpt carefully. For one thing, typical of a beta test, the goal includes finding defects that might be hard to find in test. That was a valuable objective from the test team's point of view, because one thing we could not cover well were different phone line conditions for the modems.

However, the beta program also included a marketing component. The marketing team was looking to gather testimonials and other useful marketing collateral from the project. For this reason, marketing—rather than test—managed the effort.

In Figure 7–14? you see an example of test logging from the beta testers on this project. As you can see, this would not qualify as professional test logging by a team of professional testers doing, say, a system test. However, it's hard to enforce standards on volunteers. Similar problems often exist with user acceptance test logging and with unit test logging.

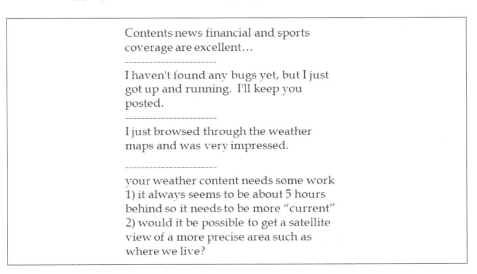

Figure 7–14   *Example: Results logging from beta testers*

However, in this case, unlike many beta tests, there was a large volume of data from the testers. It was sometimes hard to interpret due to the ambiguity of some of the comments.

In an attempt to understand how these results fit with what we had found in test, the marketing and technical support teams performed a comparison with the test results. That effort was not very conclusive, but the idea is a good one. It would be especially important in a user acceptance test to compare results against the system testing done previously.

HELLOCARMS Team Gap Analysis Exercise

Assess yourself and others in the group against the skills list from the last exercise. Use that self-assessment to identify gaps in the team. Outline an approach to fill the gaps.

HELLOCARMS Team Gap Analysis Debrief

The specific results of this exercise depend on the team. However, in general, a manager has a number of options to fill a skills gap in a team:

- Hire someone with the skill. Going forward, have that person serve as the specialist, handling the tasks that require the skill.
- Hire someone with the skill. In the short term, have that person serve as the specialist, handling the tasks that require the skill. In the long term, arrange for that person to cross-train other team members.
- Bring in a consultant with the skill. Use that person to handle the tasks that require the skill. (This makes sense only when the need is temporary and nonrecurring.)
- Bring in a consultant with the skill. Use that person to handle those urgent tasks that require the skill. Before releasing the consultant from the engagement, arrange for the consultant to cross-train other team members. (This might not strike the consultant as in his best financial interests, so be clear about it up front and make the knowledge transfer a material part of the contract.)
- Outsource the work to a company with the skill. Use that company to handle the tasks that require the skill. (This often makes sense when there are various economies-of-scale or when the skill has a particularly long learning curve or is difficult to master.)
- Send someone to be trained in an off-site course. Going forward, have that person serve as the specialist, handling the tasks that require the skill.
- Send someone to be trained in an off-site course. In the short term, have that person serve as the specialist, handling the tasks that require the skill. In the long term, arrange for that person to cross-train other team members.

- Bring in on-site training for some of your team. (This option is usually only cost effective when multiple people need the training.) Going forward, have those people serve as the specialists, handling the tasks that require the skill.
- Bring in on-site training for all of your team. In the short term, have some of the attendees who showed the most aptitude serve as the specialists, handling the tasks that require the skill. In the long term, arrange for those people to cross-train other team members.
- Rotate staff with the skill in from other areas of your company while rotating out from your team staff that need the skill. Of course, you need to make sure you don't create a new skills gap by rotating out some of your staff.
- Have the development team provide a transfer of information to the entire test team prior to the start of testing.

As you can see, some of these have implications in terms of test team organization and perhaps even company-wide human resource management decisions. Not all of these options are available to all test managers in all situations.

7.4   Fitting Testing within an Organization

Learning objectives

(K2) Explain options for independent testing.

Back in the early days of computing, there was no such specific, separately identifiable activity known as "testing." Developers debugged their code, and that was usually intertwined with some unit testing task. That didn't work. My first job was as a programmer, and where I worked, this was exactly how we approached quality assurance. It was a quality disaster.

This approach by itself still doesn't work. It does not work for those throwback, Neanderthal organizations that rely on this approach entirely. It does not work for those cutting-edge companies that think some fancy language or process or tool has solved the software quality problem at last. It does not work for anyone, unless we define "work" as "shift most costs of poor quality onto end users who are too stupid to know better or trapped in a monopolistic market without any real choice." And those organizations that rely on stupid users or a monopoly position had better hope they are right.

With the widespread advent of independent test teams in the late 1980s and early 1990s, we saw improvements. I was working in an independent test lab in the late 1980s and as a test manager in the early 1990s, and we made great strides. However, we also saw the emergence of a new dysfunction, the "hurl it over the wall to the test guys and hold them responsible for delivered quality" mistake. Every now and then, we work with organizations that still suffer from this problem.

Let's be clear. When quality matters—and shouldn't it always—everyone must play a role. We looked at the idea of a series of quality assurance filters in earlier chapters, as well as in the Foundation syllabus. Each team in the organization typically participates in and owns one or more of these filters.

Some of these filters, especially high-level testing like system test and acceptance test, work best with a high level of independence. Some of these filters, especially low-level testing like unit testing, work best with less independence. Let's survey the degrees of independence so you understand your options.

Self-testing occurs when the developers test their own code. There is no independence here, of course. The author bias problem is significant, and the developers—even if given enough time to do unit testing—often miss the important bugs because they determine that the code works as they intended. Of course, that might not match the actual requirements. The advantages are that the developers can fix any defects they find quite quickly and, being quite technical, understand the software being tested.

Buddy testing occurs when developers test each other's code but not their own. Pair programming, which is a practice in some agile techniques, is a special form of this, where development of code, continuous code review, and development and execution of unit tests by a team of two programmers evolves the code. While the author bias problem is not so acute here, when two people work closely together, it's hard to say there is much independence between the developer and the tester. In addition, there tend to be few if any usable defect metrics captured in this situation without careful cultivation of the proper mindset because when peers test each other's code, they might not want to report defects. Finally, since the average programmer has little training or formal experience with testing, the mindset is usually focused on positive tests. Once again, the advantages include a quick repair of defects and good tester understanding of the software being tested.

Having the tester or testers inside of development occurs when a development team includes one or more testers and these testers are not part of an independent team. This is rather popular these days because many proponents of agile methodologies advocate this approach. There is nothing wrong with it as part of a larger quality assurance process, but by itself it can be dangerous. The main problem is editing and self-editing.

Self-editing means that the tester does not report—or reports only informally to the developer—problems they find, leaving no official trail in a bug tracking system. This is the equivalent of an organization tearing out its eyes and flying blind with respect to quality. Defect metrics, while insufficient by themselves for all the reasons discussed earlier in this book, are certainly necessary to any balanced, meaningful picture of quality. In addition, an organization that doesn't study its mistakes is unable to learn from them.

Even if the tester does report bugs, editing can happen. The development manager or project manager does not allow the tester to release a clear, balanced, complete set of test results to the broader set of stakeholders. Furthermore, since the development manager or project manager is often focused on short-term goals like getting the product released on time and on budget, the entire mission for the testers is likely to be verifying adherence to requirements. Finally, it is often the case in these arrangements that the tester tasks are assigned to junior developers or factotums of some sort or another, along with a number of other responsibilities. Therefore, the testing is often done hurriedly and without any particular professionalism.

All those disadvantages enumerated, I do see value in having one or more testers—whose permanent positions are inside an independent test team and who are true professional testers—assigned to act as testing resources within development teams. In this role they can create good test cases, build automated test harnesses, create continuous integration build-and-smoke-test facilities, and the like. We have played this role for clients in the past, with great success. However, this too is often not sufficient by itself.

Testing by business, users, and technical support occurs, often in the context of acceptance testing and beta testing. This has the advantage of a truly independent outlook, motivated to report findings truthfully to the stakeholders. What these folks typically care about is the ability to get their job done, plain and simple, and if quality's not there, they'll suffer. This is a great approach for the final levels of testing.

Unfortunately, what we tend to see with organizations that rely on this approach for system testing is that the test team's skills are one-dimensional. They are focused entirely on domain knowledge. Technical skills, if present, are limited. Management disdains professional testing, with the usual refrain being,

"Oh, any user can test." In addition, the amateur testers tend to bring a firefighting, patch-it-until-it-works attitude to the testing work.

Test specialists in an independent test group are present in many thoughtful organizations, with the independent test team responsible for system test, system integration test, and, in some cases, component integration test. In this case, we have all the advantages of true, professional testers testing against specific test targets. Unlike the approaches mentioned earlier, we often see test targets beyond functionality, including usability, security, and performance. For all the advantages of an independent test team, it should be kept in mind that the formality usually associated with such teams does tend to slow down the process. It's also possible that reporting structures or poor management can lead to perverse incentives and a lack of focus on quality.

Finally, testing by an external test organization occurs in a number of settings. For example, in certain military contracts, independent verification and validation by a team not in any way associated with the prime contractor is required. As another example, you might hire a test lab to do compatibility testing for an e-commerce website to save the expense of having all the configurations in-house. Here, the maximum level of independence is achieved. Of course, the separation of test and development duties might mean that the knowledge transfer necessary for thorough testing might not occur. To make up for these disconnections, the organizations must put in place very clear requirements and well-defined communication structures.

Furthermore, there's a potential "who guards the guards" problem. I worked with one client once where they were doing testing for a defense contractor. One of the test managers told me that he wasn't interested in skills growth for his test team. He just wanted templates for test plans and test cases so his testers could fill in the blanks. I asked him if it mattered whether they had their brain turned on or off while they were doing that. Surely even author-biased testing by the programmer is better than some unskilled tester doing a haphazard, path-of-least-resistance job of it. Any company engaging an external test organization should plan to audit the quality of that organization regularly, including the skills and professionalism of the team.

Now, notice that I listed advantages and disadvantages for each option. This means that you can use each option for one or more of the quality filters I mentioned earlier. The advantages and disadvantages tend to be mutually correcting, so a mix of degrees of independence, with different degrees for different tasks, is often appropriate.

On Using Different Mixes of Independence

I mentioned in Chapter 5, in the context of maturity models, that reducing matters to black or white, either/or dualities, while simplifying the concept, often loses some of the important nuances. This question of independence is one where too many people have fallen into the black or white, either/or duality trap. People ask, "Should we have developers testing, or users testing, or independent test teams, or buddy testing, or outside test labs?"

The answer is not one of these options to the exclusion of all others but rather each of these options, in some mix with some or all of the other options, to the degree appropriate for the particular project, product, and software development and testing process. Independence is a matter of degree, not an either/or state.

In addition, independence is an attribute of the relationship between those developing and those testing. For any two entities—whether at the level of individual people, teams, or organizations—we can ask, "What is the relationship between them and to what extent are they independent?" The more an entity is free to act as it sees fit, without having to accept direction from the other entity, the more independent that entity is.

Notice that the distinction here is not one of disregarding how one's actions affect another but rather not having to get approval for those actions. This is important to remember because some independent test teams make the mistake of thinking that they can and should—as a sign of their independence—do whatever they think is right, and to the devil with the consequences to the project and the organization. Independent test teams that fall into this adversarial, "quality cop" mindset often end up being disbanded. Successful independent test teams act in consultation with other project stakeholders, preserving their independence, but with the goal of serving the stakeholders and the best interests of the project and organization in mind.

Increasing independence of testing is not without risks, as I discussed earlier. More independence can result in more isolation. It can reduce the level of insight and understanding of what is going on in the project. It can also lead to a loss of ownership and responsibility for quality on the part of those developing the code. These are not necessary outcomes of independent testing, as some of those who argue a dualistic view of this question suggest, but simply project risks that the manager of an independent test team must mitigate.

Decreasing independence of testing is not without risk either. It can increase insight and understanding of the project—and this is the outcome touted by many of the dualists—but it can and often does introduce conflicting goals. Decreasing independence can lead to blind spots as to what the requirements really are. Decreasing independence also decreases the degree to which testing involves people who specialize in testing and thus have an imperfect, skewed skills mix.

In some cases, the choice of software development models and other project realities can influence the choices here. For example, if you are following an agile lifecycle model, then pair programming and testing within the development team might be part of the mix. As another example, if you are seeking to have your product certified as Microsoft compatible, then using Microsoft's compatibility test lab—obviously completely independent from your organization—will be required.

Again, remember that you can mix all of these independence options that have been discussed. In a few moments, you'll see an example of a very successful organization that does just that.

When you do split up the testing across various entities with various degrees of independence, the usual rules of pervasive testing apply. Make sure you define the responsibilities and expectations for each test level and entity doing testing. A concise, clear test policy document, developed with the participation of all the entities and approved by senior management, can accomplish this. By defining the responsibilities and expectations, you'll be setting up a mix of different filters, deployed at the ideal spot in the lifecycle, which can maximize quality within the schedule and budget constraints of the project.

Outsourcing of testing is one form of external, independent testing. This can take a number of shapes. One is hiring an outside testing company to provide co-located testing services (which is sometimes called insourcing). Another is to have the testing done at an external facility located close to the development team. Yet another is to have the testing done at an external facility that is some distance away, perhaps not just miles or kilometers but also in time zones.

Many outsource services companies, RBCS included, provide a mix of all three options. We have testers who work on-site for our clients. We have the ability to provide testing services through local or in-country facilities. We also have the ability to have the testing done through partners around the world.

I discussed this topic at some length in Chapter 2, but let's review some of the challenges here.

The outsource testing team might have cultural differences with your test team, your development team, or both.

The project team and local test team might have difficulty providing timely, adequate supervision and direction, particularly on chaotic, constantly changing projects.

Due to a lack of foresight, significant communications problems can exist between the local project team and the outsource test entity. This can compound the supervision problem.

Without careful contracting, you can have problems with protection of intellectual property. Even with good contracts, in some countries your legal recourse might be quite limited.

Again, if insufficient care is taken when the testing is contracted, including especially the selection of the outsource test vendor, the skills of the testers can be questionable.

Exacerbating this skills problem can be the problem of employee turnover. Again, proper contracting and vendor selection can help reduce this.

Since companies pursuing outsourcing often forget to include their own costs of managing the relationship in the overall budget, outsourcing does not always involve accurate cost estimation.

Finally, the quality of the work can suffer.

Some of these challenges can increase with distance. Again, I'm not mentioning these as outcomes that necessarily will occur and dog your project but rather as risks that you can and should mitigate through the kinds of techniques for managing outsourced testing that I covered in Chapter 2. A lot of it comes down to careful outsource test vendor selection and careful contracting.

Example: Mixed QA Independence Options

Figure 7–15? shows the how one of our clients approaches integrating quality assurance and testing tasks, with various degrees of independence, into the entire development lifecycle.

First, let me review the lifecycle. Project teams take on projects for various business stakeholders who authorize those projects. To be deployed, projects will be included in a bundled release that will be tested with other projects and delivered into production. The bundled releases into production occur about every two months. This approach minimizes regression and interoperability risks.

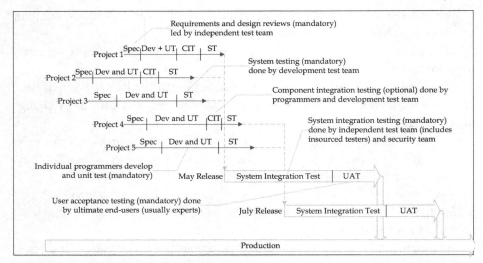

Figure 7–15   *Example: Mixed QA independence options*

For each project, as it moves through this lifecycle, a variety of quality assurance activities take place. Each has differing levels of independence, differing responsible parties, and differing focus.

Each project goes through a requirements and design specification period at the beginning. The independent test team leads mandatory reviews of these specification documents. The participants vary, with business stakeholders and business analysts heavily involved in the requirements reviews and senior programmers, system architects, network administrators, and database administrators heavily involved in the design reviews.

Each project then goes into a development phase. Each programmer unit tests their own code. Programmers review each other's code. Unit tests are subject to approval.

Each project then moves into a pre-bundle testing period. In other words, the code developed will go through separate testing prior to integration with the other projects' code. This period can—but need not necessarily—contain a component integration test level, depending on the number of modules involved. The programmers themselves handle this component integration test, assisted by a test team internal to the development team working on the project. This internal development test team is a transient team, assembled by the project manager from members of the project development team. Thus, it is not independent but does have excellent insight into the project, especially technically.

The pre-bundle test period contains a mandatory system test level. The development test team handles this test level.

At this point, all those projects that have qualified to enter the bundle will do so. When I say, "qualified to enter the bundle," what I mean is that project metrics indicated sufficient quality to be in the bundle.

The first quality filter for the bundled software is system integration testing by the independent test team. This is a mandatory activity. One of the test types during system integration testing, security testing, is done by the security team, another separate group.

The final quality filter is user acceptance testing, done by actual users, ideally expert users who know the most about the business problem to be solved by the system.

So, we have eight quality filters:

- Requirements reviews
- Design reviews
- Code reviews
- Unit test
- Component integration test
- System test
- System integration test
- User acceptance test

These filters have different levels of independence.

So, does this approach work? Well, the defect detection percentage for system integration test and user acceptance test has been consistently over 99 percent for a few years now. This is in part because the independent test team and users find very few bugs in those final filters, only those bugs that couldn't have been found earlier.

So, yes, this approach works. In fact, if what you care about is the highest quality, every time, without compromise, this not only works but indeed is one of the best ways I've ever seen it done.

7.5 **Motivation**

Learning objectives

(K2) Provide examples of motivating and demotivating factors for testers.

As test managers, we need to motivate our team members. How can we motivate testers? There are a number ways.

- Recognition. When someone does good work, tell them so. Public praise for a job well done is a major motivator for many people. The converse, by the way, is not true: Public criticism for a job poorly done will not motivate someone to do better. You should give criticism privately, and make sure that criticism is constructive and guides the tester toward the desired improvement.
- Management approval. This doesn't just mean your approval. As a test manager, promote your team and get upper management approval for your work. Then, share that with your team.
- Respect. As a test manager, you want to build a culture of mutual respect in your team. You must also ensure that the project team treats your testers with respect. Of course, that respect must be earned.
- Adequate rewards. This includes financial elements, such as salary, merit increases, and bonuses. It also includes nonfinancial elements, such as training and career growth.

Of course, it happens that project realities constrain the motivational tools available to you.

- If the team is subject to impossible deadlines, that makes the job hopeless. In addition, tight project deadlines usually mean poor quality when testing starts because everyone is taking shortcuts.
- Testers should not take bug deferral personally, if it is done thoughtfully and with an eye toward what matters to customers. However, wholesale deferral of bugs without any consideration of the impact of them is demotivating.
- Crunch time happens on projects, and testers should be ready to put in extra hours to accomplish important tasks. However, mandatory overtime that clearly accomplishes nothing is demotivating.

▓   Finally, being held responsible for quality when everyone else on the project is taking steps that actively undermine quality—being the quality scapegoat—is demotivating.

As a test manager, you can't necessarily stop these things from happening, but you should plan to expend serious political capital to try to resolve them. At the least, your team will see that you are serious about trying to maintain their motivation. Few things are more demotivating than working for a manager who doesn't care about how you feel.

Unfortunately, metrics are often misused, so many people think of metrics as demotivating. Properly used, though, product, process, and project metrics can demonstrate the value of testing.

You should remember these metrics from Chapter 2. You can measure your team's effectiveness, for example, using the defect detection percentage to measure bug finding. You can measure your team's efficiency, for example, by looking at cost of quality. You can measure your team's risk mitigation contribution. You can measure your team's cross-functional interactions, for example, by looking at bug report reject rates and surveying stakeholders about the quality of your test results reports.

Define an assessment program for your test team. You can use the models discussed in Chapter 5. In consultation with the test team and other project stakeholders, and based on what you want to see, set goals and publish progress toward those goals. This will help you demonstrate value and progress to management and will also help show testers that in spite of some daily frustrations, you are collectively, as a team, making progress.

As mentioned, recognition takes various forms. People want respect from their peers and managers, and they want peer and manager approval of their work. They want promotional opportunities. They want fair pay, relative to their peers and the industry. They want a career path.

A test team that is not respected will not be recognized. One that is respected can make meaningful contributions and will be recognized. That is a virtuous cycle, and your job as a test manager is to create and sustain that cycle.

To create and sustain this cycle of recognition and respect, you must be able to demonstrate value. Metrics are essential to demonstrated value. Test managers who insist on respect and recognition for their test teams based purely on subjective reports of good work done—or worse yet based on an assertion that the test team deserves respect—tend to be disappointed in the organization's reaction.

Example: Real Quotes from Real Projects

One thing that makes a project motivating—or demotivating—to work on is the feedback you get from your peers. So, here are some example quotes from project team members that illustrate either motivating or demotivating experiences for test teams that I've managed.

Let's start with the demotivating comments.

"We all have pain in our lives right now." This comment came from a developer in a conference call. His implication was that because developers were suffering from all the bugs found, the test team needed to have some pain in its life too. However, that's an odd idea of justice because test would be suffering for bugs it didn't create.

"Some developers are returning bugs as 'irreproducible,' even though our bug reports document them as intermittent...or reproducible only in the test environment." This is from an email I sent to the development manager to report a problem with development handling of bug reports. It was frustrating for our test team to see these responses because it was clear that the developers weren't paying attention to the reports.

Now, here are some motivating quotes.

"If you never made anyone upset, you wouldn't be doing your job." This comment came from a developer who was remarking on another developer's defensive reaction to a bug report. Seeing that understanding within the development team was motivating to us.

"As of [next week], test goes on a five-day schedule." This was a comment I sent to the test team, ending a long period of six-day weeks. They were motivated to start working normal hours again.

"I'm there, and I really like expensive tequila!" This was from a manager, agreeing to come to a test team dinner after a tough project. Getting some attention in a social setting from management sends a message to the test team that they matter.

7.6 Communication

Learning objectives

(K2) Explain the factors that influence the effectiveness of communication within a test team, and between a test team and its stakeholders.

There are three main channels of communication for most test teams:

- First, we communicate, mostly internally but also with others, about the documentation of test products. This includes discussions of test strategies, test plans, test cases, test summary reports, and defect reports.
- Second, we communicate feedback on reviewed documents, typically on a peer level both inside and outside the test group. This includes discussions about requirements, functional specifications, use cases, and unit test documentation.
- Third, we communicate as part of information gathering and dissemination. This can include not just peer level communications but communications to managers, users, and other project stakeholders. It can be sensitive, as when test results are not encouraging for project success.

It's important to remember that both internal and external communications are important to the professionalism of the testers who work for you, and for you as a test manager.

Effective communication assists you in achieving your objectives as a test manager, while ineffective communication will hinder you. It's important to be professional, objective, and effective. You want each communication you have, both inside and outside the test team, to build and maintain respect for the test team. When communicating about test results, giving feedback on issues with documents, or delivering any other potentially touchy news, make sure to use diplomacy.

It's easy to become caught up in emotions at work, especially during test execution when things are often stressful. Remember to focus on achieving test objectives. Remember also that you want to see the quality of products and processes improved. Don't engage in communication that is contrary to those goals.

It's also easy to communicate as if you were communicating with yourself or someone like you. In other words, we testers often speak in a sort of shorthand about very fine-grained details of our work and findings, and with a certain degree of skepticism. When talking to fellow testers, this is fine. However, you have to remember to tailor communication for the target audience. When talking to users, project team members, management, external test groups, and customers, you need to think carefully about how you are communicating, what you are communicating, and whether your communications support your goals.

As a test manager, I have seen a single thoughtless email, bug report, or hallway conversation do a great deal of damage to my test team's reputation and credibility. So, even with all the other work you have to do, remember to think about your communications.

Test Manager Audience

Compared to most testers, test managers have a wider audience with whom they communicate. Test managers may find themselves talking to users or customers about quality risks, important requirements or use cases, bugs, test conditions, and test coverage. Test managers have to communicate regularly—usually daily—with other project team members, such as development leads, software release engineers, system operators, and the like. Test managers usually have periodic status discussions with peer managers and supervising managers as well as having on-demand discussions when urgent matters arise. If external test groups are engaged for outsourcing some of the testing work, as discussed in Chapter 2, the test manager must manage this resource through regular communication.

Each different type of audience member has different information needs. It is a common test management worst practice to spray irrelevant details at all and sundry, giving people too much information and no way to sort it out. Instead, work with your audience to understand what information they need from you, then tailor your communication to provide just that.

Some people need the details. For example, developers, development leads, and development managers may want fine-grained analysis of the defects you've found during testing. A chart showing a correlation between defect clusters and the maximum cyclomatic complexity of a module would be useful to this audience because it would give them ideas about where to focus product quality improvements. You might go through a 20- or 30-page detailed presentation with this audience, as I have in the past when reporting test results to development teams.

Some people need the higher view. For example, senior managers overseeing a project typically need to understand what's been covered, what hasn't been covered, what risks remain, what works and doesn't work, and where the project stands in terms of defect trends and backlog. I've put together executive test dashboards that included just three or four Excel graphs.

Whether reporting details or summaries, it's important to properly present your information. This is especially true with brief executive presentations, where you need to concisely and precisely deliver your message and you won't have time to recover from a fumble. Do people need to understand trends? Current status? Underlying causes? What is the best way to display the information? Successful test managers know how to get their message across.[2]

However you are delivering your message—more about options for that in a moment—you should be sure that you are clear on what you're trying to say, what that means for each member of the audience, and why they should care. You should also consider how someone might misunderstand your message, how you would recognize such misunderstandings, and how you could correct misunderstandings with a minimum of damage.

Mastering Test Manager Communication

In addition to communicating externally, and to a wide audience, you also need to consider how to communicate internally. As I mentioned earlier, you want to build a self-directing team. Such a team needs the right information to direct themselves in a proper way. As a test manager, you'll hear news about the project, product, and organization that your testers need to know. You'll need to exercise test control actions that reprioritize tests or change existing plans or instructions.

You should also be ready to pass on the odd interesting bit of trivia, gossip, or social news, provided that doing so is consistent with maintaining the morale and alignment of the team with the larger organizational objectives. Workplaces are social places, after all, and communicating with your testers about facts alone will create a rather sterile environment. It's also useful to you as a manager to create an environment where testers feel comfortable communicating with you and with each other about what's going on in their lives, to some extent. Obviously, there are limits to the personal information you want shared, but a fuller understanding of your colleagues as human beings will make you a better manager.

---

2. Some good ideas on how to do this can be found in Edward Tufte's *The Visual Display of Quantitative Information*.

Whether communicating inward, outward, or upward, you should hold your communications to the same standard. Give people information they need or want, information that is appropriate to them and that avoids irrelevant and distracting details. You should make sure the information is delivered in a way that is effective so that the recipient gets the message. In many cases, you'll want to follow up with the recipient to make sure the message was received and understood. And, in all cases, you should maintain the proper level of professionalism and objectivity in your communications.

There are many different means of communicating, and as mentioned earlier, you'll want to carefully consider which is best for any given message. Email is fine for some information, especially routine status information that is unlikely to set off alarms or be misunderstood. For more complex, nuanced, or potentially upsetting information, verbal one-on-one delivery is usually better, either in person or, if that's not possible, by phone. Just remember that, when communicating by phone, a lot of the nonverbal communication that happens face-to-face will be lost. Video calling is a good option if you're worried about that, given the ubiquity of video telephony services available now.

Meetings are yet another means of communicating that the successful manager must master. Understand the ground rules and expectations of the meeting before you show up. Coming to a meeting underprepared or unaware of the agenda or the attendees of the meeting is a good way to look like an incompetent buffoon. Meetings differ in terms of their level of formality and also the kind of discussions that are allowed. Also, know who is chairing the meeting and understand the kind of communication style that person has. Definitely, in any meeting, be respectful of people's time by avoiding situations where you ask lots of questions that you could have answered yourself by doing your homework before the meeting.[3]

Whether as part of a meeting or as a separate deliverable, you may find that you need to produce reports. Some of these are the types of status and results reports I mentioned earlier. In some cases, such as when you're working in a regulated environment, you may have to produce or contribute to formal reports for regulators or auditors. You should understand the required content, the degree of formality, the need for supporting materials (if any), the format of delivery (e.g., document, presentation, graphics, etc.), any applicable templates

---

3. An excellent discussion of this is found in *Peopleware, 3rd Edition,* by Tom DeMarco and Tim Lister.

or structures to be followed, and any applicable version control and configuration management issues for the report.

Of course, testers often use test management tools, defect management tools, and other tools to enter, update, and communicate test-related information. As a test manager, you should define the standards for how these means of communication are used. Ultimately, you are responsible for the quality of the information in these repositories because the information is entered and updated by your team.

This same level of concern should carry over for all of your communications. As an organization that tests other people's work products, shouldn't you and your team's work products be exemplary in all ways in terms of their quality? I know that's the standard I hold my testers to. I sometimes decline to interview testers based on sloppy resumes because I don't feel like hiring someone whose work will need lots of cleaning up. This high standard of quality is true for all work products, but most especially for those you'll be showing to senior management. A test manager is a person in the quality business, and such a person has no business going into a senior project status meeting with a presentation full of typos, sloppy graphics, and incomplete analysis. By using reviews and proofreading for test work products, you and your team can avoid embarrassing yourselves this way.

Example: Acceptance Test Status Email

Figure 7–16? is an example of test communication. It is an excerpt of an email to a vendor about the results of acceptance testing our new website.

The first paragraph is to communicate that this is a carefully thought-out analysis, not just one of the dozens of fired off emails someone is likely to get. The message is, "Pay attention to this email, please, because I did." This paragraph also refers the reader to further details in the attached document.

The second paragraph—including the bullet list and closing sentence—summarizes what needs to be done to complete the acceptance testing and move into deployment.

The third paragraph clarifies the meaning of the deferral of certain bugs. I wanted to make sure that I was not waiving any legal rights RBCS had to insist on these problems being fixed later.

The final paragraph is a subtle hint that we were disappointed to be still finding problems.

> I have spent a couple hours reviewing the current status of the site and
> the acceptance test. Please see attached [documents] with deferred bug reports
> and [test status]…for pass 2.
>
> The following issues are must-fix to move forward with deployment:
>
> o   Consistency of messages and UI (for examples, see bugs 85, 91, 92, 95, 97)
>
> o   Newsletter link…not in place as agreed (see bug 98)
>
> o   Identification and resolution of internal dead links (see bug 103)
>
> While some of these issues might strike the casual reader as picayune, please
> understand that our target customers…are sensitive to any errors…
>
> In the interests of moving forward and having this critical marketing collateral in
> place…I have agreed to defer a number of bugs from pass 1 that either failed
> verification testing or which related to advertised product features that [the
> vendor] retroactively and unilaterally withdrew… Please note that deferral of
> these bugs does not indicate acceptance by RBCS of the disposition of those bugs
> for all time.
>
> Finally, please note that there were eighteen (18) new bug reports filed
> during the second pass.

Figure 7–16   *Example: Acceptance test status email*

Now, this type of email is appropriate for me to send as a customer to a vendor, explaining test results. Would you send it to your development colleagues? Probably not. The important point here is that every word and every sentence of that email had a communication objective.

7.7   Sample Exam Questions

To end each chapter, you can try one or more sample exam questions to reinforce your knowledge and understanding of the material and to prepare for the ISTQB Advanced Level Test Manager exam.

1.   Assume you have just been hired as a test manager in charge of integration testing, system testing, and acceptance testing for a bank. Most of the bank's systems involve a mix of mainframe central data repositories and services, Unix-based client-server applications in the branches and back office, and browser-based banking access for customers.

 You have inherited a testing team from your predecessor as test manager. His team was effective at finding defects and at automating most of the regression tests. However, he left under pressure due to a lack of overall business confidence in the systems after release and due to relationship problems between himself and other managers in the organization. He staffed the test team primarily with people who had extensive experience testing systems that were implemented using one or more of the same types of technologies used by the bank. He tended to hire people who were self-taught or had learned on the job.

You are now performing a skills inventory on your test team, identifying strengths and weaknesses in five major areas: technical knowledge of software systems, business knowledge related to banking applications, software testing knowledge, interpersonal skills, and education and training. Based only on the information given in the scenario here, identify the *two* results that you are most confident you will find in this skills inventory.

A. The team has broad knowledge of the banking domain.

B. The team has focused knowledge of pertinent technologies.

C. The team has targeted knowledge of testing.

D. The team has strong interpersonal skills.

E. The team has sound knowledge of testing fundamentals.

2. Continue the previous scenario.

Assume that you are in a position to hire two additional testers for your test team. In addition, you have been given a budget to provide training for the team. Your manager has asked you to submit a team development plan for the coming year. She has told you that you may provide two training courses for your team. She has also told you that you may hire two people, and you may use those new hires to cross-train your team. Which *two* choices on the following list are the *least* valuable in this situation?

A. Provide test training focused on automation skills.

B. Provide test training covering broad testing topics.

C. Provide business skills training focused on banking applications.

D. Hire a tester with experience in testing banking applications.

E. Hire a tester with experience in the underlying technologies.

F. Hire a tester with strong interpersonal skills.

3. Assume you are a test manager working on a project to create a programmable thermostat for home use to control central heating, ventilation, and air conditioning (HVAC) systems. In addition to the normal HVAC control functions, the thermostat has the ability to download data to a browser-based application that runs on PCs, tablets, and smartphones for further analysis.

    You have decided to outsource browser compatibility testing for this system to a large company that provides testing, development, and technical support services offshore. By checking this company's references, you have determined that it has done compatibility testing for e-commerce applications in the past. Which of the following is most likely to be true about the outsource organization?

    A. This organization will have the browsers and hardware required.

    B. This organization will have people who specialize in testing.

    C. This organization will have a stable test team.

    D. This organization will do a better testing job than an in-house team.

4. You are a test manager in charge of system testing on a project to update a cruise-control module for a new model of a car. The goal of the cruise-control software update is to make the car more fuel efficient. Assume that management has granted you the time, people, and resources required for your test effort, based on your estimate. Which of the following is an example of a motivational technique for testers that will work properly and is based on the concept of adequate rewards as discussed in the Advanced syllabus?

    A. Bonuses for the test team based on improving fuel efficiency by 20 percent or more

    B. Bonuses for the test team based on detecting 90 percent of defects prior to release

    C. Bonuses for individual testers based on finding the largest number of defects

    D. Criticism of individual testers at team meetings when someone makes a mistake

5. Assume you are a test manager for a banking project to upgrade an existing automated teller machine system to allow customers to obtain cash advances from supported credit cards. You have not been able to obtain a list of the supported credit cards, which are not included in the requirements specification. Which of the following is an example of a good way to communicate that problem in an email?

    A. "Until we receive a complete list of supported credit card types, I have directed the test analysts to not do any work on test design."

    B. "When will it be possible for us to know which specific credit card types will be supported? Test design is impeded by a lack of clarity here."

    C. "Here we go again. The business analysts gave us incomplete and ambiguous requirements specifications. Typical."

    D. Do not communicate the problem; just log the delaying effect of the information problem and be ready to explain the delays to the project manager later.

8   Preparing for the Exam

"Not everyone who doesn't study for the exam will fail.
But everyone who does fail didn't study enough."

A frequent warning from the author when teaching ISTQB courses.

The eighth chapter of this book is concerned with topics that you need to know in order to prepare for the ISTQB Advanced Test Manager exam. The chapter starts with a discussion of the ISTQB Advanced Test Manager learning objectives, which are the basis of the exams.

Chapter 8 of this book has two sections:

1. Learning Objectives
2. ISTQB Advanced Exams

If you are not interested in taking the ISTQB Advanced Test Manager exam, this chapter might not be pertinent for you.

8.1   Learning Objectives

National boards and exam boards develop the Advanced level exams based on learning objectives. A learning objective states what you should be able to do prior to taking an Advanced level exam. Each Advanced level exam has its own set of learning objectives and its own text. There are no shared learning objectives or text across the three separate Advanced level syllabi, so don't bother to read or study the other two Advanced level syllabi if you're studying for the Advanced Test Manager exam. I listed the learning objectives for the Advanced Test Manager exam at the beginning of each section in each chapter.

The learning objectives are at four levels of increasing difficulty. Question writers will structure exam questions so that you must have achieved these learning objectives to determine the correct answers for the questions. The exams will cover the more basic levels of remembrance and understanding implicitly as part of the more sophisticated levels of application and analysis. For example, to answer a question about how to create a test plan, you will have to remember and understand the contents of such a document. So, unlike Foundation exams, where simple remembrance and understanding often suffice to determine the correct answer, an Advanced exam requires you to apply or analyze the facts that you remember and understand in order to determine the correct answers.

Let's take a closer look at the four levels of learning objectives you will encounter on the Advanced exams. The tags K1, K2, K3, and K4 are used to indicate these four levels, so remember those tags as you review the Advanced Test Manager syllabus.

Level 1: Remember (K1)

At this lowest level of learning, you will be expected to recognize, remember, and recall a term or concept. Watch for keywords such as *remember, recall, recognize*, and *know*. Again, this level of learning is likely to be implicit within a higher-level question.

For example, you should be able to recognize the definition of *failure* as

- "non-delivery of service to an end user or any other stakeholder," and
- "actual deviation of the component or system from its expected delivery, service or result."

This means that you should be able to remember the ISTQB glossary definitions of terms used in the ISTQB Advanced Test Manager syllabus. Expect this level of learning to be required for questions focused on higher levels of learning like K3 and K4.

Level 2: Understand (K2)

At this second level of learning, you will be expected to be able to select the reasons or explanations for statements related to the topic and summarize, differentiate, classify, and give examples. This learning objective applies to facts, so you should be able to compare the meanings of terms. You should also be able to understand testing concepts. In addition, you should be able to understand test procedure, such as explaining the sequence of tasks. Watch for keywords such as *summarize, classify, compare, map, contrast, exemplify, interpret, translate, represent, infer, conclude*, and *categorize*.

For example, you should be able to explain the reason tests should be designed as early as possible:

- To find defects when they are cheaper to remove
- To find the most important defects first

You should also be able to explain the similarities and differences between integration and system testing:

- Similarities: Testing more than one component and testing nonfunctional aspects.
- Differences: Integration testing concentrates on interfaces and interactions, while system testing concentrates on whole-system aspects, such as end-to-end processing.

This means that you should be able to understand the ISTQB glossary terms used in the ISTQB Advanced Test Manager syllabus. Expect this level of learning to be required for questions focused on higher levels of learning like K3 and K4.

Level 3: Apply (K3)

At this third level of learning, you should be able to select the correct application of a concept or technique and apply it to a given context. This level is normally applicable to procedural knowledge. At K3, you don't need to evaluate a software application or create a testing model for a given software application. If the syllabus gives a model, the coverage requirements for that model, and the procedural steps to create test cases from a model in the Advanced syllabus, then you are dealing with a K3 learning objective. Watch for keywords such as *implement*, *execute*, *use*, *follow a procedure*, and *apply a procedure*.

For example, you should be able to do the following:

- Identify boundary values for valid and invalid equivalence partitions.
- Use the generic procedure for test case creation to select the test cases from a given state transition diagram (and a set of test cases) in order to cover all transitions.

This means that you should be able to apply the techniques described in the ISTQB Advanced Test Manager syllabus to specific exam questions. Expect this level of learning to include lower levels of learning like K1 and K2.

Level 4: Analyze (K4)

At this fourth level of learning, you should be able to separate information related to a procedure or technique into its constituent parts for better understanding and distinguish between facts and inferences. A typical exam question at this level will require you to analyze a document, software, or project situation and propose appropriate actions to solve a problem or complete a task. Watch for keywords such as *analyze, differentiate, select, structure, focus, attribute, deconstruct, evaluate, judge, monitor, coordinate, create, synthesize, generate, hypothesize, plan, design, construct*, and *produce*.

For example, you should be able to do the following:

- Analyze product risks and propose preventive and corrective mitigation activities.
- Describe which portions of an incident report are factual and which are inferred from results.

This means that you should be able to analyze the techniques and concepts described in the ISTQB Advanced Test Manager syllabus in order to answer specific exam questions. Expect this level of learning to include lower levels of learning like K1, K2, and perhaps even K3.

Where Did These Levels of Learning Objectives Come From?

If you are curious about how this taxonomy and these levels of learning objectives came to be in the Foundation and Advanced syllabi, then you'll want to refer to Bloom's taxonomy of learning objectives, defined in the 1950s. It's standard educational fare, though you probably haven't encountered it unless you've been involved in teaching training courses.

You might find it simpler to think about the levels this way:

- K1 requires the ability to remember basic facts, techniques, and standards, though you might not understand what they mean.
- K2 requires the ability to understand the facts, techniques, and standards and how they interrelate, though you might not be able to apply them to your projects.
- K3 requires the ability to apply facts, techniques, and standards to your projects, though you might not be able to adapt them or select the most appropriate ones for your project.

K4 requires the ability to analyze facts, techniques, and standards as they might apply to your projects and adapt them or select the most appropriate ones for your project.

As you can see, there is an upward progression of ability that adheres to each increasing level of learning. Much of the focus at the Advanced level is on application and analysis.

8.2   ISTQB Advanced Exams

Like the Foundation exams, the Advanced exams are multiple-choice exams. Multiple-choice questions consist of three main parts. The first part is the stem, which is the body of the question. The stem may include a figure or table as well as text. The second part is the distracters, the choices that are wrong. If you don't have a full understanding of the learning objectives that the question covers, you might find the distracters to be reasonable choices. The third part is the answer or answers, the choice or choices that are correct.

If you sailed through the Foundation exam, you might think that you'll manage to do the same with the Advanced exams. That's unlikely. Unlike the Foundation exam, the Advanced exams are heavily focused on questions derived from K3 and K4 level learning objectives. In other words, the ability to apply and to analyze ideas dominates the exams. K1 and K2 level learning objectives, which make up the bulk of the Foundation exam, are often covered implicitly within the higher-level questions.

In addition, unlike with the Foundation exam, the questions are weighted. K3 and K4 questions will be assigned two and three points, respectively, in most cases. K2 questions will be assigned only one point.

For example, the Foundation exam might typically include a question like this:

Which of the following is a major section of an IEEE 829 compliant test plan?

A. Test items

B. Probe effect

C. Purpose

D. Expected results

The answer is A, while B, C, and D are distracters. All that is required here is to recall the major sections of the IEEE 829 templates. Only A is found in the test plan, while C and D are in the test procedure specification and the test case specification, respectively. B is an ISTQB glossary term. As you can see, it's all simple recall.

Recall is useful, especially when you're first learning a subject. However, the ability to recall facts does not make you an expert, any more than my ability to recall song lyrics from the 1970s qualifies me to work as the lead singer for the band AC/DC.

On the Advanced Test Manager exam, you might find a question like this:

Consider the following excerpt from the Test Items section of a test plan.

> During system test execution, the configuration management team shall deliver test releases to the test team every Monday morning by 9:00 a.m. Each test release shall include a test item transmittal report. The test item transmittal report will describe the results of the auto-mated build and smoke test associated with the release. Upon receipt of the test release, if the smoke test was successful, the test manager will install it in the test lab. Testing will commence on Monday morning once the new weekly release is installed.
>
> Should the test team not receive a test release, or if the smoke test results are negative, or if the release will not install, or should the release arrive without a transmittal report, the test manager shall immediately contact the configuration management team manager. If the problem is not resolved within one hour, the test manager shall notify the project manager and continue testing against the previous week's release, if possible. If the test release fails installation, addition-ally the test analyst who attempted the installation shall file an incident report.

Assume that you are working as the test manager on this project. Suppose that you have received two working, installable, testable releases so far. On Monday of the third week, you do not receive the test release.

Which of the following courses of action is consistent with the test plan?

A. Filing a defect report describing the time and date at which you first noticed the missing test release

B. Creating a test that describes how to install a test release

C. Sending an SMS text message to the configuration management team manager

D. Sending an email to the project manager and the configuration management team manager

The answer is C. A, B, and D are distracters. A is wrong because it is not that the release didn't install, it's that it didn't even arrive. B is wrong because, while such a test might be useful for installation testing, it has nothing to do with the escalation process described in the test plan. C is consistent with the test plan. D is not consistent with the test plan because the spirit of the one-hour delay described in the test plan excerpt is that the configuration management team manager should have a chance to resolve the problem before the project manager is engaged. In addition, when time is of the essence, email is not a good escalation technique.

As you can see, this kind of question requires analysis of a situation. Yes, it helps to know the content of documents such as the test plan, defect report, and test item transmittal report. In fact, you'll probably get lost in the terminology if you don't know the standard. However, simply knowing the IEEE 829 standard for test documents will not allow you to get the right answer on this question except by chance.

Scenario-Based and Pick-N Questions

Further complicating this situation is the fact that many exam questions will actually consider a scenario. In scenario-based questions, the exam will describe a set of circumstances. It will then present you with a sequence of two, three, or even more questions based on that scenario.

For example, the questions about the scenario of the test plan excerpt and the missing test release might continue with another pair of questions:

Assume that on Monday afternoon you finally receive a test release. When your lead test analyst attempts to install it, the database configuration scripts included in the installation terminate in midstream. An error message is presented on the database server in Cyrillic script, though the chosen language is US English. At that point, the database tables are corrupted and any attempt to use the application under test results in various database connection error messages (which are at least presented in US English).

Consider the following possible actions:

I.   Notifying the configuration management team manager
II. Notifying the project manager
III. Filing a defect report
IV. Attempting to repeat the installation
V.   Suspending testing
VI. Continuing testing

Which of the following sequence of actions is in the correct order, is the most reasonable, and is most consistent with the intent of the test plan?

A. I, II, V

B. V, I, IV, III, I

C. VI, II, I, III, IV

D. II, I, V

The answer is B, while A, C, and D are distracters. A is wrong because there is no defect report filed, which is required by the test plan when the installation fails. C is wrong because meaningful testing cannot continue against the corrupted database because the project manager is notified before the configuration management team manager and because the defect report is filed before an attempt to reproduce the failure has occurred. D is wrong because the project manager is notified before the configuration management team manager and because no defect report is filed.

As you can see, with a scenario-based question it's very important that you study the scenario carefully before trying to answer the questions that relate to it. If you misunderstand the scenario—perhaps due to a rushed reading of it— you can anticipate missing most if not all of the questions related to it.

In addition to scenario questions, you'll also see another new type of question on the Advanced exams, Pick-N questions. In these questions, you will pick two or three answers out of a list of five or seven options, respectively. These questions are often a harder form of a Roman-type question, in that it is more difficult to use a process of elimination to select the right answer. And, if you only get some of the right answers—that is, one out of two or two out of three— you might not get partial credit.

Let me go back to this question of learning objectives for a moment. I said that the exam covers K1 and K2 learning objectives—those requiring recall and understanding, respectively—as part of a higher-level K3 or K4 question.

There's an added complication with K1 learning objectives: They are not explicitly defined. The entire syllabus, including glossary terms used and standards referenced, is implicitly covered by K1 learning objectives. So, you'll want to read the Advanced Test Manager syllabus carefully, a number of times.

Not only should you read the Advanced Test Manager syllabus, but you'll need to go back and refresh yourself on the Foundation syllabus. Material that is examinable at the Foundation level is also examinable at the Advanced level, especially when material in the Advanced level builds on the Foundation level. It would be smart to take a sample Foundation exam and reread the Foundation syllabus as part of studying for the Advanced Test Manager exam.

8.3   On the Structure of the Exams

So, enough about the questions on the exam, what can you expect from the exam itself? In the Advanced Test Manager exam, you will get 65 questions. You'll have three hours (180 minutes) to complete it. (If your native language is not the same as the language of the exam, you'll be allowed an extra 45 minutes, for a total of 225 minutes.) Most of our customers find that the time limitation is not an issue, unlike with the Foundation exam, where a significant percentage of people need the entire hour.

Now, with the Foundation exam, you could estimate how many questions were going to be asked on each section by using the time allocated in the syllabus for that section. This trick will not work on the Advanced Test Manager exams. In the Advanced Test Manager exams, when we wrote the exam guidelines, we used a process of weighting the learning objectives for importance. So, for Chapter 1, here are the number of questions per learning objective:

A. TM-1.2.1 (K4): 2

B. TM-1.3.1 (K3): 2

C. TM-1.3.2 (K2): 1

D. TM-1.4.1 (K3): 2

E. TM-1.5.1 (K3): 2

F. TM-1.6.1 (K2): 2

G. TM-1.7.1 (K2): 1

H. TM-1.8.2 (K3): 1

For TM-1.8.1 (K2), a question is optional, and there won't be more than one question on that learning objective. There will be at least 13 questions and at most 14 questions on Chapter 1. Remember that an exam question might cover multiple learning objectives, so it could be that a single question counts twice. For example, one question could cover both TM-1.2.1 and TM-1.3.1, so that one question would count toward coverage of each of the two learning objectives.

For Chapter 2, here are the number of questions per learning objective:

A. TM-2.2.1 (K4): 2

B. TM-2.2.2 (K2): 2

C. TM-2.2.3 (K2): 1

D. TM-2.3.1 (K2): 1

E. TM-2.3.2 (K2): 1

F. TM-2.3.3 (K4): 2

G. TM-2.3.4 (K2): 2

H. TM 2.4.1 (K4): 1

I. TM-2.4.2 (K4): 1

J. TM-2.4.3 (K2): 2

K. TM-2.4.4 (K3): 1

L. TM-2.5.1 (K3): 1

M. TM-2.5.2 (K2): 1

N. TM-2.6.1 (K2): 1

O. TM-2.6.2 (K2): 1

P. TM-2.6.3 (K2): 2

Q. TM-2.7.2 (K3): 1

R. TM-2.8.1 (K2): 1

For TM-2.7.1 (K2), TM-2.9.1 (K2), and TM-2.3.5 (K2), you will see one question that covers one of these learning objectives. There will be 25 questions on Chapter 2. Notice that Chapters 1 and 2 together account for 38 questions, about three-fifths of the exam.

For Chapter 3, here are the number of questions per learning objective:

    A. TM-3.2.1 (K2): 1

    B. TM-3.3.1 (K4): 2

    C. TM-3.3.2 (K2): 1

    D. TM-3.4.1 (K3): 1

    E. TM-3.5.1 (K2): 1

There are no optional learning objectives. For Chapter 3, you will see exactly six questions, as specified above.

For Chapter 4, here are the number of questions per learning objective:

    A. TM-4.2.1 (K3): 1

    B. TM-4.3.1 (K3): 1

    C. TM-4.3.2 (K2): 1

    D. TM-4.4.1 (K2): 1

There are no optional learning objectives. For Chapter 4, you will see exactly four questions, as specified above.

For Chapter 5, you will see one questions against TM-5.2.1 (K2). You will see two questions that address the optional learning objectives, TM-5.3.1 (K3), TM-5.4.1 (K2), TM-5.5.1 (K2), TM-5.6.1 (K2), and TM-5.7.1 (K2). For Chapter 5, you will see three questions.

For Chapter 6, here are the number of questions per learning objective:

    A. TM-6.2.1 (K2): 1

    B. TM-6.2.2 (K2): 1

    C. TM-6.2.3 (K4): 1

    D. TM-6.3.1 (K2): 1

For TM-6.4.1 (K2), a question is optional; you might see a question on that learning objective. You'll see at least four questions and at most five questions on Chapter 6.

For Chapter 7, here are the number of questions per learning objectives:

A. TM-7.2.1 (K4): 2

B. TM-7.2.2 (K4): 1

C. TM-7.3.1 (K2): 1

D. TM-7.5.1 (K2): 2

For TM-7.4.1 (K2) and TM-7.6.1 (K2), you'll see one question against one or the other of these learning objectives. You'll see seven questions for Chapter 7.

Based on the suggested point allocation—one point for a K1 question, two points for a K3 question, and 3 points for a K4 questions—there are either 112 or 113 total points available. You have to get 73 points (65 percent) to pass.

Okay, I realize that you might be panicking. Don't panic! Remember, the exam is meant to test your achievement of the learning objectives in the Advanced Test Manager syllabus. This book contains solid features to help you do that. Ask yourself the following questions:

- Did you work through all the exercises in the book? If so, then you have a solid grasp of the most difficult learning objectives, the K3 and K4 objectives. If not, then go back and do so now.
- Did you work through all the sample exam questions in the book? If so, then you have tried a sample exam question for most of the learning objectives in the syllabus. If not, then go back and do so now.
- Did you read the ISTQB glossary term definitions where they occurred in the chapters? If so, then you are familiar with these terms. If not, then return to the ISTQB glossary now and review those terms.
- Did you read every chapter of this book and the entire ISTQB Advanced Test Manager syllabus? If so, then you know the material in the ISTQB Advanced Test Manager syllabus. If not, then review the ISTQB Advanced Test Manager syllabus and reread those sections of this book that correspond to the parts of the syllabus you find most confusing.
- Are you comfortable with Chapters 1 and 2? Most of the points will be for questions about the material in these two chapters, so if you're wondering where to focus, that's the place.

I can't guarantee that you will pass the exam. However, if you have taken advantage of the learning opportunities created by this book, by the ISTQB glossary, and by the ISTQB Advanced Test Manager syllabus, you will be in good shape for the exam.

Good luck to you when you take the exam, and the best of success when you apply the ideas in the Advanced Test Manager syllabus to your next testing project.

Bibliography

Referenced Books

Boris Beizer. *Software Testing Techniques*. ITP, 1990.

Rex Black. *Critical Testing Processes*. Addison-Wesley, 2003.

———. *Managing the Testing Process, 3rd Edition*. John Wiley & Sons, 2009.

———. *Pragmatic Software Testing: Becoming an Effective and Efficient Test Professional*. John Wiley & Sons, 2007.

———. *Testing Metrics*. RBCS, 2012.

———. *The Expert Test Manager: Guide to the ISTQB Expert Level Certification*. Rocky Nook, 2014.

Rex Black and Judy McKay. *Improving the Testing Process*. RBCS, 2012.

Rex Black, et al. *Foundations of Software Testing, 3rd Edition*. Thomson Learning, 2011.

Rick Craig and Stefan Jaskiel. *Systematic Software Testing*. Artech House, 2002.

Lisa Crispin and Janet Gregory. *Agile Testing*. Addison-Wesley, 2009.

Tom DeMarco and Tim Lister. *Peopleware, 3rd Edition*. Dorset House, 2013.

Gerrit de Vries, et al. *TPI Next*. UTN Publishers, 2009.

Malcolm Gladwell. *Outliers: The Story of Success*. Back Bay Books, 2011.

Adam Goucher and Tim Riley (editors). *Beautiful Testing*. O'Reilly, 2009.

Capers Jones. *Estimating Software Costs, 2nd Edition*. McGraw-Hill, 2007.

Capers Jones. *Software Assessments, Benchmarks, and Best Practices*. Addison-Wesley, 2000.

Capers Jones and Olivier Bonsignour. *The Economics of Software Quality*. Pearson, 2011.

Daniel Kahneman. *Thinking, Fast and Slow.* Farrar, Straus and Giroux, 2013.

Tim Koomen, et al. *T-Map Next.* UTN Publishers, 2006.

Steve McConnell. *Software Estimation: Demystifying the Black Art.* Microsoft Press, 2006

Bob McFeeley. *IDEAL: A User's Guide for Software Process Improvement.* Software Engineering Institute (SEI), 1996.

Judy McKay. *Managing the Test People.* Rocky Nook, 2007.

John Musa. *Software Reliability Engineering, 2nd Edition.* Author House, 2004.

D.H. Stamatis. *Failure Mode and Effect Analysis.* ASQ Quality Press, 2003.

Edward Tufte. *The Visual Display of Quantitative Information, 2e.* Graphics Press. 2001.

Erik van Veenendaal. *Practical Risk-Based Testing: The PRISMA Approach.* UTN Publishers, 2012.

James Whittaker. *Exploratory Testing.* Addison-Wesley, 2009.

James Whittaker. *How to Break Software: A Practical Guide to Testing.* Addison-Wesley, 2002.

James Whittaker and Hugh Thompson. *How to Break Software Security.* Addison-Wesley, 2003.

Karl Wiegers. *Software Requirements 2.* Microsoft Press, 2003.

Other References

Rex Black. "What IT Managers Should Know about Testing ROI." RBCS Basic Library, RBCS, Inc. http://www.rbcs-us.com/images/documents/What-IT-Managers-Should-Know-about-Testing-ROI.pdf

Rex Black. "I Take It (Almost) All Back." RBCS Articles, RBCS, Inc. http://www.rbcs-us.com/documents/I-Take-It-All-Back.pdf

www.risks.org. *The Risks Digest,* for up-to-date information on how software defects affect real-world systems and their users.

Dictionary.com, for standard English words.

HELLOCARMS
The Next Generation of Home Equity Lending

System Requirements Document

This page deliberately blank.

I   Table of Contents

This page deliberately blank.

II   Versioning

Ver.	Date	Author	Description	Approval By/On
0.1	Nov 1, 2013	Rex Black	First Draft	
0.2	Dec 15, 2013	Rex Black	Second Draft	
0.5	Jan 1, 2014	Rex Black	Third Draft	

This page deliberately blank.

III Glossary

Term[1]	Definition
Home Equity	The difference between a home's fair market value and the unpaid balance of the mortgage and any other debt secured by the home. A homeowner can increase their home equity by reducing the unpaid balance of the mortgage and any other debt secured by the home. Home equity can also increase if the property appreciates in value. A homeowner can borrow against home equity using *home equity loans, home equity lines of credit*, and *reverse mortgages* (see below).
Secured Loan	Any loan where the borrower uses an asset as collateral for the loan. The loan is secured by the collateral in that the borrower can make a legal claim on the collateral if the borrower fails to repay the loan.
Home Equity Loan	A lump sum of money, disbursed at the initiation of the loan and lent to the homeowner at interest. A home equity loan is a secured loan, secured by the equity in the borrower's home.
Home Equity Line of Credit	A variable amount of money with a pre-arranged maximum amount, available for withdrawal by the homeowner on an as-needed basis and lent to the homeowner at interest. A home equity line of credit allows the homeowner to take out, as needed, a secured loan, secured by the equity in the borrower's home.
Mortgage	A legal agreement by which a sum of money is lent for the purpose of buying property, and against which property the loan is secured.
Reverse Mortgage	A mortgage in which a homeowner borrows money in the form of regular payments which are charged against the equity of the home, typically with the goal of using the equity in the home as a form of retirement fund. A reverse mortgage results in the homeowner taking out a regularly increasing secured loan, secured by the equity in the borrower's home.

---

1. These definitions are adapted from www.dictionary.com.

This page deliberately blank.

000 Introduction

The Home Equity Loan, Line-of-Credit, and Reverse Mortgage System (HEL-LOCARMS), as to be deployed in the first release, allows Globobank Telephone Bankers in the Globobank Fairbanks call center to accept applications for home equity products (loans, lines of credit, and reverse mortgages) from customers. The second release will allow applications over the Internet, including from Globobank business partners as well as customers themselves.

At a high level, the system is configured as shown in Figure 1. The HELLO-CARMS application itself is a group of Java programs and assorted interfacing glue that run on the Web server. The Database server provides storage as the application is processed, while the Application server offloads gateway activities to the clients from the Web server.

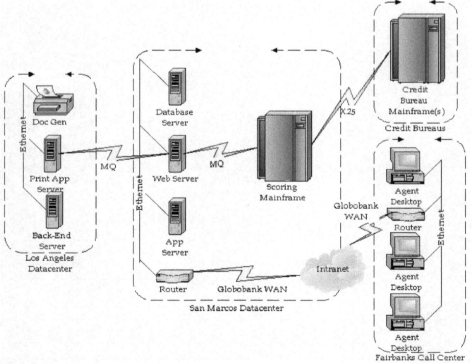

Figure 1   *HELLOCARMS System (First Release)*

001 Informal Use Case

The following informal use case applies for typical transactions in the HELLO-CARMS System:

1. A Globobank Telephone Banker in a Globobank Call Center receives a phone call from a Customer.

2. The Telephone Banker interviews the Customer, entering information into the HELLOCARMS System through a Web browser interface on their Desktop. If the Customer is requesting a large loan or borrowing against a high-value property, the Telephone Banker escalates the application to a Senior Telephone Banker who decides whether to proceed with the application.

3. Once the Telephone Banker has gathered the information from the Customer, the HELLOCARMS System determines the credit-worthiness of the Customer using the Scoring Mainframe.

4. Based on all of the Customer information, the HELLOCARMS System displays various Home Equity Products (if any) that the Telephone Banker can offer to the customer.

5. If the Customer chooses one of these Products, the Telephone Banker will conditionally confirm the Product.

6. The interview ends. The Telephone Banker directs the HELLOCARMS System to transmit the loan information to the Loan Document Printing System (LoDoPS) in the Los Angeles Datacenter for origination.

7. The HELLOCARMS system receives an update from the LoDoPS System when the following events occur:

   a. LoDoPS system sends documents to customer;

   b. Globobank Loan Servicing Center receives signed documents from customer; and,

   c. Globobank Loan Servicing Center sends check or other materials as appropriate to the Customer's product selection.

Once the Globobank Loan Servicing Center has sent the funds or other materials to the Customer, HELLOCARMS processing on the application is complete, and the system will not track subsequent loan-related activities for this Customer.

Once HELLOCARMS processing on an application is complete, HELLO-CARMS shall archive the application and all information associated with it. This applies whether the application was declined by the bank, cancelled by the customer, or ultimately converted into an active loan/line of credit/reverse mortgage.

003 Scope

The scope of the HELLOCARMS project includes:

- Selecting a COTS solution from a field of five vendors.
- Working with the selected application vendor to modify the solution to meet Globobank's requirements.
- Providing a browser-based front-end for loan processing access from the Internet, existing Globobank call centers, outsourced (non-Globobank) call centers, retail banking centers, and brokers. However, the HELLOCARMS first release will only provide access from a Globobank call center (specifically Fairbanks).
- Developing an interface to Globobank's existing Scoring Mainframe for scoring a customer based on their loan application and HELLOCARMS features.
- Developing an interface to use Globobank's existing underwriting and origination system, Loan Document Printing System (LoDoPS), for document preparation. This interface allows the HELLOCARMS system, after assisting the customer with product selection and providing preliminary approval to the customer, to forward the pre-approved application (for a loan, line of credit, or reverse mortgage) to the LoDoPS and to subsequently track the application's movement through to the servicing system.
- Receiving customer-related data from the Globobank Rainmaker Borrower Qualification Winnow (GloboRainBQW) system to generate outbound offers to potential (but not current) Globobank customers via phone, e-mail, and paper-mail.

004 System Business Benefits

The business benefits associated with the HELLOCARMS include:

- Automating a currently manual process, and allowing loan inquiries and applications from the Internet and via call center personnel (both from the current call centers and potentially from outsourced call centers, retail banking centers, and loan brokers).
- Decreasing the time to process the front-end portion of a loan from approximately 30 minutes to 5 minutes. This will allow Globobank's Consumer Products Division to dramatically increase the volumes of loans processed to meet its business plan.
- Reducing the level of skill required for the Telephone Banker to process a loan application, since the HELLOCARMS will select the product, decide whether the applicant is qualified, suggest alternative loan products, and provide a script for the Telephone Banker to follow.
- Providing online application status and loan tracking through the origination and document preparation process. This will allow Telephone Banker to rapidly and accurately respond to customer inquiries during the processing of their application.
- Providing the capability to process all products in a single environment.
- Providing a consistent way to make decisions about whether to offer loan products to customers, and if so what loan products to offer customers, reducing processing and sales errors.
- Allowing Internet-based customers (in subsequent releases) to access Globobank products, select the preferred product, and receive a tentative loan approval within seconds.

The goal of the HELLOCARMS System's business sponsors is to provide these benefits for approximately 85% of the customer inquiries, with 15% or fewer inquiries escalate to a Senior Telephone Banker for specialized processing.

010 Functional System Requirements

The capability of the system to provide functions which meet stated and implied needs when the software is used under specified conditions.

ID	Description	Priority*
010-010	Suitability	
010-010-010	Allow Telephone Bankers to take applications for home equity loans, lines of credit, and reverse mortgages.	1
010-010-020	Provide screens and scripts to support Call Center personnel in completing loan applications.	1
010-010-030	If the customer does not provide a "How Did You Hear About Us" identifier code, collect the lead information during application processing via a drop-down menu, with well-defined lead source categories.	2
010-010-040	Provide data validation, including the use of appropriate user interface (field) controls as well as back end data validation. Field validation details are described in a separate document.	1
010-010-050	Display existing debts to enable retirement of selected debts for debt consolidation. Pass selected debts to be retired to LoDoPS as stipulations.	1
010-010-060	Allow Telephone Bankers and other Globobank telemarketers and partners to access incomplete or interrupted applications.	2
010-010-070	Ask each applicant whether there is an existing relationship with Globobank; e.g., any checking or savings accounts. Send existing Globobank customer relationship information to the Globobank Loan Applications Data Store (GLADS).	2
010-010-080	Maintain application status from initiation through to rejection, decline, or acceptance (and, if accepted, to delivery of funds).	2

*   Priorities are:
    1   Very high
    2   High
    3   Medium
    4   Low
    5   Very low.

ID	Description	Priority*
010-010-090	Allow user to abort an application. Provide an abort function on all screens.	3
010-010-100	Allow user to indicate on a separate screen which, if any, are existing debts that the customer will retire using the funds for which the customer is applying. Allow user the option to exclude specific debts and to include specific debts. For debts to be retired, send a stipulation to LoDoPS that specifies which debts that the customer must pay with loan proceeds.	3
010-010-110	Exclude a debt's monthly payment from the debt ratio if the customer requests the debt to be paid off.	3
010-010-120	Provide a means of requesting an existing application by customer identification number if a customer does not have their loan identifier.	4
010-010-130	Direct the Telephone Banker to transfer the call to a Senior Telephone Banker if an application has a loan amount greater than $500,000; such loans require additional management approval.	1
010-010-140	Direct the Telephone Banker to transfer the call to a Senior Telephone Banker if an application concerns a property with value greater than $1,000,000; such applications require additional management approval.	2
010-010-150	Provide inbound and outbound telemarketing support for all States, Provinces, and Countries in which Globobank operates.	2
010-010-160	Support brokers and other business partners by providing limited partner-specific screens, logos, interfaces, and branding.	2
010-010-170	Support the submission of applications via the Internet, which includes the capability of untrained users to properly enter applications.	3
010-010-180	Provide features and screens that support the operations of the Globobank's retail branches.	4
010-010-190	Support the marketing, sales, and processing of home equity applications.	1
010-010-200	Support the marketing, sales, and processing of home equity line of credit applications.	2
010-010-210	Support the marketing, sales, and processing of home equity reverse mortgage applications.	3
010-010-220	Support the marketing, sales, and processing of applications for combinations of financial products (e.g., home equity and credit cards).	4
010-010-230	Support the marketing, sales, and processing of applications for original mortgages.	5
010-010-240	Support the marketing, sales, and processing of pre-approved applications.	4

ID	Description	Priority*
010-010-250	Support flexible pricing schemes including introductory pricing, short term pricing, and others.	5
010-020	Accuracy	
010-020-010	Determine the various loans, lines of credit, and/or reverse mortgages for which a customer qualifies, and present these options for the customer to evaluate, with calculated costs and terms. Make qualification decisions in accordance with Globobank credit policies.	1
010-020-020	Determine customer qualifications according to property risk, credit score, loan-to-property-value ratio, and debt-to-income ratio, based on information received from the Scoring Mainframe.	1
010-020-030	During the application process, estimate the monthly payments based on the application information provided by the customer, and include the estimated payment as a debt in the debt-to-income calculation for credit scoring.	2
010-020-040	Add a loan fee based on property type: 1.5% for rental properties (duplex, apartment, and vacation) 2.5% for commercial properties. 3.5% for condominiums or cooperatives. 4.5% for undeveloped property. Do not add a loan fee for the other supported property type, residential single family dwelling.	3
010-020-050	Capture all government retirement fund income(s) (e.g., Social Security in United States) as net amounts, but convert those incomes to gross income(s) in the interface to LoDoPS. [Note: This is because most government retirement income is not subject to taxes, but gross income is used in debt-to-income calculations.]	1
010-020-060	Capture the length of time (rounded to the nearest month) that the customer has received additional income (other than salary, bonuses, and retirement), if any.	3
010-030	Interoperability	
010-030-010	If the customer provides a "How Did You Hear About Us" identifier code during the application process, retrieve customer information from GloboRainBQW.	2
010-030-020	Accept joint applications (e.g., partners, spouses, relatives, etc.) and score all applicants using the Scoring Mainframe.	1
010-030-030	Direct Scoring Mainframe to remove duplicate credit information from joint applicant credit reports.	2
010-030-040	Allow user to indicate on a separate screen which, if any, are existing debts that the customer will retire using the funds for which the customer is applying. Allow user the option to exclude specific debts and to include specific debts. For debts to be retired, send a stipulation to LoDoPS that specifies which debts that the customer must pay with loan proceeds.	1

ID	Description	Priority*
010-030-060	If the Scoring Mainframe does not show a foreclosure or bankruptcy discharge date and the customer indicates that the foreclosure or bankruptcy is discharged, continue processing the application, and direct the Telephone Banker to ask the applicant to provide proof of discharge in paperwork sent to LoDoPS.	3
010-030-070	Allow user to indicate on a separate screen which, if any, are existing debts that the customer will retire using the funds for which the customer is applying. Allow user the option to exclude specific debts and to include specific debts. For debts to be retired, send a stipulation to LoDoPS that specifies which debts that the customer must pay with loan proceeds.	3
010-030-080	Capture all government retirement fund income(s) (e.g., Social Security in United States) as net amounts, but convert those incomes to gross income(s) in the interface to LoDoPS. [Note: This is because most government retirement income is not subject to taxes, but gross income is used in debt-to-income calculations.]	1
010-030-090	Pass application information to the Scoring Mainframe.	1
010-030-100	Receive scoring and decision information back from the Scoring Mainframe.	1
010-030-110	If the Scoring Mainframe is down, queue application information requests.	2
010-030-120	Initiate the origination process by sending the approved loan to LoDoPS.	2
010-030-130	Pass all declined applications to LoDoPS.	2
010-030-140	Receive LoDoPS feedback on the status of applications.	2
010-030-145	Receive changes to loan information made in LoDoPS (e.g., loan amount, rate, etc.).	2
010-030-150	Support computer-telephony integration to provide customized marketing and sales support for inbound telemarketing campaigns and branded business partners.	4
010-040	Security	
010-040-010	Support agreed upon security requirements (encryption, firewalls, etc.)	2
010-040-020	Track "Created By" and "Last Changed By" audit trail information for each application.	1
010-040-030	Allow outsourced telemarketers to see the credit tier but disallow them from seeing the actual credit score of applicants.	2
010-040-040	Support the submission of applications via the Internet, providing security against unintentional and intentional security attacks.	2

ID	Description	Priority*
010-040-050	Allow Internet users to browse potential loans without requiring such users to divulge personal information such as name, government identifying numbers, etc., until the latest feasible point in the application process.	4
010-040-060	Support fraud detection for processing of all financial applications.	1
010-050	Compliance (functionality standards/laws/regs)	
	[To be determined in a subsequent revision]	

020 Reliability System Requirements

The capability of the system to maintain a specified level of performance when used under specified conditions.

ID	Description	Priority
020-010	*Maturity*	
	[To be determined in a subsequent revision]	
020-020	*Fault-tolerance*	
	[To be determined in a subsequent revision]	
020-030	*Recoverability*	
	[To be determined in a subsequent revision]	
020-040	*Compliance (reliability standards/laws/regs)*	
	[To be determined in a subsequent revision]	

030 Usability System Requirements

The capability of the system to be understood learned, used, and attractive to the user and the call center agents when used under specified conditions.

ID	Description	Priority
030-010	*Understandability*	
030-010-010	Support the submission of applications via the Internet, including the capability for untrained users to properly enter applications.	2
	[More to be determined in a subsequent revision]	
030-020	Learnability	
	[To be determined in a subsequent revision]	
030-030	*Operability*	
030-030-010	Provide for complete customization of the user interface and all user user-supplied documents for business partners, including private branding of the sales and marketing information and all closing documents.	3
	[More to be determined in a subsequent revision]	
030-040	*Attractiveness*	
	[To be determined in a subsequent revision]	
030-050	*Compliance (usability standards)*	
030-050-010	Comply with local handicap-access laws.	5

040 Efficiency System Requirements

The capability of the system to provide appropriate performance, relative to the amount of resources used under stated conditions.

ID	Description	Priority
040-010	*Time behavior*	
040-010-010	Provide the user with screen-to-screen response time of one second or less. This requirement should be measured from the time the screen request enters the application system until the screen response departs the application server; i.e., do not include network transmission delays.	2
040-010-020	Provide an approval or decline for applications within 5 minutes of application submittal.	2
040-010-030	Originate the loan, including the disbursal of funds, within one hour.	3
	[More to be determined in a subsequent revision]	
040-020	*Resource utilization*	
040-020-010	Handle up to 2,000 applications per hour.	2
040-020-020	Handle up to 4,000 applications per hour.	3
040-020-030	Support a peak of 4,000 simultaneous (concurrent) application submissions.	4
040-020-040	Support a total volume of 1.2 million approved applications for the initial year of operation.	2
040-020-050	Support a total volume of 7.2 million applications during the initial year of operation.	2
040-020-060	Support a total volume of 2.4 million conditionally-approved applications for the initial year of operation.	2
	[More to be determined in a subsequent revision]]	
040-030	*Compliance (performance standards)*	
	[To be determined in a subsequent revision]	

050 Maintainability System Requirements

The capability of the system to be modified. Modifications may include corrections, improvement, or adaptations of the software changes in environments, and in requirement s and functional specifications.

ID	Description	Priority
050-010	*Analyzability*	
	[To be determined in a subsequent revision]	
050-020	*Changeability*	
	[To be determined in a subsequent revision]	
040-030	*Compliance (performance standards)*	
	[To be determined in a subsequent revision]	

060 Portability System Requirements

The capability of the system to be transferred from one environment to another.

ID	Description	Priority
060-010	Adaptability	
	[To be determined in a subsequent revision]	
060-020	Installability	
	[To be determined in a subsequent revision]	
060-030	Co-existence	
060-030-010	Should not interact in any non-specified way with any other applications in the Globobank call centers or data centers.	1
	[More to be determined in a subsequent revision]	
060-040	Replaceability	
	Not applicable	
060-050	Compliance	
	[To be determined in a subsequent revision]	

This page deliberately blank.

A   Acknowledgement

This document is based on an actual project. RBCS would like to thank their client, who wishes to remain unnamed, for their permission to adapt and publish anonymous portions of various project documents.

This page deliberately blank.

Correct Answers
to Sample Exam Questions

CHAPTER 1
1: A and B
2: B
3: C
4: B

CHAPTER 2
1: C
2: B
3: A
4: D
5: A
6: C
7: B
8: A and C
9: A
10: C
11: A and E
12: B
13: D
14: C
15: C and E
16: D
17: C and D
18: D
19: D
20: A
21: B
22: A

23: C
24: D

CHAPTER 3
1: B
2: D
3: A and B
4: B

CHAPTER 4
1: C
2: A

CHAPTER 5
1: A
2: D
3: A

CHAPTER 6
1: A
2: B and C
3: D

CHAPTER 7
1: B and C
2: A and E
3: A
4: B
5: B

Index